A CONSUMER'S DICTIONARY OF
HOUSEHOLD, YARD AND OFFICE CHEMICALS

ALSO BY THE AUTHOR

A CONSUMER'S DICTIONARY OF HOUSEHOLD, YARD AND OFFICE CHEMICALS

RUTH WINTER

Crown Publishers, Inc.
New York

Published by Crown Publishers, Inc., 201 East 50th Street, New York, New York 10022. Member of the Crown Publishing Group.

CROWN is a trademark of Crown Publishers, Inc.

Manufactured in the United States of America

LIBRARY OF CONGRESS CATALOGING-IN-PUBLICATION DATA

Winter, Ruth
    A consumer's dictionary of household, yard, and office
chemicals / by Ruth Winter. — 1st ed.

    1. Housing and health—Dictionaries. 2. Household supplies—
Toxicology—Dictionaries. I. Title.
RA770.5.W56 1992
615.9—dc20   91-33189
                                                    CIP

ISBN 0-517-58722-X

10 9 8 7 6 5 4 3 2 1

First Edition

CONTENTS

INTRODUCTION

Take a look around your home, yard, or office. Many of those innocent-looking, brightly packaged products you purchased at the supermarket, hardware, or stationery store and use so casually contain allergens, poisons, and cancer-causing agents.

Check around your living and working areas. Do you have a product containing methylene chloride? It is widely used as a solvent, degreaser, and paint and varnish thinner. It is in pesticide aerosols, refrigeration and air-conditioning equipment, in cleansing creams, and in paint and varnish removers. Some paint strippers, as a matter of fact, are 80 percent methylene chloride. You may be more cautious about using products containing the chemical after you read the reported health effects under the listing for it in this book. They include liver, kidney, and central nervous system damage; it increases the carbon monoxide level in the blood and people with angina (chest pains) are extremely sensitive to the chemical; methylene chloride has been linked to heart attacks and cancer.

Do you have oven cleaners in your cleaning-supply closet? Many spray types are highly irritating to the skin and lungs, particularly those with methylene chloride, sodium and potassium hydroxide (lye), and petroleum distillates.

What about your carpets and cabinets? Detergent and pesticide residues can accumulate on carpeting and vaporize, causing respiratory symptoms. In 1987, when the United States Environmental Protection Agency (EPA) installed 27,000 square yards of new styrene-butadiene-latex–backed carpet in many of the offices at its national headquarters in Washington, D.C., employees began to complain of respiratory problems, burning eyes, rashes, dizziness, and nausea within a few days. After a few months, more than 122 employees had complained of adverse health effects blamed on poor air quality and carpet emission. Six of the employees had such severe reactions that they could not enter the building without experiencing serious health effects. A chemical, 4-phenylcyclohexene, that emits gases from new carpeting and inadequate ventilation, was designated the culprits.[1,2] Most kitchen cabinets are built with

[1]Hilleman, Bette, "Multiple Chemical Sensitivity," *Chemical and Engineering News*, July 20, 1991, pp. 26–42.
[2]D. Weitzman and R. Singhvi, "Indoor Air Quality at EPA Headquarters: A Case Study," *The Practioner's Approach to Indoor Air Quality Investigations*, ed. Donald Weekes and Richard Gammage, American Industrial Hygiene Association, Akron, Oh., 1990, pp. 151–162.

particle board or hardwood plywood veneered with an attractive wood, such as oak. These materials may outgas formaldehyde.

Have you sprayed your pet with a product containing DDVP or hung a flea collar with it around your pet's neck? A study performed by the national Toxicology Program of the Department of Health and Human Services revealed a significant leukemia hazard from this common household pesticide widely used in pet, house, and yard aerosol products since the 1950s, and the EPA reported the cancer risk for applying DDVP sprays ranged from one in a hundred to one in a hundred thousand. The generally accepted "significant" threshold is one cancer incidence in one million persons.[3] The EPA, as this is being written, is moving to have DDVP banned as a pesticide for food packaging because it was found in animal tests to cause "more than a negligible risk." It may take years to get it off the market as a food package pesticide, but what about the hundreds of other products that still contain DDVP?[4] The EPA conducted a major study of nonoccupational exposure to pesticides and found indoor exposure to pesticides is widespread, with as many as ten different pesticides being detected in a single home.[5]

Edward P. Krenzelok, Pharm.D., director of the Pittsburgh Poison Center at Children's Hospital of Pittsburgh, says, "Most people are unaware that the most common and effective pesticides used on household plants and gardens contain the same agents as the chemicals used in chemical warfare."[6] The agents are organophosphates (*see* Organophosphates). "Although these products are excellent pesticides," Krenzelok points out, "they can be extremely toxic to humans if improperly used."

He says 72,336 children in the United States are exposed to these poisons and, because children lack the defense mechanisms of adults, they are generally more sensitive to pesticides.

More than half of the pesticide poisonings reported in 1990 occurred in children under the age of six years.

This book is not aimed at convincing you to forego the use of chemicals around your home, yard, or office. Its objective is to make you aware that you must select and utilize chemicals carefully

---

[3]*Chemical Regulation Reporter*, Washington, D.C., Bureau of National Affairs, 1987.
[4]Mike Beringer, United States Environmental Protection Agency, personal communication, August 8, 1991.
[5]*Report to Congress on Indoor Air Quality: Executive Summary and Recommendations*, United States Environmental Protection Agency, August 1989, p. 7.
[6]"The War Against Pesticides," American Academy of Pediatrics news release, July 1991.

and, to do that, you have to be knowledgeable about their uses, benefits, and hazards. The health and even the lives of you and your family members may depend upon such awareness.

The EPA has undertaken a long-term series of studies of human exposure to indoor air pollutants known generically as the Total Exposure Assessment Methodology (TEAM) studies. In research conducted by TEAM investigators, levels of a dozen common organic pollutants were found to be two to five times higher inside homes than outside, regardless of whether the homes were located in rural or highly industrial areas. Organic chemicals, which contain carbon and easily vaporize at room temperature, are employed widely as ingredients in household, yard, and office products because of their many useful characteristics such as the ability to dissolve substances and evaporate quickly. Paints, varnishes, and waxes all contain organic solvents, as do many cleaning, disinfecting, cosmetic, degreasing, and hobby products. Fuels are made up of organic chemicals. All of these products can release potentially harmful emanations while you are using them, and, to some degree, when they are stored.

The EPA researchers measured indoor pollutant concentrations in ten public buildings, including schools, homes for the elderly, and office buildings, and found that newly constructed building may have levels of formaldehyde, asbestos, pesticides, solvents, and other pollutants as much as a hundred times normal levels. These levels diminish rapidly during the first several months of the buildings' lives, but they are still two to four times higher than outdoor levels. The EPA points out that these buildings may contain children and the elderly, who are very sensitive to such compounds.[7]

Similar findings have been reported by other researchers. Scientists at Chicago IIT Research Institute detected more than two hundred different chemicals in a study of indoor air in thirty-six Chicago-area homes and found that, in general, indoor levels of the chemicals were significantly higher than outdoor levels. Other studies found styrene (*see* Styrene) in the air in 80 percent of sampled homes in Bayonne, New Jersey, and 150 chemicals in the air of forty houses monitored in Oak Ridge, Tennessee.[8]

TEAM studies indicate that while we are using products contain-

[7]Robert Gettlin, "Pollutants in Buildings Found High," Newhouse News Service, November 1988.
[8]"Beware 'Sick'-Building Syndrome: The deadliest pollutants of all may be the ones you breathe at home or at work," *Newsweek,* January 7, 1985, pp. 58–60.

ing organic chemicals, we can expose ourselves and others to very high pollutant levels, and elevated concentrations can persist in the air long after we finish. During and up to several hours immediately after completing activities such as paint stripping, for example, levels may be a thousand times more than the background outdoor levels. Three out of four specific organic compounds mentioned—benzene, perchloroethylene, and paradichlorobenzene—were among the most prevalent organic compounds identified in indoor air by TEAM investigators. The fourth organic compound, methylene chloride, has been cited before. As you will read under their listings, these chemicals are potentially very harmful.[9]

YARD CHEMICALS

Our lawn and garage chemicals may also be dangerous. Yard chemicals may be lethal not only to pests, but to human beings as well. The United States General Accounting Office reports that 230 million pounds of herbicides, insecticides, fungicides, and rodenticides are used each year for nonagricultural purposes, and that about 55 million pounds of pesticides—or about 30 percent of all nonagricultural pesticides—are applied around homes and gardens. Additional pesticides are applied at stores, schools, restaurants, offices, industrial workplaces, sports facilities, hotels, hospitals, and theaters.

You can buy pesticide products ranging widely in toxicity and potential effects. No special training is required to purchase these products, and no one is looking over your shoulder, monitoring your vigilance in reading and following label instructions. Yet many of these products are extremely hazardous, especially if they are stored, handled, or applied improperly. The National Academy of Sciences has found that home owners already use four to eight times as many chemical pesticides per acre as farmers, and the disparity is widening.[10]

The National Cancer Institute reported in 1991 that dogs whose owners used a common weed killer, 2, 4-D on their lawns had double the immune system cancer (lymphoma) of dogs whose owners did not have "treated lawns." The NCI said this is consistent

---

[9]*Report to Congress on Indoor Air Quality, Volume I: Federal Programs Addressing Indoor Air Quality,* United States Environmental Protection Agency, August 1989, p. 21.
[10]California Senate Office of research issue brief, "Pesticides at Home: Uncertain Risks and Inadequate Regulations," April 1988, Sacramento, Ca.

with studies that show an excess of lymphomas in humans who have frequent contact with 2,4-D.[11]

You will see described in this book under individual pesticides, under the general listing for pesticides, and for specific uses such as pet pesticides, a great deal of information. However, there are several points I would like to emphasize.

• Some insecticides, once applied, can never really be removed. The termite pesticide, chlordane, has been detected in the air of some treated homes fourteen years after application.[12]

• Many insecticides are relatively insoluble in water, and are instead dispensed in petroleum-based solvents, to which a large number of individuals are sensitive. So not only are the principal ingredients a potential source of trouble, but the vehicle is, too.

• Some rugs, as part of the manufacturing process, are treated with toxins to kill insects, and these poisons are not entirely removed by cleaning.

• Insect repellents, insecticides, or fungicides in wallpaper paste are hidden sources of human and pet exposure.

OFFICE CHEMICALS

If you develop symptoms such as headaches, nose and throat irritation, and a host of other physical problems while working at the office, you may be suffering from the effects of emissions from building materials and furnishings, equipment and tools. Office copying machines and laser printers, for example, give off ozone. Spirit duplicators emit methanol fumes, and signature machines give off butyl methacrylate, while blue print copiers emit ammonia and acetic acid. Many workers also are troubled by the odor of fresh newsprint, marking pencils, certain carbon papers, and some typewriter ribbons.[13]

[11]"A Case-Control Study of Canine Malignant Lymphoma: Positive Association with Dog Owner's Use of 2,4-D Herbicides," National Cancer Institute Release, September 3, 1991.
[12]*Report to Congress on Indoor Air Quality, Volume III: Indoor Air Pollution Research Needs Statement*, United States Environmental Protection Agency, August 1989, p. 31.
[13]Christopher M. Rch, National Institute for Occupational Safety and Health, Centers for Disease Control, Cincinnati, Oh., "NIOSH Indoor Air Quality Investigations: 1971 through 1988," presented at the Fourth National Environmental Conference, June 20–23, 1989, San Antonio, Texas, United States Department of Health and Human Services, Public Health Service.

National Institute of Occupational Safety and Health (NIOSH) researchers in their investigations of office space found problems with pesticides, such as chlordane, which were applied improperly; boiler additives that caused skin rashes; improperly diluted cleaning agents, such as rug shampoo and other detergents that vaporized and caused respiratory symptoms; tobacco smoke of all types; combustion gases from sources common to cafeterias and laboratories; and cross-contamination from poorly ventilated sources such as exhaust fumes from basement garage floors and loading docks. Formaldehyde from insulation and vinyl chloride from furnishings caused eye, nose, and throat irritation, and asbestos and fiberglass fibers were found embedded even in soft contact lenses worn by office workers.[14,15]

The quality of indoor air and the health risks resulting from poor air quality have become major concerns to building occupants, especially office workers. Unfortunately, the health risks of most indoor air exposures are poorly understood.

Originally, scientists thought indoor pollution just reflected outdoor pollution. But when an EPA team sampled air from schools in the shadow of chemical storage tanks, and in a relatively pristine suburban setting, they discovered that outside air had almost no effect on indoor pollution levels.

A committee of the World Health Organization estimates that as many as 30 percent of new or remodeled buildings may have unusually high rates of complaints, now known as Sick-Building Syndrome (SBS). New buildings, NIOSH researchers discovered, had levels of some chemicals that were a hundred times higher than outdoor levels, and the levels were still about ten times higher after six months. Even in buildings that had been occupied for a while, the presence of pollutants was two to five times worse than outside.[16]

The irony is that modern technology created the indoor air-quality problem by giving architects and engineers the tools to build tightly sealed, energy-efficient buildings. As much as 90 percent of the air is recycled in some structures. Aside from bacteria and fungi that can accumulate in humidifier systems, circulation vacuum pumps,

[14]Anna Lo Davol, M.D., "Is Your Office Making You Sick?", *Parents*, October 1986, pp. 230–232.
[15]T. A. Seitz, "NIOSH Indoor Air Quality Investigations: 1971– 1988," *The Practioner's Approach to Indoor Air Quality Investigations*, ed. Donald M. Weekes and Richard B. Gammage, American Industrial Hygiene Association, Akron, Oh., 1990, pp. 163–171.
[16]"Ventilation and Air Quality in Offices," *Indoor Air Facts No. 3*, United States Environmental Protection Agency, 20A–4002, July 1990.

blowers, ventilation ducts, and air filters, there are the chemicals that keep blowing around.

NIOSH researchers found that it is not uncommon for more than one problem to exist in a single building, but that inadequacies in ventilation systems or their operation are the major contributors to indoor air-quality problems.

If you have symptoms that disappear in the evening, never occur on weekends, and start up on Monday at the office again, you may have Building-Related Illness (BRI). Not all employees may be equally affected but if you are and the situation is not corrected, you can contact NIOSH. See listing on page 315. Experts from NIOSH will conduct health-hazard evaluations of indoor air quality (IAQ) at the request of employee groups, unions, management, and local, state, and federal agencies. Generally, these requests are in response to work health complaints and illness.[17] There is no doubt poor indoor air can adversely affect employee health and productivity. The costs to industry have been estimated to be in the tens of billions of dollars per year.[18] When improvements in the indoor air environment are made, employee morale and productivity increase, so everyone benefits.

WE LIVE IN A SEA OF CHEMICALS

There are now more than fifty thousand different chemicals in common use in the United States and about a thousand more are added each year.[19] The health effects of most of them are uncertain.

In September 1980, the National Toxicology Program (NTP) contracted with the National Research Council (NRC) and the National Academy of Sciences (NAS) for a study with two principal charges.

1. To determine toxicity-testing needs for substances to which humans are exposed so that the federal agencies responsible for the protection of public health will have the information needed to assess the toxicity of such substances.

2. To develop and validate uniformly applicable and wide-ranging criteria by which to set priorities for research on substances with potentially adverse public-health impact.

[17]Reh, Christopher M., op. cit.
[18]Report to Congress on Indoor Air Quality, United States Department of Health and Human Services, Public Health Service, 1989.
[19]"Keeping Tabs on Exposure to Environmental Chemicals," *National Research Council News Report*, Vol. XLI, Number 6, June–July 1991, p. 19.

The NRC-NAS committee found 53,500 distinct entities in common use as pesticides, cosmetic ingredients, food additives, and drugs.[20] The committee selected a hundred representative samples culled from the various categories to determine the extent of knowledge about the toxicity of chemicals in common use. The committee found that toxicity testing had been inadequate in 92 percent of the samples and that the testing often lacked the required observations (e.g., test animal description, diet analysis, chemical analysis, clinical chemistry, and histopathology), used too few doses, or lacked sufficiently detailed end points, such as data tabulation and statistical analysis of data. For pesticides alone, the committee found that some of the required tests were not done at all.

"The three greatest testing needs for health-hazard assessment of pesticides and inert ingredients of pesticide formulations were in teratology, neurobehavioral toxicity, and genetic toxicity," the committee concluded. That means the committee thought there was insufficient knowledge about the ability of pesticides to cause brain and nerve damage and birth defects.[21]

LABELS—AND YOUR RIGHT TO KNOW WHAT IS IN A PRODUCT

One way to learn more about the toxicology of ingredients is to gather information from consumers and the physicians who may treat them when an adverse reaction to a product occurs. It is very difficult to definitely link a product's ingredient with a symptom when no one except the manufacturer knows exactly what ingredients are in the product.

Food, drug, cosmetic, and medical labels are under the jurisdiction of the Food and Drug Administration (FDA).

Pesticide labeling is under the jurisdiction of the EPA. You many not think of them as pesticides, but many cleaning agents such as cleansers containing bleach, and bleaches themselves are considered pesticides because they kill tiny living things we call "germs." If the bleaches or cleansers do not claim germicidal properties, however, they do not have to submit to EPA labeling.

Household and office products that contain known hazardous substances are under the jurisdiction of the United States Consumer Product and Safety Commission (CPSC). Manufacturers are re-

---

[20]"Toxicity-Testing Strategies to Determine Needs and Priorities," United States National Research Council, National Academy Press, Washington, D.C., 1984.
[21]Ibid.

quired to list only those ingredients designated by CPSC as hazardous. Manufacturers do not have to submit labels for review before marketing.

The CPSC was founded by the Congress in 1972 to:

• Protect the public against risks of injuries associated with consumer products

• Develop standards

• Promote research concerning product safety

• Investigate the causes and to prevent product-related deaths

• Assist consumers in evaluating the comparative safety of consumer products

In 1981, Congress weakened the CPSC by requiring the commission to allow voluntary standards whenever possible, and by further restricting the disclosure of safety hazard information by brand name. Congress further weakened the CPSC by cutting back on the data-gathering activity of the National Electronic Injury Surveillance System (NEISS), which collects information on hospital emergency room visits due to injuries and fatalities associated with consumer products.

Consumer product-related injuries claim an estimated twenty-nine thousand lives each year in the United States. In addition, there are an estimated thirty-three million nonfatal consumer product injuries annually.[22]

How does the CPSC find those products that do not have labels listing their hazardous ingredients?

There are about a hundred investigators in the field to check labels, according to Charles Jacobson, compliance officer for CPSC in the area of toxic chemicals.[23]

He said that if a product is not in compliance, the agency can seize it, enjoin the packager from distributing it, and, if necessary, criminally prosecute those involved.

He admitted that it is a big job because there are thousands upon thousands of different products on the market ranging from dolls

[22]Tom Christoffel, J. D., and Katherine K. Christoffel, M. D., M.P.H., "The Consumer Product Safety Commission's Opposition to Consumer Product Safety: Lessons for Public Health Advocates," *American Journal of Public Health*, March 1989, Vol. 79, No. 3, pp. 336–339.

[23]Charles Jacobson, compliance officer, U.S. Consumer Products Safety Commission, Washington, D.C., personal communication with author, August 5, 1991.

to automobiles, not just chemicals. He added, however, that the CPSC receives complaints from consumers (*see* page 316 for the CPSC Consumer Hotline) and reports from hospital emergency rooms and coroners alerting the agency to problems.

According to Jacobson, companies are very sensitive to potential injury to consumers. If there is an ingredient linked to birth defects, cancer, or learning disabilities, the manufacturer will review the information and reformulate the product excluding the ingredient rather than keeping it in and having to list a warning on the label.

Jacobson said there is no requirement that every ingredient other than hazardous ones be on the label.

He said some argue that listing all the ingredients would lead to confusion and, if a person were injured, the situation might be muddled because medical personnel would not know which ingredient might be causing the problem.

As for allergies set off by hidden ingredients, Jacobson said it would be almost impossible to label allergenic chemicals because even in cosmetics, labels are required to carry only "coloring" and "perfumes," and a single perfume may have more than a hundred ingredients.

Industries have to provide a Material Safety Data Sheet (*see* MSDS) to employees working with a chemical product, but are not required to offer such information to the consumer. However, on product labels there is sometimes a toll-free number to call for further information. You can request an MSDS or a list of ingredients, and many manufacturers will send it to you.

Those who design labels have a difficult job. They must have a knowledge of chemistry, toxicology, the law, and consumer psychology, and be able to fit all the information into a relatively small space.

The fact remains that there are many household, yard, and office chemicals containing "hidden" ingredients that can be hazardous to our health and we, as consumers, should be able to find them listed on product labels in order to make more informed choices about what we buy and use. We must demand more informative labeling! Some companies already provide this, which means all companies could do it if pressured to do so.

When asked which household products he considered most hazardous, Jacobson answered drain cleaners and petroleum products.

"Drain cleaners are designed to destroy organic matter and, if you don't handle them properly, they can certainly injure you. Strong cleansers such as fairly concentrated laundry detergents and automatic dishwasher detergents can also be hazardous, and, of course, petroleum products such as automobile care products, paint strippers, and such are combustible."

What about methylene chloride and perchloroethylene (*see both*), two compounds that have been linked to cancer, birth defects, and other ailments?

Jacobson pointed out that methylene chloride is a substitute for benzene (*see* Benzene), a highly toxic chemical, and perchloroethylene is a substitute for carbon tetrachloride (*see* Carbon Tetrachloride), also a highly toxic compound.

He said research is being conducted to see whether methylene chloride use has declined after it was cited as a carcinogen several years ago. A study is now in progress, he added, to determine whether the health of dry cleaners has been affected by perchloroethylene.

According to Jacobson, the long-term, chronic effects of chemicals is an area that requires a great deal more knowledge, and research is under way. He pointed out, however, that if every ingredient suspected of causing cancer were banned, there would be hardly any products on the market.

Jacobson maintained that the hazards of household products are not that serious, if they are handled according to the instructions on their labels.

There is, he believes, much truth to the old adage, "When all else fails, read the label!"

"We are all guilty of not thoroughly reading labels. If vapors may be harmful, it doesn't do much good to read the label after you have used the product and inhaled the vapors. Read the labels, preferably before every use," he emphasized.

The guardians of our safety, the Environmental Protection Agency, the Federal Food and Drug Administration, the Consumer Product Safety Commission, and the other federal, state, and local agencies charged with protecting us, generally admit that researchers are just beginning to look at indoor pollution emanating from household, yard, and office chemicals.

The relative importance of any single source depends upon how much of a given pollutant it emits and how hazardous those emissions are. In some cases, factors such as how old the source is and whether it is properly maintained are significant. For example, an improperly adjusted gas stove can emit significantly more carbon monoxide than one that is properly adjusted.

Here is how chemicals you use around your home, office, and yard get into your body:

Vapor. A vapor is the gas form of a substance that is a liquid or solid at normal pressure and temperature. Most organic solvents evaporate and produce vapors. Vapors can be inhaled into the lungs, and in some cases may irritate the eyes, skin, or respiratory tract. Some are flammable, explosive, and/or toxic. Refrigerators, deep freezes, and air conditioners may leak, causing symptoms among the susceptible.

"Volatility" is the tendency of a liquid to evaporate to a gas, or, to form vapors (*see* Gas and Vapors). Most solvent exposure results from inhaling the vapors. The higher the concentration of vapors, the greater the hazard. The greater the volatility, the greater the possibility of breathing a hazardous amount of solvent. For instance, ethyl ether has an evaporation rate of 1 because it is the most volatile solvent. However, even the least volatile solvents, the glycol ethers, can evaporate at a rate sufficient to produce a hazardous level of vapors in some situations. Chemicals are less volatile in cool air than in warm air, so keep that in mind when you are using solvents!

The most common way chemicals enter your body is through your lungs. Your lungs consist of branching airways (bronchi) with clusters of tiny air sacs (alveoli) at the ends of the airways. Oxygen and other chemicals are absorbed into your bloodstream by the alveoli. Organic solvents such as toluene (*see* Toluene), depending on their size, may be deposited in the bronchi and/or alveoli. Many of these may be coughed out, but others may stay in the lungs, where they may cause damage. Some particles may dissolve and be absorbed into the bloodstream, creating symptoms such as dizziness or headache.

The more physically active you are, the harder and faster you breathe, the greater amount of a chemical you will inhale to be absorbed by your lungs. Therefore, with exposure to the same concentration of a solvent in the air, a person who is working hard will absorb more of the solvent than a person at rest, and the active person will more likely experience a toxic effect. This is one reason not all people experience the same symptoms even if they are exposed to the same concentration of a solvent.

Dust. Dusts consist of small, solid particles in the air. Dusts may be created when solids are pulverized or ground, or when powder (settled dust) becomes airborne. Dusts may be hazardous because they can be inhaled into the respiratory tract. Larger particles of dust are usually trapped in the nose and windpipe, where they can be expelled, but smaller particles (respirable dust) can reach and damage the lungs. Some, like lead dust, may then enter the bloodstream through the lungs. Organic dusts, such as grain dust, may explode when they reach high concentrations in the air.

House dust can create a big problem, particularly in dust-allergic patients. It not only contains bacteria, flakes of human skin, animal dander, disintegrated stuffing materials, and other assorted by-products of living, but also may contain pesticides, solvents, and other stuff you have used around your home or office (*see* House Dust). Some allergic people have substituted sponge-rubber pillows and mattresses to guard against exposure to dust in the bedroom, only to find the vapors from the rubber even more annoying than the dust. Other household rubber sources include rubber rug pads and rug backing, upholstery, seat cushions, typewriter pads, rubber-tiled floors, and electrical insulation of electric blankets.

Fume. A fume consists of very small, fine solid particles in the air that form when solid chemicals (often metals) are heated to very high temperatures, evaporate to vapor and, finally, become solid again. The welding or brazing of metal, for example, produces metal fumes. Fumes are hazardous because they are easily inhaled. Many metal fumes can cause an illness called "metal fume fever," consisting of flulike fever, chills, and aches. Inhalation of other metal fumes, such as lead, can cause poisoning without causing metal fume fever.

Fiber. A fiber is a solid particle whose length is at least three times its width. The degree of hazard depends upon the size of the fiber. Smaller fibers, such as asbestos, can lodge in the lungs and cause serious harm. Larger fibers are trapped in the respiratory tract, and are expelled without reaching the lungs.

Mist. A mist consists of liquid particles of various sizes that are produced by agitation or spraying of liquids. Mists can be hazardous when they are inhaled or sprayed on the skin. The spraying of pesticides and the machining of metals using metalworking fluids are two situations where mists are commonly produced and very dangerous.

Skin contact. Industrial statistics show that contact dermatitis (*see* Contact Dermatitis) accounts for more than 50 percent of all occupational illness, excluding injury, and results in about a fourth of the time lost from work. About one out of every thousand workers in the United States suffers from contact dermatitis, costing millions of dollars each year. You will note that many of the chemicals listed in this dictionary may cause contact dermatitis or an allergic reaction. Common sensitizers are nickel, which produces more allergic dermatitis than all other metals combined, dyes containing *p*-phenylenediamine, rubber compounds, the chemical ethylenediamine, insecticides, and synthetic waxes *(see all)*.

Your skin is a protective barrier that helps keep foreign chemicals out of your body. However, some chemicals can pass easily through intact skin and, of course, if the skin is cut or cracked, can penetrate even more easily. Many chemicals, particularly organic solvents, can penetrate the skin. Also, some caustic substances, such as strong acids and alkalis, can burn the skin chemically. Others can irritate the skin. Solvents dissolve the oils in the skin, leaving it dry, cracked, and susceptible to infection and absorption of chemicals.

Eye contact. Some chemicals may burn or irritate the eyes. Occasionally, they may be absorbed through the eyes and enter the bloodstream. The eyes are easily harmed by chemicals, so any eye contact with chemicals should be taken as a serious incident.

The "toxicity" of a substance is the potential for that substance to cause harm. However, this is only one factor in determining whether it is a danger to you. The degree of danger is decided by the following factors.

• Route of exposure—how the substance enters your body

• Dose—how much enters your body

• Reaction and interaction—other substances to which you are exposed

Humans vary widely in sensitivity to the effects of a chemical. A lot depends upon age, sex, inherited traits, diet, pregnancy, state of health, and use of medication, drugs, or alcohol. Depending on these characteristics, some will experience the toxic effects of a chemical at a lower or higher dose than others.

There are some people who are diagnosed as having an "environmental illness," or "multiple chemical sensitivity" (MCS). They have been labeled by conventional physicians as having a psychiatric disorder rather than a physical disorder, but the doctors who treat them, "clinical ecologists," maintain that the MCS patients have a definite physical disorder that makes them highly susceptible to the effects of environmental chemicals.[24]

---

[24]"People Diagnosed as Having 'Environmental Illness'," Office of Health Center Information and Communication, University of Iowa Health Center, February 5, 1991.

The Human Ecology Action League (HEAL) was founded in 1977 as a nonprofit organization of people affected by or concerned about the environment. According to the organization's membership information packet, "chemical sensitivities and related disorders include many medical conditions that share a common characteristic. Sufferers become ill from eating, breathing, or absorbing small amounts of widely used 'safe' chemicals."

HEAL's literature points out that many chronic illnesses, including autoimmune disorders such as lupus and rheumatoid arthritis, can be aggravated by chemicals and that people can become so sensitized from a major exposure that small amounts of chemicals in daily life can subsequently provoke symptoms. Even repeated low-dose exposure can cause gradual, subtle, but long-term damage.

The majority of people, however, do not have MCS, but can certainly be affected by chemicals that are irritants or allergens. Some chemicals cause both reactions. For example, formaldehyde gas is very irritating. Almost everyone will experience irritation of the eyes, nose, and throat, with tears in the eyes and a sore throat, at some level of exposure. If the exposure is high enough, they may even develop "chemical pneumonia." One person may be more sensitive to formaldehyde and experience irritation at lower levels of exposure than other people in the area. A few individuals may be allergic to formaldehyde and develop hives or a rash at very low levels; however, most people will not be allergic to the chemical, but be irritated by it.

LOCAL OR SYSTEMIC EFFECTS

If a toxic substance causes damage at the point where it first contacts the body, that is a "local effect." The most common points at which substances first contact the body are the skin, eyes, nose, throat, and lungs. Toxic substances can also enter the body and travel in the bloodstream to internal organs. Effects that are produced this way are called "systemic." The internal organs most commonly affected are the liver, kidneys, heart, nervous system (including the brain), and reproductive system.

A toxic chemical may cause local effects, systemic effects, or both. For example, if ammonia gas is inhaled, it quickly infiltrates the lining of the respiratory tract (nose, throat, and lungs). Almost no ammonia passes from the lungs into the blood. Since damage is caused only at the point of initial contact, ammonia is said to exert a local effect. An epoxy resin is an example of a substance with local effects on the skin. On the other hand, if liquid phenol contacts the skin, it irritates the skin at the point of contact (a local effect), and can also be absorbed through the skin, and may damage the liver and kidneys (systemic effects).

Sometimes, as with phenols, the local effects caused by a chemical provide a warning that exposure is occurring. You are then alerted that the chemical may be entering your body and producing systemic effects you cannot yet see or feel. Some chemicals, however, do not provide any warning at all, and so are particularly hazardous. For example, the solvents glycol ethers (*see* Glycol Ethers) can pass through the skin and cause serious internal damage without producing any observable effect on the skin.

The Amount Counts

In general, the greater the amount of a substance that enters your body, the greater the effect on your body. This connection between amount and effect is called the "dose-response relationship." The EPA states one of the biggest deficiencies found in the assessment of indoor environments is the inability to properly assess human risk from indoor air pollution. This shortcoming is the result of limited data on human exposure to the many different pollutants found indoors, and the inability to distinguish among multiple health end points.[25]

When evaluating the significance of exposure to airborne particles or vapors at home or work, an industrial hygienist (IH) or similarly trained professional may go to the site and collect air samples to identify the chemical and measure its concentration. If the measured concentration is higher than is considered acceptable, some action is taken to rectify the situation.

How does an IH determine what concentration is acceptable? The answer is simple, according to Sidney C. Soderholm, Ph.D., assistant professor of toxicology in biophysics at the University of Rochester. The investigator looks on one of the available lists prepared by governmental and nongovernmental organizations to see what concentration is considered acceptable in the situation, and makes a judgment based on professional training. If the contaminant identified in the air is not on the list, more analysis is needed.

The EPA and other government agencies are funding research to develop better methods of determining how indoor pollutants affect us. Dr. Soderholm and his colleagues, under a government grant,

---

[25]*Report to Congress on Indoor Air Quality: Volume III: Indoor Air Pollution Research Needs Statement,* United States Environmental Protection Agency, August 1989, p. 12.

for example, have developed a laboratory method for measuring the deposition of inhaled materials in the lung.

What does his work mean to you? It should provide the information and tools to allow IHs and others who make air concentration measurements to more accurately assess hazards, and, thus, to do their jobs better and with more confidence when evaluating particles and vapors in room air.[26]

Time Counts

The longer you are exposed to a chemical, the more likely you are to be affected by it. The dose is still important, however, because at very low levels you may not experience any effects no matter how long you are exposed. At higher concentrations you may not be affected following a short-term exposure, but repeated exposure over time may cause harm. Chemical exposure over a long period is often particularly hazardous because, over time, some chemicals can accumulate in the body, or because, through continued exposure, the damage does not have a chance to be repaired.

Sooner or Later

Health effects from indoor air pollutants fall into two categories: those that are experienced immediately after exposure, and those that do not show up until years later.

Immediate, or "acute," effects, which may show up after a single exposure or repeated exposures, include irritation of the eyes, nose, and throat, headaches, dizziness, and fatigue. These effects are usually short-term and treatable. Sometimes the treatment is simply eliminating the exposure, if the source can be identified. Symptoms of some diseases, including asthma, hypersensitivity pneumonia, and humidifier fever can also show up soon after exposure.

The likelihood of an individual developing immediate reactions to indoor air pollutants depends on several factors. Age, preexisting medical conditions, and individual sensitivity are important influences.

Some effects are similar to those from colds or other viral diseases, so it is often difficult to determine if the symptoms are a result of exposure to indoor air pollution. For this reason, it is important to pay attention to the time and place the symptoms occur. If the symptoms fade or go away when you are away from home and

[26]Sidney C. Soderholm, Ph.D., assistant professor of toxicology in biophysics, University of Rochester, personal communication, July 15, 1991.

come back when you return home, an effort should be made to identify the indoor air sources that may be the cause. Health effects may show up years after exposure has occurred, or only after long or repeated periods of exposure. These effects, which include emphysema and other respiratory diseases, heart disease, and cancer, can be severely debilitating, or fatal.

The delay between the beginning of exposure and the appearance of disease caused by that exposure is called "the latency period." Some chronic effects caused by chemicals, such as cancer, have very long latency periods. Cancer, which is the uncontrolled growth and spread of abnormal cells in the body, has been known to develop as long as forty years after a worker's first exposure to a cancer-causing chemical.

The length of the latency period for chronic effects makes it difficult to establish the cause-and-effect relationship between the exposure and the illness. Since chronic diseases develop gradually, you may have the disease for some time before it is detected. It is, therefore, important for you and your physician to know what chronic effects might be caused by the substances you use on the job.

Knowledge about the health effects of chemicals is often based on their effects on industrial workers, our "canaries," who work with or produce the chemicals. Their very high exposure to toxic chemicals and their resulting ailments serve as an early warning system to those of us exposed to those same chemicals in much lower doses.

BIRTH DEFECTS

Some of the effects of hazardous chemicals can be passed from one generation to another.

The effect of chemicals around the house, yard, and office causing birth defects has been of concern for a number of years. Each year, 250,000 children are born with birth defects, 60 percent of which are unknown in origin.

The presence of solvents in drinking water has been linked to leukemia and birth defects in California, Massachusetts, and New Jersey.[27,28,29] A schoolteacher from Rochester learned that perchloroethylene, a solvent used in caulking her new house, could

[27]S. W. Lagakos, B. J. Wessen, and M. Zelen, "An Analysis of Contaminated Well Water and Health Effects in Woburn, Massachusetts," *Journal of the American Statistical Association,* 81, no. 395, September 1986, pp. 583–596.
[28]Robert Hanley, "Women's Leukemia Rate Higher in Four New Jersey Towns," *New York Times,* December 13, 1987, p. 64.
[29]*Interim Report on Ground Water Contamination,* House Committee on Government Operations, September 30, 1980.

well have been the cause of leukemia in her newborn infant and in the family's dog. Both died. The level of perchloroethylene from the caulking, when tested by environmental investigators, reportedly was a thousand times the level in homes in industrial northern New Jersey. The family was advised to vacate the house immediately.[30]

Children and pregnant women have been known to be vulnerable to the effects of toxic chemicals but, recently, attention has been focused on the effects of common chemicals on sperm. Evidence exists that paternal exposure can also affect the developing fetus. Paternal exposures to drugs, alcohol, radiation, and workplace toxins have been reported to produce a wide spectrum of problems, including stillbirths, spontaneous abortions, fetal and neonatal growth retardation, childhood leukemia, tumors of the central nervous system, and behavioral changes.

Experiments at the Medical College of Ohio's Department of Physiology and Biophysics, for example, have shown that certain chemicals, including a variety of pesticides, markedly affect sperm cell function.[31] Men who worked in the metal industry were found to be 3.3 times more likely to have children who developed brain cancer than were those who worked in jobs with low exposure to hazardous materials, the Ohio researchers noted. A man's job during the year prior to his wife's pregnancy was particularly important in determining the risk of cancer in their children, the study found. Again, no cause-and-effect relationship could be proven.

A British Columbia study of more than twenty-two thousand children born with birth defects found that children of fire fighters were more likely to suffer from a congenital heart defect that creates an abnormal opening between heart chambers. The study noted that fire fighters are exposed to gases such as carbon monoxide, and combustion products of plastics and rubber, all of which are known to cause genetic abnormalities and cancers. However, the study could not determine whether genetic damage to fathers was responsible for birth defects.[32]

[30]Bernadette Danna-Lee, Rochester, New York, "A Mother's Search for the Truth," paper presented before The Fourth National Environmental Health Conference, United States Department of Health and Human Services and Public Health Service, San Antonio, Texas, June 20–23, 1989.

[31]Leonard Nelson, Medical College of Ohio, "Toxicants That Affect Sperm Cell Function May Have Fetal Consequences," paper presented at the American Association for the Advancement of Science meeting, Washington, D.C., February 17, 1991.

[32]Max Gates, "Dad's Toxic Exposure Studied as Pregnancy Risk," *The Star-Ledger,* May 25, 1990, p. 22.

Dr. Maureen Paul, director of the Occupational Reproductive Hazards Center, University of Massachusetts Medical Center, Worcester, says that determining the effects of exposure to toxic substances will be difficult, because the effects of low-level exposures are difficult to detect, and some effects may not appear for years, or even generations.[33]

Danger Multiplied

The common answer to persons worried about toxic chemicals in their food, water, and air is that exposure to a minute amount of a chemical will not harm you. That risk is dose related. But rarely cited is the problem of exposure to more than one chemical at a time.

Depending upon the job you have and your activities at home, you may be exposed to several or perhaps many chemicals at one time. If you are, you need to be aware of their possible reactions and interactions. A "reaction" (*see* Reaction *and* Reactivity) occurs when chemicals combine with each other to produce a new substance. This new substance may have properties different from those of the original ones, and it could be more hazardous. For example, when household bleach and lye (such as a drain cleaner) are mixed together, a highly dangerous chlorine gas is released.

An interaction of two chemicals may affect your health more adversely than the action of either one alone. For instance, carbon tetrachloride and ethanol (drinking alcohol) are both toxic to the liver. If you are overexposed to carbon tetrachloride and drink alcohol excessively, the damage to your liver may be much greater than the consequence of either chemical alone. Another example of interaction is the increased risk of developing lung cancer caused by exposures to both cigarette smoking and asbestos. If you smoke a pack of cigarettes a day or are heavily exposed the asbestos, you may increase your risk of lung cancer up to six times higher than someone who is not exposed to either. But if you smoke a pack a day and are also heavily exposed to asbestos, your risk may be ninety times higher than someone who avoids both.

Another type of interaction causes "potentiation"; this occurs when the effect of one substance is increased by exposure to a second substance, which would not cause that effect by itself. For example, although acetone does not damage the liver by itself, it can increase carbon tetrachloride's ability to harm the liver.

[33]Ibid.

A label will sometimes specify incompatible chemicals, and the Material Safety Data Sheet (MSDS) for a chemical will often list its potential hazardous reaction along with the substances with which it should not be mixed. Unfortunately, however, few chemicals have been tested to determine if interactions and potentiations with other chemicals do occur, so you should avoid mixing chemicals whenever possible.

YOUR BODY'S DEFENSES

Despite all of the chemical hazards mentioned above, your body's ability to detoxify a toxic substance is wondrous. Your body has several systems. Of prime importance are the liver, kidneys, and lungs, which "detoxify" or change chemicals to a less toxic form and then eliminate them. If your rate of exposure to a chemical exceeds the rate at which you can eliminate it, some of the chemical will accumulate in your body. For example, if you work with a chemical for eight hours a day, you have the rest of the day (sixteen hours) to eliminate it from your body before you are exposed again the next day. If your body cannot eliminate all the chemical in sixteen hours and you continue to be exposed, the amount in the body will accumulate for each day you are exposed. Illness that affects the organs used for detoxification and elimination, such as hepatitis, an inflammation of the liver, can also decrease their ability to eliminate chemicals from the body.

Accumulation does not continue indefinitely. There is a point where the amount in the body reaches a maximum and remains the same, as long as your exposure also remains the same. This point will be different for each chemical.

Some chemicals, such as ammonia and formaldehyde, leave the body quickly and do not accumulate at all. Other chemicals are stored in the body for long periods. For instance, lead is stored in the bones, calcium is stored in the liver and kidneys, and polychlorinated biphenyls (PCBs) are stored in the fat. There are a few substances, such as asbestos fibers, that, once deposited, remain in the body forever.

Solvents may be inhaled, ingested, or absorbed directly through the skin because they are soluble in fat. Many are rapidly excreted in expired air. Some may be metabolized in the liver, then excreted in the bile, and may have the potential for liver toxicity. Others are excreted through the kidneys. Accumulation in the body is dependent on fat content of specific tissue, which is greatest in fat tissue. Nerve tissues have a relatively high fat content, so brain and nerves may be affected.

In addition to your liver, kidneys, and lungs to protect you against toxic chemicals, you are armed with your senses.

Sense of smell. The "odor threshold" is the lowest level of a chemical that can be smelled by most people. If a chemical's odor threshold is lower than the amount deemed hazardous, the chemical is said to have "good warning properties." One example of a chemical with good warning properties is ammonia. Most people can smell it at 5 parts per million (ppm), far below the Permissible Exposure Level (PEL) of 25 ppm.

It is important to remember that for most chemicals, the odor thresholds vary widely from person to person. In addition, some chemicals, such as hydrogen sulfide, cause you to rapidly lose your ability to smell them (called "olfactory fatigue").

Do not depend on odor alone to warn you. If you cannot smell a chemical, it may still be present. Some chemicals cannot be smelled even at levels that are harmful, have no color, and may not cause immediate symptoms. Carbon monoxide is an example of such a "sneak" killer.

With these cautions in mind, knowing a chemical's odor threshold may serve as a rough guide to your exposure level.

Sense of taste. If you inhale or ingest a chemical, it may leave a taste in your mouth. Some chemicals have a particular taste.

Cough and sneeze reflexes. If you cough up mucous (sputum or phlegm) with particles in it, or blow your nose and see particles on your handkerchief, then you know you have definitely inhaled some chemical in particle form.

BEING ALERT TO CERTAIN SIGNS AROUND YOU

Is There Settled Dust or Mist?

If chemical dust or mist is in the air, it will eventually settle on work surfaces, or on your skin, hair, and clothing. It is likely that you inhaled some of this chemical while it was in the air.

Do You Have Immediate Symptoms?

If you or your co-workers experience symptoms known to be caused by a chemical during or shortly after its use, you may have been overexposed. Symptoms might include tears in your eyes, a burning sensation of skin, nose, or throat, a cough, dizziness, or a headache.

Do You Know What Is in a Product You Are Using?

Everyone who works with toxic substances should know the names, toxicities, and other hazards of the substances they use. Employers are required by law to provide this information, along with training in how to use toxic substances safely. As pointed out before, a worker may obtain information about a chemical's composition, physical characteristics, and toxicity from the Material Safety Data Sheet (MSDS). Unfortunately, the precise chemical composition is often proprietary information (a trade secret), and the toxicity information on an MSDS may be incomplete and unreliable.

If you are troubled by a chemical at work, check with the EPA, the Consumer Product Safety Commission, or OSHA (*see* listings on page 316) to find out more about the chemical and any rules for its use.

HINTS FOR SAFER USE OF CHEMICALS

Substitute. Use a less toxic alternative for a hazardous chemical, if possible. Many suggestions are given in this book. But before choosing a substitute, carefully consider its physical and health hazards. For example, mineral spirits (Stoddard Solvent) is less of a health hazard than perchloroethylene for dry cleaning (*see all*), but is more of a fire hazard and an air pollutant.

Ventilate, ventilate. In the zeal to save fuel and electricity, modern buildings and homes have become "sealed" containers for humans, and the result has been an increase in health problems resulting from home pollution and SBS (*see* Sick-Building Syndrome).

Good ventilation could reduce up to 75 percent of all office and home air problems. Temperatures should not vary more than four or five degrees (68 degrees to 73 degrees).

If too little outdoor air enters a home, pollutants can accumulate to levels that can cause discomfort and pose health problems. Unless they are built with special mechanical means of ventilation, homes that are designed and sealed against letting inside air out and outside air in may have higher pollutant levels than other homes. However, because some weather conditions can drastically reduce the amount of outside air that enters a home, pollutants can build up even in homes that are normally considered leaky. High temperature and humidity levels also can increase the concentration of some pollutants.

Outside air enters and leaves a house in three ways. It flows through construction joints and cracks around windows, doors, in the foundation, or from crawl spaces underneath the home; it comes in and leaves through open windows or doors; and it is exchanged through outdoor vented fans.

Local exhaust ventilation has a hood or an intake at or over the source of exposure to capture or draw contaminants from the air before they spread into a room and your breathing zone. General or dilution ventilation is continual replacement and circulation of fresh air sufficient to keep concentrations of toxic substances diluted below hazardous levels. However, concentrations will be highest near the source, and overexposure may occur in this area. If the dilution of air is not well mixed, pockets of high concentrations may exist.

The average air exchange rate of homes in the United States today is 0.7 to 1.0 air changes per hour; in relatively tight homes it can be as low as 0.2 air changes per hour (*see* Ventilation Rate). It is important to understand that an air exchange rate of 1.0 air changes per hour does not mean that all pollutants will be removed in one hour. Ventilation is a process of dilution and removal that gradually rids pollutants. In addition, pollutant removal is further slowed down by being trapped by carpets, drapes, and other surfaces, only to be released into the air later.

PROTECT YOURSELF

Use a respirator. If you must work with toxic chemicals or sand, or blow potentially harmful dust and fibers around, use a respirator. Respiratory protective equipment consists of devices that cover the mouth and nose to prevent substances in the air from being inhaled. A respirator is effective only when fitted, used, and maintained properly.

Wear protective clothing. This includes gloves, aprons, goggles, and face shields when using toxic chemicals. These should be made of materials designed to resist penetration by the particular chemical being used. Wear heavy-duty vinyl gloves with cotton liners, if possible, when hands are in contact with harsh cleansers at home or chemical irritants at work. Avoid abrasive soaps for removing grease and oil. Remove rings when using soaps and detergents, because these materials can become trapped underneath them and cause irritation. Manufacturers of protective wear usually can provide some information regarding the substances that are effectively blocked by the clothing.

Use barrier creams. Barrier creams are used to coat the skin and prevent chemicals from reaching it. They may be helpful when the type of work prevents the use of gloves. However, barrier creams are not recommended as substitutes for gloves. General skin creams and lotions (such as moisturizing lotion) are *not* barrier creams.

Be a good housekeeper. Do not leave rags soaking in solvent where they might give off vapors. Keep solvent containers closed as much as possible. Go on a toxic substances hunt! In your basement, look for paint and paint supplies, brush cleaners, paint thinners and strippers, wood preservatives, varnishes, shellacs, sealants, and oil stains. Many of these are poisons or sensitizers. Some cause cancer. Many accumulate in the environment and in people to toxic levels— and they do not go away. Some craft and hobby supplies are toxic: glues and adhesives, staining materials, photographic chemicals, soldering materials, and aerosols may be on your shelves.

In the closets and kitchen of your home look for pesticides, mothballs, and cleaning products such as bleach, ammonia, drain cleaners, oven cleaners, spot removers, furniture and floor polishes, deodorizers, disinfectants, and glass, tile and metal polishes. Many of these may cause instant death if ingested. Others may accumulate in your body and lead to illness, or cause you to develop a sensitivity after repeated exposure (*see* Sensitivity and Sensitize)

In your garage, look for fertilizers, pesticides, insecticides, herbicides, fungicides, and rodenticides. Check for antifreeze, oil, degreasers, batteries, transmission fluid, waxes and polishes, radiator/engine flush compounds, charcoal fire-starting fluid, and rustproofer. All of these are poisonous to people, pets, and wildlife.

Assume that the contents of all unlabeled containers are hazardous. Do not assume that an old, opened package contains what it says it does. People reuse containers without relabeling them. Old receptacles are hazardous because they may rust, leak and/or because their contents may have deteriorated into more harmful substances. Because gases can leak even from closed containers, your disposal of them could do much to lower the concentration of toxic chemicals in your home.

Some of the products you may find on the shelf have been banned but are still lying around your home. Do not simply toss these unwanted products in the garbage can. Find out if your local government or any organization in your community sponsors special days for collection of toxic household wastes. If such days are available, use them to dispose of unwanted containers safely. When in doubt, do not toss it out until you have contacted your local public health department, county extension of the USDA, poison control center, state EPA, hazardous waste-management office, or groundwater protection hotline.

Do not pour chemicals down the drain, and definitely do not pour a series of chemicals down the drain one after the other. You may cause an explosion in your plumbing system, or cause the plumbing to corrode.

Make sure that materials you decide to keep are stored in well-ventilated areas, safely out of reach of children and pets. Keep them in their original containers, tightly covered, in a secure area away from heat, moisture, and open flames.

Buy limited quantities. In the future, if you use products only occasionally or seasonally, such as paints, paint strippers, kerosene for space heaters, or gasoline for lawn mowers, buy only as much as you will use right away.

Never mix chemicals together. You may cause an explosion or create a material much more toxic than the original product alone.

If you must oil a machine, use medical-grade mineral oil. It is obtainable from a pharmacy. This, too, may cause respiratory problems, but fewer than those caused by commercial machine oils.

Paint and/or apply varnish in the spring. This allows you to leave the windows open all summer. Some sensitive individuals will detect paint fumes for three months or more after application.

Use polishes outdoors, if possible. Polishes—from shoe to furniture to silverware polish—should be used outdoors or with the windows wide open.

Don't get yourself in hot water—too long. Minimize use of hot water. Use warm or cool water rather than hot whenever possible particularly if there is a problem with chemicals in your water or your home. Hot water causes compounds such as benzene to vaporize more rapidly. Ventilate bathrooms before and after showering. Limit showering and bathing to less than fifteen minutes.

Cool it. Remember, as the temperature of the environment rises, any substance in the environment is more likely to evaporate to a gas or form vapors.

Take off your shoes when you enter your home. In Japanese homes, you are required to remove your shoes before entering. This is a good idea according to studies conducted by researchers from

Seattle, Washington, and Montana State University.[34] John W. Roberts, M.Sc., and Evelyn R. Warren, Ph.D., studied rug dust from twenty-nine homes in Seattle and found that twenty-five had excessive mutagenic and/or toxic levels. The concentration of dust in rugs varies with the type of carpet, vacuum cleaner, frequency of cleaning, sources of dust by the front door, and shoe removal practices. Power head vacuum cleaners picked up from 2.1 to 6.4 times more dirt than an air cleaner. The combination of a shag rug, an air cleaner, unpaved road shoulders or walkways, and vacuuming every other week, resulted in the highest amount of toxic dust. Bare floors had the lowest concentrations.

The study suggested that floor dust can be a significant source of toxins for small children who live in areas where soil has been contaminated by residues from air pollution or hazardous waste. Smoking or use of toxic products in the home add further risks, the researchers concluded. Use of entrance mats, and removal or cleaning of shoes at the door can reduce track-in dirt.

The researchers pointed out that toddlers ingest 2.5 times as much dust as adults, and because they are, on the average, only one-fifth the weight of adults, their risk will be potentially at least 12.5 times greater.

Smell a carpet before you buy it. If it smells strong, do not purchase it. It probably has not been adequately "cured."

Switch soaps. Use soaps or detergents specifically formulated for babies' wash if laundry products are suspected of causing skin inflammation. Avoid fabric softeners and antistatic products, and double-rinse the wash if you are sensitive.

Prewash new materials. If you are sensitive, wash new clothing and bed linens several times before using. Contact dermatitis caused by clothing is usually due to formaldehyde (*see* Formaldehyde) released by chemicals in the finishing of fabrics (*see* Finishing Compounds) and sometimes to the dyes. Avoid polyester blends and cottons that are labeled "permanent press" and "wrinkle resistant," and stick to natural fibers such as cotton, linen, and silk. (Although wool is a natural fiber, it can be irritating.)

Seal off the sources of pollution. It may be possible to seal off offending pollutants from the environment, such as radon, pesticides, and carbon monoxide. Covering surfaces with two coats of nitrocellulose-based varnish will reduce formaldehyde emissions by

[34]John W. Roberts, M. Sc., and Guylyn Warren, Ph.D., "Sources of Toxics in House Dust," *International Journal of Biosocial Research*, Vol. 9, No. 1, 1987, pp. 82–91.

about 79 percent. Unfortunately, most sealants contain other toxic chemicals, so they must be applied with caution.

GUARD AGAINST YARD KILLERS

Air currents may carry pesticides that were applied on adjacent property, or miles away. However, there are steps you can take to reduce your outdoor exposure to airborne pesticide residue, or drift.

Avoid applying pesticides in windy weather. (When winds exceed ten miles per hour.)

Use coarse-droplet nozzles. This reduces misting the spray and gets as close to the target as possible.

Keep the wind to your side. This prevents sprays and dusts from blowing into your face.

Protect yourself when someone else is applying pesticides. If the person is spraying near your home, stay indoors with your pets and children, keeping doors and windows closed. If it is very windy during the pesticide application, remain inside for an hour or two.

Protect your environment if pesticides are applied frequently near your home. If you live next to fields receiving regular pesticide treatment, consider planting a buffer zone of thick-branched trees and shrubs upwind, to help serve as a windbreak.

Insist on public notifications of pesticide spraying. Many governments require public notification in advance of area-wide or broad-scale pesticide spray activities, through announcements to area residents, or posting of signs in areas to be treated. Some communities have also enacted "right-to-know" ordinances, which require public notification, usually through posting, of lawn treatments and other small-scale outdoor pesticide uses. If your local government does not require notifications, either for large- or small-scale applications, you may want to work with local officials to develop such requirements.

INDOOR PESTICIDE PRECAUTIONS

Indoors, the air you breathe may bear pesticide residues long after a pesticide has been applied to objects in your home or office, or to indoor surfaces and crawl spaces. Pesticides dissipate more slowly indoors than outdoors. In addition, energy-efficient features built into many homes reduce air exchange, aggravating the problem. To limit your exposure to indoor pesticide residues:

- use pesticides indoors only when absolutely necessary.
- use only limited amounts.

• provide adequate ventilation during and after application.

• if you hire a pest control company, make sure the personnel are certified and oversee the application activities carefully.

• if pesticides are used inside your home, air out the house often, since outdoor air generally is fresher and purer than indoor air. Open doors and windows, and run overhead or whole-house fans to exchange indoor air for outside air rapidly and completely.

• if pesticides have been used extensively and an indoor air contamination problem has developed, clean-scrub all surfaces where pesticides may have settled, including cracks and crevices. Consult a knowledgeable professional for advice on appropriate cleaning materials if soap and water are insufficient.

• consider pesticide labeling to be what is is intended to be—your best guide to using pesticides safely and effectively.

• pretend that the pesticide product you are using is more toxic than you think it is. Take special precautions to ensure an extra margin of protection for yourself, your family, and pets.

• do not use more pesticide than the label says. You may not achieve a higher degree of pest control, and you will certainly experience a higher degree of risk.

• if you hire a pest control firm to do the job, ask the company to use the least toxic or any chemical-free pest control means available. For example, some home pest control companies offer an electro-gun technique to control termites and similar infestations by penetrating infested areas and "frying" the problem pests without using any chemicals.

• remember that sometimes a nonpesticidal approach is as convenient and effective as its chemical alternatives. Consider using such alternative approaches whenever possible.

IF YOU WORK IN A SICK OFFICE BUILDING

If you feel you have a problem that is not being corrected, you can call either NIOSH or your state Occupational Health Association. Both have industrial hygienists, epidemiologists, engineers, and chemists who can diagnose SBS (see Sick Building Syndrome). These agencies will investigate when several people in an office have symptoms that fit Sick Building Syndrome, and both promise anonymity. See Further Information at the back of this book. **Check with management about the kinds of products used for**

cleaning. Cleaning personnel tend to use very strong chemicals because it makes their job easier.

HOW TO USE THIS BOOK

While unique in content, this dictionary follows the format of most standard dictionaries. The following are examples of entries with any explanatory notes that may be necessary.

FORMALDEHYDE • **Formalin. Methaldehyde. Methanal. Methyl Aldehyde. Methylene Glycol. Methylene Oxide. Oxomethane. Oxymethylene. Paraform. Paraformaldehyde. Trioxane. BFV®. Fannoform®. Formalith®. Formol®. Fyde®. Ivalon®. Karsan®. Lysoform®. Morbicid®. Superlysoform®.** A colorless gas obtained by the oxidation of methyl alcohol and, generally, used in watery solution. Vapors are intensely irritating to mucous membranes. It has been estimated that 4 to 8 percent of the general population may be sensitized to formaldehyde. It is used in more than three thousand products, including disinfectants, cosmetics, fungicides, leather tanners, platers, defoamers, preservatives, and adhesives. It is also used in pressed-wood products such as hardwood, plywood, wall paneling, particle board, fiberboard, and furniture. Some surfactants, such as the widely used lauryl sulfate, may contain formaldehyde as a preservative, and others may have it without listing it on the label. Formaldehyde is used in the manufacture of commercial products such as resins, wrinkleproof fabrics, rubber products, dyes, durable press drapes, carpets, and other textiles, plastics, and paper products such as paper towels. It is also present in insulation materials such as urea-formaldehyde foam, and combustion products, such as fuel exhaust and tobacco smoke. Any of these materials may give off formaldehyde vapors. The eyes, nose, and throat are irritated by formaldehyde vapors at levels as low as one part formaldehyde per million parts of air. Some people are more easily affected than others. Formaldehyde levels in the indoor air depend mainly on what is releasing the formaldehyde, temperature, humidity, and the air exchange rate (the amount of air entering or leaving the indoor area). Average concentrations in older homes without urea-formaldehyde insulation are generally well below 0.1 ppm. In homes with signifcant amounts of new pressed-wood products, levels can be greater than 0.3 ppm. Increasing the flow of outdoor air into a room decreases formaldehyde levels. Sealing a residence or office, conversely, increases the formaldehyde level in the air. Some sources such as pressed-wood products containing urea-formaldehyde glues, urea-formaldehyde foam insulation, durable press fabrics, and draperies, release more formaldehyde when new. As they age, the formaldehyde decreases.

Formaldehyde is an inexpensive and effective preservative, but there are serious questions about its safety. Ingestion can cause severe abdominal pain, internal bleeding, loss of ability to urinate, vertigo, coma, and death. Skin reactions after exposure to formaldehyde are very common because the chemical can be both irritating and an allergen. Physicians have reported severe reactions to nail hardeners containing formaldehyde. Its use in cosmetics is banned in Japan and Sweden. It is a highly reactive chemical that is damaging to the hereditary substances in the cells of several species. Researchers from the Division of Cancer Cause and Prevention of the National Cancer Institute recommended in April 1983, that formaldehyde be "further investigated" since it is involved in DNA damage and inhibits its repair, potentiates the toxicity of X rays in human lung cells, and may act in concert with other chemical agents to produce mutagenic and carcinogenic effects. Formaldehyde causes cancer in test animals. Some studies have suggested that formaldehyde exposure can cause cancer of the lungs and respiratory tract in humans, although other studies have not found this effect, according to the Hazard Evaluation System and Information Service of California (HESIS).

You can reduce your exposure to high levels of formaldehyde in the following ways:

• Make sure there is plenty of fresh air coming into the room from outside, and increase ventilation after bringing new sources of formaldehyde into the home.

• Purchasing low formaldehyde-releasing pressed-wood products for use in construction or remodeling, and for furniture, cabinets, and other wood items. These include oriented strand board and softwood plywood for construction, low formaldehyde-emitting pressed-wood products or solid wood for furniture and cabinets. Some products are labeled as low emitting, or ask for help in identifying low-emitting products. The "exterior grade" pressed-wood products are lower emitting because they contain phenol resins, not urea resins.

• Use alternative products such as lumber or metal.

• Avoid the use of foamed-in-place insulation containing formaldehyde, especially urea-formaldehyde foam insulation.

• Wash new clothing and bed linens several times before using.

• Do not wear clothing with a stiff finish, or with fabrics labeled as permanent press, wrinkle or crease resistant, waterproof, wash-and-wear, mothproof, mildew proof, sweat repellant, or fire retardant.

• Wear clothing made of silk, 100 percent synthetic fiber, or wool (unless it is shrinkproof). Fabrics that are mercerized, sanforized, or sized do not utilize formaldehyde.

See also Fabric Softeners, Finger Paint, Flame Retardants, Waterproof Adhesives, Waterproofing, Water Repellants, and Wrinkleproof Finishes.

You have learned that formaldehyde is a colorless gas obtained by the oxidation of methanol, and that it has other names, such as Formalin and Methaldehyde. You have also learned some of the names under which it is sold, such as Formol® and Lysoform®. The products in which it is commonly used are described, and the benefits and known hazards are listed. The means of reducing exposure to formaldehyde are given, along with a listing of other products in which it may be "hidden."

You may also look up products under general categories such as:

DISINFECTANTS • Household products may contain acids, alkali, alcohol, pine oil, phenol, or cationic detergents such as quaternary compounds *(see all)*. In some disinfectants, the vehicle is more toxic than the germicide. For example, Lysol® contains 79 percent ethanol, which is more toxic than the 0.1 percent concentration of *o*-phenylphenol *(see both)*. Skin contact and vapors can be irritating and corrosive to the skin and respiratory system, respectively. These products are more hazardous when dispersed from aerosol cans, because the disinfectant can be inhaled through the nose and mouth. Avoid aerosol dispensers. Make sure there is adequate ventilation. Use gloves and, if necessary, goggles. Less toxic alternatives are soap, isopropyl alcohol, white vinegar, or a mixture of one-half a cup of borax *(see* Borax) in one gallon of hot water. Keep all disinfectants stored away where children cannot reach them.

The alternatives listed here are offered as options and are not presented as recommended courses of action. Several listed alternatives are also potentially hazardous if handled improperly.

Commercial products as examples are listed throughout the dictionary. Be aware, however, that formulas change and not all ingredients may be listed on labels.

Terminology generally has been kept to a middle road between technician and average interested lay person, while at the same time avoiding oversimplification of data. A single chemical may have many names and some manufacturers, when forced to list an ingredient on the label for consumers, do so in the most complicated form. If in doubt, look up any general terms such as cleaning fluids, pesticides, floor cleaners, brake fluid, or wrinkleproof finishes, which are listed alphabetically, in the same manner as the chemicals.

With *A Consumer's Dictionary of Household, Yard, and Office Chemicals,* you will be able to make wiser choices at the store and use chemicals more safely.

You may not have any control over outdoor pollution or hidden additives in your food and water, but you do have control over the products you purchase and use in your household, yard, and office.

A

ABIETIC ACID • **Sylvic Acid.** A widely available natural acid, water-insoluble, prepared from pine resin, usually yellow, and comprised of either glassy or crystalline particles. It is used in making resins, adhesives, typewriting paper, denture adhesive powder, and varnishes. It is a texturizer in the making of soaps and in the manufacture of vinyls, lacquers, and plastics. Little is known about abietic acid toxicity; it is harmless when injected into mice, but causes paralysis in frogs, is slightly irritating to human skin and mucous membranes, and causes contact dermatitis. May also cause allergic reactions.

ABIETO-FORMO-PHENOLIC RESIN • Used in printing inks. Can cause contact dermatitis. *See* Abietic Acid, Phenol, and Printing Inks.

ABIETYL ALCOHOL • *See* Abietic Acid.

ABITOL • **Dihydroabietyl Alcohol.** Found in plastics, adhesives, and cosmetics. Can cause contact dermatitis. *See* Abietic Acid.

ABRASIVE CLEANERS OR POWDERS • Contain trisodiumphosphate, ammonia, or alcohol *(see all)*. For less toxic alternative, rub area with one-half lemon dipped in borax, rinse and dry or make a paste of baking soda and lemon juice, and rub it on.

ABRASIVES • Fine, hard-surfaced materials used to reduce, smooth, clean, or polish the surfaces of other, less hard substances such as glass, plastic, stone, and wood. Natural, abrasive materials include diamond dust, sand, emery, and pumice. *See also* Aluminum Oxide and Silicon Carbide.

ACACIA GUM • **Gum Arabic. Catechu.** Acacia is the odorless, colorless, tasteless dried exudate from the stem of the acacia tree grown in Africa, the Near East, India, and the southern United States. Its most distinguishing quality among the natural gums is its ability to dissolve rapidly in water. The use of acacia dates back four thousand years, when the Egyptians employed it in paints. It is used today in ink, matches, lithography, mucilages, offset sprays in printing, adhesives, stiffeners for rayon, pastry, and denture-adhesive powder. Its principal use in the confectionery industry is to retard sugar crystallization, and as a thickener for candies, jellies, glazes, and chewing gum. It is used as a demulcent to soothe irritations, particularly of the mucous membranes. It can cause allergic reactions such as skin rash and asthmatic attack. Oral toxicity is low. *See also* Vegetable Gums.

ACARABEN • *See* Chlorobenzilate.

ACARACIDES • Chemicals that kill mites and ticks, such as dinobuton, acricid, fenitothion, chlorfensulphide, or ethion *(see all)*. For ear mites in pets, methoxychlor, piperonyl butoxide, and pyrethrins may be used in mineral oil *(see all)*. *See also* Pesticides.

ACCELERATOR • A substance added to a compound to speed the final result of the mixture. For example, zinc oxide may be added to accelerate the vulcanization of rubber.

ACCENT™ • A grass-killing sulfonylurea herbicide for cornfields, made by DuPont. It reportedly requires a lower dose and is less toxic than older chemicals. Farmers who have switched to the new product need use only 0.5 to 1 percent as much herbicide per acre as they did before.

ACCLAIM™ • A crabgrass control. *See* Fenoxaprop-Ethyl.

ACEPHATE • An organophosphorus insecticide of moderate persistence in the environment and of relatively low toxicity for humans and other warm-blooded animals. It interferes with transmission of nerve signals, but is less toxic than parathion and many other organophosphates.

ACETAL • A volatile liquid derived from acetaldehyde *(see)* and alcohol, used as a solvent, a fruit flavoring, and in medicine as a hypnotic. It is a central nervous system depressant, similar in action to paraldehyde, but more toxic. Paraldehyde is a hypnotic and sedative whose side effects are respiratory depression, cardiovascular collapse, and possible high blood pressure reactions.

ACETALDEHYDE • **Ethanal.** A flammable, colorless liquid, with a characteristic fruity odor, occurring naturally in apples, broccoli, cheese, coffee, grapefruit, and other vegetables and fruits. An intermediate *(see)* and solvent in the manufacture of perfumes. Also used in the manufacture of synthetic rubber and in the silvering of mirrors. It is irritating to the mucous membranes, and ingestion of large doses may cause death by respiratory paralysis. Inhalation, usually limited by intense irritation of lungs, can also be toxic. Acetaldehyde can damage the kidneys, liver, lungs, and eyes. A fire hazard, it should be kept away from heat and flame.

ACETAMIDE • **Ethanamide; Acetic Acid Amide.**Colorless, deliquescent crystals derived from ethyl acetate and ammonium hydroxide. Odorless when pure, but can have a mousy scent. Used as a general solvent in lacquers, explosives, soldering flux; as a hygroscopic, wetting, or penetrating agent; and to denature alcohol. Has caused liver cancer when given orally to rats in doses of 5,000 milligrams per kilogram of body weight. A mild skin irritant with low toxicity.

ACETANILIDE • Trimethylactanilide. White, shiny, odorless leaflets or powder, derived from aniline *(see)*. Used as a rubber accelerator, as an inhibitor in hydrogen peroxide, a stabilizer for cellulose ester coatings, a synthetic camphor, and in pharmaceutical chemicals and dyestuffs. It is also a precursor of penicillin, and is used as an antiseptic. It caused tumors when given orally to rats in doses of 3,500 milligrams per kilogram of body weight, and can cause contact dermatitis in humans.

ACETATE • A manufactured fiber made by combining cellulose with acetate from acetic acid and acetic anhydride *(see both)*. The cellulose acetate is dissolved in acetone *(see)*, and as the threads emerge from the spinner, the solvent is evaporated in warm air. The result is a fast-drying, supple, inexpensive fabric that is shrink resistant, able to take a wide range of colors and to resist wrinkles. Special dyes were developed for acetate since it does not accept the dyes ordinarily used for cotton and rayon. The uses of acetate fabrics, which usually have to be dry-cleaned, are foundation garments, lingerie, dresses, knitted jerseys, shirts, slacks, sportswear, satin, faille, crepe, lace, and tricot fabrics, taffeta, brocade, draperies, upholstery, filling for comforters and pillows, and cigarette filters. Acetate is adversely affected by acetone *(see)* and other organic solvents such as nail polish remover and perfumes containing solvents.

ACETIC ACID • Bromo, Chromium Salt, Diazo- and Dehydro-Acetyl Oxide, Acetic Oxide. The number one organic chemical produced in the United States. A clear, colorless liquid with a pungent odor, derived from oxidation of acetaldehyde *(see)*. It occurs naturally in apples, cheese, cocoa, grapes, skimmed milk, oranges, peaches, pineapples, strawberries, and a variety of other fruits and plants. An organic acid solvent for gums, resins, and volatile oil. Used as a dehydrating and acetylating agent *(see both)*, in the production of dyes, perfumes, plastics, food starch, and aspirin, in blueprint copiers, and as a wart remedy. Also used as a synthetic flavoring agent, it is one of the earliest-known food additives. Vinegar is about 4 to 6 percent acetic acid, and essence of vinegar is about 14 percent. In its glacial form (without much water) it is highly corrosive and its vapors are capable of producing lung obstruction. Less than 5 percent acetic acid in solution is mildly irritating to the skin. It caused cancer in rats and mice when given orally or by injection.

ACETIC ACID AMIDE • *See* Acetylamide.

ACETIC ANHYDRIDE • **Acetyl Oxide. Acetic Oxide.** Colorless, with a strong odor, it mixes with water and alcohol. It is derived from acetaldehyde *(see)* and is used to make cellulose acetate fibers and plastics, and in the production of dyes, perfumes, explosives, aspirin, and food starch. May cause skin burns and eye damage. In vapor state, acetic anhydride produces irritation and necrosis of tissues, and carries a warning against contact with skin and eyes. Inhalation can cause lung injury.

ACETIC OXIDE • *See* Acetic Acid and Acetic Anhydride.

ACETONE • **Dimethyl Ketone. 2-Propanone.** A colorless, ethereal liquid derived by oxidation or fermentation and used to clean and dry parts of precision equipment, a nail polish remover, and a solvent for celluloid material in dentifrices, airplane glue, fats, oils, and waxes. It is among the top five organic chemicals produced in the United States. Can cause contact dermatitis, with skin rashes on the fingers and elsewhere. It can cause peeling, brittleness, and splitting of the nails. Inhalation may irritate the lungs, and in large amounts it is narcotic, causing symptoms of drunkenness similar to ethanol *(see)*. It is highly flammable and explosive and should be kept away from heat and flame.

ACETONE PEROXIDE • Acetone *(see)* to which an oxygen-containing compound has been added. It has a sharp, acrid odor similar to hydrogen peroxide. A strong oxidizing agent, it can be damaging to the skin and eyes.

ACETYL BENZOYL PEROXIDE • White crystals decomposed by water and organic matter. Used in medicine as a germicide and disinfectant. Also used to bleach flour. Toxic when ingested.

ACETYL CHLORIDE • **Ethanol Chloride.** A colorless, fuming liquid with a strong odor, derived by mixing acetic acid and phosphorous trichloride. Used to remove water from compounds, and in dyestuffs and pharmaceuticals. It is very irritating to the skin and mucous membranes, and a particularly strong eye irritant. Highly flammable, and reacts violently with water and alcohol. *See* Acetylated.

ACETYLATED • Any organic compound that has been heated with acetic anhydride or acetyl chloride to remove its water. Acetylation is used to coat candy and other products in order to hold in moisture.

ACETYLENE • A colorless gas with a garliclike odor, derived from petroleum or calcium carbide. Used in welding operations and in the manufacture of vinyls, acrylates, trichloroethylene, and carbon black. Highly flammable and explosive, it is irritating to the lungs and narcotic to the system.

ACGIH • American Conference of Governmental Industrial Hygienists, a professional organization that recommends exposure limits for toxic substances.

ACID AEROSOL • Acidic liquid or solid particles that are small enough to become airborne. High concentrations of acid aerosols can be irritating to the lungs and have been associated with some respiratory diseases, such as asthma.

ACIDS • Substances capable of turning blue litmus paper red and of forming hydrogen ions when dissolved in water. An acid aqueous solution is one that has a pH *(see)* of less than 7. Most accidents with acids around the home occur from inadvertent exposure to household products such as toilet bowl and metal cleaners. *See* Toilet Bowl Cleaners, Drain Cleaners, Metal Cleaners and Anti-Rust Compounds, Soldering Fluxes, Automobile Battery Fluid, Swimming Pool Sanitizers, and Bleaches. *See also* Chromic Acid, Hydrochloric Acid (Muriatic Acid), Nitric Acid, Phosphoric Acid, Hydrofluoric Acid, Sulfuric Acid, Acetic Acid, Formic Acid, Oxalic Acid, and Carbolic Acid.

ACONITIC ACID • **Citridic Acid. Equisetic Acid. Achilleic Acid.** A flavoring agent found in beetroot and cane sugar. Most of the commercial aconitic acids, however, are manufactured by sulfuric acid dehydration of citric acid. It is used in fruit, brandy, and rum flavorings for beverages and confections. Also used in the manufacture of plastics and Buna™ rubber. No known toxicity.

ACRICID • *See* Acaracides.

ACRILAN® • A brand of acrylic fiber *(see* fiber). It is unaffected by common solvents and is resistant to alkalies, sunlight, and weathering. It is easily dyed and wears longer than wool but not nylon. It is unaffected by mildew, molds, moths, and carpet beetle larvae. Exposure to warm temperatures for a long time causes some yellowing. It is not very flammable and melts before it burns. It is used in fabrics, sweaters, blankets, and carpets.

ACROLEIN • A yellow, transparent, liquid by-product of petroleum produced by the oxidation of propylene. Sources include combustion of wood, paper, cotton, petroleum products, and polyolefins. Used in making plastics and metal products. Very toxic. It causes tearing and intense irritation of the upper respiratory tract, and is also a skin irritant. It is a fire hazard, and should be kept away from heat and flame.

ACRYLAMIDE • Colorless, odorless crystals soluble in water and derived from acrylonitrile and sulfuric acid. It is used in the manufacture of dyes and adhesives, in soil conditioning agents, waterproofing agents, grout, permanent press fabrics, nail enamels, and face masks. Toxic by skin absorption. Long-term exposure produces nerve and brain damage, fatigue, and other neurological disorders. The OSHA permissible exposure limit is 0.3 mg/m^3 per 8 hours for the skin but the polymer *(see)* is nontoxic. Toxicity can result from handling the crystalline powder, primarily through long-term skin exposure. It causes peeling skin on the palms. Onset time is one month to eight years.

ACRYLAMIDE COPOLYMER • A polymer *(see)* of two or more monomers *(see)* consisting of acrylamide and/or its simple alkyl derivatives. *See* Acrylamide.

ACRYLAMIDE/SODIUM ACRYLATE • A polymer of acrylamide and sodium acrylate monomers. *See* Acrylamide and Acrylates.

ACRYLAN™ • *See* Acrylic Fiber.

ACRYLATES • **Acrylic Monomer. Methyl Methacrylate.** Salts or esters of acrylic acid used as a thickening agent and as a constituent of nail polish, paint, paper, leather finisher, and many other coatings. Acrylates are also used in adhesives, paints, plastics, and glass sealers of screws in the automobile industry. To be effective the compounds must be stiff at room temperature. If inhaled, acrylates can cause allergic reactions. Also, as acrylates can penetrate rubber gloves, they may cause hives. Strong irritants. *See also* Clothing.

ACRYLATE-ACRYLAMIDE RESIN • *See* Acrylic Resins.

ACRYLIC ACID • **2-Propanoic Acid.** Prepared from acrylonitrile or by oxidation of acrolein, it is a corrosive liquid with an acrid odor. It is used in the manufacture of plastics. A strong irritant.

ACRYLIC FIBER • A man-made fiber from acrylonitrile *(see),* coal, air, water, petroleum, and limestone. The acrylonitrile is usually combined with small amounts of other chemicals to improve the ability of the fiber to absorb dyes. The fabrics made from the fibers are soft, light, warm, and hold their shape. They are quick drying and resistant to sunlight, weather, oil, and chemicals. The fabrics are used in work clothes, sweaters, socks, skirts, dresses, baby garments, blankets, fleece fabrics, ski and snow suits; also draperies, carpeting, upholstery, work clothes, and slacks. They usually can be washed either by hand or machine and, if pressing is required, a moderately warm iron is recommended.

ACRYLIC RESINS • Polymers *(see)* of acrylics. Acrylic resins vary from hard, brittle solids to fibrous, elastic structures to thick liquids, depending on the method of polymerization. Used in waxy oils, base coats, dyes, protective coatings, and waterproofing of fabrics and paper. Also used as a glass substitute, in decorative illuminated signs, contact lenses, dentures, medical instruments, and furniture. Also used in the automobile industry. Can cause allergic reactions in humans.

ACRYLONITRILE • **Vinyl Cyanide. Propenenitril.** A colorless liquid with a mild odor derived from propylene oxygen and ammonia. It is among the top five organic chemicals produced in the United States each year. About 1.5 billion pounds of this substance are produced in the United States each year and used in acrylic and other synthetic fibers with such trade names as Orlon, Acrilan, Creslan, Acrylan, Elura, and Verel. It is also used in resin, plastics, latexes, and fumigants. In January 1978 the U.S. Department of Labor announced an "emergency action" to reduce worker exposure, saying that 10,000 workers were directly exposed and that another 125,000 workers were indirectly exposed. Health effects in workers have been found to be brain tumors, and lung and bowel cancer. NIOSH *(see)* requires periodic chest X rays of employees and methods to prevent skin contact. Officials said there was little risk that users of the finished products made with acrylonitrile were in danger. The emergency action was touched off when E. I. Du Pont de Nemours & Co. conducted a survey of a group of workers at its plant in Camden, South Carolina, and found that the incidence of cancer among those exposed to acrylonitrile for a long period of time was nearly three times the "expected" rate. The emergency standards permitted a worker to be exposed to only 2 parts per million of air (ppm) in an eight-hour period. The previous standard set before the carcinogenic effects of the chemical were understood was 20 ppm. Exposure causes flushing of the face, salivation, irritation of the eyes, photophobia, vomiting, weakness, headache, and diarrhea. Absorbed through the skin. Flammable. *See also* Vinyl Chloride.

ACTINOL • *See* Tall Oil.

ACTIVATED CHARCOAL • *See* Carbon Black.

ACTIVATED CHARCOAL (CARBON) • Used to remove impurities that cause undesirable color, taste, or odor in liquid. The major sources are lignite, coal, and coke. The Select Committee of the Federation of American Societies for Experimental Biology (FASEB), under contract to the FDA, concluded that it is not a hazard to human health at current or possible future use levels. However, the committee said because the substance is used extensively in the food industry, it would be prudent to have purity specifications for food grade-activated carbon to assure the absence of any cancer-causing hydrocarbons in food.

ACUTE TOXICITY • The capacity of a substance to cause a poisonous effect (such as skin or eye irritation, or damage to an organ), or death, as a result of a single or short-term exposure.

ADHESIVES • Substances, inorganic or organic, natural or synthetic, capable of bonding other materials together by surface attachment. *See* Casein Glues, China Cement, Contact Fabric, Film, Glue, General Purpose; Leather; Metal; Model Cement; Paste, Library; Patching; Pipe Joint; Plastic; Resins; Roofing; Rubber; Shoe Cement; Thermoplastic; Tile; Wallpaper; Waterproof. *See also* Abietic Acid and Acacia Gum.

ADHESIVE TAPE • A frequent cause of skin reactions, it is thought to be the cause of irritation more than allergy. However, some tapes do contain rosins, turpentine, and lanolin *(see all)*, which are known to cause allergic contact dermatitis.

ADIPIC ACID • **Hexanedoic Acid.** Colorless needlelike formations, fairly insoluble in water; found in beets. A buffering and neutralizing agent impervious to humidity. Used in hair color rinses, nylon manufacture, and plastics. Also used in food flavorings and in the manufacture of nylon, artificial resins, urethan foams and lubricating oil. Lethal to rats in large oral doses. No known human toxicity.

AEROSOL • Small particles of material suspended in gas.

AEROSOLS • The first aerosol patent was actually issued in 1899, but was not used until 1940, when insecticides were first packaged in self-dispensing gas-pressurized containers. It is estimated that the average home has forty-five aerosol products, ranging from hair spray to bathroom cleaners. More than a hundred people in the United States, mostly young Americans, have died from sniffing aerosol gases for "kicks." These gases can cause severe, irregular heartbeats. Freon®, the most commonly used group among aerosol gases, is a lung irritant, central nervous system depressant, and in high concentrations can cause coma. In addition to Freon®, hair sprays contain PVP (*see* Polyvinylpyrrolidone), or shellac. PVP is believed to be cancer-causing. In addition, thesaurosis, a condition in which there are foreign bodies in the lungs, has been found in persons subjected to repeated inhalation of hair sprays. In powder products (*see* Talc) the inhalation of powder or its component silicones, can damage the lungs. In 1972, the Society of Cosmetic Chemists reported that powder aerosols evidenced a high particle retention in the lungs and profound pulmonary effects. Tests showed large powder particles in twenty-three separate areas of the lungs.

The aerosol container can become a lethal weapon: a flamethrower if near a fire, and a shrapnel bomb when heated. It has been known to explode when placed too near a radiator or heater. Also, aerosol gases turn into toxic gases: fluorine, chlorine, hydrogen fluoride, and chloride, or even phosgene, a military poison gas.

In 1974, Dr. F. S. Rowland, professor of chemistry at the University of California, Irvine campus, and Dr. Mario J. Molina, a University of California research associate, reported in *Nature,* the international scientific journal published in England, that man-made chemicals used extensively in aerosol spray cans and refrigeration units pose a threat to the fragile layer of stratospheric ozone that shields the earth from much of the sun's ultraviolet radiation. The result could be a great increase in skin cancers. Do not buy aerosols when other methods of application are available. Many products have been placed in hand-pump containers because of the concern about aerosols.

AGENT ORANGE • *See* 2,4,5-T, 2,4-D, and Dioxin.

AIR FRESHENERS • May contain cresol, phenol or formaldehyde (*see all*). For a less toxic alternative, leave an open container of baking soda in room; add cloves and cinnamon or vanilla to boiling water and simmer, or use fresh flowers, or herbs. Open windows and use exhaust fan to exchange stale air for fresh. *See* Deodorants.

AIRPLANE MODEL CEMENTS • May contain toluene, acetone, naphtha, alcohols, aliphatic acetates, tricresyl phosphate, and hexane. Chronic hexane glue sniffers develop nerve damage. Some acute effects of inhalation abuse are similar to those of alcohol. Most affect the brain and may cause sudden death by disrupting the rhythm of the heart.

ALAR™ • *See* Daminozide.

ALCOHOLS • **Ethanol, Methanol, Isopropanol.** Alcohol is manufactured by the fermentation of starch, sugar, and other carbohydrates. It is clear, colorless, and flammable, with a somewhat pleasant odor and burning taste. Medicinally, used externally as an antiseptic and internally as a stimulant and hypnotic. "Absolute alcohol" is ethyl alcohol to which a substance has been added to make it unfit for drinking. "Rubbing alcohol" contains not less than 68.5 percent and not more than 71.5 percent by volume of absolute alcohol and a remainder of denaturants, such as perfume oils. Since it is a fat solvent, alcohol can dry the hair and skin when used in excess. Toxic in large doses. Used in window cleaners, paints, thinners, cosmetics, adhesives, and mimeograph correction fluids. Wood alcohol and isopropyl alcohol are used in antifreeze. Alcohols are used as solvents in shellac, varnish, paint remover, and many other consumer products. *See also* Methanol and Ethanol.

ALDEHYDES, ALIPHATIC • A class of organic chemical compounds that falls between an acid and an alcohol. Aldehyde contains less oxygen than acids and less hydrogen than alcohols. Generally colorless, volatile liquids, some examples are formaldehye, benzaldehyde, pentanal and nonanal *(see all)*. Formaldehyde, a preservative, is used widely in cosmetics and building products. Indoor sources of aldehydes are fungicides, germicides, solvents, nail polish remover, waterproofing, disinfectants, artificial and permanent-press textiles, paper products, particle boards, cosmetics, flavoring agents, insulation, carpet backings, floor coverings, combustion devices, fire retardants, inks, and dyes. Toxic sources at work can involve the treatment of wood, cotton, and paper. Most are irritating to the skin and gastrointestinal tract. Aldehydes are soluble in fat and exert toxicity by altering the cell membrane fat fraction. If they reach the lungs, they produce swelling. They also cause irritation of the eyes and throat.

ALDOL • Made from acetaldehyde, which occurs naturally in apples, broccoli, cheese, coffee, grapefruit, and other vegetables and fruits. A thick, colorless liquid used in the manufacture of rubber, and in perfumes. Has also been used as a sedative and hypnotic in medicine. May cause contact dermatitis.

ALGICIDE • A chemical agent added to water to destroy algae. Copper sulfate *(see* Copper Salts) is usually added for the purpose to large bodies of water. Algicides for fish tanks can be very toxic. They may contain monuron, a herbicide that has been curtailed in the United States because of its cancer-causing potential; the herbicides simazine and atrazine, which are not as toxic, and dichlone, a fungicide used on food crops that is a central nervous system depressant. *See* Pool Chemicals for algicides used in swimming pools.

ALGINIC ACID • Obtained as a highly gelatinous precipitate from seaweeds. Resembles albumin or gelatin *(see both)*. Alginic acid is slowly soluble in water, forming a very thick liquid. Odorless and tasteless, it is used in sizing paper and textiles and as a stabilizer in cosmetics. Also used as a stabilizer in ice cream and salad dressing. Capable of absorbing 200 to 300 times its weight of water and salts. No known toxicity.

ALIPHATIC HYDROCARBONS • Derived from petroleum, most are mixtures such as gasoline, kerosene, and natural gas. In the home and office, they are in cooking and heating fuels, aerosol propellants, cleaning compounds, refrigerants, lubricants, detergents, deodorizers, waxes and polishes, flavoring agents, and perfumes. Mild to moderate mucous membrane and respiratory tract irritation may occur depending on the amount of vapor inhaled. These affect breathing and the heart in concentrations as low as 15 percent. Higher molecular-weight aliphatic hydrocarbons, such as gasoline, are central nervous system depressants at high concentration. Aspiration of liquid aliphatic hydrocarbons produces severe chemical pneumonia. Prolonged skin contact with liquid aliphatic hydrocarbons causes a contact dermatitis secondary to the drying and defatting action of these solvents. Acute toxicity does not occur with solid aliphatic hydrocarbons such as paraffin. *See also* Propane, Butane, Hexane, Undecane, Limonene, and Isobutane.

ALIZARIN DYES • **Turkey Red.** Occurs in the root of the madder plant, a climbing herb of the genus *Rubia,* and was known and used in ancient Egypt, Persia, and India. Today, it is produced synthetically from anthracene, a coal tar. It yields different colors depending upon the metals mixed with it. Colors produced include orange, red, Turkey red, rose, blue, black, violet, lilac, yellow, and dark brown. It is also used to dye wool, cosmetics, and red paints. Can cause contact dermatitis.

ALKALI • The term originally covered the caustic and mild forms of potash and soda. Now a substance is regarded as an alkali if it produces hydroxyl ions in solution. An alkaline aqueous solution is one with a pH *(see)* greater than 7. Ingestion of alkali corrosives from household products ranging from pH 7 to 14 is more common and usually more serious than ingestion of acids, because of the deeper, more intense irritant effects. Most have good safety packaging but problems have arisen because some formulas have been changed to liquid instead of to granular lye. This makes it more likely to be swallowed by children or adults accidentally. *See* Ammonia, Drain Cleaners, Oven Cleaners, and Bleaches.

ALKANET ROOT • A red coloring extracted from the root of the herblike alkanet, a plant root of Asia Minor and the Mediterranean. Used as a copper or blue coloring (when combined with metals) for hair oils, wines, inks, and sausage casings. May be mixed with synthetic dyes for color tints. Formerly used as an astringent. No known toxicity.

ALKANOLAMINES • Compounds such as ethanolamine in which nitrogen is attached directly to the carbon of alcohols from alkene (a saturated fatty hydrocarbon) and amines (from ammonia). These compounds are viscous, colorless liquids that are used as solvents and to form soaps from fatty acids *(see)*. No known toxicity.

ALKYL • Meaning "from alcohol"; usually derived from alkane. Any one of a series of saturated hydrocarbons such as methane. The introduction of one or more alkyls into a compound is for the purpose of making the product more soluble. The mixture is usually employed with surfactants *(see)*, which have a tendency to float when not alkylated.

ALKYL DIMETHYL BENZYL AMMONIUM CHLORIDE • Used in Lysol™ Pine Action cleanser. *See* Alkyl and Ammonium Chloride.

ALKYL ETHOXY SULFATE • Used in liquid dishwashing products and may cause contact dermatitis. *See* Dishwashing Products.

ALKYL RESINS • A class of polyester resins derived from alcohol and acids. They have a low shrinkage rate and good resistance to electricity. Used as laminating adhesives and coatings, especially by impregnation of layered material. Also used in varnishes, on metal, ceramics, and heat-resistant furniture. *See* Clothing.

ALKYL SULFATES • These sulfates were developed by the Germans during World War II, when vegetable fats and oils were scarce. A large number have been made. They are prepared from primary alcohols by treatment with sulfuric acid. The alcohols are usually prepared from fatty acids *(see)*. For example, lauric acid makes a soap effective in hard water. If it is reduced to lauryl alcohol and sulfated, it makes sodium lauryl sulfate, a widely used detergent. Alkyl sulfates are used in detergents to thicken and improve foaming. The alcohol sulfates are low in acute and chronic toxicity, but they may cause skin irritation.

ALL™ CONDENSED PHOSPHATE LAUNDRY DETERGENT • A nonionic detergent containing sodium polyphosphate and sodium sulfate *(see both)*.

ALLERGEN • A substance that provokes an allergic reaction in the susceptible but does not normally affect other people. Plant pollens, fungi spores, and animal danders are some of the common allergens.

ALLERGIC CONTACT DERMATITIS • ACD. Skin rash caused by direct contact with a substance to which the skin is sensitive. Symptoms include a red rash, swelling, and intense itching. Blisters may develop and break open, forming a crust. In severe cases, the rash and blisters may spread all over the body. A variety of substances can cause the condition. The most common is poison ivy *(see)*. Others include industrial chemicals, metals, cosmetics, deodorants, mouthwashes, dyes, certain types of textiles, and medicines, as well as local treatments with ointments and local application of antibiotics. ACD may develop at any age. Its precise prevalence is unknown, but it is thought to affect a significant percentage of the population. The disease may be acute or chronic. It is less common than skin rashes caused by irritants but more serious because relapses commonly occur and may force a person to change jobs. Symptoms may appear seven to ten days after the first exposure to an allergen. More often, the allergic reaction does not develop for many years, and may require many repeated low-level exposures. Once the sensitivity does develop, however, contact with the triggering allergen will produce symptoms within twenty-four to forty-eight hours. An attack builds in severity from one to seven days. Even without treatment, healing often occurs in one or two weeks, although it may take a month or longer.

The rash does not spread on the body, nor can it be spread to another person. The extension of the rash is caused by renewed contact with whatever triggered the initial outbreak.

Some substances such as film developers, rubber chemicals, and beryllium, can cause symptoms other than the classic red rash and blisters. In some cases, ACD may look like hives. Detailed questioning about work, leisure activities, and the pattern of the rash often reveals its source. Patch tests may confirm the diagnosis.

ALLERGIC REACTION • An adverse immune response following repeated contact with otherwise harmless substances such as pollens, molds, foods, cosmetics, and drugs.

ALLERGY • An altered immune response to a specific substance, such as ragweed or pollen, on reexposure to it.

ALLERGY STANDARD PATCH-TEST SCREENING TRAY • Physicians place patches containing chemicals that are selected from a screening tray usually containing twenty-two common allergens. The chemicals are: Benzocaine; Imidazolidinyl Urea; Thiram Mix;

Wool (lanolin) alcohols; Neomycin sulfate; p-Phenylenediamine; Mercaptobenzothiazole; p-tert-Butylphenol Formaldehyde; Thimersol; Formaldehyde; Carba Mix; Rosin (Colophony); Black rubber mix; Ethylenediamine Dihydrochloride; Quaternium-15' Mercapto Mix; Epoxy Resin; Fragrance mix; Ammoniated Mercury; Potassium Dichromate; Paraben mix and Nickel Sulfate.

ALLOY • Metallic solid produced by dissolving two or more molten metals in each other. The alloy then has properties different from those of its constituents.

ALUM • **Potash Alum. Aluminum Ammonium. Potassium Sulfate.** A colorless, odorless, crystalline, water-soluble solid used in astringent lotions, after-shave lotions, and as a styptic (stops bleeding). Also used in antiperspirants to prevent aluminum chloride *(see)* from causing skin irritation. A double sulfate of aluminum and ammonium potassium, it is also employed to harden gelatin, size paper, or waterproof fabrics. In concentrated solutions alum has produced gum damage and fatal intestinal hemorrhages. It has a low toxicity in experimental animals, but ingestion of 30 grams (an ounce) has killed an adult human. It is also known to cause kidney damage. Liquid alum has been found by Pennsylvania State University researchers to be capable of removing over 99 percent of phosphates from waste water effluent.

ALUMINA • *See* Aluminum Oxide.

ALUMINUM • A silvery white, crystalline solid that is frequently used in food additives and cosmetics. Ingestion or inhalation of aluminum can aggravate kidney and lung disorders. Aluminum deposits have been found in the brains of Alzheimer's victims but its part, if any, in this degenerative brain disorder is not clear. Aluminum poisoning can cause spinal cord and brain disease, skeletal pain, and binding of phosphate, an essential body chemical, making it useless.

ALUMINUM ACETATE • **Burow's Solution.** A mixture including acetic acid and boric acid, with astringent and antiseptic properties. Used in astringent lotions, antiperspirants, deodorants, and protective creams. Also used as a fur dye, in fabric finishes, waterproofing, and as a disinfectant by embalmers. Ingestion of large doses can cause nausea and vomiting, diarrhea, and bleeding. Prolonged and continuous exposure can produce severe sloughing of the skin. It also causes skin rashes in some persons.

ALUMINUM AMMONIUM SULFATE • Odorless, colorless crystals with a strong astringent taste. Used in purifying drinking water, in baking powders, as a buffer and neutralizing agent in milling, and in the cereal industry. Used also for fireproofing, and in the manufacture of vegetable glue and artificial gems. In medicine, it is an astringent and styptic (stops bleeding). Ingestion of large amounts may cause burning in the mouth and pharynx, vomiting, and diarrhea.

ALUMINUM CHLOROHYDRATE • An ingredient of commercial antiperspirant and deodorant preparations. Also used for water purification and treatment of sewage.

ALUMINUM CLEANER • Many aluminum cleaners contain hydrofluoric acid *(see)*, which is very corrosive and dangerous. If you can avoid products with this ingredient—it is listed on the label—do so. If you do use a product that contains this ingredient, protect your skin, wear safety goggles, and do not inhale the fumes. A safer alternative to remove stains and discoloration from aluminum cookware is to fill the pot with two tablespoons of cream of tartar to a quart of water. Bring the solution to a boil and simmer ten minutes. Wash as usual and dry. To clean an aluminum coffeepot, boil equal parts of water and white vinegar. Boiling time depends upon how heavy deposits are.

ALUMINUM HYDRATE • Usually obtained as a white mass or powder, it is almost insoluble in water but forms a gel when exposed to water. It is used as an adsorbent and emulsifier in the manufacture of glass, clay, paper, pottery, cosmetics, printing inks, lubricants, and dentfrices. It is also used as an antacid.

ALUMINUM OLEATE • A yellow, thick, acidic mass practically insoluble in water. Used in packaging, as lacquer for metals, in waterproofing, and for thickening lubricating oils. Low toxicity.

ALUMINUM OXIDE • **Alumina. Emery.** Derived from bauxite, which is hydrated aluminum oxide. Coal mine waste waters are used to obtain aluminum sulfate, which is then reduced to aluminum oxide. The mineral, corundum, is natural aluminum oxide, and emery, ruby, and sapphire are impure crystalline varieties. Used in the production of aluminum and the manufacture of abrasives, ceramics, electrical insulators, catalysts, paper, spark plugs, as an adsorbent for gases and water vapors, in light bulbs, artificial gems, heat-resistant fibers, and as a dispersing agent in food. Inhalation of the dust is toxic.

ALUMINUM PHOSPHATE • **Aluminum Orthophosphate.** White crystals insoluble in water. Used in ceramics, dental cements, and cosmetics as a gelling agent. Corrosive to tissue.

ALUMINUM PHOSPHIDE • **AIP.** Dark gray or yellow crystals used as an insecticide and fumigant. Dangerous fire risk. *See* Phosphine and Fumigants.

ALUMINUM SALTS • **Aluminum Acetate. Aluminum Caprylate. Aluminum Chloride. Aluminum Chlorohydrate. Aluminum Diacetate. Aluminum Distearate. Aluminum Glycinate. Aluminum Hydroxide. Aluminum Lanolate. Aluminum Methionate. Aluminum Phenolsulfonate. Aluminum Silicate. Aluminum Stearate. Aluminum Sulfate. Aluminum Tristearate.** The strong and weak acids of aluminum, used primarily in antiperspirants to combat body odors. The strong salts may cause skin irritation and damage fabrics, particularly linens and cottons. *See* Aluminum Acetate, Aluminum Chlorohydrate, Aluminum Silicate, Aluminum Sulfate, and Aluminum Stearates.

ALUMINUM SILICATE • A white mass, insoluble in water, obtained naturally from clay, or synthesized. Used as an anticaking and coloring agent in powders. Essentially harmless when given orally and when applied to skin. *See* Aluminum Salts.

ALUMINUM STEARATES • Hard, plasticlike materials used in waterproofing fabrics, thickening lubricating oils, as a chewing gum-base component, and as a defoamer component used in processing beet sugar and yeast. No known toxicity.

ALUMINUM SULFATE • **Cake Alum.** Colorless crystals, soluble in water, used as an antiseptic, astringent, and detergent in antiperspirants, and deodorants. Also used to purify water. It is among the top five inorganic chemicals produced in the United States each year. May cause allergic reactions in some people.

AMBERGRIS • Concretion from the intestinal tract of the sperm whale found in tropical seas. About 80 percent cholesterol, it is a gray to black waxy mass and is used for fixing delicate odors in perfumery. It is also used as a flavoring for food and beverages. No known toxicity.

AMES TEST • Dr. Bruce Ames, a biochemist at the University of California, developed a simple, inexpensive test, using bacteria, that reveals whether or not a chemical is a mutagen. Almost all chemicals that are known carcinogens also have been shown to be mutagenic on the Ames Test. Whether the test can identify carcinogens is still controversial.

AMIDE • Derived from ammonia *(see)*.

AMIDO- • Denoting a compound derived from ammonia in which at least one hydrogen atom of ammonia has been replaced by an acid.

AMINES • A class of organic compounds derived from ammonia.

They are basic in nature—synthetic derivatives of ammonium chloride, a naturally occurring salt. Quaternary ammonium compounds *(see)* used in detergents are examples.

AMINO-AZOBENZENE • Yellow to tan crystals soluble in alcohol and slightly soluble in water, derived from benzene. Used in leather dyes, textiles, and in insecticides. A suspected cancer-causing agent.

AMINO-AZOTOLUENE HYDROCHLORIDE • Reddish brown to yellow crystals derived from toluene and used in leather dyes and medicines. A suspected cancer-causing agent.

4-AMINOBENZOIC ACID. • *p*-**Aminobenzoic Acid.** *See* Para-Aminobenzoic Acid.

3-AMINO-1,2,4-TRIAZOLE • Light yellow crystals made from vinyl acetate and thiourea, and used as a herbicide, defoliant, and a thyroid inhibitor. Not permitted for use on food crops. It has been linked to cancer in humans, and may cause contact dermatitis *(see)*.

AMITROLE • *See* 3-Amino-1,2,4-Triazole.

AMMONIA • Obtained by blowing steam through incandescent coke, ammonia is extremely toxic when inhaled in concentrated vapors, and is irritating to the eyes and mucous membranes. It is among the top five inorganic chemicals produced in the United States. Used in refrigerants, in the manufacture of detergents, permanent wave lotions and hair bleaches, and in cleaning preparations. Also used in the manufacture of explosives and synthetic fabrics, herbicides, fertilizers, and pesticides. Has been shown to produce cancer of the skin in humans, in doses of 1,000 milligrams per kilogram of body weight. It is also irritating to the lungs, and may cause swelling of lung tissue. Many incompatibilities. For example, it may cause explosions if mixed with silver or mercury. *See* Household Ammonia.

AMMONIA-BASED CLEANERS • *See* Household Ammonia.

AMMONIA WATER • Ammonia gas dissolved in water. Used as an alkali *(see)*. Colorless with a very pungent odor, it is irritating to the eyes and mucous membranes. In strong solution can cause burns and blistering.

AMMONIATED NITROGEN FERTILIZER • Ammonia is formed as an end-product of animal metabolism by decomposition of uric acid. It is added to fertilizer to speed up decomposition to enrich the soil. Inhalation can be toxic. *See* Ammonia.

AMMONIUM BICARBONATE • An alkali used as a leavening agent in the production of baked goods. Also used in compost heaps to accelerate decomposition. Usually prepared by passing carbon dioxide gas through concentrated ammonia water. Shiny, hard, colorless or white crystals; faint odor of ammonia. No known toxicity.

AMMONIUM BORATE • Used in joint compounds. *See* Borates.

AMMONIUM BROMIDE • Colorless crystals or white powder, derived by the action of an acid on ammonium hydroxide. Used in hair conditioners, and as an anticorrosive agent and fire-retardant agent. *See* Bromides.

AMMONIUM CARBONATE • A white, solid alkali derived partly from ammonium bicarbonate *(see)*, and used as a neutralizer and buffer in permanent wave solutions and creams. Decomposes when exposed to air. Also used in baking powders, for defatting woolens, in fire extinguishers, and as an expectorant. Ammonium carbonate can cause skin rashes on the scalp, forehead, or hands.

AMMONIUM CHLORIDE • An ammonium salt that occurs naturally. Colorless, odorless crystals or white powder, saline in taste, and incompatible with alkalies. Used as an acidifier in permanent wave solutions, and eye lotions, it is employed industrially to freezing mixtures, batteries, dyes, safety explosives, and in medicine as a urinary acidifier and diuretic. Also used to keep snow from melting on ski slopes. If ingested, can cause nausea, vomiting, and acidosis. Lethal as an intramuscular dose in rats and guinea pigs. As with any ammonia compound, concentrated solutions can be irritating to the skin.

AMMONIUM CUMENESULFONATE • **Benzenesulfonic Acid. Methylated Ammonium Salt.** Derived from coal tar or petroleum, it is used as a solvent. *See* Coal Tar.

AMMONIUM DICHROMATE • Orange needles used in red dyes and synthetic perfumes. Irritating to the eyes and skin. A suspected carcinogen.

AMMONIUM DODECYLBENZENESULFONATE • **Ammonium Lauryl Benzene Sulfonate.** *See* Quaternary Ammonium Compounds and Surfactants.

AMMONIUM GLYCYRRHIZATE • The ammonium salt of glycyrrhizic acid. *See* Quaternary Ammonium Compounds.

AMMONIUM HYDROXIDE • **Ammonia Water.** A weak alkali formed when ammonia dissolves in water. Exists only in solution. A clear, colorless liquid with an extremely pungent odor. Used as an alkali *(see)* in metallic hair dyes, hair straighteners, and protective skin creams. Also used in detergents, stain removers, ceramics, wood fireproofing, inks, explosives, and pharmaceuticals. Irritating to the eyes and mucous membranes.

AMMONIUM LAURYL SULFATE • The ammonium salt of lauryl sulfate derived from the natural coconut alcohols, it is a mild anionic surfactant *(see)* cleanser that is widely used at mild acidic pH values. *See* Lauryl Alcohol.

AMMONIUM MOLYBDATE • A colorless, green or white, crystalline salt. *See* Ammonia.

AMMONIUM NITRATE • Odorless, transparent, water-absorbing crystals used to make fertilizers, laughing gas, matches, and firecrackers. Dangerous explosion hazard. It is among the top five inorganic chemicals produced in the United States.

AMMONIUM NONOXYNOL-4-SULFATE • A cleansing material that breaks up and holds oils and soils so that they may be removed easily from skin or hair. *See* Ammonium Sulfate.

AMMONIUM OLEATE • The ammonium salt of oleic acid *(see)*. Used as an emulsifying agent.

AMMONIUM OXALATE • Used in joint compounds, which are used during construction and building repair.

AMMONIUM PERSULFATE • **Ammonium Salt.** Colorless, odorless crystals soluble in water. Used as an oxidizer and bleach in dyes, and as a disinfectant and preservative. May be irritating to the skin and mucous membranes. Lethal to rats in large oral doses.

AMMONIUM PHENOSULFONATE • The ammonium salt of phenolsulfonic acid. *See* Quaternary Ammonium Compounds.

AMMONIUM PHOSPHATE • **Ammonium Salt.** Odorless crystals or powder with a cool, saline taste, used to fireproof textiles, paper, wood, and vegetable fibers, for soldering tin, copper, brass, and zinc, and in corrosion inhibitors. No known toxicity.

AMMONIUM RHODANILATE • **Ammonium Salt.** Used in photography. Can cause contact dermatitis *(see)*.

AMMONIUM SULFATE • **Ammonium Salt.** A neutralizer in permanent wave lotions. Odorless and colorless; either crystals or powder. Industrially used in freezing mixtures, fireproofing fabrics, and tanning. Used medicinally to prolong analgesia. No known toxicity when used cosmetically. Rats were killed when fed large doses.

AMMONIUM SULFIDE • A salt derived from sulfur and ammonium. Used as a neutralizer in permanent wave lotions, and to apply patina to bronze. Also used in spice flavorings. It has been reported to have caused a death when ingested in a permanent wave solution. Irritating to the skin when used in depilatories.

AMMONIUM THIOCYANATE • **Thiocyanic Acid. Ammonium Salt. Ammonium Rhodanide.** Water-absorbing crystals derived from ammonium cyanide. Used in matches, for dyeing fabrics, in photography, for increasing the strength of silks, and in pesticides and adhesives. *See* Cyanide.

AMPHO- • Prefix from Greek meaning "double," or "both."

AMPHOTERIC • A material that can display both acidic and basic properties. Used primarily in surfactants *(see)*, it contains betaines and imidazoles *(see both)*.

AMPHOTERIC-2 • A cleansing compound that breaks up and holds oils. *See* Amphoteric.

AMSONIC ACID • Yellow needles, slightly soluble in water, used in the manufacture of dyes and bleaching agents.

AMYL ACETATE • **Banana Oil. Pear Oil. Amyl Cinnamic Alcohol. Amyl Cinnamic. Isoamyl Acetate. 1-Pentanol Acetate.** Derived from amyl alcohol, it is used as a solvent for lacquers and paints, in photographic film, leather polishes, nail polishes, as a warning odor added to gas, flavoring agent, printing and finishing fabrics, perfuming shoe polish, to cover unpleasant odors, in waterproofing, in bronzing liquids, and as a solvent for phosphorus in fluorescent lamps. Flammable and potentially explosive.

AMYL CINNAMIC • *See* Amyl Acetate.

AMYL CINNAMIC ALCOHOL • *See* Amyl Acetate.

ANAPHYLAXIS • Means, literally, "without protection." A dramatic allergic reaction that can result in collapse and, sometimes, death. Chemicals in the body are suddenly released that overwhelm it. The onset is usually rapid, and symptoms develop within minutes after exposure to the allergen; death may occur almost immediately, or within hours. The first evidence may be swelling and redness of the skin, often accompanied by hives. The victim may have a feeling of great anxiety. Other symptoms may include swelling of the throat and upper airway, bronchospasm, overproduction of mucus, a drop in blood pressure, shock, irregular heartbeat, nausea, vomiting, intestinal cramps, diarrhea, skin rash, angioedema *(see)*, uterine cramps, and urgency to urinate. Treatments that may control the reaction are epinephrine, oxygen, and intravenous fluids. Why some people react so severely to this allergen is unknown.

ANGIOEDEMA • A reaction in the skin and underlying tissue marked by swelling and red blotches.

ANHYDRIDE • A residue resulting from water being removed from a compound. An oxide—combination of oxygen and an element—that can combine with water to form an acid, or that is derived from an acid by the abstraction of water. Acetic acid *(see)* is an example.

ANHYDROUS • Describes a substance that contains no water.

ANILAZINE • **Dyrene. Bonide. F&B. Mobay.** White or tan crystals prepared from aniline and used as a turfgrass fungicide. *See* Fungicides.

ANILINE • A colorless to brown liquid that darkens with age. Slightly soluble in water, it is one of the most commonly used of the organic bases, the parent substance for many dyes and drugs. Derived from nitrobenzene or chlorobenzene, it is among the top five organic chemicals produced each year in the United States. Used as a rubber accelerator to speed vulcanization, an antioxidant to retard aging, and as an intermediate *(see)*. Also used in dyes, photographic chemicals, the manufacture of urethane foams, pharmaceuticals, explosives, petroleum refining, resins and adhesive products, paint removers, herbicides, and fungicides, crayons, diaper markings, and shoe polishes. It causes allergic reactions, and contact dermatitis *(see)*, and is toxic when ingested, inhaled, or absorbed through the skin. A potential human cancer-causing agent, it caused cancer in mice when injected under the skins or administered orally. In an April 1991 report in the *Journal of the National Cancer Institute* of a study of 1,749 workers at the Goodyear Tire and Rubber Company plant in Niagara Falls, New York, it was revealed that workers exposed directly to aniline had 6.5 times the rate of bladder cancer than the average resident in the state.

ANILINE DYES • **Coal Tar Dyes.** Aniline is a colorless to brown liquid that darkens with age. A synonym for coal tar dyes *(see)*, it refers to a large class of synthetic dyes made from intermediates *(see)* based upon or made from aniline. It is among the top five organic chemicals produced in the United States. Used in the manufacture of hair dyes, medicinals, resins, and perfumes. Also used in carbons, fur dyeing, rubber, photographics, inks, colored pencils, and crayons. Most are somewhat toxic and irritating to eyes, skin, and mucous membranes, but are generally much less toxic than aniline itself. These dyes caused tumors in animals whose skins were painted with them.

ANIMAL GLUE • Used in wallpaper paste.

ANIONIC SURFACTANTS • A class of synthetic compounds used as emulsifiers in about 75 percent of all hand creams and lotions. An "anion" is a negatively charged ion that is "surface active." These detergents usually consist of an alkali salt as soap, or ammonium salt of a strong acid. Anionic compounds—which include sodium, potassium, and ammonium salts of fatty acids and hydrocarbons with sulfur or phosphates—are the most common surfactants used in detergents. Can be irritating to the skin, depending on alkalinity. Used in shampoos, irritation to the eyes depends on the compound. Sodium laureth sulfate, for example, is very irritating, whereas triethanolamine (TEA) coco hydrolyzed animal protein is the least irritating. *See* Emulsifiers and Ammonia Water.

ANISIC ACID • Prepared from benzene *(see)* or anethole, it is used in weed killers, repellents, and to kill insect eggs. Toxic.

ANT PASTES • *See* Antimony Compounds.

ANT POISONS • To kill ants, pour household ammonia down the center of an ant hill, and make a circle around the hill and fill it with ammonia. *See* Insecticides.

ANTHOPHYLLITE • *See* Asbestos.

ANTHRACENE • **Tar.** Yellow crystals with blue fluorescence, derived from crude anthracene oil. Used in dyes, calico printing, and in smoke screens. It is a cancer-causing agent, and may also cause contact dermatitis.

ANTHRAQUINONE • A coal tar color produced industrially from phthalic anhydride and benzene *(see both)*. Light yellow, slender prisms, which are insoluble in water. It is used widely as a starter for the manufacture of vat dyes. Also used as an organic inhibitor to prevent growth of cells, and a repellent to protect seeds from being eaten by birds. Caused tumors when given orally to rats in doses of 72 milligrams per kilogram of body weight. May cause skin irritation and allergic reactions.

ANTIBODY • Protein in blood formed in response to invasion by a germ, virus, or other foreign body. In sensitive individuals, a special antibody, IgE, is responsible for the allergic reaction.

ANTIFREEZE • **Coolant. Deicer.** Contains glycols, alkalies such as borates *(see)*, toluene, methanol, xylene, and acetone. Sodium or calcium chloride (salt) may also be added. *See all.* Extremely harmful if swallowed. Toxic to kidneys and the central nervous system.

ANTIGEN • Any substance that provokes an immune response when introduced into the body.

ANTIMONY COMPOUNDS • **Antimony Potassium Tartrate. Tartar Emetic. Antimony Potassium Tartrate.** A silver-white, brittle metal obtained from ore mined in China, Mexico, and Bolivia. Used in alloys, batteries, foils, ceramics, safety matches, ant pastes, textiles, bases for paints and enamels, in matches, putty, fireproofing, in the manufacture of bullets, metal bearings, hair dyes, and plastics. Also used medicinally as an emetic and to combat worms. It can cause contact dermatitis, eye and nose irritation, and ulceration by contact, fumes or dust; also, can cause dizziness, diarrhea, nervous complaints such as sleeplessness, fatigue and muscle pain. When reacting with moisture or acids it evolves a hydrogen mist that can cause fluid in the lungs, if inhaled. It has been linked to skin cancer, particularly among those exposed to it, who also smoke.

ANTIOXIDANTS • Preservatives that prevent fats from spoiling. Vitamins C and E are examples.

ANTI-RUST COMPOUNDS • *See* Acids, Epoxy Resins, and Chromium.

ANTISAPSTAIN • An antifungal for timber. Can cause irritant and allergic reactions, including contact dermatitis *(see)*.

ANTISTATIC AGENTS • Polyethylene glycol and ethylene oxide compounds as well as acrylic esters and iodides provide antistatic properties in clothing *(see all)*.

ANTIWRINKLE • *See* Clothing.

AQUARIUM PRODUCTS • Compounds to kill algae without killing the fish include monuron and one or more of the following: simazine, atrazine, dichlone and dehydroabietylamine acetate. Potassium permanganate and copper sulfate are used as a disinfectant for aquariums. To dechlorinate water for aquariums sodium thiosulfate is used with methylene blue, potassium phosphate permanganate, quinine sulfate, and sodium carbonate. Sodium perborate is used in some water treatment compounds as are polyvinylpyrrolidone and sulfites. To clear cloudy water, potassium permanganate is used. Almost all the ingredients mentioned can be toxic if ingested by humans with the exception, of course, of sodium chloride.

ARABIC GUM • *See* Acacia.

ARACHIDIC ACID • **Eicosanoic Acid.** A fatty acid that is widely distributed in peanut oil fats and related compounds. Used in lubricants, greases, waxes, and plastics. No known toxicity.

ARALDITE • May cause contact dermatitis. *See* Epoxy Resin.

ARAMITE • **Sulfurous Acid. Acaracide. Ortho-Mite.** A liquid; practically insoluble in water. Can be mixed with many organic solvents. Used for plants, as an insecticide. In undiluted form it may cause skin irritation. Large doses may cause central nervous system depression. Caused cancer when given orally to mice in doses of 130 milligrams, and to dogs in doses of 35 milligrams per kilogram of body weight.

AREGINAL • *See* Fumigants.

AROMATIC AMINES • Compounds derived from aniline, benzene, naphthalene, xylene, ethyl benzene, styrene, and raw anthracene. They may be found in paints, varnishes, glues, enamels, lacquers, cleaners, printed paper, adhesives, paint strippers, plastics, and insulation. Many of them have similar effects on the body; but they vary greatly in toxicity. All the liquids in the group are irritants. The vapors are irritating and can lead to lung and kidney damage. Among the compounds associated with bladder cancer in workers are I-NA, 2-NA, benzidine, 4-aminobiphenyl, magenta, and auramine. Although "aromatic" implies distinctive odors, these chemicals may be difficult to detect by smell: odor cannot be depended upon to warn of their presence. Exposure to aromatic amines can occur not only in industrial environments, but also through the air, foodstuffs, plastics, and drinking water. *See* Aromatic Compounds.

AROMATIC COMPOUNDS • Any organic compound, such as benzene, toluene, xylene, ethylbenzene, and styrene. The vast majority are obtained from petroleum and coal tar. *See all.* They are called "aromatic" because of the strong but not unpleasant odor of the chemicals. Found in paints, varnishes, glues, enamels, lacquers, cleaners, printed paper, adhesives, paint strippers, plastics, and insulation.

ARSENATE, POTASSIUM • **Fowler's Solution.** Colorless crystals, soluble in water, used in the manufacture of fly paper, insecticidal preparations, preserving hides, and in printing textiles. Can cause contact dermatitis. *See* Arsenic Compounds.

ARSENATE, SODIUM • Clear, colorless crystals with a mildly alkaline taste; derived from arsenic. Used in dyeing, printing, insecticides, ant poisons, weed killers, wallpaper paints, glass, and ceramics. Can cause contact dermatitis. Toxic by inhalation or ingestion.

ARSENIC COMPOUNDS • Arsenic is a grayish white element that occurs in the earth's crust and is highly toxic in most forms. An estimated 1.5 million American workers and countless consumers are exposed to arsenic, which is used in the manufacture of metal alloys, ceramics, dyes, drugs, glass; in garden and farm pesticides; as a defoliant during cotton harvesting; as a growth stimulant for livestock and poultry; as a wood treatment to prevent rot; and for the control of sludge in lubricating oils. High rates of lung cancer have been found among both men and women in two Montana cities with copper mining and smelting facilities. The best explanation seems to be that the airborne arsenic, to which the men are exposed on the job, has also polluted the air in the community, contributing to a rise in lung cancer among women. The incubation period for arsenic is believed to be eleven to twenty years. Target organs are the bladder, skin, lung, vulva, eyelids, face, neck, and larynx. Ingestion causes nausea, vomiting, and death. Chronic poisoning can result in pigmentation of skin and kidney and liver damage, weakness, loss of appetite, and diarrhea. Arsenic can also cause the skin to be sensitive to light and break out in a rash or to swell.

Read the labels of pesticides, ceramic clays, and other products to see if they contain arsenic. If they do, do not buy them, or if you must buy them, exercise extreme caution when using them. If you are using them to kill rodents, remove food attractants and substitute traps for poisons.

ARSENIC TRIOXIDE • **White Arsenic. Arsenious Oxide.** Derived from smelting of copper and lead concentrates, it is used in pigments, ceramic enamels, aniline colors, insecticides, soaps, hair tonics, depilatories, caustics, weed killers, poison baits, fungicides, glasses, alloys, sheep and cattle dips, hide preservatives, wood preservative, and in the preparation of other arsenic compounds. A cancer-causing agent in humans. Also a powerful allergen, and a deadly poison via all routes of the body.

ARSINE • **Arsenic Hydride.** Colorless gas derived from arsenic and used for organic synthesis, war gas, and as a doping agent in the manufacture of electronic parts. It is poisonous upon inhalation. *See also* Arsenic.

ART MATERIALS • Modeling clays, water-soluble pastes, glues, and school paints are generally nontoxic. Water colors and poster paints contain resin gums (gamboge), which are irritating to mucous membranes, and are laxatives. Large ingestion of gamboge-containing products requires forced vomiting. Chemicals that can be hazardous if inhaled, absorbed, or swallowed are found in permanent felt-tipped markers (unless labeled otherwise), rubber cement, spray fixatives, powdered clay, and instant papier-mâché. Children should not use these compounds because they may easily mishandle them. Youngsters should use liquid tempera paints, crayons, oil pastels or dustless chalks, water-based markers, papier-mâché made from black-and-white newspaper, and library paste, or flour-and-water paste. Children should not use epoxy, instant glue, airplane glue, or solvent-based adhesives. Instead, they should be given white glue, school paste, or preservative-free wheat paste. The Center for Safety in the Arts (CSA) is a national clearinghouse for research and education on hazards in the visual arts, performing arts, museums, and school art programs. CSA is partially funded with public support from the National Endowment for the Arts, the New York State Council on the Arts, the New York City Department of Cultural Affairs, and the New York State Department of Labor Safety and Health Training and Education Program. For more information write to Center for Safety in the Arts, 5 Beekman Street, Suite 1030, New York, NY 10038. The Arts and Crafts Materials Institute in Boston has a certification program. Products that are nontoxic and meet quality and performance standards receive the CP (certified product) or AP (approved product) seal. This means the products are safe for children, even if ingested. Among the items that may have these certifications are crayons, watercolors, tempera colors, finger paints, chalks, modeling materials, block-printing inks and media, drawing inks, etching inks, screenprinting inks, school pastes and adhesives, acrylic and oil paints, marking crayons, and other art materials. Further information on arts and crafts products used by children can be obtained by requesting *Children's Art Supplies Can Be Toxic,* published by the Center for Safety in the Arts. To obtain a copy, send a self-addressed, stamped envelope with your request to 5 Beekman Street, New York, NY 10038. A list of certified and approved products can be obtained from the Arts and Crafts Materials Institute by sending your request and a self-addressed, stamped envelope to 715 Boylston St., Boston, MA 02116. *See* listings, Further Information, page 312.

ARTIFICIAL • A substance not duplicated in nature. A scent, for instance, may have all natural ingredients, but it must be called artificial if it has no counterpart in nature.

ARTIFICIAL ANT OIL • *See* Furfural.

ART SUPPLIES • *See* Art Materials.

ASBESTOS • **Actinolite. Amosite. Anthophyllite. Crocidolite. Chrysotile. Tremolite.** From the Greek *asbestos,* meaning "inextinguishable." These naturally occurring fibrous silicates classified as "asbestos" are now believed to be the most important cancer-causing agents in the workplace. There has been a thousandfold increase in output of asbestos during the past sixty years, and although it has been known for more than half a century that persons who inhaled large amounts of asbestos dust in the course of their work sometimes developed disabling or fatal fibrosis of the lungs, only within the last half of the twentieth century has it been found to cause cancer. An estimated three thousand different products in daily use throughout the world contain some asbestos. The total world production each year is approximately 4 million tons. Canada accounts for about 30 percent of the total, and the United States for about 3 percent. Asbestos is used in so many products because it inhibits combustion, is acid resistant, has great tensile strength, and is lightweight.

Workers exposed to high levels of asbestos in factories and shipyards and people exposed to air containing asbestos have been shown to develop

• lung cancer;

• mesothelioma, a cancer of the lining of the chest and the abdominal cavity;

• asbestosis, in which the lungs become scarred with fibrous tissue.

The risk of lung cancer and mesothelioma increases with the number of fibers inhaled. Those who also smoke greatly increase the odds they will develop such problems. The symptoms of lung cancer and mesothelioma take about twenty to thirty years to develop.

Most products today do not contain asbestos and the few that do are required to print that fact on the label. However, until the 1970s, many types of building products and insulation materials used in homes and offices contained asbestos. Common products that you may still have in your home or office, and which may release fibers are:

• steam pipes, boilers, and furnace ducts insulated with an asbestos blanket or asbestos paper tape. These materials may release asbestos fibers if damaged, repaired, or removed improperly.

• resilient floor tiles (vinyl, asbestos, asphalt, and rubber), the backing on vinyl sheet flooring, and adhesives used for installing floor tile. Sanding tiles can release fibers. So may scraping or sanding the backing of sheet flooring during removal.

• cement sheet, millboard, and paper used as insulation around furnaces and wood-burning stoves. Repairing or removing appliances may release asbestos fibers. So may cutting, tearing, sanding, drilling, or sawing insulation.

• door gaskets in furnaces, wood stoves, and coal stoves. Worn seals can release asbestos fibers during use.

• soundproofing or decorative material sprayed on walls and ceilings. Loose, crumbly, or water-damaged material may release fibers. So will sanding, drilling, or scraping the material.

• patching and joint compounds for walls and ceilings, and textured paints. Sanding, scraping, or drilling these surfaces may release asbestos.

• asbestos cement roofing, shingles, and siding. These products are not likely to release asbestos fibers unless sawed, drilled, or cut.

• artificial ashes and embers sold for use in gas-fired fireplaces. Also other older household products such as fireproof gloves, stovetop pads, ironing board covers, and certain hair dryers.

• automobile brake pads and linings, clutch facings, and gaskets.

Asbestos that is not damaged will usually not cause a problem. If damaged items are small, such as gloves, stovetop pads, or ironing covers, get rid of them. If you are going to remodel or in any way disturb an area containing asbestos, it is best to get a licensed professional to do so. To find a professional, check with your local air pollution control board, the state agency responsible for worker safety, and your local Better Business Bureau. Ask if the firm has had any safety violations. Find out if there has been any legal action against it. The workers should be equipped with approved respirators, gloves, and other protective clothing. Before work begins, you should contact your regional Environmental Protection Agency office to find out what the regulations are for removing asbestos. Be sure the contractor does not track asbestos dust throughout other areas of your home. The work area should be sealed and plastic sheeting used. Turn off the heating and air conditioning system during work. Upon completion, make sure the contractor cleans the area well with wet mops, rags, sponges, or high-efficiency particle air vacuum cleaners. A regular vacuum cleaner must never be used.

For more information on asbestos in other consumer products, call the CPSC Hotline or write to the U.S. Consumer Product Safety

Commission, Washington, D.C. 20207. The CPSC Hotline has information on certain appliances and products such as the brands and models of hair dryers that contain asbestos. Call CPSC at (800) 638-CPSC. A teletypewriter for the hearing impaired is available at (800) 638-8270. The American Lung Association, the U.S. Consumer Product Safety Commission, and the U.S. Environmental Protection Agency have published a very useful document, "Asbestos In Your Home," which may be obtained from your local chapters of these organizations. *See* listings, Further Information, page 312.

ASPHALT • Mineral pitch. Bitumen. Found naturally and also produced by distillation of crude petroleum. Asphalt coatings usually contain mineral spirits, and also may contain aluminum, solvents, and silicates. Hot asphalt can cause burns, and the fumes are highly irritating to the eyes and skin. Asphalt can cause skin cancer.

ASPHYXIANT • A vapor or gas that can cause loss of consciousness and death due to lack of oxygen.

ASTHMA • Constriction of the airways (bronchial tubes) to the lungs, producing symptoms of cough and shortness of breath. May be an allergic response.

ATOPIC DERMATITIS • A chronic, itching inflammation of the skin, also called "eczema" *(see)*.

ATRAZINE • One of the most widely used pesticides in the United States. It reacts with nitrate *(see)* under acidic conditions, such as those found in the stomach, to form *N*-nitrosoatrazine, a cancer-causing compound. Atrazine is used as a weed-control agent for corn, and for noncrop and industrial sites. Sodium nitrite is used as a meat preservative, and may also be present in acid soils because of the large amounts of nitrite fertilizers used. Atrazine may cause birth defects. It has moderately acute toxicity via oral, skin, or inhalation routes. Poisoned animals show muscular spasms, stiff gait, and lung problems.

AURAMINE • Yellow dye for paper, textiles, leather. Also used as an antiseptic and fungicide. Those involved in the manufacture and use of dyestuffs, as well as workers in rubber and paint plants, risk getting cancer of the bladder and pancreas. The incubation period is from twelve to thirty years. *See* Aniline.

AUTOMATIC DISHWASHER DETERGENTS • *See* Dishwasher Detergent (Automatic).

AUTOMATIC TRANSMISSION FLUID • Mainly composed of mineral oil, it is used to pull the clutches and lubricate automobile transmissions. It is highly flammable at high temperatures and relatively nontoxic unless swallowed and inhaled during vomiting. Used automatic transmission fluid contains toxic heavy metals including lead. When draining fluid wear gloves and avoid skin contact.

AUTOMOBILE BATTERIES • *See* Batteries, Automobile and Boat.

AUTOMOBILE BATTERY FLUID • *See* Acids and Battery Acid.

AUTOMOBILE BRAKES • Studies with an electron microscope—an instrument that has ten thousand times the resolution of ordinary microscopes—have shown that automobile brakes give off a dust containing filaments of deformed "chrysotile" asbestos, a type of asbestos that many researchers consider a health hazard. According to public health officials, these fibers may not be particularly dangerous to the average consumer because when you drive a car, you breathe in only small amounts of the brake-drum dust. However, there may be a real risk factor for workers such as brake repairmen, who use compressed air to blow asbestos fibers from the brakes. Wear of break linings is, however, a major source of asbestos in the ambient air, according to the National Cancer Institute. Chrysotile fiber concentrations near highways range from 0 to 12,000 fibers per cubic meter in Los Angeles. The OSHA eight-hour standard is 2 fibers (greater than 5 microns in length) per milliliter of air.

AUTOMOBILE BRAKE FLUID • *See* Brake Fluid.

AUTOMOBILE CLEANERS • *See* Car Wash Compounds.

AUTOMOBILE POLISH • Usually contains carnauba or petroleum waxes, silicone, petroleum distillates, abrasives, emulsifiers *(see all)*, dye, and perfume.

AUTOMOBILE TRANSMISSION FLUID • *See* Transmission Fluid.

AUTOMOBILE WAX • *See* Car Wax.

AVOIDANCE • Measures taken to avoid contact with allergy-producing substances. Since there are no cures for allergies as of yet, avoiding allergens is the best way to combat them.

AZINPHOS-METHYL • **Guthion**™. Crystals from methanol used as an insecticide and acaracide on fruits and vegetables. *See* Organophosphates.

AZLON • A man-made fiber produced from proteins found in nature such as casein from skim milk, peanuts, and corn kernels. Azlon fibers are extremely soft and somewhat weak, and may be susceptible to bacteria and mildew damage unless specially treated.

AZO DYES • An estimated 60 percent of all coloring agents used are azo dyes. They are found in food, drugs, cosmetics, clothes, ballpoint pens, and ink. Human exposure to these compounds occurs not only via commercial products, but also via past and present disposal practices. Azo dyes are made from diazonium compounds and phenol *(see)* and belong to a large category of colorings that are characterized by the way they combine with nitrogen. The dyes usually contain a mild acid, such as citric or tartaric acid. It can cause allergic reactions. People who become sensitized to permanent hair dyes containing *p*-phenylencdiamine *(see)* also develop a cross-sensitivity to azo dyes. That is, a person who is allergic to permanent *p*-phenylenediamine dyes will also be allergic to azo dyes. There are reports that azo dyes are absorbed through the skin. They can cause contact dermatitis, and are suspected cancer-causing agents. *See also* Diazo Dyes.

B

BAK • The abbreviation for benzalkonium chloride *(see)*.

BAKING POWDER • In baking, any powders used as a substitute for yeast. It is usually a mixture of sodium bicarbonate with starch as a filler, and a harmless acid such as tartaric (cream of tartar). Nontoxic.

BAKING SODA • A common name for sodium bicarbonate *(see)*.

BALLPOINT INK • Contains glycols, dyes, resins, and sometimes benzyl alcohol *(see all)*. *See also* Inks.

BALLPOINT PEN REMOVER • May be removed by using hair spray and then washing with soap and water. *See* Ink Eradicator.

BALSAM PERU • A dark brown viscous liquid with a pleasant lingering odor and a warm bitter taste for use in cosmetics and odorants. Obtained from Peruvian balsam in Central America near the Pacific coast. Mildly antiseptic and irritating to the skin, it may cause contact dermatitis and a stuffy nose. It is one of the most common sensitizers and may cross-react with benzoin, rosin, benzoic acid, benzyl alcohol, cinnamic acid, essential oils, orange peel, eugenol, cinnamon, clove, Tolu balsam, storax, benzyl benzoate, and wood tars.

BANANA OIL • *See* Amyl Acetate.

BANOL • *See* Promecarb.

BARIUM HYDROXIDE • *See* Barium Sulfate.

BARIUM SULFATE • Blanc Fixe. Crude Barite. The salt of the alkaline earth metal, it is a fine, white, odorless, tasteless powder used as a white coloring and as a base for depilatories and other cosmetics. Also used for paper coatings, paints, filler, and to take the shine off textiles; in rubber, plastics, lithograph inks, X-ray photography, and battery plates. Barium hydroxide is also used in a similar manner. The barium products are poisonous when ingested and frequently cause skin reactions when applied. Symptoms of poisoning include severe abdominal pain, vomiting, shortness of breath, rapid pulse, paralysis of limbs and, eventually, coma, and death.

BARIUM SULFIDE • A yellowish green or gray powder that is soluble in water. Used to dehair hides, as a flame retardant, and in luminous paints. *See* Barium Sulfate.

BASE • *See* Alkali.

BATTERIES • Devices that generate electric current by converting chemical energy to electrical energy. Dry-cell and disc or button batteries are used in flashlights, radios, hearing aids, watches, cameras, calculators, toys, and other items in the home and office. These batteries may contain mercuric oxide (*see* mercury), lead, zinc, alkalines, nickel, cadmium, silver, and electrolytes. If the batteries leak or explode the chemical substances contained in these batteries can cause internal and external burns and irritations. Batteries may explode if an attempt is made to recharge nonrechargeable batteries or when batteries are thrown into a fire. Batteries that are chewed or punctured can also leak, and the small button batteries are particularly hazardous to children who may swallow them. At this writing, the New Jersey Senate is trying to ban them. The senate was also trying to make manufacturers gradually reduce the levels of mercury in common alkaline-manganese dry-cell batteries, the most common batteries found in flashlights and other consumer goods. If successful, by 1996, the batteries could contain no mercury. Also manufacturers would be required to set up collection and proper disposal system for nickel-cadmium and sealed-lead batteries.

BATTERIES, WET CELL • Automobile, boat, and tractor batteries contain lead and a solution of sulfuric acid, hence the title "wet cell." When activated, the solution in the battery produces explosive gases that are flammable. Manufacturers of these batteries must use labels that warn you of the dangers from battery acid and accumulated gases. Sulfuric acid is extremely caustic and contact can cause burning and charring of the skin. If a battery should leak, wash the area with plenty of water. Fumes are very irritating. Battery acid is devastating to the eyes. Lead is poisonous in all forms. Improper disposal of batteries presents an enviromental hazard. Contact your local waste disposal department or look under "batteries" in your phone book. You may find a company not only willing to take the batteries off your hands but pay you a small amount of money for the opportunity.

BAYGON™ • **Propoxur. DDVP. Phenol Methylcarbamate.** White to tan crystals, a carbamate *(see)* pesticide that decomposes at high temperatures to emit very toxic methyl isocyanate. A poison by mouth and skin. Possible mutagen.

BBC12 • *See* Dibromochloropropane.

BEHENALKONIUM CHLORIDE • *See* Quaternary Ammonium Salts.

BEHENAMIDOPROPYL DIMETHYLAMINE • *See* Quaternary Ammonium Compounds.

BEHENETH-5,-10,-20,-30 • The polyethylene glycol ethers of behenyl alcohol. *See* Polyethylene Glycol and Behenyl Alcohol.

BEHENYL ALCOHOL • **1-Docosanol.** Colorless wax that is insoluble in water but soluble in alcohol and chloroform. It is made from behenic acid, lithium, and aluminum. Used in synthetic fibers, lubricants, and to stop evaporation from the surface of water.

BELMARK™ • *See* Fenvalerate.

BENOMYL • **Methyl-1-(butyl carbamoyl)-2-benzimidazole-carbamate. Tersan 1991. Bonide.** A white, crystalline solid; a carbamate *(see)*. The generic name for a fungicide used on peaches, apples, and other fruits after they are picked. Also used as an oxidizer in sewage treatment. A mild skin irritant, it is extremely toxic by ingestion, and may cause birth defects.

BENTONITE • A white clay found in the midwestern United States and Canada. Used to thicken lotions, to suspend makeup pigments, and emulsify oils. Also used in liquid makeup, and in facial masks to absorb oil on the face and reduce shine; as a thickener in lubricating greases and fireproofing agents; a filler in ceramics, paper coatings, asphalt, polishes, and abrasives; as a food additive to thicken and color products; and in cement and in oil-well drilling. Inert and generally nontoxic.

BENZALDEHYDE • **Artificial Almond Oil.** A colorless liquid that occurs in the kernels of bitter almonds. Lime is used in its synthetic manufacture. As the artificial essential oil of almonds, it is used in cosmetic creams and lotions, perfumes, soaps, and dyes. May cause allergic reactions. Highly toxic.

BENZALKONIUM CHLORIDE • BAK. A widely used ammonium detergent (*see* Ammonium) and germicide with an aromatic odor and a very bitter taste. Soluble in water and alcohol. It is used as a fungicide, and in medicine as a topical antiseptic. Allergic conjunctivitis (red, irritated eyes) has been reported when used in eye lotions. Highly toxic.

BENZENE • Benzol. Derived from toluene or gasoline, it is used in the manufacture of detergents, nylon, artificial leather, as an antiknock in gasoline, in airplane fuel, dope, varnish, lacquer, and as a solvent for waxes, resins, and oils. Although its use in consumer products has been greatly reduced, it is still among the top five organic chemicals produced in the United States each year. Highly flammable. Poisonous when ingested and irritating to the mucous membranes. Harmful amounts may be absorbed through the skin. Also can cause sensitivity to light in which the skin may break out in a rash or swell. Inhalation of the fumes may be toxic. It has been linked to anemia, cancer in humans (particularly leukemia), liver damage, and kidney damage. May contaminate other solvents. The Consumer Product Safety Commission voted unanimously in February 1978 to ban the use of benzene in the manufacture of many household products. The commission took the action in response to a petition filed by the Consumer Health Research Group, an organization affiliated with consumer advocate Ralph Nader. Earlier in the year, OSHA and the EPA both cited benzene as a threat to public health. For more than a century, scientists have known that benzene is a powerful bone-marrow poison, causing such conditions as aplastic anemia. In the past several decades evidence has been mounting that it also causes leukemia. It has a chronic effect on bone marrow, destroying the marrow's ability to produce blood cells. Safety standards for cosmetic manufacturing workers and other workers have been set at 10 parts per million during an eight-hour day, but OSHA wants it reduced to 1 part per million. Prior to a ten-year Environmental Protection Agency study, a report of which was made public in the early 1990s, it was believed that most individuals were exposed to benzene through living in urban-industrial areas with heavy concentrations of petroleum refining. It is estimated that 2 to 3 million workers may be exposed to benzene in the petrochemical, rubber, and coke plants. Shoemakers, furniture finishers, and gas station attendants are also exposed to it.

The new findings reported by EPA's TEAM Study, "Major Sources of Benzene Exposure," in 1989, however, indicate that personal exposure to cigarette smoke, using solvents that emit benzene, pumping gasoline, and inhaling exhaust vapors seeping from attached garages, is four times as great as open-air exposure. A nonsmoker who lives with a smoker is exposed to twice the level of benzene as someone who resides in a nonsmoking household. The traditional sources of atmospheric emissions (auto exhaust and industrial emissions), the EPA found, account for only about 20 percent of total exposure. Exposure to various personal activities such as driving, using attached garages, emissions from consumer products, building materials, paints, and adhesives probably account for 20 percent. To reduce your exposure to benzene, stop smoking, use care around gasoline and car exhaust, and make sure your house is well ventilated and insulated from vapors that might arise from an attached garage. Avoid use of solvents containing benzene.

BENZETHONIUM CHLORIDE • *See* Quaternary Ammonium Compounds.

BENZIDINE DYES • A group of azo dyes *(see)* that are derived from nitrobenzene and zinc. They include yellow and orange colors. They are highly toxic and cause cancer. Body contact should be avoided.

BENZOIC ACID • A preservative that occurs in nature in cherry bark, raspberries, tea, anise, and cassia bark. First described in 1608, when it was found in gum benzoin. Used in chocolate, lemon, orange, cherry, fruit, nut, and tobacco flavorings. Also used in margarine and as an antifungal agent. A mild irritant to the skin, it can cause allergic reactions.

BENZOL • Obsolete name for Benzene *(see)*.

BENZOYL PEROXIDE • A bleaching agent for flours, blue cheese, fats, oils, and milk. A catalyst for hardening certain fiberglass resins. A drying agent in cosmetics. Used for acetate yarns and for embossing vinyl flooring. Highly toxic by inhalation. A skin allergen and irritant.

BENZYL CHLORIDE • A colorless liquid with a pungent odor that causes eye tearing. Derived by passing chlorine over boiling toluene. Intensely irritating to the eyes and skin; a poison via inhalation. Used in the manufacture of benzyl compounds, synthetic tannins, perfumes, pharmaceuticals, photographic developer, gasoline gunk inhibitors, and quaternary ammonium compounds. There is an OSHA standard for it pertaining to air in the workplace. A NIOSH review reported it to be a carcinogen.

o-BENZYL-p-CHLOROPHENOL • Chlorophene. Prepared from benzyl chloride and phenoxide followed by chlorination. Used in Lysol® Brand Disinfectant. *See* Phenol for toxicity.

BERYLLIOSIS • A lung inflammation caused by inhaling fumes or dust of the metal beryllium. This is an ongoing problem in the nuclear, aerospace, telecommunications, and computer industries. Researchers at The National Jewish Hospital and Respiratory Center are working under a government grant to develop a screening test for beryllium disease.

BERYLLIUM • *See* Beryllium Nitrate.

BERYLLIUM NITRATE • White to slightly yellow water-absorbing crystals used in electroplating, fluorescent and neon lighting, and in some ceramics. Can cause contact dermatitis. Beryllium is a suspected human cancer-causing agent. A poison via inhalation, and moderately toxic when ingested.

BETAINE • Occurs naturally in beets and many other vegetables as well as in animal substances. It is used in resins. Has been employed medically to treat muscle weakness. No known toxicity.

BHC • HCH, 666. Hexachlor. *See* Lindane.

BICHLORIDE OF MERCURY • *See* Mercury Compounds.

BIG WALLY FOAM CLEANER™ **•** Contains ammonia and ethyl alcohol *(see both)*.

BINDER • A substance such as gum arabic, gum tragacanth, glycerin, and sorbitol *(see all)*, which dispenses, swells, or absorbs water, increases consistency, and holds ingredients together. For example, binders are used to help powders in compacts retain their shape; binders in toothpaste provide for the smooth dispensing of the paste.

BIOCIDE • The general name for any substance that kills or inhibits the growth of microorganisms such as molds, slime, bacteria, and fungi. Many biocides are also toxic to humans. Those you may find around the house, office, or yard include chlorinated hydrocarbons, metallic salts, quaternary ammonium compounds, and phenolics *(see all)*.

BIOXIRAN • *See* Butane.

BIRDS • If birds such as starlings, pigeons, or woodpeckers are a nuisance on your property, use a child's pinwheel, tin can lids strung together, or beribbon a string with tin foil to scare the birds away.

BIS- • From the Latin *duis,* meaning "twice" or "again."
2,3,4,5-BIS(2-BUTENYLENE)TETRAHYDROFURFURAL • An insect repellent. *See* Insecticides.
BIS (2-BUTYLENE)TETRAHYDRO-2-FURALDEHYDE • An insect repellent in pet shampoos. *See* Pet pesticides.
BISMARCK BROWN • A basic brown color prepared from phenylenediamine and nitrous acid, and used in dyeing silk, wool, and leather. Can cause contact dermatitis.
BISMUTH COMPOUNDS • **Subgallate. Subnitrate. Oxychloride.** Bismuth is a gray-white powder with a bright, metallic luster. It occurs in the earth's crust, and for many years was used to treat syphilis. Bismuth subgallate, a dark gray, odorless, tasteless form, is used as an antiseptic and in dusting powder. Bismuth subnitrate is both odorless and tasteless, and is used in bleaching and freckle creams, and hair dyes. Bismuth oxychloride is "synthetic pearl." Bismuth is also used in alloys, magnets, and semiconductors, to coat selenium, and to make luminous paints. Bismuth subsalicylate is used as a surface coating for plastics and copying paper. It is flammable in powder form. Most bismuth compounds have a low toxicity when ingested, but may cause allergic reactions when applied to the skin. Bismuth poisoning can cause neurological disorders, lack of appetite, headache, rash, kidney damage, and ulcers of the stomach, mouth, and lips.
BISPHENOL-A • White flakes with a phenolic odor made from phenol and acetone with hydrochloric acid. It is used in the manufacture of epoxy resins, flame retardants, rubber chemicals, and fungicides. *See* Phenol.
BIS (TRIBUTYLTIN) OXIDE • **TBTO.** An organic tin compound, it is a yellow liquid that kills fungi, and is widely available in commercial paint fungicides. EPA registrations for paint fungicide products permit their use in interior paints. In animal studies, a variety of toxic responses have been associated with exposure to TBTO. Dietary exposure of experimental animals to the chemical has resulted in weight loss, immunosuppression, and anemia. Inhalation exposure has produced bleeding and swelling in the lungs of mice and guinea pigs. In humans, skin exposure produces irritation, including redness and itching. Industrial exposure to vapors or fumes of organic tin compounds causes eye and throat irritation. Workers so exposed have developed sore throats and coughs within several hours. In January 1991, a Wisconsin family became ill after the landlord used paint containing TBTO on the walls and ceilings

of two rooms of their apartment. Reported symptoms included a burning sensation in the nose and forehead, headache, nosebleed, cough, loss of appetite, nausea, and vomiting. The tenant, a woman who was in her third trimester of pregnancy, also complained of a persistent odor from the paint, and provided investigators with an empty bottle of a paint additive used for mildew control. The label indicated that the product contained 25 percent TBTO as its only active ingredient. In February 1988, the Washington Department of Health issued a health advisory against using TBTO in interior paint, based on its investigation of six incidents of illness among persons who painted one or more walls with interior paint containing this fungicide. Complaints and reported symptoms included respiratory problems, sore throat, weakness, headaches, and swollen glands. In July 1988, the Washington Department of Agriculture established regulations banning the sale of this product in the state for use in interior paints. The investigation in Wisconsin suggests that the use of this product as an additive for interior paints represents a source of toxic, short-term exposure. The health effects of chronic, low-level exposure are unknown. (*Centers for Disease Control Morbidity and Mortality Weekly Report,* May 3, 1991, vol. 40, no. 17, pp. 280–281)

BLANC FIXE • *See* Barium Sulfate.

BLEACHES • Sodium hypochlorite is used in household bleach products such as Clorox™, in 3 to 6 percent concentrations, and has a pH of up to 11. Some bleaches such as Purex™, contain silicate (15 to 17 percent), and sodium carbonate (60 percent), and have a pH of approximately 10.5. Among other popular bleaches are: peroxide (hydrogen peroxide, 3.0 percent), Minute Mildew Remover™ (calcium hypochlorite, 48 percent), and Tilex™ Instant Mildew Remover (sodium hypochlorite, 5 percent and calcium hypochlorite, 48 percent). Household bleaches may produce erosions but rarely penetrate through lining of the throat to cause constriction of the windpipe. Granular and commercial bleaches may contain higher concentrations of hypochlorite or sodium carbonate, leading to greater tissue destruction. For less toxic alternatives for laundry, use half a cup of white vinegar, baking soda, or borax per load. *See* Alkali.

BOLD™ GRANULAR LAUNDRY DETERGENT • An anionic detergent containing sodium alkyl benzene sulfonate, sodium tripolyphosphate, and sodium silicate (*see all*).

BONIDE • *See* Benomyl and Anilazine.

BORATES • Used as corrosion inhibitors, borates may cause ear, nose, and throat irritation. Acute poisonings have followed ingestion, injections, enemas, irrigation of the bladder, and application of powders and ointments to burned, abraded skin. The biochemical mechanism of borate poisoning is unknown. The highest concentrations of borates in poisoning have been found in the brain, gastrointestinal tract, kidneys, liver, and skin. Borates are rapidly absorbed from mucous membranes and abraded skin, but not from intact skin. Infants and young children are thought to be more sensitive to borate intoxication than adults. Borate poisoning symptoms include nausea, vomiting, diarrhea, stomach pain, weakness, lethargy, headache, restlessness, tremors, and convulsions. *See* Perborate and Borax.

BORAX • **Sodium Borate. Tincal. Sodium Tetraborate Dehydrate. Disodium Tetraborate Decahydrate.** A mild alkali found in the Far West, particularly in Death Valley, California. Used in cold creams, foundation creams, hair-color rinses, permanent waves, and shaving creams. Also used as a water softener, a wood preservative, an herbicide, in wallpaper removers and cleaning compounds, and to prevent irritation of the skin by the antiperspirant aluminum chloride *(see)*. Borax is recommended as a cleaning agent and pesticide by those who seek to use less toxic alternatives to commercial products, but it can be toxic. *See* Boric Acid and Borates for toxicity.

BORDEAUX MIXTURE • Aqua-colored powder made from copper sulfate and calcium hydroxide and used as a fungicide. *See* Copper Salts and Calcium Hydroxide.

BORIC ACID • An antiseptic with bactericidal and fungicidal properties, used in baby powders, bath powders, liquid powders, mouthwashes, eye creams, protective creams, after-shave lotions, soaps, and skin fresheners. It is still widely used despite repeated warnings of possible toxicity from the American Medical Association. Severe poisonings have followed both ingestion and topical application to abraded skin. Boric acid is used as a fungal control on citrus fruit (FDA tolerance, 8 ppm boron residues) and for heat-resistant glass, glass fibers, porcelain enamels, welding flux, brazing copper, flame retardant in cellulose insulation, mattress batting and cotton textile products, and in nickel-plating baths. *See* Borates.

BORIC ACID ESTERS • Colorless to yellow liquids used as dehydrating agents, special solvents, stabilizers, plasticizers, or adhesion additives to latex paints, ingredients of soldering and brazing fluxes. *See* Boric Acid, Esters, and Borates.

BORIC ANHYDRIDE • *See* Boron Oxide.

BORIC OXIDE • *See* Boron Oxide.

BORNEOL • Occurs naturally in coriander, ginger oil, oil of lime, rosemary, strawberries, thyme, citronella, and nutmeg. Used in perfumery, it has a peppery odor and a burning taste. Toxicity is similar to camphor *(see)*.

BORON OXIDE • **Boric Anhydride. Boron Trioxide. Boric Oxide.** Colorless crystals or water-absorbing lumps, derived by heating boric acid *(see)*. It is used in the production of heat-resistant glass, as a fire-resistant additive for paints, electronics, and as a herbicide. Used in medicine and household and industrial products, it is a poison that is often ingested accidentally and, sometimes, fatally. Ingestion causes central nervous system and blood circulation depression, diarrhea, vomiting, profound shock, and coma. It also causes a drop in body temperature and a rash covering the whole body.

BORON TRIOXIDE • *See* Boric Oxide.

BOTRAN™ • *See* Dichloran.

BP 300™ • A pesticide containing pyrethrins, piperonyl butoxide, and petroleum distillate *(see all)*.

BRAKE FLUID • Made up of a lubricant (such as castor oil), or a glycol plus a solvent (such as methyl or butyl ethers of ethylene glycol), and inhibitors (such as potash soap or borax) plus an antioxidant (such as hydroquinone). May also contain heavy metals and a dye. Flammable and toxic. Used brake fluid contains lead and other heavy metals in addition to solvents.

BRAKES • *See* Automobile Brakes.

BRAN OIL • *See* Furfural.

BREATHING ZONE. • The area or space (as in a room) surrounding occupants.

BRODIFACOUM • Rat and mouse poison.

BROMATED • Combined or saturated with bromine, a nonmetallic, reddish, volatile, liquid element. *See* Bromine.

BROMEX • *See* Naled.

BROMIDES, POTASSIUM AND SODIUM • Potassium bromide is used in the manufacture of photographic paper and plates and in engraving. It is used medically as a sedative and anticonvulsant. Sodium bromide is also used in the manufacture of photographic equipment and as a sedative and sleep inducer. Bromides can cause skin rashes. Large doses of the bromides can cause central nervous system depression, and prolonged intake may cause mental deterioration.

BROMINE • A dark, reddish brown liquid derived from seawater and natural brines by oxidation of bromine salts with chlorine. It is soluble in organic solvents, and slightly soluble in water. Attacks most metals. Used in the manufacture of anti-knock gasolines, in bleaching, water purification, fumigants, fire-retardant plastics, dyes, photography, in shrink-proofing wool, and as a solvent. It is toxic by ingestion and inhalation, and is a severe skin irritant. Can cause spontaneous fires on contact with combustible materials.

BROMOSALICYLANILIDE • A fungicide used in deodorant sprays. *See* Salicylanilide and Deodorant Sprays.

BUFFER • Usually a solution with a relatively constant acidity/alkalinity ratio, which is unaffected by the addition of comparatively large amounts of acid or alkali. A typical buffer solution would be hydrochloric acid and sodium hydroxide *(see both).*

BUHACH® • An insecticide that contains pyrethrin *(see),* and is sold as a "natural insecticide." Prospectors in Alaska in the late 1800s reportedly used it to fight off Klondike mosquitoes.

BUILDING-RELATED ILLNESS • A term referring to any discrete, identifiable disease or illness that can be traced to a specific pollutant or source within a building.

BURNT LIME • *See* Calcium Oxide.

BUTADIENE • A colorless gas produced from petroleum gases. It can also be obtained by cracking naphtha and light oil. The thirty-sixth most common chemical produced in the United States, it is widely used in industry in the manufacture of synthetic rubber, plastics, resins, rocket fuels, and many other products. It is irritating to the skin and mucous membranes, and is narcotic in high concentrations. The long-term human health effects are unknown and are now being investigated by the Chemical Industry Institute of Toxicology. Investigators at Johns Hopkins University under a government grant are also studying the chemical and its possible link to cancer, including leukemia and other lymphatic and blood cancers, gastrointestinal cancers, and sarcomas. The chemical was in the carpeting installed in new Environmental Protection Agency offices in Washington, D.C., and was thought to contribute to the "building-related illnesses" suffered by employees. The carpeting had to be removed. *(See* pages 5–7.)

BUTANE • *N*-Butane. Methylsulfonal. Bioxiran. Dibutadiene Dioxide. A flammable, easily liquefiable gas derived from petroleum. It is the raw material for motor fuels and is used in the manufacture of synthetic rubber. A solvent, refrigerant, and food additive. Also used as a propellant or aerosol in cosmetics. The principal hazards are fire and explosion, but it may also be narcotic in high doses and cause asphyxiation. It has been determined by the National Institute of Occupational Safety and Health to be an animal carcinogen.

BUTOXYETHANOL • Butyl Cellosolve®. A solvent for nitrocellulose *(see)*, resins, grease, oil, and albumin. See Polyethylene Glycol for toxicity.

BUTOXY PROPYLENE GLYCOL • Propylene Glycol Monobutyl Ether. An insect repellent. *See* Propylene Glycol for toxicity.

BUTYL ACETATE • Acetic Acid. Butyl Ester. A colorless liquid with a fruity odor, prepared from acetic acid and butyl alcohol *(see both)*, and used in perfumery, nail polish, nail polish remover, and food flavorings. Also used in the manufacture of lacquer, artificial leather, plastics, and safety glass. It is an irritant; may cause eye irritation (conjunctivitis). A narcotic in high concentrations, and toxic when inhaled at 200 ppm.

BUTYL ACID PHOSPHATE • White liquid soluble in alcohol and acetate but not in water and naphtha. It is used as a curing agent and accelerator in resins and coatings and in some strong detergents. It is irritating to the skin and tissue.

BUTYL ALCOHOL • A colorless liquid with an unpleasant odor, used as a clarifying agent *(see)* in shampoos, as a flavoring for beverages and ice cream, and as a solvent for waxes, fats, resins, and shellac. Also used in enamel paint *(see)*. When ingested, it may cause irritation of the mucous membranes, headache, dizziness, and drowsiness. Inhalation of as little as 25 ppm causes lung problems in humans. When applied to the skin, it can also cause contact dermatitis.

n-BUTYL ALCOHOL • *See* Butyl Alcohol.

t-BUTYL ALCOHOL • *See* Butyl Alcohol.

BUTYL CELLOSOLVE® • Ethylene Glycol, Monobutyl Ether. 2-Butoxyethanol. Liquid derived from ethylene glycol soluble in water, mineral oil, and most organic solvents. Used as a solvent for nitrocellulose, resins, grease, oil, and in dry cleaning. Toxic; may cause anemia and central nervous system depression. Can be absorbed easily through the skin.

1,3-BUTYLENE GLYCOL • A clear, colorless, viscous liquid with a slight taste. A solvent and humectant most resistant to high humidity and, thus, valuable in foods and cosmetics. It retains scents, and preserves against spoilage. It has a similar toxicity to ethylene glycol *(see),* which when ingested may cause transient stimulation of the central nervous system, followed by depression, vomiting, drowsiness, coma, respiratory failure, and convulsions. Renal damage may proceed to kidney failure and death. One of the few humectants not on the FDA's Generally Recognized As Safe list (GRAS), although efforts to place it there have been made through the years.

BUTYL METHACRYLATE • **Methyacrylic Acid. Butyl ester.** Derived from methacrylic acid, and used for resins, solvent, coatings, adhesives, oil additives, emulsions for textiles, leather and paper finishing. Toxic by ingestion. May cause allergic reactions when inhaled.

BUTYL OLEATE. • The ester of butyl alcohol and oleic acid *(see both),* it is a plasticizer, particularly for polyvinyl chloride *(see),* and is used in waterproofing, as a solvent, a lubricant, and in polishes. No known toxicity.

BUTYL PARABEN • The ester of butyl alcohol and p-hydroxybenzoic acid, it is widely used as an antifungal, especially in cosmetics. It is also used as a preservative.

p-tert-BUTYL PHENOL • White crystals insoluble in water and soluble in alcohol and ether; derived from phenol and ether. Used in rubber compounds, plastics, resins, and adhesives. An irritant to eyes and skin, it can cause allergic contact dermatitis.

BUTYL RUBBER • A synthetic rubber, a combination of isobutylene and isoprene, used to line tractor tires and other oversize vehicles, and for electric wire insulation, steam hoses, and other industrial rubber goods. It is a pond and reservoir sealant. Latex is used for paper coating, textile and leather finishing, adhesive formulations, air bags, for self-curing cements, pressure-sensitive adhesives, and sealants. It is also used as a chewing gum-base component. No known toxicity.

BUTYL TIN • See Organotin Compounds.

BUTYRALDEHYDE • A synthetic flavoring agent found naturally in coffee and strawberries. Used in food flavorings, solvents, in the manufacture of rubber, gas accelerators, synthetic resins, and plasticizers. May be an irritant and a narcotic.

BUTYROLACTONE • **Butanolide.** Prepared from acetylene and formaldehyde, it is an oily liquid lactone used chiefly as a solvent for plastics. It is also an intermediate *(see)* in the manufacture of polyvinylpyrrolidone *(see),* a constituent of paint removers, textile aids, and drilling oils, and a solvent for nail polish. Toxic by ingestion.

C

CABINETMAKING • *See* Woodworking.

CADMIUM • A naturally occurring metal used to control molds and diseases that attack home lawns, golf-course turfs, and other grasses. However, less than 0.1 percent of the annual U.S. consumption of 12 million pounds of cadmium is used in pesticides— most of it is used in industries that produce electroplating and rubber, nickel-cadmium batteries, brazing-soldering alloys and pigments, and chemicals that act as stabilizers in plastics, in the manufacture of rubber tires, and the solder employed in plumbing. Other sources of human exposure are cigarette smoke, air pollution, drinking water, and sludge. Cadmium in drinking water has been correlated with cancer of the pharynx, esophagus, intestines, larynx, lungs, and bladder. Cadmium is believed to cause mutations: This conclusion is based upon findings of chromosome and DNA damage resulting from the presence of cadmium in the blood of industrial workers. In addition, exposure to home-lawn treatment products containing cadmium may be dangerous to women of childbearing age. It is a potential carcinogen. Ingestion causes sudden nausea, salivation, vomiting, diarrhea, and abdominal pain. It is poisonous when ingested, but irritation and vomiting are so violent that little cadmium is absorbed. Cadmium is considered an environmental and occupational hazard known to cause kidney damage after chronic exposure and to adversely affect the reproductive organs and liver in acute exposure situations. Researchers believe that females may be at greater risk than males because of the role of sex hormones in liver metabolism. Inhalation of dust and fumes affects mainly the respiratory system. The dust is a great fire hazard. In addition to the adverse effects mentioned above, cadmium poisoning can cause emphysema, fatigue, headache, anemia, deranged mineral metabolism, and loss of smell.

CADMIUM CHLORIDE • A white powder, soluble in water, used in photography and dye, particularly hair dye. Inhalation of the dust and fumes is highly toxic, and ingestion can cause death. It produced tumors when injected under the skins of rats and when given intravenously, and also caused cancer in mice when injected. NIOSH review determined it to be an animal carcinogen.

CAKE ALUM • *See* Aluminum Sulfate.

CALCIUM ACETATE • **Brown Acetate of Lime.** A white, amorphous powder used medicinally as a source of calcium. It is also used in the manufacture of acetic acid and acetone *(see both)*, in dyeing, tanning, and curing skins, and as a corrosion inhibitor in metal containers. Used cosmetically for solidifying fragrances, and as an emulsifier and firming agent. Low oral toxicity.

CALCIUM ACID PHOSPHATE • *See* Calcium Phosphate.

CALCIUM ARSENATE • **Tricalcium Arsenate.** A colorless powder used as an insecticide and herbicide. It is a human cancer-causing agent, and a skin irritant. *See* Arsenic Compounds.

CALCIUM CARBONATE • **Chalk.** A tasteless, odorless powder that occurs naturally in limestone, marble, and coral, it is an absorbent that removes shine from talc. Used as a white coloring in cosmetics and food, an alkali to reduce acidity, a neutralizer and firming agent, and a carrier for bleaches. Also used in dentifrices as a tooth polisher, in deodorants and depilatories as a filler, and in face powder as a buffer. A gastric antacid and antidiarrheal medicine, it may cause constipation. No known toxicity. *See* Chalk.

CALCIUM CHLORIDE • The chloride salt of calcium, used in its waterless form as a drying agent for organic liquids and gases. It is an emulsifier and texturizer in cosmetics, an antiseptic in eye lotions, and is employed medicinally as a diuretic and a urinary acidifier. It is also used in fire extinguishers, to preserve wood, and to melt ice and snow.

CALCIUM HYDROXIDE • **Slaked lime. Limewater. Lye.** Used in cream depilatories, mortar, plaster, cement, pesticides, fireproofing, and as an egg preservative. Also used as whitewash, in the dehairing of hides, in water softening, and as a soil conditioner. Employed as a topical astringent and alkali in solutions or lotions. Accidental ingestion can cause burns of the throat and esophagus, as well as death from shock and asphyxia due to infection, and swelling of the glottis. Calcium hydroxide also can cause burns of the skin and eyes.

CALCIUM HYPOCHLORITE • A germicide and sterilizing agent, it is the active ingredient of chlorinated lime, and is used in the curd washing of cottage cheese, in sugar refining, as an oxidizing and bleaching agent, as a bactericide, deodorant, disinfectant, and fungicide, and to kill algae. Fruits and vegetables are sterilized by washing in a 50 percent solution. Under various names, dilute hypochlorite is found in homes as laundry and household bleaches. Household mildew removers contain 5 percent calcium hypochlorite, which is twice as toxic as common household sodium hypochlorite bleach. Industrial-strength hypochlorite bleaches contain 15 to

20 percent solutions. Occasionally, cases of poisoning occur when people mix household hypochlorite solution with various other household chemicals, causing the release of poisonous chlorine gas. As with other corrosive agents, the toxicity of calcium hypochlorite is determined by its concentration. Highly corrosive to skin and mucous membranes. Ingestion may cause pain and inflammation of the mouth, pharynx, esophagus, and stomach, with erosion particularly of the mucous membranes of the stomach.

CALCIUM HYPOPHOSPHITE • Crystals of powder slightly acid in solution, and practically insoluble in alcohol. A corrosion inhibitor, and has been used as a dietary supplement in veterinary medicine. *See* Phosphine.

CALCIUM OLEATE • Yellowish crystals soluble in benzene and chloroform, but not in water, alcohol, or acetone. It is used as a grease-thickening agent, emulsifying agent, and in waterproofing concrete. *See* Oleic Acid.

CALCIUM OXIDE • **Quicklime. Burnt Lime.** A hard, white or grayish white, odorless mass or powder commercially obtained from limestone. It is used as a yeast food and dough conditioner for bread, as an alkali for neutralizing dairy products, and to clarify beet and cane sugar juices. Industrial uses are for bricks, plaster, mortar, stucco, dehairing hides, fungicides, and insecticides. A strong caustic, it may severely damage skin and mucous membranes, and can cause both thermal and chemical burns.

CALCIUM PHOSPHATE • **Dibasic, Monobasic, and Tribasic.** White, odorless, tasteless powders used as yeast foods, dough conditioners, firming agents, and in fertilizers, glass, and plastics. Tribasic is an anticaking agent used in table salt. Dibasic is used to improve bread, as a carrier for bleaching, as a mineral supplement in cereals, in dental products, and in fertilizers. Monobasic is used in bread, and as a fertilizer. Nontoxic.

CALCIUM SILICATE • **Okenite.** An anticaking agent, white or slightly cream-colored, free-flowing powder used in face powders, baking powder, and salt because it has extremely fine particles and good water absorption. Also used as a coloring agent, in road construction, and in lime glass. Practically nontoxic if ingested, but inhalation may cause irritation of the respiratory tract.

CALCIUM STEARATE • Prepared from limewater *(see)*, it is an emulsifier used in hair-grooming products. Also used as a coloring agent, in waterproofing, in paints, and printer's ink. Nontoxic.

CALCIUM STEAROYL LACTYLATE • The calcium salt of the stearic acid ester of lactyl lactate. A free-flowing powder used to improve the flow of powders. No known toxicity.

CALCIUM SULFATE • **Plaster of Paris.** A fine, white to slightly yellow, odorless, tasteless powder that occurs in nature as anhydrate or gypsum. It is used in cement, tile and plaster, paints, paper, wallboard, dyeing and calico printing, metallurgy, insecticides, and as a soil conditioner. It is also used in toothpaste and tooth powders as an abrasive and firming agent, as a coloring agent in cosmetics, and as an alkali in creamed cottage cheese. Because it absorbs moisture and hardens quickly, its ingestion may result in intestinal obstruction. Mixed with flour, it has been used to kill rodents. No known toxicity on the skin.

CALCIUM SULFIDE • A yellow powder formed by heating gypsum with charcoal at 1,000°F (523°C). It is used in luminous paints, lubricants, as a food preservative, in depilatories, and acne preparations. Can cause allergic reactions.

CALGON™ • *See* Sodium Hexylmetaphosphate.

CALGONITE™ **ELECTRONIC DISHWASHER DETERGENT** • A strong irritant containing complex sodium phosphates, chlorinated trisodium phosphate, and sodium silicate *(see all)*.

CAMEL HAIR • Hair from the beast of burden. It may be found in rugs and fabrics, and can cause contact dermatitis.

CAMPHOR OIL • **Japanese White Oil. Camphor Tree.** Distilled from trees at least fifty years old grown in China, Japan, Taiwan, Brazil, and Sumatra. The camphor tree is used in spice flavorings and in cosmetics to give a "cool" sensation to the skin. It is also used in horn-rimmed glasses, as a drug preservative, in embalming fluid, in the manufacture of explosives, in lacquers, as a moth repellent, in cold medications and anesthetics, and topically in liniments. It can cause contact dermatitis. In 1980, the FDA banned camphorated oil as a liniment for colds and sore muscles due to the work of a New Jersey pharmacist who collected case reports of poisonings through skin absorption and accidental ingestion, and testified before the FDA's Advisory Review Panel on Over-the-Counter Drugs. Camphor is readily absorbed through all sites of administration. Ingestion of 2 grams generally produces dangerous effects in an adult. Ingestion by pregnant women has caused fetal deaths.

CANCELLATION • The Federal Insecticide, Fungicide, and Rodenticide Act (FIFRA), section 6 (b), authorizes cancellation of registration if, when used according to widespread and commonly recognized practice, a pesticide generally causes unreasonable, adverse effects on the environment, or if its labeling or other material required to be submitted does not comply with FIFRA provisions.

CANDELILLA WAX • Obtained from candelilla plants for use in lipsticks, solid fragrances, and liquid powders to give them body. Brownish to yellow-brown, hard, brittle, easily pulverized, practically insoluble in water, slightly soluble in alcohol. Used in emollients to protect the skin against moisture loss. Also used in the manufacture of rubber, polishes, cements, varnishes, candles, electric insulating compositions, sealing wax, paper sizes, phonograph records, in waterproofing and writing inks, and to harden other waxes. Used as a coating for foods. No known toxicity.

CANVAS ADHESIVES • May contain polyvinyl acetate, silicones, methylcellulose, phenols, petroleum solvents, and ammonia *(see all)*. Nitrocellulose adhesives may also contain acetone and camphor *(see both)*.

CAPAM • *See* Fungicides.

CAPRIC ACID • Obtained from a large group of American plants. Solid crystalline mass with a rancid odor used in the manufacture of artificial fruit flavors in lipsticks, and to scent perfumes. No known toxicity.

CAPROAMPHOACETATE • *See* Surfactants.

CAPROAMPHODIACETATE • *See* Surfactants.

CAPROAMPHODIPROPIONATE • *See* Surfactants.

CAPROAMPHOHYDROXYPROPYLSULFONATE • *See* surfactants.

CAPRYLIC ACID • An oil liquid made by the oxidation of octanol *(see)* for use in perfumery. Occurs naturally as a fatty acid in sweat, fusel oil, in the milk of cows and goats, and in palm and coconut oil. No known toxicity.

CAPRYLOAMPHOACETATE • *See* Surfactants.

CAPRYLOAMPHODIACETATE • *See* Surfactants.

CAPRYLAMPHODIPROPIONATE • *See* Surfactants.

CAPRYLOAMPHOHYDROXYPROPYLSULFONATE • *See* Surfactants.

CAPTAFOL • *See* Phthalimides.

CAPTAN • **Merpan™. Orthocide™. Vanicide 89.** White- to creamy-colored powder, practically insoluble in water, derived from tetrahydrophthalimide and trichloromethylmercaptan. Used to treat seeds, to preserve fruit, and as a fungicide in paint, plastic, leather, and fabric. Also used as a preservative in cosmetics. It is a fungicide of lower toxicity than most, but in large doses can cause diarrhea and weight loss. A skin and lung irritant, and a suspected cause of human birth defects. Pregnant women should avoid exposure to it. *See* Phthalimides.

CAR WASH COMPOUNDS • These usually contain a detergent such as alkyl aryl sodium sulfonate *(see)*, and emulsifiers and creams with petroleum distillates such as benzene or phenol *(see both)*.

CAR WAX • Paste wax for automobiles usually contains 75 to 85 percent naphtha *(see)*, and 15 to 25 percent wax. *See* Waxes.

CARBA MIX • A mixture of carbamates *(see)* used in rubber and lawn and garden fungicides. A common skin sensitizer. *See* Fungicides and Carbamates.

CARBAMATES • Compounds based on carbamic acid, which is used only in the form of its numerous derivatives and salts. Carbamates are used in pesticides. Among the carbamate pesticides are aldicarb, 4-benzothienyl-methylcarbamate (moban), bufencarb (BUX), carbaryl, carbofuran, isolan, 2-isopropyl phenyl-*N*-methylcarbamate, 3-isopropyl phenylmethylcarbamate, maneb, propoxur, thiram, Zectran, zineb, and ziram. Carbamic acid, which is colorless and odorless, causes depression of bone marrow, degeneration of the brain, nausea, and vomiting. It is moderately toxic by many routes.

CARBAMIC ACID ETHYL ESTER • See Urethane.

CARBARYL • **Sevin**™. A pesticide used on corn and other vegetables and fruits. It can cause nausea, vomiting, diarrhea, lung damage, blurred vision, excessive salivation, muscle twitching, cyanosis, convulsions, coma, and death. An eye and skin irritant, and a poison via ingestion and skin absorption. Absorption through skin is slow. It does not accumulate in the tissues, and is much less toxic than parathion *(see)*. *See* Pesticides.

CARBIDE • *See* Carbitol®.

CARBITOL® • **Carbide. Carbon.** Trade name for a group of glycol ethers *(see)* that are used in solvents and abrasives. Absorbs water from the air and is mixable with acetone, benzene, alcohol, water, and ether. More toxic than polyethylene glycol *(see)*.

CARBOLIC ACID • Legal label for phenol. *See* Phenol.

CARBON BLACK • Several forms of artificially prepared carbon or charcoal, including animal charcoal, furnace black, channel (gas) black, lamp black, and activated charcoal. Animal charcoal is used as a black coloring in confectionery. Activated charcoal is used as an antidote for ingested poisons, and as an adsorbent in diarrhea. The others have industrial uses. Carbon black, which was not subject to certification *(see)* by the FDA, was reevaluated and then banned in 1976. It was found in tests to contain a cancer-causing byproduct that was released during dye manufacture. It can no longer be used in candies such as licorice and jelly beans, in drugs or cosmetics. Studies of employees in the carbon black industry indicate there are no physiologic effects from contact, inhalation, or ingestion.

CARBON DIOXIDE • A colorless, odorless, noncombustible gas with a faintly acidic taste. Used as a pressure-dispensing agent in aerosol creams. Also used in the carbonation of beverages and as dry ice for refrigeration in the frozen food industry. Used on stage to produce harmless smoke or fumes. Handling the solid can cause frostbite because it is very cold. Inhalation may cause shortness of breath, vomiting, high blood pressure, and disorientation if inhaled in sufficient amounts. It is damaging to the skin.

CARBON DISULFIDE • A clear, odorless, faintly yellow liquid derived from natural gas or petroleum, which is used as a fumigant *(see)*, and to make viscose rayon, cellophane, and flotation agents. It is also used in the manufacture of carbon tetrachloride *(see)* and solvents. An extremely dangerous compound, poisonous if ingested, toxic by skin contact, and highly flammable.

CARBON MONOXIDE • CO. Carbon monoxide is the leading cause of poisoning deaths in the United States, accounting for 3,500 to 4,000 deaths per year. An estimated 10,000 people a year lose a day's work and/or seek medical attention due to carbon monoxide poisoning. Roughly two-thirds of fatalities occur in fire victims; most of the remaining fatalities result from exposure to products of inadequate combustion of organic compounds in automobile cylinders or kerosene heaters. Carbon monoxide may be in the air of offices, restaurants, bars, arenas at 2.5–2.8 ppm, and in kitchens with gas stoves at 3.1–7.8 ppm. The source is combustion equipment, engines, stoves, faulty heating systems, water heaters, and dryers. If you have an attached garage, always make sure the door to the house is closed and the garage door is open when the car is running. The effects of carbon monoxide have been known since early times. In mild to moderate toxicity, symptoms may be nonspecific such as nausea, fatigue, and headache, and resemble the flu. Patients with preexisting brain or heart disease appear more sensitive to carbon monoxide. As many as 15 to 40 percent of victims of serious, nonfatal carbon monoxide poisoning develop symptoms such as personality changes and memory impairment, which can appear after apparent recovery. Perceptible clinical effects occur with two-hour exposure to concentrations of CO as low as 100 ppm. The maximum to which a worker in the United States may be transiently exposed without altering blood levels of CO is 200 ppm.

CARBON PAPER • From the Latin word *carbo,* meaning "coal," it is a paper that may be coated with the plasticizer triphenyl phosphate and nigrosine, which is present in special carbon paper used for computers, and an ink that consists basically of waxes, oils, and colors. The oils are nondrying to produce softness and compactness of the ink. The waxes keep the ink hard and dry at room temperature and are the carriers for color. The most common causes of allergic reactions to carbon paper have been reported to be nigrosine and triphenyl phosphate *(see both).*

CARBON TET • *See* Carbon Tetrachloride.

CARBON TETRACHLORIDE • **Carbon Tet. Tetrachloromethane. Perchloromethane.** A colorless, clear, heavy, nonflammable liquid obtained from carbon disulfide and chlorine. Used as a fire extinguisher; for cleaning clothing; for rendering benzene nonflammable; as a drying agent for wet spark plugs in automobiles; as a solvent for oils, fats, lacquers, varnishes, rubber waxes, resins; for extracting oil from flower seeds; for exterminating insects; as a solvent; and for starting material in the manufacture of many organic compounds. It is used to kill hookworms and tapeworms. Poisonous by inhalation, ingestion, or skin absorption. Acute poisoning causes nausea, diarrhea, headache, stupor, kidney damage, and can be fatal. Chronic poisoning involves liver damage, but can also cause kidney injury. When absorbed through the skin it can cause a defatting action. It has caused cancer in animals. Because it is so toxic, the FDA banned its use in products for the home in 1970. It is still used in industry.

CARBONIC ACID • A weak acid formed by the reaction of carbon dioxide *(see)* and water, it is a liquid with a pleasant, ethereal odor that is a solvent for nitrocellulose and is used in the manufacture of radio tubes. It is also used to fix rare earths to cathodes. An animal carcinogen.

CARBONLESS COPY PAPER • Pressure-sensitive paper that copies text and/or drawing produced by a typewriter or writing utensil.

The principal coating is made up of microcapsules of ink. The top surface of the second sheet is coated with a material that absorbs the ink when the capsules are broken by pressure. The inks are mostly triphenyl methane dyes such as gentian violet or malachite green. They are dissolved in organic solvents inside capsules that include kerosene, di-arylethanes, alkyl naphthalenes, cyclohexane, and di-butyl phthalate. Some of these papers contain formaldehyde or ammonia. Carbonless paper can cause itchy eyes, throat irritation, fatigue, and skin rash. *See* Papers.

CARBOPHENOTHION • *See* Organophosphates.

CARBORUNDUM™ • *See* Silicon Carbide.

CARBOWAX • *See* Polyethylene Glycol Monostearate.

CARBOXYMETHYLCELLULOSE • Made from cotton by-products, it occurs as a white powder or in granules. A synthetic gum used in detergent, soap, in textile manufacturing, for coating paper and paperboard, emulsion paints, and as a stabilizer in ice cream, beverages, and other foods. It is employed in bath preparations, beauty masks, dentifrices, hair-grooming aids, hand creams, rouge, shampoos, and shaving creams. As an emulsifier, stabilizer, and foaming agent, it is a barrier agent *(see)*. Used medicinally as a laxative or antacid. It has been shown to cause cancer in animals when ingested. Toxicity on the skin is unknown.

CARBURETOR CLEANERS • These contain ethylene dichloride, potassium hydroxide, cresol, and perhaps ammonium oxalate. May also contain sodium chromate, water, and alcohol. *See all*.

CARCINOGEN • A chemical or physical agent capable of causing cancer. A substance that causes cancer is called "carcinogenic."

CARNAUBA WAX • The exudate from the leaves of the Brazilian wax palm tree, used in shoe polishes, leather finishes, varnishes, electric insulating compounds, furniture and floor polishes, carbon paper, waterproofing of rubber and plastic products to prevent sun damage, and in candy and cosmetics. No known toxicity.

CARPET • Made of synthetics, vegetable fibers, or animal hair, carpets often arrive permeated with pesticides to prevent molds and moths. Normal wear will cause particles to break off and become airborne. In winter, these microscopic bits of synthetic carpet circulate through the heating system, where they are vaporized into gases. A heated synthetic may produce dozens of different compounds ranging from sulfuric acid to hydrogen cyanide. If the home or office is not properly ventilated, the occupants will breathe these minute amounts of gases over and over again.

CARRAGEENAN • Irish Moss. A stabilizer, emulsifier, and stiffener for cloth, it has a seaweedlike odor, and is derived from Irish moss. It is completely soluble in hot water and not coagulated by acids. Nontoxic.

CASCADE™ ELECTRIC DISHWASHER DETERGENT • A strong irritant containing chlorinated trisodium phosphate and sodium silicate *(see both)*.

CASEIN • The principal protein in milk, a white, tasteless, odorless solid used in plastic items, paper coatings, water-dispersed paints, adhesives, food, animal feed, and textile fibers. Nontoxic.

CASEIN GLUES • Contain casein, the principal protein of cow's milk, urea, zinc oxide, ammonium hydroxide, sodium o-phenylphenate *(see all),* and water. *See also* Adhesives and Casein.

CASTOR OIL • Palm Christi Oil. The seed of the castor-oil plant. After the pale yellow, viscous, acrid-tasting oil is expressed from the beans, a residual castor pomace remains, which contains a potent allergen. This may be incorporated in fertilizer, which is the main source of exposure. Castor oil is used as a flavoring, a release and anti-sticking agent in hard candy products, a raw material in embalming fluid, a laxative, and a cosmetic ingredient. It is also used in detergents, industrial lubricants, electrical insulating compounds, and the manufacture of Turkey-red oil *(see).* Ingestion of large amounts may cause pelvic congestion and induce abortions. Soothing to the skin.

CAT BOX LITTER • Most litters contain aluminum magnesium silicate, and iron oxide, plus deodorants and perfumes.

CATALYST • A substance that causes or speeds up a chemical reaction, but does not change in of itself.

CATECHU • *See* Acacia Gum.

CATIONIC • A group of synthetic compounds employed as emulsifiers, wetting agents, and antiseptics in special hand creams. Their positively charged ions (cations) repel water. Any class of synthetic detergents usually consisting almost entirely of quaternary ammonium compounds *(see)* with carbon and nitrogen. Used also as wetting and emulsifying agents in acid to neutralize solutions, as a germicide, or fungicide. Toxicity depends upon ingredients used.

CATTLE HAIR • The hair of these animals may be used in blankets, brushes, ozite, rugs, and rug pads, and can cause skin rashes in those who are hypersensitive to it.

CAULKING COMPOUNDS • There are frequently many ingredients and changes in these mixtures. Among the materials commonly used are calcium carbonate, titanium dioxide, polyvinyl acetate, vegetable oils, silicates, polydimethylsiloxane, xylene, rosin, and epoxy resins *(see all)*.

CAUSTIC • Something alkaline that is strongly irritating or corroding to tissue.

CAUSTIC SODA • *See* Sodium Hydroxide.

CD • The abbreviation for Completely Denatured alcohol, meaning a poison has been added so that it is not drinkable.

CD ALCOHOL 19 • A denatured alcohol used as a solvent. *See* Denatured Alcohol.

CDEC • **2-chloroallyl diethyldithiocarbamate.** Amber liquid that is a carbamate *(see)*, herbicide, and pesticide.

CEDAR • **Cedar Wood Oil.** The colorless or yellow oil from white, red, or various other cedars, obtained by distillation from fresh leaves and branches. It is often used in perfumes, soaps, and sachets for its warm, woodsy scent. Used frequently as a substitute for oil of lavender. There is usually a strong camphor odor that repels insects. Cedar oil can be a photosensitizer, causing reactions on the skin when exposed to light. Similar toxicity to camphor *(see)*.

CEDAR WOOD OIL • *See* Cedar.

CEDRO OIL • *See* Lemon Oil.

CEILING LIMIT • In air, the maximum concentration of a material that must never be exceeded, even for an instant.

CELLOPHANE • Film made from wood pulp. It is transparent, strong, flexible, and resistant to grease, oil, and air. Used for wrapping and protective packaging. *See also* Rayon and Viscose.

CELLOSOLVE™ • *See* Ethylene Glycol Monobutyl Acetate and Ether.

CELLULOID® • A substance composed essentially of cellulose nitrate and camphor *(see both)* or other plasticizers. It is used as a nail finish, for brushes and combs, as well as for photographic films and various household products. No known toxicity.

CELLULOSE • The chief constituent of the fiber of plants, the basic material for cellulose gums *(see)*. Cotton contains about 90 percent. Used as an emulsifier in cosmetic creams. Cellulose is flammable. *See also* Rayon and Carboxymethylcellulose.

CELLULOSE GUMS • Any of several fibrous substances consisting of the chief part of the cell walls of plants. Ethylcellulose is a film-former in lipstick. Methylcellulose (Methocel®) and hydroxyethylcellulose (Cellosize®) are used as emulsifiers in hand creams and lotions. They are resistant to bacterial decomposition and give uniform viscosity to products. No known toxicity.

CERESIN • **Ceresine®. Earth Wax.** A white or yellow, hard, brittle wax used in protective creams. It is made by purifying ozokerite *(see),* a mineral found in the Ukraine, Utah, and Texas. It is used as a substitute for beeswax and paraffin *(see both);* also used to wax paper and cloth, as a polish, and in dentistry for taking wax impressions. May cause allergic reactions.

CERAMICS • Products manufactured by heating earthy raw materials in which sand and other compounds are mixed. Ceramics include brick, tile, terra-cotta, dinnerware, porcelain, floor tile, glass products, enamels, cement, plaster, and aluminum silicate fibers.

CERTIFIED • Each batch of coal tar or petrochemical colors, with the exception of those used in hair dye, must be certified by the FDA as "harmless and suitable for use" in foods, drugs, and cosmetics. The manufacturer must submit samples of every batch for testing and the lot test number accompanies the colors through all subsequent packaging.

CESSPOOL CLEANER • *See* Septic Tank and Cesspool Cleaners.

CETEARALKONIUM BROMIDE • The quaternary ammonium salt that is a blend of cetyl and stearyl radicals. *See* Quaternary Ammonium Compounds.

CETETH-2 • **Polyethylene (2) Cetyl Ether.** A compound of derivatives of cetyl, lauryl, stearyl, and oleyl alcohols *(see)* mixed with ethylene oxide, a gas used as a fungicide and a starting material for detergents. Oily liquids or waxy solids. Used as surface-active agents *(see),* and as emulsifiers, allowing oil and water to mix to form smooth cosmetic lotions or creams. *See* individual alcohols for toxicity.

CETETH-2, -4, -6, -10, -30 • *See* Ceteth-2.

CETETHYL MORPHOLINIUM ETHOSULFATE • *See* Quaternary Ammonium Compounds.

CETRIMONIUM BROMIDE • A cationic *(see)* detergent, antiseptic, disinfectant, and cleansing agent in skin-cleaning products and shampoos. It masks or decreases perspiration odors. Can be irritating to the skin and eyes, can be fatal if swallowed.

CETRIMONIUM CHLORIDE • A quaterary ammonium compound *(see).*

CETRIMONIUM TOSYLATE • A quaternary ammonium compound *(see).*

CETYL • Means wax *(see).*

CETYL ALCOHOL • An emollient and emulsion stabilizer used in many cosmetics preparations including baby lotion, brilliantine hairdressing, deodorants and antiperspirants. It is spread on reservoirs and growing plants to inhibit evaporation of water. Also used in detergents. Cetyl alcohol is waxy, crystalline, and solid, and found in spermaceti *(see)*. It has a low toxicity for both skin and ingestion and is sometimes used as a laxative. Can cause hives.

CETYL AMMONIUM • An ammonium compound, germicide, and fungicide used in cuticle softeners, deodorants, and baby creams. Used medicinally as an antibacterial agent. *See* Quaternary Ammonium Compounds for toxicity.

CETYL PALMITATE • Produced by the reaction of cetyl alcohol and palmitic acid. Used in the manufacture of soaps and lubricants. Nontoxic.

CETYL PHOSPHATE • A mixture of esters of phosphoric acid and cetyl alcohol *(see both)*.

CETYL RICINOLEATE • Salt derivative of castor oil used in tanning preparations. *See* Ricinoleic Acid.

CETYLARACHIDOL • A suds and foam stabilizer used in hair and body shampoos, and in various types of household detergents. It has mild conditioning properties, and in some instances may be used as an emulsifier. *See* Quaternary Ammonium Compounds for toxicity.

CETYLTRYMETHYLAMMONIUM BROMIDE • An antimicrobial preservative that helps destroy germs and prevent their growth. *See* Quaternary Ammonium Compounds.

CHALK • Purified calcium carbonate *(see)* used in nail whiteners, powders, and liquid makeup to assist in spreading and to give a characteristic smooth feeling. Also used for drawing on slate, or marking containers. A grayish white, amorphous powder usually molded into cones for the cosmetics industry. Used medicinally as a mild astringent and antacid. Nontoxic.

CHARCOAL • Made by burning wood, it is used as a filtering medium, to absorb gas, in explosives and fuel, and to purify and decolorize oils. It is also a deodorant. Nontoxic but, of course, can be a fire hazard.

CHEER™ GRANULE LAUNDRY DETERGENT • An anionic detergent that contains sodium alkyl benzene sulfonate *(see)*.

CHELATING AGENT • Any compound, usually that binds and precipitates metals, such as ethylenediamine tetraacetic acid (EDTA), which removes trace metals. *See* Sequestering Agent.

CHEMICAL SENSITIVITY • Evidence suggests that some people can develop health problems characterized by such effects as dizziness, eye and throat irritation, chest tightness, and nasal congestion that appear whenever they are exposed to certain chemicals. People may react to even minute amounts of chemicals to which they have become "sensitized."

Such people generally fall into four groups:

1. Industrial workers who are exposed to chemicals in the workplace and suffer acute and/or chronic effects.

2. "Tight" building occupants (those in buildings with inadequate ventilation) who are exposed to off-gassing from construction materials, office equipment or supplies, or tobacco smoke.

3. Members of communities that are contaminated with toxic waste, community-wide pesticide spraying, groundwater contamination, and/or air pollution.

4. Individuals who, because of genetics or prior exposure, are hypersensitive to consumer products, drugs, and pesticides.

CHICLE • The gummy, milky resin obtained from trees grown in Mexico and Central America. Rubberlike and quite soft at moderate temperatures. Used in the manufacture of chewing gum, insulation, and waterproofing. No known toxicity.

CHINA CEMENT • The water type contains polyvinyl acetate and dibutyl phthalate *(see both)*. The solvent type usually contains cellulose nitrate, isopropyl alcohol, acetone, toluol, butyl acetate, and dibutyl phthalate *(see all)*. May also contain methyl ethyl ketone, butyl alcohol, hexane, ethyl acetate, camphor, methyl acetate, ethyl alcohol, methyl isobutyl ketone (MIK), and heptane *(see all)*.

CHINA CLAY • *See* Clays.

CHITIN • A white powder similar in structure to cellulose *(see)*. It is the principal constituent of the shells of crabs, lobsters, and beetles, and is also found in some fungi, algae, and yeasts. It is used in wound-healing emulsions and tanning products.

CHLORACETAMIDE • *See* Quaternary Ammonium Compounds.

CHLOROACETIC ACID • Made by the chlorination of acetic acid *(see)* in the presence of sulfur or iodine. Used in the manufacture of soaps and creams. It is irritating to the skin and mucous membranes and can be toxic and corrosive when swallowed.

CHLORAMINE • A colorless, unstable, pungent liquid that is used as a water disinfectant. Can cause contact dermatitis. *See* Chlorine.

CHLORAMINE T • *See* Sodium *p*-Toluene Sulfochloramine.

CHLORDANE • An organochlorine pesticide introduced in 1945 that was among the first to be developed for insect control. Because of its persistence in the environment, most of its uses were suspended by order of the EPA in 1975. Several specified uses are still permitted, including pest control on pineapple, strawberries, and Florida citrus crops. It also can be used to remedy a number of other pest-control problems that plague certain areas of the United States. Chlordane causes cancer of the liver in mice. It is less toxic than other similar pesticides, but acute exposure has the effect of stimulating the central nervous system. It also has been implicated in acute blood dyscrasia (abnormalities) such as aplastic anemia. Can be absorbed through the skin.

CHLORDIMEFORM • Colorless crystals derived from ethyl formate and ammonia. It is a fumigant, a miticide, and an insecticide that kills insect eggs. Sold for use on cotton and vegetable crops, it is less toxic than organophosphates, and is biodegradable.

CHLORINATED HYDROCARBONS • Hydrocarbons in which one or more of the hydrogen atoms have been replaced by chlorine *(see)*. Many members of the group have been shown to cause cancer in animals, and some to cause cancer in humans. Among the designated carcinogens: chloroform, vinyl chloride, bis chloromethyl ether, trichloroethylene, aldrin, chlordane, dieldrin, heptachlor, lindane, methoxychlor, toxaphene, terpene polychlorinates, and carbon tetrachloride *(see all)*. Concern about the potential hazard of certain chlorinated hydrocarbons is based on their ubiquity; their persistence in the environment; their capacity to accumulate in living organisms including humans and the human fetus; and the experimental evidence of a potential carcinogenic effect.

CHLORINE • A nonmetallic element found in the earth's crust; a heavy, diatomic gas, noncombustible, and greenish yellow, with a pungent, suffocating odor. In liquid form it is a clear amber color with an irritating odor. It does not occur in a free state but as a component of the mineral halite (rock salt). Toxic and irritating to the skin and lungs, it has a tolerance level of 1 ppm in air. It is used in the manufacture of flame-retardant compounds, and in processing fish, vegetables, and fruit. It is also used in the manufacture of carbon tetrachloride, trichloroethylene, and ethylene dichloride *(see all)*, in shrink-proofing wool, and in lithium or zinc batteries. The chlorine used to kill bacteria in drinking water may contain carcinogenic carbon tetrachloride, a contaminant formed during the production process. In water, chlorine also has been found to sometimes form undesirable "ring" compounds such as toluene, xylene, and the suspected carcinogen styrene—these have been observed in drinking water and waste-water plants in the Midwest. Chlorine is a powerful irritant, and can be fatal upon inhalation. In fact, it is stored in military arsenals as a poison gas. A National Cancer Institute study published in 1987 linked bladder cancer to people who had been drinking chlorinated surface water for forty or more years.

CHLORINE BLEACH • This usually contains chlorine *(see)* with sodium tripolyphosphate and sodium silicate *(see both)*. Prolonged exposure to chlorine bleach can damage the lungs. *See also* Dishwashing Detergents.

CHLORINE DIOXIDE • A reddish yellow gas with an unpleasant odor. It is a strong oxidizer used to bleach wood pulp, fats, oils, and flour, to remove flavor from and to purify drinking water, and to treat swimming pool water. Highly irritating and corrosive to the skin and mucous membranes of the respiratory tract. Reacts violently with organic materials. It can kill.

CHLORINE GAS • *See* Chlorine.

CHLORITE • *See* Calcium Hypochlorite.

CHLOROACETIC ACID • Made by the chlorination of acetic acid *(see)* in the presence of sulfur or iodine. Used in the manufacture of soaps and creams. It is irritating to the skin and mucous membranes and can be toxic and corrosive when swallowed.

2-CHLOROALLYL DIETHYL DITHIOCARBAMATE • *See* CDEC.

CHLOROBENZENE • **Monochlorobenzene. MCB. Benzene Chloride.** A colorless, flammable liquid with a mild, aromatic odor. It is used as a solvent in the manufacture of dyestuffs and many pesticides, and is also used in the production of other chemicals, such as phenol. It is absorbed through inhalation, ingestion, and eye and skin contact. Acute chlorobenzene poisoning can affect the respiratory system, eyes, skin, liver, and central nervous system. The EPA has classified it as a possible human carcinogen.

CHLOROBENZILATE • **Arcaraben™.** A thick, yellow liquid that is used as a pesticide, and to kill spite-mites. *See* Miticides.

CHLOROETHANE • *See* Ethyl Chloride.

CHLOROFLUOROCARBONS • **CFCs.** A class of chemicals made from carbon, fluorine, chlorine, and hydrogen, and sold under such names as Freon™, Genetron™, Isotron™, and Styrofoam™. These were once widely used in manufacturing, as solvents in the electronics industry, in foaming agents, aerosol propellants, fire extinguishers, dry-cleaning solvents, degreasing agents, rigid foam insulation for homes and household appliances, and foam packaging. Chlorofluorocarbons are highly volatile compounds and inhalation of high concentrations of CFCs may affect the lungs and central nervous system. Deliberate inhalation of CFCs from aerosol has killed teenagers looking for a "high." CFCs have been linked to depletion of the protective ozone layer in the earth's atmosphere, permitting harmful rays of the sun to penetrate to the earth. The increase in ultraviolet radiation escalates the chances of developing skin cancer and cataracts. In 1977, the EPA and the FDA banned the use of CFCs in most aerosol cans in the United States. In 1979, the U.S. government banned their use except in a few specialized products. In 1987, thirty-five countries followed suit. There are still several sources of CFCs in many homes and offices. Check air conditioning and refrigeration systems for leaks and have them sealed if they are emitting CFCs. Do not use rigid foam insulation that is blown between the walls with CFCs to insulate the home, and avoid purchasing Styrofoam containers.

CHLOROFORM • **Trichloromethane.** A colorless liquid with a characteristic odor and sweet taste, made from chlorinated lime or methane gas. It is used as a solvent, in plastics, as a fumigant, in insecticides, and to clean wool or synthetic fabrics. It has many serious side effects and is considered a carcinogen. Exposure to it may also cause respiratory and skin allergies. Complaints received by the FDA about blisters and inflammation of the gums caused by toothpaste were found to be due to the amount of chloroform in the product. The manufacturer was asked to reduce the amount of the substance. Large doses may cause low blood pressure, heart stoppage, and death. In April 1976, the FDA determined that chloroform may cause cancer and asked drug and cosmetics manufacturers who had not already done so to discontinue using it immediately, even before it was officially banned. In June 1976, the National Cancer Institute made public the finding that chloroform caused liver and kidney cancers in test animals. Home exposure to chloroform still occurs from vapor released from chlorinated water while taking showers, and washing clothes and dishes. The best way to reduce exposure from water vaporization is to open windows or use the bathroom fan when showering.

CHLOROMETHOXYPROPYLMERCURIC ACETATE • A preservative. *See* Mercury.

CHLORONEB • **Teremec SP. Scott's No. II.** A turf fungicide. *See* Fungicides.

CHLOROPHENOL • **Biocide.** Causes ear, nose, and throat irritations, skin rashes, and reproductive problems. *See* Phenols and Biocide.

CHLOROPHENOXY DERIVATIVES • Highly toxic herbicides made from chlorine and phenol *(see both)*.

CHLOROPHYLL • The green coloring matter of plants, which plays an essential part in the photosynthesis process. Used in antiperspirants, dentifrices, deodorants, and mouthwashes as a deodorizing agent. It imparts a greenish color to certain fats and is used to color soaps, oils, fats, waxes, liquors, and perfumes. It can cause a sensitivity to light.

CHLOROPICRIN • **Chlorpicrin.** Derived from the action of picric acid on calcium, it is used to make violet coloring, as a fumigant, fungicide, insecticide, rat killer, and tear gas. Very toxic by ingestion and inhalation including skin and eye contact. Causes tearing, vomiting, bronchitis, and fluid in the lungs. It is used as a poison by the military.

CHLOROTHALONIL • **Decanil 2787. Bonide.** A fungicide, bactericide, and nematocide used in turfgrass and on plants. *See* Fungicides.

CHLOROXYLENOL • Made from benzene, it is the active ingredient in germicides, antiseptics, fungistats, mildew preventatives, and preservatives. Toxic by ingestion, a strong irritant, and can be absorbed by the skin. Claimed to be sixty times as potent as phenol.

CHLORPENTAFLUOROETHANE • A gas used alone or with carbon dioxide as a propellant, and as an aerating agent in foods. *See* Fluoroethane and Propellant.

CHLORPROPHAM • A pesticide similar to DDT, used on potatoes and other vegetables. *See* Pesticides.

CHLORPYRIFOS • **Dursban™. Lorsban™.** White granular powder used as an insecticide and acaracide on corn and other vegetables. Moderately toxic pesticide, it is poisonous via ingestion, inhalation, and contact with skin. It inhibits the sending of nerve signals. *See* Pesticides.

CHLORTHIALDIMETHYL™ • *See* DCPA.

CHOLINESTERASE • An enzyme that helps regulate nerve impulses. Cholinesterase inhibition is associated with a variety of acute symptoms such as nausea, vomiting, blurred vision, stomach cramps, and rapid heart rate and, in severe cases, can lead to death.

CHROMATE SALTS • Sodium Chromate. Potassium Chromate. Highly corrosive salts of chromium *(see).* Used in enamels, finishing leather, and for rust-proofing metals. National Cancer Institute researchers reported that nasal cancers were associated with exposure to chromates. They said chromate exposure did not appear to be related to the manufacturing of chromates, but to their use in the building industry and in painting.

CHROME CLEANERS • These contain an abrasive, an alcohol, an ammonium and/or an acid such as oxalic or hydrochloric *(see all).*

CHROMIC ACID • Chromium trioxide. Chromic anhydride. Consists of dark, purplish red crystals that are soluble in water, alcohol, and mineral acids. Used in chemicals, chromium plating, process engraving, anodizing, ceramic glazes, colored glass, metal cleaning, inks, tanning, and paints, and as a textile mordant. Highly toxic and corrosive to the skin. The tolerance level is 0.1 milligram per cubic meter of air, according to an OSHA standard. A powerful oxidizing agent, it may explode on contact with reducing agents and may ignite on contact with organic metals.

CHROMIUM COMPOUNDS • Oxides. Chromium occurs in the earth's crust. It is used for plating metals and plastics, for corrosion resistance, in stainless steels, as a protective coating for automobile parts, and as a coloring in paint. Chromic oxide is used for green eye shadow and chromium oxide for greenish mascara. Inhalation of chromium dust can cause irritation and ulceration. Ingestion results in violent gastrointestinal irritation. Application to the skin may result in allergic reaction. It is also a skin irritant. The most serious effect of chromium reported, however, concerns lung cancer, which may develop twenty to thirty years after exposure to the metal. One study showed that the death rate from lung cancer among exposed chromium workers is twenty-nine times that of the normal population. It may also cause kidney damage.

CHROMIUM OXIDE GREENS • Coloring. *See* Chromium Compounds.

CHROMIUM SULFATE • Chromic Sulfate. A violet or red powder used in the textile industry, in green paints and varnishes, green ice, ceramics, in tanning, and in green eye shadows. Can cause contact dermatitis. *See* Chromium Compounds.

CHROMOSOME • The part of a cell that contains genetic material.

CHRONIC TOXICITY • The capacity of a substance to cause harmful health effects after long-term exposure.

CHRYSOTILE • A form of asbestos used in paving roads, playgrounds, and parking lots throughout the United States. It has been reported to cause similar problems as asbestos *(see)*.

CINNAMENE • *See* Styrene.

CINNAMOL • *See* Styrene.

CIPC • *See* Chloropropham.

CIS TRANS ISOMER RATIO PERMETHRIN (3-PHENOXY CARBOX-YLATE) • A pesticide used in yard sprays. *See* Permethrin.

CITRAL • A light, oily liquid that occurs naturally in citrus and other fruits, and can be made synthetically. Used in flavorings, chewing gums, perfumes, soaps, and colognes for its lemon and verbena scents. Also found in detergents and furniture polish. The compound has been reported to inhibit wound healing and tumor rejection in animals.

CITRIC ACID • One of the most widely used acids in the cosmetics industry, it is derived from citrus fruit by fermentation of crude sugars. It is used as a water-conditioning agent and detergent builder, in cleaning and polishing stainless steel and other metals, and in cultured dairy products. In cosmetics, it is employed as a preservative, a sequestering agent *(see),* to adjust acid-alkali balance, as a foam inhibitor, and plasticizer. Also used as an astringent, alone, or in astringent compounds. No known toxicity.

CITRONELLA OIL • Almost colorless with a pleasant odor, it is a natural food flavoring extract from fresh grasses grown in Asia. Used in perfumes, toilet waters, and perfumed cosmetics and as an insect repellent. It may cause allergic reactions such as stuffy nose, hay fever, asthma, and skin rash when used in cosmetics. When ingested, it can cause vomiting, cyanosis, convulsions, damage to intestinal mucosa, and, when taken in sufficient amounts, death.

CLARIFICATION • Removal from liquid of small amounts of suspended matter as, for example, the removal of particles and traces of copper and iron from vinegar and certain beverages.

CLARIFYING AGENT • A substance that removes from liquids small amounts of suspended matter. Butyl alcohol, for instance, is a clarifying agent for clear shampoos.

CLAYS • **Kaolin. China Clay.** Used to clarify liquids *(See* Clarification), and as a filler for paper. Also used in the manufacture of porcelain and pottery, as an emollient, a poultice, and a gastrointestinal adsorbent. Nontoxic.

CLEANING COMPOUNDS • Household cleaning products cause from 5 to 10 percent of childhood poisonings each year, with soaps, detergents, bleaches, and corrosive cleaning agents being those most commonly involved. Soaps are the salts of fatty acids produced by the action of alkali on natural fats and oils. If swallowed, they may produce an upset stomach. Deodorant bars contain bacteria killers, perfumes, and detergents, but in amounts too low to cause serious trouble, according to Matthew J. Ellenhorn and Donald G. Barceloux in *Medical Toxicology: Diagnosis and Treatment of Human Poisoning* (New York: Elsevier, 1988). Detergents contain synthetic, organic, surface-active agents known as surfactants *(see)*. Surfactants are derived from petroleum, and are designed to lower the surface tension of water and thereby make substances in the solution more soluble. Surfactant classification is based on the ability to increase water solubility. "Anionic" compounds—which include sodium, potassium, and ammonium salts of fatty acids and hydrocarbons with sulfur or phosphates—are the most common surfactants used in detergents. They possess irritating properties. Ajax Cleanser®, which contains sodium alkyl benzene sulfonate, is an example of an anionic detergent. "Nonionic" surfactants include alcohols or sulfonates such as alkyl ethoxylate *(see)*, which are heavy-duty laundry products. Nonionic surfactants produce less local irritation than anionic ones. Mr. Clean®, which contains sodium alkyl ethoxylate sulfate, is an example of a nonionic detergent. "Cationic" surfactants include quaternary ammonia compounds *(see)* such as benzalkonium chloride *(see)*, and are used in disinfectants, industrial and institutional products, fabric softeners, antistatic compounds, and swimming pool algicides. Concentrated cationic solutions (10 to 15 percent) are caustic, and even dilute solutions (0.1 to 0.5 percent) may cause mucosal irritation. Downy Fabric Softener®, which contains alkyl dimethyl ammonium chloride, is an example of a cationic detergent. Large ingestion may produce central nervous system symptoms. "Amphoteric" surfactants contain both anionic and cationic surface-active molecules, and are used mostly in industrial products. "Builders" are added to detergents to improve their wetting and emulsifying properties. Because of concern about the environment and the lasting effects of phosphates, a greater number of products now contain silicates or carbonates *(see both)*. Death has occurred after intentional ingestion of low-phosphate detergent. Detergents also contain a variety of additives such as bleaches, anti-bacteria agents, enzymes, perfumes, colorants, whitening agents, and softeners, which may cause allergic reactions but are not used in sufficient amounts to cause irritation. Liquid household cleansers contain more toxic ingredients such as acids, glycol ethers, petroleum distillates *(see all)* than synthetic detergents. They may contain pine oil or turpentine *(see both)*. Abrasive cleaners contain pumic or silica *(see* Pumice and Silicates) and have a minimal toxicity. A few powdered cleaners contain borax, which may cause boric acid poisoning. *See* Boric Acid. It is best to avoid products with borax or pine oil *(see both),* particularly if you have young children around the house.

CLEANING FLUIDS • May contain trichloroethane, naphtha, perchloroethylene, trichloroethylene, carbon tetrachloride, toluene, or methylene chloride *(see all)*. May be subject to inhalation abuse and can cause nerve and brain damage, and sudden death due to disruption of heart rhythm.

CLOROX™ • A bleach that contains sodium hypochlorite *(see).* *See also* Bleaches.

CLOTHING • Articles of clothing are frequently involved in allergic contact dermatitis. Sensitization may be due to the fabric itself, the chemicals used in processing it, or the dyes, metallic, rubber, or synthetic stitched into or onto it.

"Sanforizing" involves shrinking the material under controlled conditions, and generally no additives are used.

"Mercerizing" involves the impregnation of fabric to strengthen or add luster, and to increase the affinity for dyes.

"Sizing" is a process in which stiffeners are added to produce a glaze as in sheeting or organdy. Often starches, glues, vegetable gums, resins, or shellacs *(see all)* are used.

"Antiwrinkle" finishes are achieved through the use of resins, which make clothes crush resistant, shrink resistant, and water repellent. The formaldehyde type is the one most often involved in allergic contact dermatitis, but any of the resins can be a source. Among them, ester gums, acrylate, methacrylate, polystyrene, vinyl resins, glycol resins, alkyl resins, ketone, coumarins, phthalic and maleic anhydride, and rosin. Your allergist may make a patch test from a suspected piece of fabric by dipping it in synthetic sweat and applying it to your skin. *See also* Coated Fabric.

COAL TAR • A thick liquid or semisolid tar obtained from bituminous coal. It contains many constituents including benzene, xylenes, naphthalene, pyridine, quinolineoline, phenol, and cresol *(see all)*. Used in adhesives, creosotes, insecticides, phenols, woodworking, preservation of food, and dyes to makes colors used in cosmetics, including hair dyes. The main concern about coal tar derivatives is that they cause cancer in animals, but they are also frequent sources of allergic reactions, particularly skin rashes and hives.

COAL TAR DYES • *See* Aniline Dyes and Coal Tar.

COATED FABRIC • A fabric that has been impregnated with a coating of resin, rubber, pyroxylin, oil, starch, lacquer, varnish, synthetic plastic, or other material.

COBALT • A metal occurring in the earth's crust; gray, hard, and magnetic. Used in electroplating, ceramics, lamp filaments, fertilizers, glass, as a drier in printing inks, paints and varnishes, in colors, and in magnets. Also used as a food supplement. Excess administration can cause overproduction of red blood cells and gastrointestinal upset. Poisoning causes nausea, vomiting, lack of appetite, ear ringing, nerve damage, respiratory diseases, goiter, and heart and kidney damage. Hazardous by inhalation. Flammable.

COBALTOUS SULFATE • The salt of the metal occurring in the crust of the earth. Used as a mineral supplement and in food processing, as an insecticide, in fertilizers, fur dyeing, ceramics, and paints, as a drier for paint and ink, and in storage batteries. May cause contact dermatitis. *See* Cobalt.

COCARCINOGEN • Any agent that increases or augments the effect of a carcinogen *(see)*.

COCONUT OIL • The white semisolid, highly saturated fat expressed from the kernels of the coconut. Used in the manufacture of baby soaps, shampoos, shaving lathers, cuticle removers, preshaving lotions, hairdressings, soaps, ointment bases, and massage creams. Stable when exposed to air. Lathers readily and is a fine skin cleaner. Usually blended with other fats. May cause allergic skin rashes.

COLLOIDAL SILICA GEL • *See* Silica.

COLLODION • A mixture of nitrocellulose, alcohol, and ether in a syrupy liquid, colorless or slightly yellow. It is used as a skin protectant, in clear nail polish, as a corn remover, and in the manufacture of lacquers, artificial pearls, and cement. May cause allergic skin reactions. Highly flammable.

COLORS • There are approximately twelve hundred dyes used to color textiles and products. For textiles alone, there is a seven-volume compendium used by dyers and chemists. Among the dyes used for coloring oils, greases, waxes, paints, plastics, soaps, solvents, and textiles are: nitroso compounds (contain one atom of nitrogen and two of oxygen), azo dyes, stilbene derivatives (optical brighteners used in detergents and on fabrics), diphenyl methane derivatives, triphenylmethane derivatives, xanthene dyes (very brilliant colors), acridines, cyanines, thiazole, sulfur dyes, anthraquinone dyes (widely used because they are not affected by light), and quinolines. Many of the dyes are derived from petroleum or coal tar. Acid dyes are used to dye wool, silk, and polyamides. Mordant dyes are used on animal fibers. Direct dyes are used on cotton, cellulosics, wool, leather, and paper. They are also used for home dyeing. Basic dyes are used on fur, wool, silk, cotton cellulosics, and other man-made fibers. Sulfur dyes are used for cotton. Reactive dyes are used for cellulose, wool, and polyamides. Pigments differ from dyes in that they have no fiber affinity. Determining an allergy to a dye or fiber is very difficult. For example, polyester may be fine for a patient who is allergic to a durable-press finish but intolerable to a person who is allergic to a disperse dye. Most dye-related clothing skin problems are caused by disperse dyes, according to Alexander Fisher, M.D., author of *Contact Dermatitis,* Lea & Febiger, Philadelphia, Pa., 1986. Women's nylon stocking dye rash is usually due to disperse dyes, Dr. Fisher maintains. He says those allergic to disperse dyes should usually avoid 100 percent cellulosics (cotton and rayon), and natural fibers such as linen, silk, and wool. He says that in the past, fabrics that "leached" out color most often caused contact allergic dermatitis; although this problem seldom occurs today, it is still to be considered.

When the letters "FD & C" precedes a color it means the color can be used in a food, drug, or cosmetic. When "D & C" precedes a color, it signifies that it can be used only in drugs or cosmetics, not in food. "Ext. D & C" before a color means that it is certified for external use only in drugs and cosmetics and may not be used on the lips or mucous membranes. The bulk of food, drug, and cosmetic colors are also derived from coal tar, to which many people are allergic. Another big problem with coal tar colors, of course, is their potential for causing cancer.

"Permanent listing" means that the FDA is convinced a color is safe to use as it is now employed. Batch-by-batch certification is used to determine how well the concoction matches the FDA standards and the chemical formula that was approved. The color additives for which certification is not required are mostly dyes or pigments of vegetable, animal, or mineral origin, and generally require less processing. Many of the colors are vegetable compounds such as beet powder, caramel, beta carotene, and grape-skin compounds. A few are of animal origin such as cochineal extract, taken from the body of certain insects. Among the natural colors used are alkanet, annatto, carotene, chlorophyll, saffron, and turmeric.

COMBUSTIBLE • Able to catch on fire and burn. The National Fire Protection Association and the U.S. Department of Transportation generally define a "combustible liquid" as one having a flash point *(see)* of 100°F (37.8°C) or higher.

COMET™ CLEANSER WITH CHLORINOL • An anionic detergent and bleach containing dodecyl benzenesulfonate and sodium hypochlorite *(see both)*.

COMPLEX SODIUM PHOSPHATES • *See* Phosphates and Dishwashing Detergents (Automatic).

CONCENTRATION • The amount of a specific substance mixed into a given volume of air or liquid.

CONTACT CEMEMT • The latex type contains neoprene latex, resin gum, water, casein, and a little bit of ammonium hydroxide, sodium *o*-phenylphenate, sodium pentachlorophene, 2,2-methylencbis (4-methyl-6-tertiary-butylphenol). The solvent type contains neoprene rubber, modified phenolic resin, magnesium oxide, zinc oxide, a solvent blend of toluene, hexane and methyl ethyl ketone, and, possibly, 1,1,1-Trichloroethane, if the cement is listed as nonflammable *(see all)*. *See also* Rubber Cement.

CONTACT DERMATITIS • Skin outbreaks caused by direct contact with a substance.

COOLANT • *See* Antifreeze.

COPPER AND ITS SALTS • One of the earliest known metals. An essential nutrient for all mammals. Used as a coloring agent in cosmetics, in coins, alloys, insecticides, and fungicides. Naturally occurring or experimentally produced, copper deficiency in animals leads to a variety of abnormalities including anemia, skeletal defects, and muscle degeneration. It is used in electric wiring, switches, plumbing, heating, roofing and building construction; alloys, protective coatings, cooking utensils, corrosion-resistant piping, insecticides, antifouling paints, and as insulation for liquid fuels.

Copper salts include copper carbonate, chloride, gluconate, hydroxide, orthophosphate, oxide, pyrophosphate, and sulfate. Copper itself is nontoxic, but soluble copper salts, notably copper sulfate, are highly irritating to the skin and mucous membranes and when ingested cause serious vomiting. Poisoning can cause a flulike reaction called "metal fume disease" *(see),* plus blood disturbances.

COPPER CLEANER • Use a paste of lemon juice, salt, and flour, or rub with vinegar and salt.

COPYING PAPER • *See* Bismuth Compounds.

CORN • **Corn Sugar. Dextrose.** Used in maple, nut, and root beer flavorings for beverages, ice cream, ices, candy, and baked goods. The oil is used in emollient creams and toothpastes. The syrup is used as a texturizer in cosmetics. It may be found in capsules, lozenges, ointments, suppositories, aspirin, vitamins, and laxatives. It is also used for paper, envelopes, stamps, sticker tapes, plastic food wrappers, and foods and beverages, including sherbets, ale, whiskeys, and American wines. May cause allergic reactions such as skin rashes and asthma.

CORROSION INHIBITORS • One type contains a chromium salt, borax, phosphates, silicates *(see all),* and water. Another type contains an oil base, mineral oil, potash, alkaline salts such as borax, and petroleum waxes. Still another type contains borax, borates, sodium carbonate, sodium metasilicate, and sodium phosphate *(see all).* An organic type contains ammonium nitrite and phosphate or borax, and the last type contains polyoxyethylene glycol ether, a detergent, and alcohol.

CORROSIVE • A liquid or solid that causes visible destruction or irreversible alterations in human skin tissue or another substance at the place where it touches.

COTTON • A soft, white, cellulosic substance composed of the fibers surrounding the seeds of various plants of the Mallow family. The world's major textile fiber, it blends well with other fibers. Special finishes on cotton fabrics, either alone or in blends, impart durable press and stretch characteristics.

COTTONSEED • The water-soluble, protein material in cottonseed contains one of the most powerful allergens for humans. Occasionally, it contaminates inexpensive cotton stuffing in upholstery, mattresses, and cushions. More often, exposure to the allergen arises from the use of cottonseed meal, which may be found in fertilizers, and as a constituent of feed for cattle, hogs, poultry, and dogs. Symptoms usually result from inhalation, but allergic reactions also can occur from ingesting cottonseed meal used in pan-greasing compounds and in foods such as some fried cakes, fig bars, and cookies.

COTTONSEED OIL • The fixed oil from the seeds of the cultivated varieties of the plant. Pale yellow, oily, odorless liquid used in the manufacture of soaps, creams, nail polish removers, and lubricants. The oil is used in most oleomargarines, mayonnaises, and salad oils and dressings. Lard compounds and substitutes are made with cottonseed oil. Also used for leather dressing, and waterproofing compounds, in cotton wadding or batting for cushions, comforters, mattresses, and upholstery, and in varnishes, fertilizers, and animal feeds. Known to cause many allergic reactions, but because of its wide use in cosmetics, foods, and other products, it is hard to avoid.

COUMARINS • Used in over three hundred products in the United States including rodent killers, acne preparations, antiseptics, deodorants, skin "fresheners," hair dyes, and shampoos. Coumarin is present in several plants that are sources of essential oils such as balsam of Peru *(see)*. It has been widely used as a fragrance in soaps, detergents, perfumes, and sunscreens, and is used in deodorizing and odor-enhancing agents. May produce allergic contact dermatitis and photosensitivity *(see both)*.

CRAYONS • Children's crayons are made of pressed wax and coloring. The wax is usually paraffin and is nontoxic. Industrial crayons may be made with lead chromate, which is not harmless *(see)*.

CREAM OF TARTAR • **Sodium Potassium Tartrate.** Described in ancient times as being a residual of grape fermentation. Widely distributed in nature. Consists of colorless or translucent crystals or powder, which is odorless and has an acid taste. It is used to acidify baked goods, frozen dairy products, and other foods. It is used in bath salts, denture powders, and other cosmetics. In strong solutions, it may be mildly irritating to the skin.

CREOSOL • Obtained from coal tar and wood, it is used in hair-grooming preparations and eye lotions. An antiseptic and disinfectant, it is also used as a herbicide, in detergents, and as a textile scouring agent. Chronic poisoning may occur from ingestion or absorption through the skin. It also may produce digestive disturbances and nervous disorders, with fainting, dizziness, mental changes, skin eruptions, jaundice, uremia, and lack of urine. It caused cancer when given orally to rats in doses of 1,000 ppm. *See* Coal Tar.

CREOSOTE • Obtained from wood and tar, it is almost colorless, or yellowish. It is used as a wood preservative for railroad ties, telephone poles, and marine pilings as a disinfectant, fungicide, and bactericide. It is used on skin as an antiseptic; internally as an expectorant. Also used as a mild insect repellent. It has a smoky odor and a caustic, burning taste. Large doses internally may cause stomach irritation, heart problems, and death.

CRESLAN • *See* Acrylic.

CRESOL • Obtained from coal tar, it occurs naturally in tea and is used as a flavoring in beverages and confections as a disinfectant, and in resins, herbicides, and surfactants. It is more powerful than phenol, but less toxic. It is irritating and corrosive to skin and mucous membranes, and can be absorbed through the skin. Can cause ear, nose, and throat irritation, central nervous system depression, and liver and kidney damage. *See* Phenol.

CRESYLIC ACIDS • Mixtures of phenols that are derived from petroleum and coal tar. They are used as sanitizers, in solvents, resins, plasticizers, as gasoline additives, laminates, coating for electromagnet and inductor wire, in metal cleaning compounds, scouring compounds, and in pesticides. They are corrosive to the skin and can be absorbed through it.

CROSS-REACTIVITY • When the body mistakes one compound for another of similar chemical composition.

CRYSTAL • A solid in which the particles—molecules, atoms, ions—are arranged in a definite pattern.

CRYSTALLINE QUARTZ • *See* Silica.

CUPRIC CHLORIDE • **Copper Chloride**. A copper salt used in hair dye. A yellow to brown water-absorbing powder that is soluble in diluted acids. It is used in pigments for glass and ceramics, and as a feed additive, disinfectant, and wood preservative. Irritating to the skin and mucous membranes. Irritating when ingested, causing vomiting. *See* Copper and Its Salts.

CUPRIC SULFATE • Copper sulfate occurs in nature as hydrocyanite. Grayish white to greenish white crystals. Used as agricultural fungicide and herbicide, and in the preparation of azo dyes *(see)*. Used in hair dyes as coloring, and medicinally, as a skin fungicide. No known toxicity on the skin, but very irritating if ingested. *See* Copper and Its Salts.

CUTTING FLUID • **Cutting Oil.** A liquid applied to cutting tools to help wash away chips, or to serve as a lubricant or coolant. Among the substances used are water, detergents, mineral oils, fatty oils, or a mixture of the above.

CYANIDE • **Prussic Acid. Hydrocyanic Acid.** An inorganic salt, it is one of the most rapid poisons known. Poisonings may occur when any compound releases cyanide. Cyanide is used as a fungistat, insecticide, rodenticide, and is in metal polishes (especially silver), in electroplating solutions, art materials, photographic processes, and metallurgy.

CYANOACRYLATE • **Krazy Glue®**. An adhesive derived from formaldehyde and cyanoacetates. To prevent premature bonding, inhibitors are added. They are eye irritants and may bond skin instantly. Surgical separation of fingers and eyelids may be necessary if extreme caution is not used. The glues are not toxic, however.

CYANURIC ACID • Crystals with a strong odor, slightly soluble in water, derived from urea *(see)*. It is used to make the melamine in sponge rubber. It is also used as a herbicide and as algicides in swimming pools. Toxic by ingestion and inhalation. *See* Pool Chemicals.

CYCLOHEXANE • **Hexamethylene.** A hydrocarbon *(see)* solvent widely used in industry in the manufacture of nylon, for cellulose, fats, oils, waxes, resins, and in paint and varnish removers, glass substitutes, and fungicides. Moderately toxic by inhalation and skin contact.

CYCLOHEXANONE • A yellowish white liquid with a peppermintlike odor, derived from copper and an alcohol. Used as a solvent for polyvinyl chloride, acrylates, wood stains, paint and varnish removers, spot removers, degreasing of metals, polishes, waxes, and resins. Toxic by inhalation and skin absorption.

CYGON™ • A pesticide. *See* Organophosphates.

CYTHION • *See* Malathion.

D

2,4-D • **(2,4-Dichlorophenoxy)acetic acid.** Prepared from phenol and chloroacetic acid *(see both)*, it is a herbicide that belongs to the same class as Dioxin *(see)* and is widely used by home gardeners and farmers. Does not cause acute toxicity, but its long-term effects are a matter of controversy, and it has been linked to cancer. An excess of non-Hodgkin's lymphoma among farmers, for example, has been strongly associated with its use. It does cause eye irritation and gastrointestinal upsets. *See also* Farming.

DACRON • A polyester fiber made from polyethylene terephthalate, it is insect resistant, fire resistant, and has good elasticity. Used for textiles, often combined with wool and other fibers, in fire hoses, cordage, pillows, and many other products. Can cause allergic contact dermatitis and respiratory allergies.

DACTHAL™ • *See* DCPA.

DAMINOZIDE • **Alar**™. **Butanedioic Acid Mono(2,2-dimethylhydrazide).** An apple-growth regulator was a particular focus of alarm in 1988 and '89, when its residues were reported to be hazardous to children. Probable human carcinogen. Causes multiple tumors in animals.

DANDELION • *See* Weed Killer and Ortho Weed-B-Gon® Jet Weeder Formula II.

DANDER • A common allergen consisting of small scales from animal skin.

DASH™ • A laundry detergent. Contains sodium alkyl benzene sulfonate, and sodium alkyl ethoxylate sulfate *(see both)*. *See also* Detergents.

DBCP • The abbreviation for 1,2-dibromo-3-chloropropane. *See* Fumigants.

DCNA • *See* Picloram.

DCPA • **Dacthal**™. **Chlorthalidmethyl.** Derived from methanol, it is used as a preemergent pesticide on vegetables and fruits. *See* Methanol.

DDVP • *See* Dichlorvos.

DEA • The abbreviation for diethanolamine *(see)*.

DEA-COCOAMPHODIPROPIONATE • *See* Coconut Oil and Quaternary Ammonium Compounds.

DEA-DODECYLBENZENESULFONATE • *See* Quaternary Ammonium Compounds.

DEA-ISOSTEARATE • *See* Quaternary Ammonium Compounds.

DEA-LAURAMINOPROPIONATE • *See* Quaternary Ammonium Compounds.

DEA-LAURETH SULFATE • *See* Quaternary Ammonium Compounds.

DEA-LAURYL SULFATE • *See* Quaternary Ammonium Compounds.

DEA-LINOLEATE • *See* Quaternary Ammonium Compounds.

DEA-METHYL MYRISTATE SULFONATE • **Biterge.** *See* Quaternary Ammonium Compounds.

DEA-MYRETH SULFATE • *See* Quaternary Ammonium Compounds.

DEA-MYRISTATE • *See* Quaternary Ammonium Compounds.

DEA-OLETH-10 PHOSPHATE • *See* Quaternary Ammonium Compounds.

DEA-STYRENE/ACRYLATES/DIVINYLBENZENE COPOLYMER • The diethanolamine salt of a polymer of styrene, divinylbenzene, and two or more monomers consisting of acrylic acid, and methacrylic acid, or their esters. Used as an opacifier. *See* Acrylates, Styrene, Vinyl, and Benzene.

DECYL ALCOHOL • An intermediate *(see)* for surface-active agents, an antifoam agent, and a fixative in perfumes. Occurs naturally in sweet orange and ambrette seed. Derived commercially from liquid paraffin *(see)*. Colorless to light yellow liquid. Used also for synthetic lubricants and as a synthetic fruit flavoring. Low toxicity in animals. No known toxicity for the skin.

DEEP WOODS OFF!® • *See* DEET.

DEET • **Diethyl Toluamide.** An insect repellent that is especially active against mosquitoes, biting flies, gnats, chiggers, ticks, and fleas. DEET is present in most repellents, ranging in concentration from 7 to 100 percent. It is listed on the labels as *N*,*N*-diethyl-*m*-toluamide. Some products are 100 percent DEET. DEET is absorbed through the skin. In 1991, New York State health officials warned consumers not to use insect repellents with high levels of the chemical because of health risks. They also proposed that such products be banned. DEET-related health problems include skin rashes and scarring in adults, and in a few cases produced neurological problems in children such as loss of coordination and mental confusion. Application of a spray containing 15 percent DEET on ten occasions to the skin of a six-year-old girl was associated with the development of a fatal syndrome similar to Reye's syndrome. Four other cases of toxic brain damage have been reported after the use of DEET in children. The New York State officials claimed that products with lower concentrations of DEET were just as effective as those with high concentrations. Major producers of DEET have maintained that DEET formulas have been used since the 1950s, and are safe and effective when used as directed. If you must use products containing DEET, use a minimum amount, do not put on irritated or sunburned skin, and do not put on a child's hands. Keep all insect repellents out of reach of children. A safer alternative may be products containing citronella oil as the active ingredient. You also may try rubbing bath oil on the skin. Some people have found that it works as an insect repellent. *See* Insect Repellents.

DEGBE • *See* Glycol Ethers.

DEGREASERS • *See* Grease Removers.

DEHYDRATED. • With the water removed.

DEICER • *See* Antifreeze.

DELNAV • *See* Dioxathion.

DEMETRON • One of the most toxic insecticides, it should not be used by the untrained. *See* Insecticides.

DEMETON-METHYL • *See* Organophosphates.

DENATONIUM BENZOATE • A denaturant for alcohol that is to be used in cosmetics. It is intended to make alcohol unpalatable for drinking purposes and, therefore, is unpleasant to smell and taste. *See* Denatured Alcohol.

DENATURANT • A poisonous or unpleasant substance added to alcohols to make them undrinkable.

DENATURED ALCOHOL • Ethyl alcohol must be made unfit for drinking before it can be used in cosmetics and other commercial products. Various substances such as denatonium benzoate *(see)* are added to alcohol to make it malodorous and obnoxious in order to completely prevent its use or recovery for drinking purposes.

DEODORANT, SOLIDS • May contain dichlorobenzene, naphthalene, or paraformaldehyde, which was toxic *(see all)*, plus cedarwood, essential oils, or activated charcoal.

DEODORANT, SPRAYS • A common formula is an alcohol (ethyl or isopropyl), glycol ethers, a detergent, perfume, water, and a propellant. Other ingredients may be petroleum distillates, aluminum chlorohydrate, bromsalicylanilide, 2,3,4,5-Bis(2-butylene) tetrahydrofurfural, Cellosolve™ acetate, dichlorodifluoroethanol, fatty esters, formaldehyde, lauryl methacrylate, methoxychlor, methylene chloride, *o*-phenylphenol, *p*-dichlorobenzene, pine oil, piperonyl butoxide, pyrethrin, trichloromonofluoromethane, wax or zinc phenolsulfonate. The most toxic ingredients are *p*-dichlorobenzene and formaldehyde, but it is wise not to inhale any of the sprays.

DEODORANTS • Bathroom deodorants may contain naphthalene, paradichlorobenzene, and sodium bisulfate *(see all)*, which are quite toxic. The cleanser type almost always has pine oil *(see)* plus a soap or detergent. Deodorants may also contain phosphates, metasilicates, EDTA, isopropanol, magnesium sulfate, *(see all)* or synthetic phenols. *See also* Garbage Can Deodorants, Deodorant, Sprays, Wick Deodorants, and Deodorant, Solids.

DEQUALINIUM CHLORIDE • A bactericide and antiseptic. *See* Quaternary Ammonium Compounds.

DERMATITIS • Inflammation of the skin. *See also* Contact Dermatitis.

DETERGENTS • Any of a group of synthetic, organic, liquid, or water-soluble cleansing agents that, unlike soap, are not prepared from fats and oils and are not inactivated by hard water. Most of them are made from a petroleum derivative but vary widely in composition. The major advantage of detergents is that they do not leave a hard-water scum. They also have wetting-agent and emulsifying-agent properties. Quaternary ammonium compounds *(see)*, for instance, through surface action, exert cleansing and antibacterial effects. pHisoDerm® is an example of a liquid detergent and Dove® is an example of a solid detergent. Toxicity of detergents depends upon alkalinity. Dishwasher detergents, for instance, can be dangerously alkaline with a pH of 10.5 to 12.0, while detergents used in cosmetics products have an acidity-alkalinity ratio near to that of normal skin, 5 to 6.5 pH. Detergents have caused many poisonings because they are in brightly colored, attractive containers, and often are stored where children can reach them. There is a common misconception that low-phosphate detergents are less "dangerous" than other detergents. While low-phosphates are safer for the environment, they are much more caustic than phosphate detergents, and may cause serious burns if even a small amount is swallowed. Since powdered granules are more difficult to swallow, if you have small children, they may be a better choice for your home. *See also* Cleaning Compounds; Dishwasher Detergent (Automatic); Dishwasher Detergents (Hand); and Enzyme Detergents.

DEXTRIN • **British Gum. Starch Gum.** A white or yellow powder produced from starch and used as foam stabilizer for beer, diluting agent for dry extracts and pills, in polishing cereals, for preparing emulsions and dry bandages, for thickening industrial dye pastes, and in matches, fireworks, and explosives. Also used as a thickener in cream and liquid cosmetics. May cause an allergic reaction.

DIACETIN • A mixture of the diesters *(see)* of glycerin and acetic acid *(see both),* used as a plasticizer, softening agent, or as a solvent for cellulose derivatives, resins, and shellacs. No known toxicity.

DIACETONE ALCOHOL • A liquid with a sweet odor. It is used as a solvent for nail enamels, fats, oils, waxes, and resins, and as a preservative. Prepared by the action of an alkali such as calcium hydroxide or acetone *(see).* Highly flammable, it mixes easily with other solvents. May be narcotic in high concentrations and, when given orally, has caused kidney and liver damage, as well as anemia in experimental animals. It is a human skin irritant. Moderately toxic by ingestion.

2,4-DIAMINOPHENOXYETHANOL HCL • An aromatic amine salt used as a fixative, bactericide, and insect repellent. *See* Phenol and Quaternary Ammonium Compounds.

DIAMMONIUM LAURYL SULFOSUCCINATE • The ammonium salt of lauryl alcohol. *See* Quaternary Ammonium Compounds.

DIAMMONIUM OLEAMIDO-PEG-2-SULFOSUCCINATE • An ammonium soap used as an emulsifying agent. *See* Quaternary Ammonium Compounds.

DIAMMONIUM SODIUM SULFOSUCCINATE • The sodium salt of the diester of amyl alcohol and sulfosuccinic acid. A wetting agent and emulsifier. *See* Surfactants.

DIAMYLHYDROQUINONE • **Santovar A®.** An antioxidant for resins and oils and a polymerization inhibitor. *See* Hydroquinone.

DIATOMACEOUS EARTH • **Kieselguhr.** A porous and relatively pure form of silica formed from fossil remains of diatoms—one-celled algae with shells. Used in filtration and decolorizing; in insulation; as a mild abrasive; as a thickener in paints, rubber and plastics products; in ceramics, paper coating, asphalt compositions, and acid-proof liners. Also used in pomades, dentifrices, nail polishes, face powders, as a clarifying agent, and as an absorbent for liquids, because it can absorb about four times its weight in water. Inert when ingested. The dust can cause lung damage after long exposure to high concentrations. *See* Silica.

DIATOMITE • *See* Silica.

DIAZO- • A compound containing two nitrogen atoms such as diazolidinyl urea *(see)*, one of the newer preservatives, or diazepam (Valium®), a popular muscle relaxant and tranquilizer.

DIAZO DYES • Coloring agents that contain two linked nitrogen atoms. *See* Heliotropin.

DIAZOLIDINYL UREA • **Oxymethurea. 1,3-Bis(hydroxy-methyl)urea.** Crystals from alcohol, very soluble in water. Used in the textile industry in cotton crease- and shrink-proofing, as a pesticide, in cosmetics as an antiseptic, and in photographic developers. May release formaldehyde *(see)*.

DIAZINON • **Diazajet™. Diazatol™. Diazide™. Diazol™. Spectrocide™. Sarolex™. Ø,Ø-Diethyl Ø-(2-isopropyl-4-methyl-6-pyrimidyl)thiophosphate, Phosphorothioate.** A popular organophosphate insecticide in use since 1952. It is very toxic and inhibits the transmission of nerve signals. It has killed waterfowl and squirrels, and is harmful to the human nervous system. Read directions carefully and do not spray indoors if directions on label say that it should not be done. Cases of poisoning due to indoor use of too highly concentrated sprays have been reported. See Organophosphates.

DIBEHENYL/DIARACHIDYL DIMONIUM CHLORIDE • *See* Quaternary Ammonium Compounds.

DIBROM • *See* Naled.

DIBROMOCHLOROPROPANE • **DBCP. BBC12.** A brown liquid with a pungent odor derived from propane and bromine. It is used as a soil fumigant and to kill worms. May be irritating to the skin and mucous membranes, and may cause central nervous system depression. It is also a suspected cancer causing agent.

1,2-DIBROMO-2,2-DICHLOROETHYL DIMETHYL PHOSPHATE • *See* Naled.

2-DIBROMOMETHANE • *See* Methylene Bromide.

DIBROMOPROPAMIDINE DIISETHIONATE • The salt of isethionic acid mixed with propane. Almost insoluble in alcohol, water, and fixed oils, it is used as an antiseptic and antimicrobial. May be irritating to the skin.

DIBROMOSALAN • **4,5-Dibromosalicylanilide.** An antibacterial agent used as an antiseptic and fungicide in detergents, toilet soaps, creams, lotions, and powders. No oral toxicity reported in humans, but has caused skin sensitivity to light, causing rash and swelling.

DIBUTYL PHTHALATE • The ester of the salt of phthalic acid *(see)*, which is isolated from a fungus. The colorless liquid is used as a plasticizer in nail polish, as a perfume solvent, fixative, antifoam agent, and insect repellent. Has a low toxicity, but if ingested can cause gastrointestinal upset. The vapor is irritating to the eyes and mucous membranes. A possible cause of birth defects.

DICAMBA • **3-6-Dichloro-*o*-anisic acid (2-methoxy-3,6-dichlorobenzoic acid).** Crystals made from pentane *(see)*. It is used widely today in weed killers, and as a pesticide. Toxic.

DICAPRYL/DICAPRYLOYL DIMONIUM CHLORIDE • *See* Quaternary Ammonium Compounds.

DICAPRYLSODIUM SULFOSUCCINATE • The sodium salt of the diester of capryl alcohol and sulfosuccinic acid. *See* Quaternary Ammonium Compounds.

DICETYLDIMONIUM CHLORIDE • *See* Quaternary Ammonium Compounds.

DICHLOFENTHION • An organophosphate insecticide and worm killer that is widely used for home gardens. It is absorbed in the fat, and has been found present in human tissue forty-eight days after exposure. Human poisonings have resulted in death. *See* Insecticides.

DICHLORAN • **Dichlorobenzalkonium Chloride.** A pesticide used on fruits and vegetables. Derived from ammonium and benzene, it affects the livers of animals. *See* Pesticides.

DICHLOROBENZALKONIUM CHLORIDE • *See* Dichloran.

DICHLOROBENZENE • **P-.O-. M-.** Colorless liquid with a pleasant odor made from benzene and chorine *(see both)*. Used as a solvent for many products, as a fumigant and insecticide, for degreasing hides and wool, in metal polishes, and industrial odor control. It is widely used in moth repellents. Toxic by inhalation and ingestion, and is irritating to the eyes.

DICHLOROBENZYL ALCOHOL • An insecticide. *See* Benzyl Alcohol.

DICHLOROBUTANE • *See* Butylidene Chloride.

DICHLORODIFLUOROMETHANE • **Freon 12.** A colorless, odorless gas used to freeze foods by direct contact, and for chilling cocktail glasses. Also used as a solvent. Narcotic in high doses, and an eye irritant. When heated it emits highly toxic fumes of phosgene and fluorides.

DICHLOROETHANE • *See* Ethylene Dichloride.

DICHLOROMETHANE • *See* Methylene Chloride.

DICHLORO-*m*-XLENOL • **Dichloroxylenol.** A phenol used as a bactericide in soaps and as a mold inhibitor and preservative. *See* Phenol.

(2,4-DICHLOROPHENOXY)ACETIC ACID • *See* 2,4-D.

DICHLOROPROPANE • *See* Propylene Chloride.

DICHLOROPROPYLENE • Derived from propane *(see),* it is used to kill worms and as a soil fumigant. Irritating to skin, eyes, and mucous membranes. Has caused liver and kidney injury in animals.

DICHLOROTETRAFLUOROETHANE • **Freon® 114. Cryofluorane.** A colorless, practically odorless, noncorrosive, nonirritating, nonflammable gas. Used as a refrigerant and aerosol propellant. Is practically nontoxic, and does not affect the central nervous system. *See* Fluorocarbons.

2,2-DICHLOROVINYL • *See* Dichlorvos.

DICHLOROXYLENOL • *See* Dichloro-*m*-Xlenol.

DICHLORVOS • **DDVP. Vapona. 2,2-Dichlorovinyl. Dimethylphosphate.** An organophosphate insecticide with contact and vapor action. It has been widely used for control of agricultural, industrial, and domestic pests since the 1950s. It is used in pet flea collars and flea sprays. DDVP is available in oil solutions, emulsifiable concentrations, and aerosol formulations. It is also impregnated in polyvinyl-chloride-based pellets, strips, and blocks for delayed release. It is used as a dewormer, administered orally to dogs, cats, and puppies. Its topical (skin) application has been approved for beef and dairy cattle, goats, sheep, swine, and chickens to control fleas, flies, and mites. It is also used in tomato greenhouses and applied to mushrooms, lettuce, and radishes. Aerosols and strips are used domestically for control of ants, bedbugs, ticks, cockroaches, flies, mosquitoes, silverfish, spiders, and wasps. It is also used as a disinfectant in airplanes. Exposure to high concentrations for 30 to 60 minutes did not reportedly cause a decrease in cholinesterase activity in humans. (Cholinesterase is used to send signals between nerves.) Nerve gases used in wars include organophosphates. It is a suspected cancer-causing and birth defect–producing agent. Heat decomposition causes highly toxic fumes to be emitted. As of this writing, the EPA is moving to have the use of dichlorvos on food packaging banned because it poses "more than a negligible risk." It is in at least 350 other products, and it may take years to get this pesticide off the market. Check to see whether you have any DDVP around your home, yard, or office and get rid of it, if you do. Do not purchase products containing it. *See* Organophosphates.

DICHROMATE • A salt of chromium *(see)*, used in tanning, corrosion inhibition, plating, glassware-cleaning solutions, safety match manufacture, and pigments. Highly toxic, acute poisonings are often fatal regardless of efforts to save the victim. There is an increased incidence of lung cancer in workers exposed to chromate dust, according to a report by P. E. Eaerline, "Respiratory Cancer Among Chromate Workers," Journal of Occupational Medicine 1974, 16:523. The relative risk among chromate workers is more than twenty times that of the ordinary population, and the time it takes cancer to develop is relatively short. Chromate also produces a chronic ulcer in the exposed.

DICLOFOP • A herbicide. *See* Chlorophenoxy.

DICOCODIMONIUM CHLORIDE • *See* Quaternary Ammonium Compounds.

DICROTOPHOS • A highly toxic pesticide that interferes with nerve signals and can be absorbed through the skin. It is poisonous via ingestion, inhalation, and injection. Heat decomposition emits very toxic fumes. *See* Organophosphates.

DICYCLOHEXYL SODIUM SULFOSUCCINATE • *See* Quaternary Ammonium Compounds.

DIDECYL DIMETHYL AMMONIUM CHLORIDE • A quaternary ammonium compound used in Lysol® Brand Pine Action™ cleanser. *See* Quaternary Ammonium Compounds.

DIELDRIN • Manufacture of this pesticide used on fruits and vegetables has been discontinued in the United States.

DIESEL FUEL • A fuel obtained from distillation of petroleum, composed chiefly of paraffins *(see)*, with volatility similar to that of gas oil. It is used as fuel for ships, trucks and other automotive equipment, drilling muds, and to coat waters where mosquitoes breed. Diesel exhaust contains chemicals that can alter DNA, genetic materials that are the body's basic building blocks. The changes are believed by researchers at Baylor College of Medicine to be similar to those that lead to cancer from cigarette smoke. The Baylor study, funded by the U.S. Health Effects Institute, reported the greatest concern for factory workers, truck drivers, and others chronically exposed to diesel exhaust. (Baylor College of Medicine News Report, February 8, 1991, Houston, Tex.)

DIESTER • A compound containing two ester groupings. An ester is formed from an alcohol and an acid by eliminating water. Usually employed in fragrant liquids for artificial fruit perfumes and flavors.

DIETHANOLAMIDOOLEAMIDE DEA • *See* Quaternary Ammonium Compounds.

DIETHANOLAMINE • A colorless liquid or crystalline alcohol. It is used as a solvent, emulsifying agent, and detergent. Also employed in emollients for its softening properties, and as a dispersing agent and humectant in other cosmetic products. It is moderately irritating to the skin; very irritating to the eyes. *See* Ethanolamines.

DIETHANOLAMINE BISULFATE • *See* Ethanolamines.

***N,N*-DIETHYL META-TOLUAMIDE** • Insecticide in Deep Woods OFF!®. *See* DEET and Insecticides.

DIETHYL PHTHALATE • Made from ethanol and phthalic acid *(see both)*. Used as a solvent, a fixative for perfume, and a denaturant *(see)* for alcohol. It has a bitter, unpleasant taste. Irritating to mucous membranes. Produces central nervous system depression when absorbed through the skin.

DIETHYL PROPYLMETHYLPYRIMIDYL THIOPHOSPHATE • An organophosphorous insecticide related to diazinon *(see)*. *See also* Insecticides.

DIETHYL TOLUAMIDE • *See* DEET.

***N,N*-DIETHYL-*m*-TOLUAMIDE** • *See* DEET and Insecticides.

***N,N*-DIETHYL-*n*-TOLUAMIDE ISOMERS** • Insecticide in Deep Woods OFF!®. *See* DEET.

DIETHYLAMINE • Used in detergent soaps. Prepared from menthol and ammonia *(see both)*. Very soluble in water, forms a strong alkali, and has a fishy odor. Irritating to the skin and mucous membranes.

DIETHYLAMINE • **Salt of Dicamba. 3-6-Dichloro-*o*-Anisic Acid.** Weed killer. *See* Dicamba.

DIETHYLENE GLYCOL • Made by heating ethylene oxide and

glycol. A clear, water-absorbing, almost colorless liquid; it is mixable with water, alcohol, and acetone. Used as a solvent, humectant, and plasticizer in cosmetic creams and hair sprays. A wetting agent *(see)* that enhances skin absorption. Also used in the production of polyurethane *(see)* and other polyester resins. It is a textile softener, a plasticizer, and is used in cork compositions, bookbinding adhesives, and antifreeze solutions. Can be fatal if swallowed. Not usually irritating to the skin, but can be absorbed through the skin, and the use of glycols on extensive areas of the body is considered hazardous.

DIETHYLENE GLYCOLAMINE/EPICHLOROHYDRIN PIPERAZINE COPOLYMER • A polymer formed by the reaction of a mixture of diethylene glycolamine and piperazine with epichlorohydrin, used as a solvent. *See* Epichlorhydrin.

DIHEXYL ADIPATE • A low-temperature plasticizer. *See* Adipic Acid.

DIHEXYL SODIUM SULFOSUCCINATE • *See* Quaternary Ammonium Compounds.

DIHYDROABIETYL ALCOHOL • *See* Abietyl Alcohol and Abietic Acid.

DIHYDROABIETYL METHACRYLATE • *See* Abietyl Alcohol and Acrylates.

DIMETHOATE • **Cygon**™. **Rogon**™. Insecticide used on fruits and vegetables. *See* Organophosphates.

DIMETHYL BRASSYLATE • Used in polyethylene films and water-resistant products. *See* Polyethylene.

DIMETHYL KETONE • *See* Acetone.

DIMETHYL OCTYNEDIOL • *See* Citronella Oil.

DIMETHYL PHOSPHATE • *See* Fumigants.

DIMETHYL PHTHALATE • **Phthalic Esters.** A colorless, aromatic oil insoluble in water. A solvent, especially for musk *(see)*. Used to compound calamine lotion, and as an insect repellent. It may cause birth defects. It is moderately toxic by inhalation and ingestion. It is an eye and mucous membrane irritant, and ingestion causes central nervous system depression.

DIMETHYL SULFATE • **Sulfuric Acid. Dimethyl Ester.** A colorless, oily liquid used as a methylating agent (to add methyl) in the manufacture of polyurethane adhesive, cosmetic dyes, perfumes, and flavorings. Methyl salicylate is an example *(see)*. Extremely hazardous, dimethyl sulfate has delayed lethal qualities. Liquid produces severe blistering, necrosis of the skin. Sufficient skin absorption can result in serious poisoning. Vapors hurt the eyes. Ingestion can cause paralysis, coma, prostration, kidney damage, and death. Has been linked to cancer in humans.

DIMETHYLAMINE • Prepared from methanol and ammonia *(see both)*, it is very soluble in water and in alcohol. Used in the manufacture of soaps, detergents, and weed killers. It also promotes hardening of plastic nails. Irritating to the skin and mucous membranes.

DIMETHYLAMINE SALT OF 2-4-D DICHLOROPHENOXY ACETIC ACID • Used in weed and feed products. *See* 2,4-D.

DIMETHYLAMINE SALT OF 2(2-METHYL-4-CHLOROPHENOXY) PROPIONIC ACID • A weed killer. *See* Diethylamine, Propionic Acid, and Weed Killer.

DIMETHYLAMINOETHYL METHYLACRYLATE • Binders for coatings, textiles, dispersing agents, antistatic agents, and emulsifying agents. Irritating to skin, eyes, and mucous membranes. *See* Acrylates.

DIMETHYLFORMAMIDE • **DMF.** NIOSH *(see)* estimates that about one hundred thousand workers in the United States may be exposed to DMF, an organic solvent that is readily absorbed through the skin. The chemical is toxic to the liver and can cause skin problems and alcohol intolerance. Some reports also suggest an increase in cancer among workers exposed to DMF, but the evidence is not conclusive. DMF is used in acrylic fiber spinning, chemical manufacturing, and pharmaceutical production; it is also present in textile dyes and pigments, paint-stripping solvents, in coating, printing, and adhesive formulations.

DIMILIN® • An insect-growth regulator that is hazardous to humans and by law should be used only by certified applicators. It is used against gypsy moths. Its active ingredient is *N*-[[(4-chlorophenyl)amino)carbonyl)-2-6-difluorobenzamide.

DINITROCRESOL • A herbicide. *See* Phenol.

DINITROPHENOL • Yellow crystals derived from phenol and sulfuric acid, it is used for dyes, preservation of lumber, in the manufacture of photographic chemicals, and explosives. A dangerous compound, it is an explosive hazard when dry and poisonous when absorbed through the skin. Inhalation may be fatal.

DINOSEB • A herbicide. *See* Phenol.

DIOCTYL • Containing two octyl groups. Octyl is obtained from octane, a liquid paraffin found in petroleum.

DIOCTYL DIMETHYL AMMONIUM CHLORIDE • *See* Ammonium Chloride.

DIOXANE • **1,4Dioxane.** A colorless liquid derived from ethylene glycol. It is a solvent used for cellulose, lacquers, paints, varnishes, paint and varnish removers, dyes, stain and printing compositions, cosmetics, deodorants, fumigants, polishing compositions, and cements. Toxic by inhalation, absorbed by the skin, and an animal carcinogen. It can be fatal.

DIOXATHION • **Navadel. Delnav.** A nonvolatile, very stable, dark liquid used as a miticide, a type of insecticide that kills mites. It is an organophosphate *(see)*, and heat decomposition emits very toxic fumes.

DIOXIN • *See* TCDD.

DIPALMETHYL HYDROXYETHYLMONIUM METHOSULFATE • *See* Quaternary Ammonium Compounds.

DIPENTENE • Colorless liquid with a lemony odor, it is derived from various essential oils or wood turpentine. A solvent used for rosins, resins, rubber compounds, and gums. It is also used in pigments, paints, enamels, lacquers, furniture polish, and floor waxes. It is a moderate fire risk but is combustible.

DIPHACIN • *See* Diphacinone.

DIPHACINONE • **Diphacin.** A low-toxicity rat poison.

DIPHENYLAMINE • **DPA.** Sweet-smelling crystals made from aniline, and used in the manufacture of dyes, and to kill screwworms. A poison, it has an action similar to aniline *(see)*. Can cause liver, spleen, and kidney damage, bladder symptoms, irregular heartbeat, high blood pressure, and eczema.

DIQUAT • A herbicide and plant-growth regulator made from petroleum and bromide *(see both)*. Less toxic than paraquat *(see)*, humans are poisoned by oral and, rarely, lung routes. Poisoning complications include vomiting, mucosal ulcers, diarrhea, and other intestinal tract problems. Heart damage and irregular beats occur in severe poisonings.

DISHWASHER DETERGENTS (AUTOMATIC) • Most automatic dishwashing detergents are strongly alkaline with pH values of 10.5 to 12.0. Usually contain a water softener such as complex sodium phosphates and sodium carbonate, and chlorine bleach to prevent water spots. Also contain sodium silicate to "protect" the dishwasher and china, a thickening agent, suds-control agent, colorant, and perfume. Dishwasher detergents often carry a warning about swallowing, and contact with eyes, and caution not to put stainless steel and silverware in the same dishwasher compartment, to avoid using with ammonia-containing products, and to avoid contact with fabric. Skin irritation or burns may occur following exposure to dissolved detergents. Toxicity may range from mild tissue damage to tissue death. Swallowing automatic dishwasher detergent can cause severe burns.

DISHWASHING DETERGENTS (HAND) • Hand dishwashing detergents are much less toxic than automatic dishwashing detergents. They are combinations of anionic and nonionic detergents *(see both)*, glycols, alcohols, and salts. Swallowing them can cause irritation, but not usually burns. They are considered low in toxicity.

DISINFECTANTS • Household products may contain acids, alkali, alcohol, pine oil, phenol, or cationic detergents such as quaternary compounds *(see all)*. In some disinfectants, the vehicle may be more toxic than the germicide. For example, Lysol® contains 79 percent ethanol, which is more toxic than the 0.1 percent concentration of *o*-phenylphenol *(see both)*. Skin contact and vapors can be irritating and corrosive to the skin and respiratory system, respectively. These products are more hazardous when dispersed from aerosol cans, because the disinfectant can be inhaled through the nose and mouth. Avoid aerosol dispensers. Make sure there is adequate ventilation. Use gloves and, if necessary, goggles. Less toxic alternatives are soap, isopropyl alcohol, white vinegar, or a mixture of a half cup of borax *(see)* in one gallon of hot water. Keep all disinfectants stored away where children cannot reach them.

DISODIUM C12-15 PARETH SULFOSUCCINATE • *See* Surfactants.

DISODIUM ISOSTEARAMINO MEA-SULFOSUCCINATE • *See* Surfactants.

DISODIUM LAURAMIDO MEA-SULFOSUCCINATE • *See* Surfactants.

DISODIUM LAURETHSULFOSUCCINATE • *See* Surfactants.

DISODIUM LAURIMINIDIPROPIONATE • *See* Surfactants.

DISODIUM LAURYL SULFOSUCCINATE • *See* Surfactants.

DISODIUM NONOXYNOL-10 SULFOSUCCINATE • *See* Surfactants.

DISODIUM OLEAMIDO MIPA-SULFOSUCCINATE • *See* Surfactants.

DISODIUM OLEAMIDO PEG-2 SULFOSUCCINATE • *See* Surfactants.

DISODIUM OLEYL SULFOSUCCINATE • *See* Surfactants.

DISODIUM PARETH-25 SULFOSUCCINATE • *See* Surfactants.

DISODIUM PEG-4-COCAMIDO MIPA-SULFOSUCCINATE • *See* Surfactants.

DISODIUM PYROPHOSPHATE • **Sodium Pyrophosphate.** An emulsifier and texturizer used to decrease the loss of fluid from a compound. It is GRAS *(see)* for use in foods as a sequestrant. *See* Sodium Pyrophosphate.

DISODIUM RICINOLEAMIDO MEA-SULFOSUCCINATE • Widely used as a surfactant, it is the disodium salt of ethanolamide and sulfosuccinic acid *(see both).*

DISODIUM STEARMIDO MEA-SULFOSUCCINATE • *See* Surfactants.

DISODIUM TALLAMIDO MEA-SULFOSUCCINATE • *See* Surfactants.

DISODIUM TALLOWAMINODIPROPIONATE • *See* Surfactants.

DISODIUM WHEAT GERMAMIDO MEA-SULFOSUCCINATE • *See* Surfactants.

DISPERSANT • A dispersing agent, such as polyphosphate, for promoting the formation and stabilization of a dispersion of one substance in another. An emulsion, for instance, would consist of a dispersed substance and the medium in which it is dispersed.

DISPERSE DYES • These compounds are only slightly soluble in water but are readily dispersed with the aid of sulfated oils. Used on nylon knit goods, sheepskin, and fur, they are in human hair dyes as well as resins, oils, fats, and waxes. Not permanently listed as safe.

DISPOSAL • Getting rid of garbage has become a problem in our modern, throwaway society. A particularly difficult aspect of that problem is the disposal of hazardous waste. The following waste, potentially dangerous to humans and the environment should not be put out for regular garbage collection or dumped in the sewer or down the kitchen sink or bathroom toilet:

- Automotive paint
- Batteries
- Brake fluid
- Dry-cleaning fluid
- Engine degreaser
- Epoxies and adhesives
- Flea powder
- Gasoline
- Herbicides

- Insecticides
- Mothballs
- Motor oil
- Oil-based paints
- Paint stripper
- Photographic chemicals
- Polishes containing nitrobenzene
- Wood preservatives

Call your community waste-collection agency for disposal procedures.

DISTILLED • The result of evaporation and subsequent condensation of a liquid, as when water is boiled and steam is condensed.

DITALLOWDIMONIUM CHLORIDE • *See* Quaternary Ammonium Compounds and Tallow.

DITHANE M-45 (80W) • *See* Mancozeb.

DMC • **Dimite. Di-(*p*-chlorophenyl)ethanol.** *See* Pesticides.

DMF • *See* Dimethylformamide.

DMHF • The abbreviation for the resin formed by heating hydantoin and formaldehyde *(see both)*.

DODECYLAMMONIUM METHENARSONATE • A crab grass killer. *See* Octyl Ammonium Metharsonate.

DODECYLBENZENE SULFONIC ACID • A sulfonic acid anionic *(see)* surfactant. Made from petroleum. May cause skin irritation. If swallowed will cause vomiting.

DODECYLBENZYLTRIMONIUM CHLORIDE • *See* Quaternary Ammonium Compounds.

DODOXYNOL-5,-6,-7,-9,-12 • *See* Phenols.

DOG AND CAT REPELLENTS • The liquid type usually contains alcohol, water, lemongrass oil, eucalyptus oil, diethyl phthalate, and ammonia *(see all)*. The spray type usually contains lemongrass oil, citronella oil, mustard oil (synthetic), and a propellant *(see all)*. One popular spray product for use either indoors or out contains methyl nonyl ketone *(see)* and a propellant. The powder type contains diethyl phthalate, mineral oil, oil of allspice, oil of mustard, phenols, pine tar, soap, and wood creosote *(see all)*. May also contain nicotine.

DOG AND CAT SHAMPOOS (Waterless) • May contain a detergent such as sodium lauryl sulfate, and coconut oil *(see both)*, or naphthalene, calcium carbonate, magnesium carbonate, sulfur, and aluminum silicate. May also contain borax, starch, glycerine, kerosene, phenol, pine oil, sodium carbonate, detergents, and zinc oxide *(see all)*.

DOG FLEA COLLAR • *See* Flea Collar, Pet Pesticides, and Dichlorvos.

DOG FLEA POWDER • *See* Flea Powder, Dogs, Pet Pesticides, and Dichlorvos.

DOG EAR MITES • *See* Ear Mites.

DOG FLEA FOAM SHAMPOO (Waterless) • May contain pyrethrins, N-octyl Bicycloheptene Dicarboximide, 2,3,4,5 Bis-(2-butylene) tetrahydro-2-furaldehyde, petroleum distillates, a detergent, diethanolamide, and hexylene glycol. Some products may contain methoxychlor as well as isocetyl phenoxy polyethoxy ethanol, pine oil, and piperonyl butoxide *(see all)*.

DOLOMITE • A common mineral, colorless to white or yellowish gray, containing calcium, phosphorus, and magnesium. It is one of the most important raw materials for magnesium and its salts. Used in toothpaste as a whitener, in paper making, ceramics, mineral wool, and the removal of sulfur dioxide from stackpole gases. No known toxicity.

DOVE® • *See* Sodium Lauroyl Isethionate.

DOWFUME • **D-D™**. *See* Fumigants.

DOWICIDE™ • **Orthoxyenol.** White, flaky crystals made from phenol *(see)*, practically insoluble in water. Used in the rubber industry as an agricultural fungicide and a disinfectant. *See* Phenol for toxicity.

DOWNY FABRIC SOFTENER™ • A cationic detergent that contains alkyl diethyl ammonium chloride *(see)*. *See also* Detergents.

DPA • *See* Diphenylamine.

DPGME • *See* Glycol Ethers.

DRAGON'S BLOOD EXTRACT • The resinous secretion of the fruit of trees grown in Sumatra, Borneo, and India. Almost odorless and tasteless, and available in the form of red sticks, pieces, or cakes. Makes a bright crimson powder. Used in bitters flavoring for beverages. Also used to color lacquers and varnishes. No known toxicity.

DRAIN CLEANERS • Drain cleaners are among the most potentially lethal products around the house. The most popular products contain sodium or potassium hydroxide *(see both)* to unclog stuffed drains and cut grease buildup. Red Devil Drain Opener and Lye®

contains 96 to 100 percent sodium hydroxide and has a pH of 14. Drano Liquid® contains 9.5 percent sodium hydroxide and the professional Drano Liquid® contains 32 percent. Crystal Drano® contains 54 percent sodium hydroxide. Liquid Plumr® contains 0.5 to 2 percent sodium hydroxide and 5 to 10 percent sodium hypochlorite. Some drain cleaners have been reformulated to contain trichloroethane, which is a hydrocarbon and suspected cancer-causing agent *(see* Carcinogen) rather than a caustic. To prevent a clogged drain, try pouring down the drain once a week a cup of baking soda followed by a cup of cider vinegar. As it foams, flush the drain with a potful of boiling water. Another "home remedy" is to pour a half cup of salt and a half cup of baking soda down the drain. Follow with a quart of boiling water. Let sit overnight and then flush with water. Do not forget the old methods of a plunger (but do not use after employing a commercial drain cleaner), or a mechanical snake and garden hose. A flexible metal snake can be purchased or rented. It is threaded down the clogged drain and manually pushes the clog away. If you withdraw the snake and then turn on a garden hose full force, you may solve your problem safely and inexpensively. *See also* Acids.

DRAT • **Chlorphacinone.** A low-toxicity rat poison. *See* Pesticides.

DRION™ • *See* Dry-Die™.

DRY CLEANING • Garments are immersed in a solvent and agitated until general soil and some oily-type stains are released. Then a "spotter" at the dry-cleaners evaluates any remaining spots and chooses a chemical to remove the stain. The garment then moves on to the finishing (pressing) department. Compounds used in dry cleaning include amyl acetate, benzene, carbon tetrachloride, dichloroethylene, naphtha, oxalate, tetrachloroethane, tetrachloroethylene, trichloroethylene, perchloroethylene, turpentine, and waterproofing compounds *(see all)*. Preliminary data from EPA studies showed that elevated levels of perchloroethylene are present in indoor air after dry-cleaned clothing is brought home. The Chlorinated Solvents Project of the EPA is currently working with dry cleaners to evaluate what can be done to decrease the residual levels of perchloroethylene in dry-cleaned clothes before consumers pick them up. In the meantime, dry-clean only those garments that absolutely cannot be laundered. After you bring home dry-cleaned clothes, hang them outside before storing or wearing. You can reduce your exposure to chemicals by 20 to 30 percent.

DRY-CLEANING FLUID • If you are using dry-cleaning products yourself, proceed with great caution. Toxic chemicals found in dry-cleaning fluids are trichloroethane, ethylene dichloride, naphtha, benzene, and toluene *(see all)*. These solvents are toxic by inhalation, ingestion, and skin absorption. Wear nitrile rubber gloves and apply the fluid outside or in a well-ventilated room. Do not allow children or pets in the room while you are working. Keep the lid on the product as much as possible. If you get any on your skin, wash it off immediately with soap and water. Do. not use dry-cleaning or spot removing fluids in a washing machine, or put clothes still damp with the cleaner in the dryer.

DRY-DIE™ • A pesticide containing pyrethrins, silica gel, piperonylbutoxide, and petroleum distillates *(see all)*.

DRY JOINT COMPOUND • *See* Joint Compound.

DSMA • **Disodium Methanearsonate.** A herbicide. *See* Arsenic.

DURABLE PRESS • **Permanent Press.** The emphasis is on launderability and avoiding the need for ironing. Durable press is achieved through pre-curing fabrics, where a special resin finish is applied to them before garments are made and then permanently pressed in with a hot-heat process after the garments are completed. In the post-cured technique, resin-impregnated garments are pressed in the conventional method, and the no-iron finish baked in by placing finished garments in the open and subjecting them to heat. Tumble drying gives the best appearance. It is important, however, to remove articles from the dryer as soon as the tumbling cycle has stopped. If not taken out immediately, the resulting wrinkles may be removed by sprinkling items and tumble-drying them again for a short period of time. If articles are to be drip-dried, remove them from the washing machine before the spin-dry cycle. Do not wring or twist excess water from the articles. Place garments on nonrust hangers to dry.

DURSBAN™ **TC, 4E, LO** • *See* Chlorpyrifos and Pesticides.

DUST MITES • Microscopic bugs that cannot be seen but can cause a lot of trouble in the allergic. Dust mites thrive in sofas, stuffed chairs, carpets, and bedding, open shelves, fabric, wallpaper, knickknacks, and venetian blinds. Dust mites live deep in the carpet and are not removed by vacuuming. Allergists recommend that washable area rugs rather than wall-to-wall carpet be used. They also recommend washing bedding in hot water (at least 130°F) to kill dust mites. Cold water does not do the job. Launder bedding at least every seven to ten days. Use synthetic or foam rubber mattress pads and pillows, and plastic mattress covers if you are allergic. Vacuum and dust frequently, but bear in mind that vacuuming may not remove all dust mites because some particles of dust carrying them are so small they whisk through vacuum bags and remain in the air.

DYES • In addition to the various colors, dyers are exposed to acetone, aniline, aminobenzene derivatives, bleaches, mercury, solvents, titanium, zinc, nickel, nitrous fumes, potassium hydroxide, silver, sulfuric acid, and zinc. The dyes on fabrics most likely to cause allergic reactions are disperse, vat, azo, and basic dyes, all derived from coal tar. Basic dyes are used on fur, wool, silk, cotton, cellulose, and polyacrylics; in home dye kits; and some food dyes. Vat dyes are used for cellulose products and some wool, and also come from coal tars, but are the least allergenic of the group. They are used to color some blue jeans. Disperse dyes, which reportedly account for most allergic reactions due to fabrics, are used on synthetics such as nylon and polyester. Azo dyes *(see)* are used on cotton and other natural and synthetic fabrics. Two common types of dyes used in the home are *natural* and *direct* dyes. Natural dyes, which are prepared from plants and insects, require the use of a mordant to bind the dye to the cloth fibers. Since most natural dyes are prepared by soaking the natural product, there is no hazard due to inhalation. However, since the mordant may be hazardous, you should not get it on your skin. Direct dyes are used for coloring cotton, linen, or viscose rayon. Table salt is used to help the process and the dyes require heat in order to set. Many direct dyes are benzidine dyes *(see),* which are highly toxic by inhalation and ingestion, and possibly through skin absorption. Benzidine is a cancer-causing agent. Do not use cooking utensils to mix or hold dyes since enough of the chemical can be left on the items to be hazardous, even though it cannot be seen with the naked eye. Do not use bleach, organic solvents, or other strong chemicals to clean dye-stained skin. Do not use chemical dyes, including all-purpose or household dyes, where children are present, or if you are pregnant. Do not let children under twelve years of age use dyes. Use food coloring and natural plant and vegetable dyes with children. Do not let children apply mordants.

DYLOX • Insecticide. *See* Trichlorfon.

DYNAMO™ LAUNDRY DETERGENT • **Sodium Alkyl Benzene Sulfonate** *(see)*. *See* also Detergents.

DYRENE • *See* Anilazine.

E

EAR MITES IN PETS • *See* Acaracides and Pet Pesticides.

EARTH WAX • General name for Ozocerite, Ceresin, and Montana Waxes. *See* Waxes and Ceresin.

EASY-OFF OVEN CLEANER™ • A caustic that contains sodium hydroxide *(see)*.

EDB • Abbreviation for ethylene dibromide.

EDCO • A fumigant. *See* Methyl Bromide.

EDTA • *See* Ethylenediamine Tetraacetic Acid.

EGBE • *See* Ethylene Glycol Ethers.

EGPE • *See* Ethylene Glycol Ethers.

EICOSANOIC ACID • *See* Arachidic Acid.

ELASTOMERS • Rubberlike substances that can be stretched from two to many times their lengths. Upon their release they return rapidly to almost their original lengths. Synthetic elastomers have similar properties and are actually superior to the natural ones. They have been in use since 1930. Neoprene and silicone rubber are examples.

ELECTROSOL™ **ELECTRIC DISHWASHER DETERGENT** • A strong irritant containing sodium carbonate, sodium silicate, and sodium tripolyphosphate *(see all)*.

ELEMENT • The simplest form of matter.

ELEMI • A soft, yellowish, fragrant, plastic resin from several Asiatic and Philippine trees. Slightly soluble in water but readily soluble in alcohol. An oily resin derived from the tropical trees. The gum is used in fruit flavorings. The oil is used in citrus, fruit, vermouth and spice flavorings, for gloss and adhesion in nail lacquer, and to scent soaps and colognes. The resins are used industrially for making varnishes and inks. No known toxicity.

ELURA • *See* Spandex.

EMERY • *See* Aluminum Oxide.

EMPIRE™ • *See* Chlorpyrifos and Pesticides.

EMULSIFIERS • Agents used to assist in the production of an emulsion *(see)*. Among common emulsifiers are stearic acid soaps such as potassium and sodium stearates, sulfated alcohols such as sodium lauryl sulfate, polysorbates, and poloxamers, and sterols such as cholesterol.

EMULSIFYING OIL • **Soluble Oil.** An oil that produces a milky emulsion when mixed with water. Sodium sulfonate is an example.

EMULSIFYING WAX • Waxes that are treated so that they mix more easily.

EMULSION • What is formed when two or more nonmixable liquids are shaken thoroughly together, or held in suspension by substances called "emulsifiers," so that the mixture appears to be homogenized.

ENAMEL PAINT • **Krylon.** Contains acetone, propane, methyl ethyl ketone, PM acetate, xylene, toluene, methyl isobutyl ketone, and butyl alcohol. Does not contain lead, fluorocarbons, methylene chloride, hexane, methoxy- or ethoxyethanol. Labels carry the warning the "reports have associated repeated and prolonged occupational overexposure to solvents with permanent brain, nervous system, and other internal organ damage. Pregnant women should avoid exposure to solvents. Intentional misuse by deliberately concentrating and inhaling the contents may lead to addiction, and may be harmful or fatal." Latex- or water-based paints are safer choices.

ENAMELING • Compounds used include amyl acetate, antimony, arsenic, chromium, cobalt, lead, nickel, and silica *(see all)*. *See also* Porcelain Enamel.

ENCAPSULATION • Scents, or substances such as pesticides, can be encapsulated in coatings that can be slowly dissolved. Some microencapsulated products contain coated perfume granules that are so small they give the impression of free-flowing powder.

ENDOSULFAN • **Thiodan™.** Brown crystals made from methane and benzene, and used as an insecticide. Toxic by ingestion, inhalation and skin absorption.

ENDOTHION • *See* Organophosphates.

ENGINE AND MOTOR CLEANERS • One type contains ethylene dichloride, cresol, oleic acid, and potassium hydroxide *(see all)*. Another type contains methylene chloride, perchloroethylene, and stoddard solvent *(see all)*. Others contain petroleum solvents as well as perchloroethylene, trichloroethane, and a detergent, plus corrosion inhibitors, lubricants, pine oil, and versene.

ENGRAVING • Compounds used in engraving include acids, alkalies, benzene, copper, cyanide, and solvents *(see all)*.

ENZYME • Any of a unique class of proteins that catalyze a broad spectrum of biochemical reactions. Enzymes are formed in living cells. One enzyme can cause a chemical process that no other enzyme can do.

ENZYME DETERGENTS • Enzymes *(see)* are found in many laundry detergents and pre-soaks to loosen soil and remove stains. The enzymes are obtained from strains of bacteria. Products that contain enzymes may cause irritation and contact dermatitis in sensitive people. Asthma and dermatitis are more likely to occur from industrial exposure to enzymes than to exposure in detergent products. Granulated detergents, which encapsulate the enzyme, are less likely to produce a reaction than powdered formulations in those who have become sensitized to enzyme detergents.

EO • *See* Ethylene Oxide.

EPICHLOROHYDRIN • A colorless liquid with an odor resembling chloroform. It is soluble in water but mixes readily with alcohol and ether. Used as a solvent for cosmetic resins and nitrocellulose *(see),* and in the manufacture of varnishes, lacquers, and cements for celluloid articles. Also a modifier for food starch. A strong skin irritant and sensitizer. Daily administration of 1 milligram per kilogram of body weight to skin killed all of a group of rats in four days, indicating a cumulative potential. Chronic exposure is known to cause kidney damage, and is suspected of causing cancer.

EPIDEMIOLOGY • The study of the pattern of disease in a population.

EPN • Pale yellow crystals that constitute a very poisonous pesticide. Extremely hazardous on contact with skin, inhalation, or ingestion. Heat decomposition emits very toxic fumes. *See* Organophosphates.

EPOXY RESINS • The versatile epoxy resins are used widely in manufacturing electrical equipment, in automobile plants, in paints for surface coating, and in aircraft and other industries for adhesive purposes. Epoxy glues are used for household purposes. They are often made available in two parts, the hardener and the resin. Such products are advertised as being able to cement anything including metals, rubber, polyester resins, glass, and ceramics. Among the many other uses are beads in necklaces, model making, flame retardants, dental cement, flooring, plastic gloves, adhesive tapes, plastic panties, and handbags. They are used to coat household appliances, in wall panels, cements and mortars; in road surfaces; in rigid foams, as a matrix for stained-glass windows; as a metal finish; in anti-rust paints; and as fillers for cracks in cement.

There are many epoxy resins; most are based on bisphenol-A and epichlorhydrin *(see both).* Another type is made from polyolefins oxidized with peracetic acid *(see* Olefins). There are many modifications of these two types. They are often used in jobs where tough, durable coatings or adhesive are needed. Epoxies can be powders or thick, clear, or yellow liquids. Some common epoxy resins are the diglycidyl ether of bisphenol A (DGEBA); novolak resins; cycloalphiatic epoxy resins; brominated resins; epoxidized olefins; Epon®; and Epikote®.

Epoxy resin systems are basically made up of an epoxy resin and a curing agent (also called a hardener or catalyst). Many epoxy products also contain such additives as organic solvents, fillers such as fiberglass or sand, and pigments.

When epoxy resin systems are used, the resin is combined with a curing agent. As the mixture "cures," it becomes hard. Some epoxies cure in a few minutes at room temperature. Others need additional time or heat to harden.

In a two-component epoxy product, the epoxy resin and the curing agent are packaged separately and must be mixed together just before being used. Each component can be hazardous. In a single-component product, the resin and the curing agent are supplied in a premixed form. Single-component systems are usually safer because the hazardous chemicals are already partly combined into less toxic polymers and because they do not evaporate into the air as easily.

Epoxies are one of the most common causes of occupational health complaints. The Hazard Evaluation System and Information Service of California, for example, cites frequent effects of over-exposure to the chemicals used in epoxy resins as eye, nose, throat, and skin irritations, skin allergies, and asthma. The problems may be caused by one or more of the added ingredients such as solvents or pigments. Diaminodiphenyl sulfone (DDS), a curing agent in some epoxy resin system, is carcinogenic in laboratory animals. Two solvents sometimes found in epoxy resin systems (2-ethoxyethanol and 2-methoxyethanol) caused birth defects in laboratory animals and reduced sperm counts in men. Some glycidyl ethers also damage the testes and cause birth defects in test animals but it is not known whether the same effects occur in humans. There is no medical or laboratory test that can accurately measure the amount of epoxies in the body. The HESIS suggests the following precautions if you must work with epoxies: select premixed compounds that have a reduced solvent content; remove clothing contaminated with epoxy resins and wash off any epoxies that get on the skin; pay particular attention to fingernails and the area around the nail bed as dry or irritated skin can absorb chemicals and become sensitized to epoxies more easily; use soap and water—not solvents—to clean hands. After washing, use a skin conditioner or lotion on the hands to help keep the skin in good condition.

Hardened epoxy products are practically nontoxic unless they are cut, sanded, or burned, according to HESIS.

EPOXYETHANE • A fumigant. *See* Ethylene Oxide.

EPOXYPROPANE • **Propane Oxide. Oxetane. Trimethylene Oxide.** Prepared from potassium hydroxide solution. *See* Fumigants.

ERA® LAUNDRY DETERGENT • A nonionic detergent containing sodium alkyl ethoxylate sulfate.

ERUCAMIDE • **Erucylamide.** An aliphatic amide slightly soluble in alcohol and acetone. Used as a foam stabilizer, a solvent for waxes and resins, emulsions, and an antiblock agent for polyethylene.

ERUCIC ACID • **Cis-13-docosenoic acid.** A fatty acid derived from mustard seed, rapeseed, and carambe seed. Used in polyethylene film and water-resistant nylon.

ERUCYL ALCOHOL • A white, soft, semisolid, almost odorless alcohol derived from erucic acid *(see)*. Used as a lubricant, surfactant, and in plastics, textiles, and rubber.

ERUCYL ARACHIDATE • The ester of erucyl alcohol and arachidic acid. *See* Arachidic Acid.

ESSENCE OF MIRBANE • **Nitrobenzene.** Used to scent cheap soap. A colorless to pale yellow, oily, poisonous liquid (nitric acid and benzene). It is rapidly absorbed through the skin. Workers are warned not to get it in their eyes or on their skins, and not to breathe the vapor. Exposure to essence of mirbane may cause headaches, drowsiness, nausea, vomiting, lack of oxygen in the blood (methemoglobinemia), and cyanosis.

ESTER • A compound such as ethyl acetate *(see)*, formed from an alcohol and an acid by elimination of water. Esters are fragrant liquids often used for artificial fruit perfumes and flavors. Esterification of rosin, for example, reduces its allergy-causing properties. Toxicity depends on the ester.

ESTER GUMS • *See* Clothing.

ETCHING • Compounds used in etching include acids, alkalies, arsine, hydrofluoric acid, and picric acid *(see all)*.

ETHANAL • *See* Acetaldehyde.

ETHANAMIDE • *See* Acetamide.

1,2-ETHANEDIOL • See Ethylene Glycol.

ETHANOL • **Ethyl Alcohol. Rubbing Alcohol. Grain Alcohol. Ordinary Alcohol.** An antibacterial used in mouthwash, nail enamel, astringent, liquid lip rouge, and many other cosmetic products. Clear, colorless, and very flammable, it is made by the fermentation of starch, sugar, and other carbohydrates. Used medicinally as a topical antiseptic, sedative, and blood vessel dilator. Ingestion of large amounts may cause nausea, vomiting, impaired perception, stupor, coma, and death. When deliberately denatured *(see),* it is poisonous.

ETHANOL CHLORIDE • *See* Acetyl Chloride.

ETHANOLAMINES • Three compounds—monoethanolamine, diethanolamine, and triethanolamine—with low melting points, colorless, and solid, which readily absorb water, form viscous liquids, and are soluble both in water and alcohol. They have an ammonia smell and are strong bases. Used in cold permanent-wave lotions as a preservative. Also used to form soaps with fatty acids *(see),* widely used as detergents and emulsifying agents, and have been used medicinally to treat varicose veins. Very large quantities are required for a lethal oral dose in mice (2,140 milligrams per kilogram of body weight). Can be irritating to skin if very alkaline.

ETHAZOLE • **Koban.** *See* Fungicides.

ETHENYLBENZENE • *See* Styrene.

ETHER • **Diethyl Ether. Ethyl Ether.** An organic liquid compound, water and fat insoluble, with a characteristic odor; the most volatile of the solvents. It is obtained from olefins or alcohol and is used as a solvent and anesthetic. A mild skin irritant. Inhalation or ingestion causes central nervous system depression.

ETHOHEXADIOL • *See* Ethylhexanediol.

2-ETHOXYETHANOL • **Ethylene Glycol Monoethyl Ether.** Used extensively as a solvent in industrial products such as surface coatings, inks, dyes, cleaning fluids, metalworking fluids, degreasing agents, and hydraulic brake fluids. The permissible human exposure level of this ether has been lowered from 25 ppm to 5 ppm, and a further reduction has been proposed. May cause birth defects. *See* Glycol Ethers and Metalworking Fluids.

ETHYL ACETATE • **Acetic Ether. Acetic Ester. Vinegar Naphtha.** Colorless, fragrant liquid, soluble in alcohol and ether and derived by heating acetic acid and alcohol with sulfuric acid. Used as a solvent in coatings, plastics, in smokeless powders, medications, and flavorings. Toxic by inhalation and skin absorption and irritating to the eyes and skin. Highly flammable.

ETHYL CELLULOSE • **Cellulose Ether.** White granules prepared from wood pulp or chemical cotton and used as a binder and filler in dry vitamin preparations, chewing gum, and confectionery. Also used in the manufacture of plastics and lacquers, and in wire insulation, adhesives and coatings for cables, in printers' inks, molding powders, and casings for rocket propellants. Not susceptible to bacterial or fungal decomposition. No known toxicity.

ETHYL CHLORIDE • **Chloroethane.** A gas at room temperature, but when compressed turns into a colorless liquid with an etherlike odor. It is derived from ethylene and hydrogen chloride and is highly flammable. Used in the manufacture of tetraethyl lead, and in anesthetics, and refrigeration, as a solvent for fats, oils, and waxes, and as an insecticide. Least toxic of all chlorinated hydrocarbons, it can still cause a transient narcosis. It can be absorbed through the skin and eyes, and is a skin, eye, and mucous membrane irritant. It is moderately toxic by ingestion. Acute chloroethane poisoning can affect the liver, kidneys, respiratory system, and heart.

ETHYL ETHER • *See* Ether.

ETHYL LACTATE • A colorless liquid with a mild odor. Derived from lactic acid with ethanol. Used as a solvent for nitrocellulose, lacquers, resins, enamels, and flavorings. *See* Lactic Acid.

ETHYL LAURATE • The ester of ethyl alcohol and lauric acid, used as a synthetic flavoring. A colorless oil with a light, fruity odor. Also used as a solvent. No known toxicity.

ETHYL PELARGONATE • Derived from rice bran, the ester of ethyl alcohol and pelargonic acid *(see both)*, used in the manufacture of lacquers and plastics. Pelargonic acid is a strong irritant.

ETHYL PHTHALYL ETHYL GLYCOLATE • **Aromatic Ester.** A solvent, a fixative for perfumes, and a denaturant. *See* Polyethylene and Phthalic Acid for toxicity.

ETHYL TOLUENESULFONAMIDE • A plasticizer for cellulose acetate, and for ethylating. *See* Toluene.

ETHYLENE DIBROMIDE • A colorless, nonflammable liquid with a sweetish odor, derived from bromine and ethylene. Used as a scavenger for lead in gasoline, as a fumigant, general solvent, and in waterproofing products. A cancer-causing agent, toxic by inhalation, ingestion, and skin absorption; a strong irritant to eyes and skin.

ETHYLENE DICHLORIDE • **EDC.** The halogenated aliphatic hydrocarbon derived from the action of chlorine on ethylene. Used in the manufacture of vinyl chloride and polyvinyl chloride *(see both);* as a solvent for fats, waxes, and resins; as a lead scavenger in antiknock gasolines; in paint, varnish, and finish removers; as a wetting agent; as a penetrating agent; in organic synthesis; and as a fumigant. EDC is also used as an ingredient in cosmetics, and as a food additive. One of the highest-volume chemicals produced, it is irritating to the mucous membranes, and can be highly toxic whether taken into the body by ingestion, inhalation, or skin absorption. In testing, the National Cancer Institute found this compound caused stomach cancer, vascularized cancers of multiple organs, and cancer beneath the skins of male rats. Female rats exposed to EDC develop mammary cancer—in some high-dose animals, as early as the twentieth week of the study. The chemical also caused breast cancer and uterine cancer in female mice, and respiratory tract cancer in both sexes.

ETHYLENE GLYCOL • 1,2-Ethanediol. Monoethyl Ether. Cellosolve. 2-Ethoxy Ethanol. A slightly viscous liquid with a sweet taste. Absorbs twice its weight in water. Used as an antifreeze and humectant *(see);* also as a solvent. Its sweet taste attracts children and animals. Toxic when ingested, causing central nervous system depression, vomiting, drowsiness, coma, respiratory failure, kidney damage, and, possibly, death. To prevent poisonings, wash down puddles of antifreeze or absorb with sawdust or kitty litter. Sweep into a garbage bag and dispose of the sealed bag in the trash.

ETHYLENE GLYCOL MONOBUTYL ACETATE AND ETHER • Cellosolves. Colorless liquids with a mild odor, derived from cracking petroleum. The ethers are used as solvents for resins, oils, gums, varnishes, and inks. They also are used in painting, pastes, cleaning compounds, and hydraulic fluid. The acetates are used as solvents for oils, greases, and inks, and to dissolve plastics and resins. The ethers are mildly irritating to the skin, but vapors may cause eye and upper respiratory problems. Temporary clouding of the eye may last for several hours. They may also damage the central nervous system, blood, skin, and kidneys. Acetate derivatives cause greater eye irritation. Symptoms of repeated overexposure include fatigue, lethargy, nausea, loss of appetite, and tremors.

ETHYLENE OXIDE • EtO. ETO. EO. Epoxyethane. Oxirane. Dihydrooxirane. Dimethylene Oxide. Anprolene®. Carboxide®. Cry-Oxide®. Oxyfume®. T-Gas®. Steroxide®. Pennoxide®. A fumigant used on ground spices and other processed natural seasonings. A colorless gas, liquid at 12°C, derived from the oxidation of ethylene in air or oxygen with silver catalyst. It is used as a fungicide, rocket propellant, industrial sterilant, in surfactants *(see),* and in the manufacture of ethylene glycol *(see).* It is an irritant to the eyes and skin. A suspected human carcinogen. Women exposed to EtO during pregnancy may have a higher rate of spontaneous abortion. EtO damages the sperm and testicles of test animals, reducing their fertility. Short-term overexposure to EtO can irritate your nose, throat, and eyes, and cause nausea, vomiting, and headache. Longer-term overexposure can damage the nerves in your feet and legs. Liquid EtO or EtO mixed with water is extremely irritating, and lengthy contact can burn your skin or cause allergic skin reaction.

ETHYLENEDIAMINE • Colorless, clear, thick, and strongly alkaline, it is used as a fungicide, solvent, emulsifying agent, and in antifreeze. Also used as a solvent for casein, albumin, and shellac, and has been used as a urinary acidifier. Toxic by skin absorption and inhalation, it can cause sensitization leading to asthma, and allergic skin rashes. Highly flammable.

ETHYLENEDIAMINE TETRAACETIC ACID (EDTA) • An important compound in cosmetics used primarily as a sequestering agent *(see),* in carbonated beverages. EDTA salts are used in crab meat (cooked and canned) to retard struvite (crystal) formation and promote color retention. It is also used in nonstandardized dressings. It may be irritating to the skin and mucous membranes and cause allergies such as asthma and skin rashes. Also used as a sequestrant in carbonated beverages. When ingested, it may cause errors in a number of laboratory tests, including those for calcium, carbon dioxide, nitrogen, and muscular activity. It is on the FDA list of food additives to be studied for toxicity. It can cause kidney damage. The trisodium salt of EDTA was fed to rats and mice for nearly two years. According to a summary of the report, "Although a variety of tumors occurred among test and control animals of both species, the test did not indicate that any of the tumors observed in the test animals were attributed to EDTA. The tests were part of the National Cancer Institute's Carcinogenesis Bioassay Program."

ETHYLENE/MALEIC ANHYDRIDE COPOLYMER • Plastic material made from ethylene and maleic anhydride. Maleic anhydride is a powerful irritant causing burns. Contact with skin should be avoided. Ethylene is used in the manufacture of plastics and alcohols. High concentrations can cause unconsciousness.

ETHYLHEXANEDIOL • **Ethohexadiol.** A colorless, slightly viscous, odorless, water-absorbing liquid that is soluble in alcohol and partially soluble in water, and is derived from petroleum. Used as an insect repellant, in cosmetics, and as a solvent in printers' inks. Moderately irritating to eyes and mucous membranes, but not to skin. Ingestion causes central nervous system depression. In 1991, Canada's Agriculture Department banned four insect repellents containing the liquid, because laboratory tests showed it caused birth defects in animals. There were not known to be any reports of birth defects in humans. The products banned were BF-100 Black Fly Repellent Solution, X-IT Insect Repellent, X-IT, and X-IT Stick.

2-ETHYLHEXOIC ACID • A mild-scented liquid, slightly soluble in water, it is used in paint and varnish driers and to convert some mineral oils to greases. Its esters *(see)* are used as plasticizers. No known toxicity.

ETO • *See* Ethylene Oxide.

ETS • Abbreviation for Environmental Tobacco Smoke. *See* Tobacco.

EYE ALLERGY • There are many forms of allergy of the eye. The mucous membranes of the eye may be involved in allergic rhinitis. Such allergic conjunctivitis may also occur by itself without irritation of the nose. Another form, pinkeye, common during the spring, is probably due to allergens in the air. Dust, mold spores, foods, and eye medications may all cause conjunctivitis. There is also a less severe, chronic form of allergic conjunctivitis. Symptoms include sensitivity to light, causing eye pain; also itching, burning, a feeling of dryness, or maybe a watery discharge. Finding the source of allergy is often difficult.

EYEGLASS CLEANER • *See* Lens Cleaner.

F

FAB™ GRANULAR LAUNDRY DETERGENT • An anionic detergent that contains sodium alkyl benzene sulfonate *(see)*.

FABRIC CEMENT • Most fabric cements contain rubber latex with a little sulfur and zinc. They may also contain toluene, xylene, and petroleum distillates *(see all)*. The polyvinyl acetate emulsion contains diethyl phthalate, silicone, methylcelluose, water, and phenol. The nitrocellulose type contains acetone, ethyl acetate, and camphor. The neoprene latex contains water, casein, Dowicide™, and ammonia. *See all*.

FABRIC SOFTENERS • Anionic, nonionic, and cationic *(see all)* detergent softeners are used to modify fabric stiffness. Sulfated natural oils and fatty esters (anionic); fatty acid diethanolamines, quaternary ammonium salts, and cetyl trimethyl bromide (cationic); ethylene oxide, and oleic acid alcohols and esters (nonionic) all are used in softeners. Occasionally, these softeners are preserved with formaldehyde or formaldehyde-releasing preservatives, which may be too low to cause a skin rash. The softener is added to a finishing bath at a clothing factory. Nonwoven fabrics are impregnated with the softening agents and a perfume, and are added to the dryer tub. In the home, softeners may be be added during the rinse cycle or in the dryer. Among the ingredients used in home laundry softeners are dialkyldimethyl ammonium methyl sulfate and fatty acid esters of alcohols. Some dermatologists report that some heavily scented softening sheets can cause skin rashes, but others do not. For a possible alternative, try one cup white vinegar or one-quarter cup baking soda in the final rinse water.

FABRICS • Among the fabrics known to cause allergies are asbestos, rock wool, rubber, spandex, nylon, rayon, plastic, silk, hemp, sheep wool, cotton, linen, and mohair. *See* Clothing and Wrinkleproof Finishes.

FARMING • Farm workers have been found by National Cancer Institute (NCI) researchers to have elevated death rates for blood and lymph cancers. Cancers of the blood and lymphatic system— leukemia, the lymphomas, and multiple myeloma—have been studied the most, because some agricultural chemicals are known to affect these systems. Correlation studies indicate that death rates for leukemia are elevated in areas where certain agricultural commodities, including corn, cotton, and wheat, are heavily produced and where pesticides are used extensively. In a study of non-Hodgkin's lymphoma in Kansas, NCI researchers found that farmers who use herbicides have a 1.6-fold greater risk than nonfarmers. Among frequent users, those who mix or apply the herbicides themselves have eight times the risk. These above-average rates are associated with the use of phenoxy herbicides, especially 2,4-D *(see)*.

FASTNESS • Refers to the ability of a dye or pigment that is not very much affected by light, steam, high temperature, or other environmental conditions. Pigments usually exhibit more fastness than organic dyes.

FAT DISSOLVERS • *See* Turpentine Gum.

FATIGUE • Everyone's nose becomes "fatigued" when smelling a certain odor. No matter how much you like a fragrance or how much you hate a bad odor, you can only smell them for a short interval. It is nature's way of protecting humans from overstimulation of the olfactory sense.

FATTY ACIDS • One, or any mixture of liquid and solid acids: capric, caprylic, lauric, myristic, oleic, palmitic, and stearic. In combination with glycerin, they form fat, which is necessary for normal growth and healthy skin. Fatty acids are used in bubble baths and lipsticks, but chiefly for making soaps, detergents, paints and lacquers, candles, salad oils, shortenings, and lubricants. See Stearic Acid. No known toxicity.

FATTY ALCOHOLS • Cetyl. Stearyl. Lauryl. Myristyl. Solid alcohols made from acids and widely used in hand creams and lotions. Cetyl and stearyl alcohols form an occlusive film to keep skin moisture from evaporating, and they impart a velvety feel to the skin. Lauryl and myristyl are used in detergents and creams. Very low toxicity. The alcohols are also used for textile antistatic and finishing agents, and in plasticizers. No known toxicity.

F&B • *See* Anilazine.

FEDERAL INSECTICIDE, FUNGICIDE, AND RODENTICIDE ACT • FIFRA. It gives the Environmental Protection Agency (EPA) the authority and responsibility for registering pesticides for specific uses, provided that such uses do not pose an unreasonable risk to human health or to the environment. The EPA also has the authority to suspend or cancel the registration of a pesticide if subsequent information indicates that the use of the pesticide would pose unreasonable risk.

FENITROTHION • *See* Acaracides.

FENOXAPROP-ETHYL • Acclaim™. Furore™. Puma™. Whip™. Postemergent crabgrass control derived from propanoic acid. Related to Silvex™, a herbicide and plant-growth regulator that has been restricted because of its toxicity and long-lasting effects in the environment.

FENSULFOTHION • A brown, liquid pesticide that is poisonous via oral, skin, and inhalation. Heat decomposition emits very toxic fumes. *See* Organophosphates.

FENTHION • Mercaptophos™. A pesticide that is poisonous by mouth or skin. It is also a suspected cancer-causing agent. *See* Organophosphates.

FENVALERATE • Pyridin™. Belmark™. Derived from benzene and cyanide, it is a pesticide used on cabbage and other vegetables. An eye and skin irritant. *See* Pesticides.

FERBAM • Vanicide 89. Fermocide. Ferradow. An odorless,

black solid used as a fungicide. A suspected cancer-causing and mutagenic agent. When heated, it emits very toxic fumes. *See* Carbamates.

FERMOCIDE • *See* Ferbam.

FERRADOW • *See* Ferbam.

FERTILIZERS • Most contain an ammonium salt such as ammonium nitrate or ammonium phosphate *(see both)*. They may also contain ground bone, hoof and/or horn, or fish meal and blood meal. Sewage sludge and manure are also used as fertilizers. Urea, cobalt salts, copper salts, potassium chloride, and potassium sulfate are in some fertilizers. Among the most potentially harmful ingredients are phosphoric acid, boron salts, and liquid phosphoric acid, but it depends on what is in the mixture, and other factors in the compounds. For house and yard use, the numbers on the fertilizer bag (10–4–8) refer to the percentages by weight of nitrogen, phosphorus, and potassium, respectively. In general, liquid and granular fertilizers used for houseplants and in the garden have a low degree of toxicity unless ingested in large quantities. Single ingredient fertilizers such as ammonium nitrate or lime are more likely to be toxic or corrosive. Composting is a good alternative to chemical fertilizers, and also helps recycling. *See also* Ammoniated Nitrogen Fertilizer.

FIBER • *See* page 13, Introduction.

FIBERGLASS • There are several types of fiberglass belonging to the category of synthetic mineral fibers. The main distinction among different types of fiberglass is fiber diameter. Ordinary fiberglass insulation (glass wool) typically has a diameter between 3 and 10 microns. Asbestos fibers, which are known to cause cancer, are, on the average, much finer than synthetic fibers, and it is their shape that leads to malignancy. Also, the fine, light fibers of asbestos are more prone to become airborne, and can more easily penetrate deep into the respiratory tract. Certain types of fiberglass and other synthetic mineral fibers (SMFs) can cause cancer in animals if placed directly into the lungs, trachea, or abdominal cavity, but, according to the Hazard Evaluation System and Information Service of California (HESIS), it is not clear whether this artificial route of exposure is relevant to human exposure. There is suggestive evidence that workers exposed to large amounts of SMFs over long periods of time have higher rates of lung cancer. While it is believed that fiberglass and other synthetic mineral fibers are less cancer-causing than asbestos, common sense says that precautions should be taken if you must work with them. In June 1991, the U.S. Department of Labor reported several medical studies showed "a statistically significant increase" in respiratory tract cancer among fiberglass production workers. The Labor Department ruled that all synthetic mineral fibers products, including insulation, should carry cancer warning labels. In California, legislation was introduced to ban the production, sale, and installation of blown-in fiberglass insulation.

FICAM™ W,D, AND PLUS • **Bendiocarb**. A contact insecticide. Toxic by ingestion and skin absorption. *See* Pesticides.

FIFRA • *See* Federal Insecticide, Fungicide, and Rodenticide Act.

FILM CEMENT • May contain cotton, acetone, methanol, methyl cellosolve acetate, methylene chloride, ethylene dichloride, esters, ketones, acetate, dioxane, nitrocellulose, ethanol, secondary butyl acetate, methyl ethyl ketone (MEK), and isopropanol *(see all)*.

FINGER PAINT • Contains bentonite or titanium oxide *(see both)* plus nontoxic colors, and preservatives (perhaps a trace of formaldehyde or dimethoxane). Look for the "AP" or "CP" "nontoxic" seal on products bearing the label of The Crayon, Water Color, and Craft Institute.

FINISHING COMPOUNDS • Substances that impart softness, flexibility, wrinkle-resistance, flame-proofing, or waterproofing to products, usually textiles. Formaldehyde is an example of a chemical added to fabrics to increase wrinkle resistance and Fyrol-2® is an example of a chemical added for flame-proofing.

FIRE EXTINGUISHERS • Most contain sodium bicarbonate (baking soda). Foam types contain ethylene glycol, salts, and protein. Powder foams contain metal salts. Liquid foams contain licorice extracts, glues, and egg albumin. Liquid extinguishers contain chlorobromopropene, dichlorodifluoromethane, and dichlorofluoroethane. Some hard-to-put-out fires may also be killed by extinguishers containing sodium hydroxide and sodium dichromate. Powder extinguishers may also contain silicones, ammonium monophosphate, borax, clay, potassium sulfate, and graphite.

FIRE RETARDANTS • *See* Fireproofing and Flame Retardants.

FIREPROOFING • There are three basic methods of retarding flames. One is the coating of a surface with a substance that can be removed. The second is in solution form, to penetrate the fibers, and the third is to permanently integrate a substance into the fibers. Among the substances used are inorganic salts such as ammonium and zinc salts, antimony, and chlorinated organic compounds such as alumina trihydrate. Those products most often flame-proofed are carpets, rugs, upholstery, plastics used in construction, and some apparel.

FIXATIVE • A chemical that reduces the tendency of an odor or flavor to vaporize, by making the odor or flavor last longer.

FLAME RETARDANTS • Some fabrics such as nylon and wool are naturally flame resistant. Polyvinyl chloride fiber is flame-proof and, to some extent, the modacrylics. Glass and carbon fiber also resist fire but are not suitable for apparel. An emulsion of polyvinyl chloride with added polyvinyl alcohol is a Japanese fiber that is flame-proof. The use of melamine-formaldehyde resins on polyester blends also gives some flame resistance. Flame-retardant chemicals are used in textiles, carpets, home furnishings, plastics, paints, adhesives, and construction materials. The most widely used compound is aluminum oxide, which is employed to make carpets flame retardant. More than 150 flame retardants are available for textiles. Durable, flame-retardant chemicals contain phosphorus, nitrogen, chlorine, or bromine. Most children's sleepwear no longer contains specific chemicals but relies on synthetic fibers such as polyesters, which are flame resistant.

FLAMMABLE • Catches on fire easily and burns rapidly. The National Fire Protection Agency and the U.S. Department of Transportation define a flammable liquid as having a flash point below 100°F (37.8°C).

FLASH POINT • The lowest temperature at which a liquid emits enough flammable vapor to ignite and produce a flame when an ignition source is present.

FLAXSEED • The seed of the flax plant may be "hidden" in cereals and the milk of cows fed flaxseed; also in flaxseed tea, and the poultices and laxatives. A frequent allergen when ingested, inhaled, or in direct contact. Flaxseed is the source of linseed oil. Among other hidden sources are: dog food, muffins, Roman meal, wave-setting preparations, shampoos, hair tonics, cough remedies, depilatories, patent leather, insulating materials, rugs, and some fabrics.

FLEA COLLAR • Usually contains 2,2-Dichlorovinyl dimethyl phosphate or related compounds (*see* Dichlorvos), or a derivative of lindane *(see)*. Dichlorvos (DDVP) was restricted in food packaging by the EPA in February 1991, because it posed "more than a neglible risk." DDVP is a suspected carcinogen and birth defect–producing agent. Check whether you still have any DDVP around your pet's neck. Less toxic alternatives are herbal collars or ointments with eucalyptus or rosemary, a flea comb, or brewer's yeast (call your veterinarian for the amount).

FLEA POWDER, DOGS • May contain one or more of the pesticides carbyl, dichlorophene, piperonyl butoxide, pyrethrins, pyrophyllite, methoxychlor, chlordane, benzene hexachloride, hexachlorophene, rotenone, malathion, or 2-chloro-tetrachlorovinfos, as well as silica gel, sulfur, talc, and butoxy polypropylene glycol *(see all)*. For an alternative, feed two tablespoons of brewer's yeast and one clove of raw garlic to your animals daily. Sprinkle fennel, rue, and rosemary on carpets and bedding areas to repel fleas. Place eucalyptus seeds and leaves, and cedar chips around the animals' sleeping areas.

FLEABANE OIL • **Oil of Canada Fleabane. Erigeron Oil.** The pale yellow, volatile oil from a fresh flowering herb that takes its name from its supposed ability to drive away fleas. Used in fruit and spice flavorings. No known toxicity.

FLOOR CLEANERS • The pine oil type contains detergents and ammonia. The petroleum-solvent type contains waxes, detergents, and, perhaps, glycol ether, potassium hydroxide, and sodium perborate *(see all)*.

FLOOR POLISH • Usually contain a synthetic polymer such as styrene, acrylate or polystyrene plus waxes, a perfume, a preservative, and emulsifiers such as glycols, and benzoates. A solvent type may contain petroleum naphtha with a wax, and a liquid type usually contains petroleum distillate and resins. The aerosol type also contains synthetic polymers and waxes, along with a propellant and a preservative. Floor polishes may also contain fatty acids and ammonia. Among the ingredients used are diethylene glycol, petroleum distillates, mineral spirits, and nitrobenzene. A less toxic alternative is one part lemon juice plus two parts linseed oil; toothpaste may also be used to remove water stains. You can also mix one part lemon oil with two parts olive or vegetable oil as a polish. *See* Petroleum, Naphthas, and Glycols.

FLOOR WAX • Contains emulsifiers, preservatives, perfumes, solvents, and waxes such as paraffin and carnuba, styrene or acrylates.

FLORAL NOTE • A distinct odor or flavor of flowers.

FLUORESCENT BRIGHTENERS • **(46, 47, 52).** Colorless, water- or solvent-soluble, aromatic compounds with an affinity for fibers. They are usually violet, blue, or blue-green colors, and are capable of increasing both the blueness and the brightness of a substrate, resulting in a marked whitening effect. They improve the brightness of tints, and are included in detergents of all kinds to enhance cleansing action.

FLUORIDE • Sodium. Barium. Zinc. Acid salts used in insecticides, particularly for roaches and ants, and in other pesticides, enamel and glass mixes, electroplating fluxes, wood preservatives, as a disinfectant, in the manufacture of coated paper, and in the fluoridation of drinking water, and preparations to prevent tooth decay. The sodium salt is very toxic. In 1991, a report was released by the Public Health Service, the National Institutes of Health, the Centers for Disease Control, and the Food and Drug Administration. Researchers from these agencies studied fifty human epidemiology studies and several other animal studies and concluded that the use of fluoride be continued to help prevent tooth decay, because there is no evidence it causes cancer in humans. Dr. James Mason, U.S. Assistant Secretary for Health, said, "If fluoride presents any risk to the public at levels to which the majority of us are exposed, those risks are so small that they have been impossible to detect in the epidemiological studies to date." The agencies undertook the review after a U.S. National Toxicology Program study showed that four male rats fed high doses of fluoride over their lifetimes developed osteosarcoma, a rare bone cancer. NIOSH requires urine monitoring in workers exposed to fluorides, because the chemicals may affect kidney and bone. Chronic endemic fluorosis due to high concentrations of natural fluoride in local water supplies involves mottling of the teeth, bone changes, and, rarely, brain and nerve involvement. Acute fluoride poisoning can cause heart, brain, nerve, and gastrointestinal damage.

FLUOROACETATE • *See* Sodium Fluoroacetate.

FLUOROCARBONS • Freon®. CFC. Algofrene®. Blaco-Tron®. Genesolv®. Ucon®. FC. Arcton®. Genetron®. Halon®. Arklone®. Frigen®. Isotron®. Fluorocarbon is a general name for a class of widely used industrial solvents that generally share similar properties. They are used for cleaning and degreasing, air conditioning and refrigeration, foam-blowing, aerosol propellants, plastics manufacture, and fire extinguishers. Fluorocarbons can affect your nervous system, causing symptoms similar to drunkenness. According to the Hazard Evaluation System and Information Service of California, if used with adequate ventilation, the commonly used fluorocarbons rarely cause human health problems other than mild skin irritation (the most common effect of overexposure to fluorocarbons). During overexposure, however, the heart becomes more sensitive to adrenaline. Warning symptoms may include dizziness and skipped heartbeats.

FLUVALINATE • A synthetic pyrethrin *(see)* insecticide. Harmful if swallowed, inhaled, or absorbed through the skin. May cause allergic reactions. A respirator should be worn when it is applied.

FLYING INSECT KILLER • **Raid**®. Products such as Raid® should be used according to instructions on their labels. For this insecticide, it is a violation of federal law not to do so. You should always point spray nozzle away from face, and press button, holding the container as upright as possible. Keep out of reach of children. Do not reuse empty container. Wrap it and throw it away.

FOLPET • Crystals from benzene *(see)*, it is used as a fungicide on fruits and vegetables. May irritate mucous membranes. *See* Pesticides and Phthalimides.

FORE (80W) • *See* Mancozeb.

FORMALDEHYDE • **Formalin. Methaldehyde. Methanal. Methy Aldehyde. Methylene Glycol. Methylene Oxide. Oxomethane. Oxymethylene. Paraform. Paraformaldehyde. Trioxane. BFV**®. **Fannoform**®. **Formalith**®. **Formol**®. **Fyde**®. **Ivalon**®. **Karsan**®. **Lysoform**®. **Morbicid**®. **Superlysoform**®. A colorless gas obtained by the oxidation of methyl alcohol and, generally, used in watery solution. Vapors are intensely irritating to mucous membranes. It has been estimated that 4 to 8 percent of the general population may be sensitized to formaldehyde. It is used in more than three thousand products, including disinfectants, cosmetics, fungicides, leather tanners, platers, defoamers, preservatives, and adhesives. It is also used in pressed-wood products such as hardwood, plywood, wall paneling, particle board, fiberboard, and furniture. Some surfactants, such as the widely used lauryl sulfate, may contain formaldehyde as a preservative, and others may have it without listing it on the label. Formaldehyde is used in the manufacture of commerical products such as resins, wrinkle-proof fabrics, rubber products, dyes, durable press drapes, carpets, and other textiles, plastics, and paper products. It is also present in insulation materials such as urea-formaldehyde foam, and combustion products, such as fuel exhaust and tobacco smoke. Any of these materials may give off formaldehyde vapors. The eyes, nose, and throat are irritated by formaldehyde vapors at levels as low as one part formaldehyde per million parts of air. Some people are more easily affected than others. Formaldehyde levels in the indoor air depend mainly on what is releasing the formaldehyde, temperature, humidity, and the air exchange rate (the amount of air entering and leaving the indoor area). Average concentrations in older homes without urea-formaldehyde insulation are generally well below 0.1 ppm. In homes with significant amounts of new pressed-wood products, levels can be greater than 0.3 ppm. Increasing the flow of outdoor air into a room decreases formaldehyde levels. Sealing a residence or office, conversely, increases the formaldehyde level in the air. Some sources such as pressed-wood products containing urea-formaldehyde glues, urea-formaldehyde foam insulation, durable press fabrics, and draperies, release more formaldehyde when new. As they age, the formaldehyde decreases.

Formaldehyde is an inexpensive and effective preservative, but there are serious questions about its safety. Ingestion can cause severe abdominal pain, internal bleeding, loss of ability to urinate, vertigo, coma, and death. Skin reactions after exposure to formaldehyde are very common because the chemical can be both irritating and an allergen. Physicians have reported severe reactions to nail hardeners containing formaldehyde. Its use in cosmetics is banned in Japan and Sweden. It is a highly reactive chemical that is damaging to the hereditary substances in the cells of several species. Researchers from the Division of Cancer Cause and Prevention of the National Cancer Institute recommended in April 1983 that formaldehyde be "further investigated" since it is involved in DNA damage and inhibits its repair, potentiates the toxicity of X rays in human lung cells, and may act in concert with other chemical agents to produce mutagenic and carcinogenic effects. Formaldehyde causes cancer in test animals. Some studies have suggested that formaldehyde exposure can cause cancer of the lungs and respiratory tract in humans, although other studies have not found this effect, according to the Hazard Evaluation System and Information Service of California (HESIS).

You can reduce your exposure to high levels of formaldehyde in the following ways.

• Make sure there is plenty of fresh air coming into the room from outside, and increase ventilation after bringing new sources of formaldehyde into the home.

• Purchase low-formaldehyde-releasing pressed-wood products for use in construction or remodeling, and for furniture, cabinets, and other wood items. These include oriented strand board and softwood plywood for construction, low-formaldehyde-emitting pressed-wood products or solid wood for furniture and cabinets. Some products are labeled as low-emitting, or ask for help in identifying low-emitting products. The "exterior grade" pressed-wood products are lower-emitting because they contain phenol resins, not urea resins.

• Use alternative products such as lumber or metal.

• Avoid the use of foamed-in-place insulation containing formaldehyde, especally urea-formaldehyde foam insulations.

• Wash new clothing and bed linens several times before using.

• Do not wear clothing with a stiff finish, or with fabrics labeled as permanent press, wrinkle or crease resistant, waterproof, wash-and-wear, moth proof, mildew proof, sweat repellent, or fire retardant.

• Wear clothing made of silk, 100 percent synthetic fiber, or wool (unless it is shrink proof). Fabrics that are mercerized, sanforized, or sized do not utilize formaldehyde.

See also Fabric Softeners, Finger Paint, Flame Retardants, Waterproof Adhesives, Waterproofing, Water Repellents, and Wrinkle-proof Finishes.

FORMALIN • *See* Formaldehyde.

FOWLER'S SOLUTION • *See* Arsenate, Potassium.

FREON 12 • *See* Dichlorodifluoromethane and Fluorocarbons.

FREON 114 • *See* Dichlorotetrafluoroethane and Fluorocarbons.

FULLER'S EARTH • A white or brown, naturally occurring, earthy substance, a nonplastic variety of kaolin *(see)* containing an aluminum magnesium silicate. Used for lubricants and soaps, as an absorbent, to decolorize fats and oils, as an insecticide carrier, in floor-sweeping compounds, and as a filter.

FUMIGANTS • Toxic compounds in vapor form that destroy rodents, insects, and infectious organisms. The most effective temperature for their use is approximately 79°F. They are used chiefly in enclosed or limited areas. Some commonly used fumigants are formaldehyde, sulfur dioxide, and other sulfur compounds. Among others are chloropicrin, aluminum phosphide, areginal, BBC12 (DBCP), ethylene dichloride (EDC), 1,2-Dibromomethane, methyl bromide, carbon tetrachloride (carbon tet), carbon disulfide, hydrocyanic acid, dichloropropane, propylene dichloride, Vorlex, Dorlone, Dowfumes (D-D™), EDCO (methyl bromide), epoxyethane (ethylene oxide), epoxypropane (propane oxide), ethylene dibromide, ethylene oxide (EtO), chlordimeform, hydrocyanic acid (HCH), hydrogen cyanide, DBCP, *p*-dichlorobenzene, phosphine gas and solid, capam, vernolate, and vapam. Fumigants are very dangerous and should be handled with extreme care, preferably by licensed pesticide professionals.

FUNGI • A member of the class of relatively primitive vegetable organisms, including mushrooms, yeasts, rusts, molds, and smuts. Fungi grow indoors and can cause year-round hay fever. The most common found in homes are penicillium, aspergillus, rhizopus, and mucor. They love to multiply in vegetable bins, refrigerator drip trays, garbage pails, house plants, and planters, as well as in sinks, humidifiers, laundry areas, and in carpets, upholstery, and bedding. To reduce indoor fungi as much as possible, a dehumidifier should be installed and the water tray emptied frequently and scrubbed periodically with household ammonia solutions. If not, calcium chloride suspended in a burlap or other porous bag may be hung in damp areas, with a pan placed underneath. The pan should be emptied frequently and scrubbed with ammonia solutions. Walls and ceilings should be scrubbed with antimildew solutions available in supermarkets.

FUNGICIDES • Any substances that kill or inhibit the growth of fungi. Older types include a mixture of lime and sulfur, copper oxychloride, and Bordeaux mixture. Copper naphthenate has been used to impregnate textile fabrics such as tenting and military clothing. Copper undecylenate with zinc undecylenate is used in foot powders and sprays. Chlorine solutions are used in swimming pools and water-cooled heat exchangers. Boric acid with hydroxyquinoline sulfate is used, but is toxic to humans *(see both)*. Captain, folpet, anilazine, and zinc copper compounds are common ingredients of fungicides for your plants. If you do not overwater, and keep the soil clean and dry, you can prevent the development of fungus. *See also* Bis(tributyltin) Oxide.

FURFURAL • **Artificial Ant Oil.** A clear to yellowish liquid with an almondlike odor, derived from oat hulls, rice hulls, corncobs, and other cellulose-type waste materials. It is used as a solvent for many products including shoe dyes, and lubricants, in brake linings, weed killers, fungicides, road construction, and as a flavoring. Poisonous when inhaled, can be absorbed by the skin, and is irritating to the eyes, skin, and mucous membranes. A fire hazard and explosive compound when heated.

FURNITURE GLUE • Animal wood glue usually contains water, animal glue and Dowicide A®. Vinyl wood glue contains polyvinyl acetate and dibutyl phthalate; dry casein glue contains casein, calcium hydroxide, sodium fluoride, and kerosene *(see all)*.

FURNITURE POLISH • The solvent type may contain petroleum distillates and Turkey-red oil *(see both)* plus coloring and a perfume. The wax solvent type will contain mineral spirits and silicone *(see both)* plus a wax such as carnauba or ozokite, and, sometimes, amyl acetate and turpentine. The emulsion type also contains petroleum distillate, an emulsifier, an alcohol, water, perfume, and a preservative. The wax type usually contains mineral spirits and a wax plus an emulsifier, perfume, and dye. It may also contain alkyl sodium sulfate, bentonite, ethylene glycol, glycerine, gums, hydroxyethyl cellulose, an alcohol, pine oil, a detergent, shellac, silicones, synthetic resins, and turpentine. The aerosol type usually contains a wax, silicone oils, mineral oils, petroleum or synthetic naphthas, perfumes, preservatives, and emulsifiers plus a propellant. A less toxic alternative is one part lemon juice plus two parts linseed oil; toothpaste may be used to remove water stains. You can also try mixing one part lemon oil and two parts olive or vegetable oil as a polish. For unfinished wood, try mineral oil. For mahogany, mix equal parts white vinegar and warm water. Wipe onto wood, then polish with a soft cloth. For water spots, try toothpaste on a damp cloth. *See also* Liquid Furniture Polish.

FURNITURE STRIPPERS • May contain acetone, methyl ethyl ketone, alcohols, xylene, toluene, and methylene chloride *(see all)*. A less toxic alternative is sandpaper or a heat gun. You can also try equal portions of boiled linseed oil, turpentine, and vinegar with steel wool. Handle all solvents with extreme care.

FURNITURE WORKERS • A correlation study suggested a possible link between risk for nasal cancer (adenocarcinoma) and the location of furniture manufacturing. National Cancer Institute researchers found that men who worked in the furniture industry had nearly a sixfold increased risk for nasal cancer. Those who worked in other occupations that might involve exposure to wood dust, including carpentry and construction work, had a threefold increased risk for cancer.

FUTURE® ACRYLIC FLOOR FINISH™ • A nontoxic floor wax containing acrylic *(see)*.

FYROL FR-Z™ • **Tris (1,3-dichloroisopropyl) phosphate.** A flame retardant derived from phosphate that is used on polyester and polyurethane foam. Some chromosome abberations have been reported.

G

g • The abbreviation for gram *(see)*.

GAIN™ ENZYME LAUNDRY DETERGENT • A nonionic detergent containing sodium alkyl ethyoxylate sulfate, sodium sulfate, and sodium tripolyphosphate *(see all)*.

GARAGE • Compounds to which there may be exposure in a garage include benzine, carbon monoxide, detergents, epoxy resins, gasoline, glass fiber, lead, paints, and solvents. National Cancer Institute researchers found an excess risk of bladder cancer in garage and gas station workers, and for truck drivers and/or delivery men. Gas station workers had more than a twofold increased risk for bladder cancer and men who were drivers and/or delivery men for ten years or more had a 1.8-fold increase.

GARBAGE CAN DEODORANTS • Many contain dichlorobenzene and pine oil *(see both)*. They may also contain petroleum derivatives, salt, lime, methyl salicylate, or sodium hypochlorite *(see all)*.

GARBAGE DISPOSAL • *See* Disposal.

GARDENING • An infinite number of chemicals are used in gardens. Among the most common are fertilizers, fungicides, herbicides, insecticides, lead, and pesticides *(see all)*.

GAS • The state of matter in which atoms and molecules are in a continual state of motion and bumping into each other. The molecules are not packed as closely together as they are in liquids and solids.

GAS STATION • *See* Garage and Gasoline.

GASOLINE • A mixture of volatile hydrocarbons with an octane number of at least 60. Made by "cracking" petroleum, it is highly flammable, with a characteristic odor. Evaporates quickly. Antiknock gasoline has methyl-tert-butyl ether (MBTE) *(see)* added to eliminate knocking and increase octane number. Gasoline for automobiles has an octane number of approximately 90, and airplanes use gasolines of octane number 100 or more. Heavy abusers who inhale gasoline develop brain damage. Fifteen to twenty breaths of gasoline vapor produce five to six hours of intoxication, and can affect gait, cause hallucinations, confusion, lack of oxygen, and pneumonia. Ingestion causes vomiting, vertigo, fever, drowsiness, and confusion.

GEL • A semisolid, apparently homogenous substance that may be elastic and jellylike (gelatin), or more or less rigid (silica gel), and that is formed in various ways such as by a coagulation or evaporation.

GELATINS • A protein obtained by boiling in water skin, tendons, ligaments, or bones. Colorless or slightly yellow, tasteless, it absorbs five to ten times its weight of cold water. Used in photographic film, sizing, textile and paper adhesives, cements, matches, filters, and in cosmetics and food as a thickener. Employed medicinally to treat malnutrition and brittle fingernails. No known toxicity.

GENE • The part of the chromosome *(see)* that carries a particular inherited characteristic.

GERMICIDES • **Bactericides.** Agents that kill bacteria, especially those causing disease. These compounds vary greatly in their potency and specificity. Germicides of the pine or mint types may contain waterless soap, pine oil or methyl salicylate, alcohol, o-benzyl-p-chlorophenol, and water. *See* Phenols, Pine Oil, and Quaternary Ammonium Compounds.

GILSONITE • An asphaltlike material, a hydrocarbon *(see)* found only in Utah and Colorado. Used in wood stains, in waterproof coating, black varnishes, lacquers, baking enamels, and wire coatings. Also used in linoleum and floor tile, paving, insulation, and low-grade rubber compounds. A skin irritant.

GIZMO RAT KILLER™ • *See* Thallium.

GLASS PLUS™ • Contains isopropyl alcohol and glycol ethers *(see both)*.

GLASS WINDOW CLEANERS • Usually contain butyl cellosolve, alcohol, a wetting agent, silicone *(see all),* and water. May also contain perfume, ammonia, an alkali, glycol ethers, naphtha, an organic solvent, phosphate waxes, and ammonium hydroxide *(see)*. Alternate cleaners are plain rubbing alcohol, car-windshield washer, or one cup of household ammonia in a gallon of water. (Do not mix the alcohol and ammonia or any other cleaning products.) You can also use a quarter cup to one cup of white vinegar in one quart warm water, and rub dry with newspaper.

GLAUBER'S SALT • **Sodium Sulfate Decahydrate.** Crystalline sodium sulfate that occurs in nature as mirabilite and is made by the crystallization of sodium sulfate from water solutions; named for German chemist Johann R. Glauber, who died in 1668. Used in solar heat storage, air conditioning, as an opacifier in shampoos, a detergent in bath salts, and medicinally, as a laxative. Skin irritations may occur.

GLAZING COMPOUNDS • *See* Putty.

GLORY CONCENTRATED RUG SHAMPOO™ • An anionic *(see)* detergent that contains sodium lauryl sulfate *(see)*.

GLUE • General-purpose glue usually contains dextrin, borax, phenol, and water. Nitrocellulose cements contain, in addition to nitrocellulose, acetone, methyl acetate, and camphor. Polyvinyl acetate wood glue contains, in addition to polyvinyl acetate, dibutyl phthalate, silicone defoamers, methyl cellulose, water, and formalin. May also contain diethylene glycol dibenzoate. Gum arabic mucilage contains, in addition to gum arabic, formaldehyde, phenol, glycerin, oil of wintergreen, and water. The flexible glue type contains animal glue, sucrose, polyethylene glycol, sodium *o*-phenylphenate, phenol, methyl salicylate, and water. May also contain alkali. The polychloroprene latex type contains water, casein, sodium *o*-phenylphenate, and ammonia *(see all)*. Natural glues are made of collagen, leather, fish, gelatin, casein, blood albumin, and soybean and other vegetable adhesives that usually do not cause skin reactions. Synthetic glues, particularly those used for hobbies, and epoxy resins are common causes of nonoccupational epoxy *(see)* resin skin rashes. Cyanoacrylate adhesives such as Krazy Glue™ or Miracle Glue™, do not usually cause skin reactions, but can seal the skin of the hands or other parts together, and if soap and water or acetone do not get them apart, medical intervention might be necessary. Pressure-sensitive adhesives, adhering by application of light pressure, are used on adhesive tapes and labels that contain natural rubber or acrylates. They may cause irritation or allergic reactions.

GLUTARALDEHYDE • **Glutaral. Glutaric Aldehyde. Glutaric Dialdehyde. 1,5-Pentanedial. 1,5-Pentanedione. Cidex®. Glutarex®. Glutarol®. 1,3-diformylpropane.** A pale yellow liquid that smells like rotten apples, and is most often available in water solutions. Used as a chemical sterilant, leather-tanning agent, resin or dye intermediate, and embalming fluid. Glutaraldehyde affects you when you breathe its vapor or touch the liquid. It reacts quickly with the first body tissue it contacts. Its effects occur mainly in the areas that are directly contacted. The most common effect of overexposure is irritation of the eyes, nose, throat, and skin. Glutaraldehyde causes genetic mutations in laboratory tests, which suggests that it might cause cancer. California's Division of Occupational Safety and Health set a limit in the workplace of 0.2 parts of glutaraldehyde per million parts of air (about equal to 0.8 milligrams of glutaraldehyde per cubic meter of air).

GLYCERIDES • **Monoglycerides, Diglycerides, and Monosodium Glycerides of Edible Fats and Oils.** Any of a large class of compounds that are esters *(see)* of the sweet alcohol glycerin. They are also made synthetically. Emulsifying and defoaming agents. Used in bakery products to maintain "softness," in beverages, ice cream, ices, ice milk, milk, chewing gum base, shortening, lard, oleomargarine, confections, sweet chocolate, chocolate, rendered animal fat, and whipped toppings. The diglycerides are on the FDA list of food additives to be studied for possible mutagenic, teratogenic, subacute, and reproductive effects. The Glycerides are also used in cosmetic creams as texturizers, emulsifiers, and emollients. The final report to the FDA of The Select Committee on GRAS Substances stated in 1980 that it should continue its GRAS status with no limitations other than good manufacturing practices.

GLYCEROL • **Glycerin.** A by-product of soap manufacture, it is a sweet, warm-tasting, oily fluid obtained by adding alkalies *(see)* to fats and fixed oils. A clear, colorless, odorless, syrupy liquid. Used as a solvent, humectant, and emollient in many cosmetics, it absorbs moisture from the air and, therefore, helps keep moisture in creams and other products, even if the consumer leaves the cap off the container. Also helps the products to spread better. Among the many cosmetic products containing glycerin are cream rouge, face packs, and masks, and hand creams. Also used in resins, dynamite, printers' ink rolls, liquors, germicides, hydraulic fluid, and in polyurethane, as a humectant in foods, and as a solvent for food colors and flavors. In concentrated solutions it is irritating to the mucous membranes, but as used, is nontoxic, nonirritating, nonallergenic. Contact with strong oxidizing agents such as chromium trioxide, potassium chlorate, or potassium permanganate *(see)* may produce an explosion.

GLYCOL ETHERS • **Cellosolve®. Carbitol®. Dowanol®. Ektasolve®. EGME. EGMEA. EGEE. EGEEA. EGPE. EGDME. EGDEE. DEG. DEGME. DEGEE. DEGBE. DEGDME. TEGDME. PGME. DPG. DEPGME. 2-Methoxyethanol. 2-Methoxyethyl Acetate. 2-Ethoxyethanol. 2-Ethoxyethyl Acetate. 2-Propoxyethanol. 1,2-Dimethoxyethane. 2-(2-Methoxyethoxy)Ethanol. 2-(2-ethoxyethoxy)Ethanol. 2-(2-Butoxyethoxy)Ethanol. Bis(2-Methoxyethyl)Ether. Ethylene Glycol Monomethyl Ether. Ethylene Glycol Monopropyl Ether. Diethylene Glycol. Dipropylene Glycol. Dipropylene Glycol Monomethyl Ether.** Glycol ether is the name for a large class of chemicals. Most glycol ether compounds are clear, colorless liquids. Some have mild, pleasant odors or no smell at all; others (mainly the acetates) have strong odors. The common belief that glycol ethers never evaporate fast enough to create harmful levels in the air is false, according to HESIS, the Hazard Evaluation System and Information Service of California. Some evaporate quickly and easily can reach hazardous levels in the air; others evaporate very slowly and, therefore, are less hazardous by inhalation. EGME and EGEE are two that evaporate very quickly. The glycol ethers are used widely industrial solvents. Each may be used alone, or as an ingredient in products such as paints, varnishes, dyes, stains, inks, deodorant sprays, and semiconductor chip-coatings; as cleaners for degreasing, dry cleaning, film cleaning, and circuit board manufacture; as jet fuel deicing additives, brake fluids, in metalworking fluids *(see);* and in perfumes and cosmetics. Glycol ethers enter your body when they evaporate into the air you breathe, and they are rapidly absorbed into your body if the liquids contact your skin. Cases of poisoning have been reported where skin contact was the main route of exposure, even though there was no effect on the skin itself. The effects of overexposure can include anemia, mild intoxication, and irritation of the skin, eyes, nose, and throat. Some glycol ethers are hazardous to the reproductive system (EGPE, EGBE, DEGBE, PGME, PGMEA, and DPGME). Within the class of glycol ethers, toxicity varies. All propylene glycol ethers are currently believed to be relatively safe, according to HESIS. Most ethylene glycol ethers with "methyl" in their names are relatively toxic.

GLYCOL RESINS • *See* Clothing.

GLYCOLIC ACID • Contained in sugarcane juice, it is an odorless, slightly water-absorbing acid used to control the acid/alkali balance in cosmetics, and whenever a cheap organic acid is needed. Also used in copper brightening, decontamination procedures, and in dyeing. A mild irritant to the skin and mucous membranes.

GLYCOLS • **Propylene Glycol. Glycerin. Ethylene Glycol. Carbitol. Diethylene Glycol.** Literally, means "glycerin" plus "alcohol." A group of syrupy alcohols derived from hydrocarbons *(see)* and widely used in cosmetics as humectants and as solvents. Also used in antifreeze, hydraulic brake fluids, as solvents for paints and plastics, in printing inks, stamp pad inks, and inks for ballpoint pens, softening agent for cellophane, in fire extinguishers for gasoline and oil fires, and in synthetic fibers and waxes. The FDA cautions manufacturers that glycols may cause adverse reactions in users. Propylene glycol and glycerin *(see both)* are considered safe. Other glycols in low concentrations may be harmless for external application, but ethylene glycol, carbitol, and diethylene glycol are hazardous in concentrations exceeding 5 percent even in preparations for use on small areas of the body. Wetting agents *(see)* increase the absorption of glycols and, therefore, their toxicity.

GOLD • The soft, yellow metal occurring in the earth's crust, and used as a coloring, to give shine to cosmetics, in jewelry, gold plating, and in medicine to treat arthritis. The pure metal is nontoxic but the gold salts can cause allergic skin reactions. Ingestion can cause bone marrow depression, jaundice, stomach and intestinal bleeding, headache, and vomiting.

GRAM • **g.** A metric unit of mass. One U.S. ounce equals 28.4 grams; one U.S. pound equals 454 grams. There are 1,000 milligrams (mg) in one gram.

GRAPHITE • **Black Lead.** Obtained by mining, especially in Canada. Usually soft, black, lustrous scales. Also used in lead pencils, stone polish, and as an explosive. The dust is mildly irritating to the lungs. No longer permitted in cosmetics.

GRAS • The Generally Recognized As Safe List was established in 1958 by Congress. Those substances that were being added to food over a long time, which under conditions of their intended used were generally recognized as safe by qualified scientists, would be exempt from premarket clearance. Congress had acted on a very marginal response—on the basis of returns from those scientists sent questionnaires. Approximately 355 out of 900 responded, and only about 100 of those responses had substantive comments. Three items were removed from the originally published list. Since then, developments in the scientific fields and in consumer awareness have brought to light the inadequacies of the testing of food additives and, ironically, the complete lack of testing of the Generally Recognized as Safe List. President Nixon directed the FDA to reevaluate items on the GRAS list. The reevaluation was completed and a number of items were moved from the list. Although there were a number of others on the list, some of them top priority, to be studied in 1980, nothing has been reported by the FDA on their status since then.

GREASE REMOVERS • May contain soap, mineral spirits, oleic acid, potash, butyl alcohol, ethylene glycol monobutyl acetate (cellosolve), methyl chloroform, alkyl aryl sulfonate, and methyl ethyl ketone *(see all)*. In addition, may contain alkaline soap, alkalies such as trisodium phosphate, isophorone, isopropanol, and phosphoric acid.

GTA RAT BAIT™ • See Thallium.

GUANIDINE CARBONATE • Colorless crystals, soluble in water, found in turnip juice, mushrooms, corn germ, rice hulls, mussels, and earthworms. Occurs as water-absorbing crystals, which are very alkaline and are used to adjust pH *(see)* in compounds. Used in organic synthesis and as a rubber accelerator. A muscle poison if ingested. No known toxicity to the skin.

GUM ARABIC • *See* Acacia Gum and Glue.

GUM KARAYA • **Sterculia Gum. India Tragacanth.** The dried exudate of a tree native to India. Karaya came into wide use during World War I as a cheaper substitute for gum tragacanth *(see)*. Karaya swells in water and alcohol, but does not dissolve. Used in textile coatings, adhesives, protective coatings, and as a stabilizer, thickener, and emulsifier in food and cosmetic products. It can cause allergic reactions such as hay fever, dermatitis, gastrointestinal diseases, and asthma.

GUMS • The true plant gums are the dried exudates from various plants obtained when the bark is cut or otherwise injured. Natural gums are produced principally in Africa or Asia and include seaweed extracts, plant exudates, gums from seeds or roots, and gums obtained by microbial fermentation. They are soluble or swell in hot or cold water, and sticky. Today, the term *gum* usually refers to water-soluble thickeners, either natural or synthetic; thickeners that are insoluble in water are called "resins." Gums are used in cosmetics, as protective coatings, in adhesives, and as emulsifying agents. Also used as sizing for textiles. No known toxicity other than individual allergic reactions to specific gum.

GUTHION™ • See Azinphos-Methyl.

GUTTA-PERCHA • **Gummi Plasticum.** The purified, coagulated, milky exudate of various trees grown in the Malay Archipelago. Related to rubber; on exposure to air and sunlight, becomes brittle. Used in dental cement, in fracture splints for broken bones, and to cover golf balls. No known toxicity.

GYPSUM • A mineral that consists of calcium sulfate *(see)* with water or the rock that consists primarily of this mineral. Used in cement.

GYPSUM CEMENT • **Plaster of Paris. Calcium Sulfate.** A group of cements produced by the partial removal of water from gypsum. They usually contain other ingredients such as alum or aluminum sulfate or borax. *See* Calcium Sulfate.

H

HALONITRILES • Mutagenic and carcinogenic substances that have been detected in chlorinated drinking water supplies as a by-product of disinfectant. University of Texas researchers have found that acrylonitrile (VCN) and haloacetonitriles (HAN) injure the gastrointestinal tract.

HAMAMELIS WATER • *See* Witch Hazel.

HAZARDOUS WASTE DISPOSAL • *See* Disposal.

HCl • The abbreviation for hydrochloride.

HCH 666 • *See* Lindane.

HDPE • **High-Density Polyethylene.** Plastic is commonly used to make milk jugs and is recycled to make trash cans, flowerpots, piping, traffic cones, decking, and fencing. *See* Polyethylene.

HEDTA • **Hydroxyethyl Ethylenediamine Triacetic Acid.** A liquid with an ammonia odor used in textile-finishing compounds, antiquing agents, dyestuffs, cationic surfactants, resins, rubber products, insecticides, and medicines. Low toxicity.

HELIUM • A colorless, odorless, tasteless gas derived from natural gas. Used as propellant in pressurized containers, in welding, inflation of balloons, leak detection, luminous signs, and in diving and space vehicle-breathing equipment. No known toxicity.

HEPTANE • An aliphatic hydrocarbon *(see)*, it is a volatile, colorless liquid derived from petroleum and used as an anesthetic and solvent. Highly flammable. Toxic by inhalation.

HEPTANOIC ACID • **Enanthic Acid.** Found in various fusel oils and in rancid oils, it has the faint odor of tallow. Derived from grapes, it is a fatty acid chiefly used in making esters *(see)* for food flavoring materials. Also used in special lubricants for aircraft and brake fluids. No known toxicity.

HERBICIDES • **Weed Killers.** Pesticides used to destroy unwanted vegetation, especially various types of weeds, grasses, and woody plants. Herbicides can be very toxic. Paraquat, which was introduced in 1962, is among the most toxic, producing multisystem organ failure upon ingestion. In Japan, reportedly thirteen hundred people die each year from paraquat poisoning. Herbicides include inorganic, nonmetallic ones such as salt and ammonium sulfate; derivatives of arsenic such as DSMA (disodium methanearsonate) and arsenic trioxide; chlorophenoxy derivatives such as 2,4,5-T and silvex; nitroaniline derivatives such as benefin and fluchoralin; carbamate derivatives such as metham and chlorpropham; dipyridyl deriviatives such as diquat and paraquat; substitute amide derivatives such as alachlor and pronamide; substituted urea derivatives such as linuorn and sulfometuron methyl; triazine derivatives such as cyanazine and metribuzin; and other miscellaneous organics such as chloramben and endothall. Any ingestion of a herbicide product must be considered potentially fatal and medical aid should be sought at once. Absorption through the skin can also be toxic and, therefore, herbicides should be handled with extreme caution. *Read the entire label each time before use!*

HEXACHLOR • *See* BHC.

1,2,3,4,5,6-HEXACHLOROCYCLOHEXANE • *See* Lindane.

HEXADECYL METHICONE • A silicone wax. *See* Silicones.

HEXADIMETHRINE CHLORIDE • *See* Polymers.

HEXAMETHYLDISILOXANE • *See* Silicates.

HEXAMETHYLENE • *See* Cyclohexane.

HEXANE • **Cetane.** A colorless, volatile liquid derived from distillation of petroleum, and used as a solvent and thinner in rubber, food, pharmaceutical, paint, and perfume industries, a glue in shoe, tape, and bandage manufacturing, and a cleaning agent for textile, furniture, and leather industries. Also used in low-temperature thermometers instead of mercury, usually with a blue or red dye. Ingestion of pure hexane is rare. Short-term, high-dose inhalation exposure produces narcotic-like symptoms with headache, and nausea occurring at 1,500 ppm, and confusion and dizziness at 5,000 ppm for ten minutes. Long-term exposure to levels of 190 ppm were associated with nerve damage in exposed workers. Symptoms of chronic exposure include fatigue, numbness, pain, and other sensory abnormalities. Typically, symptoms develop two to six months after continuously being heavily exposed to hexane and progress two to six months after cessation. *See* Enamel Paint.

HEXANEDOIC ACID • *See* Adipic Acid.

HEXANEDIOL DISTEARATE • The diester of hexanediol and stearic acid, derived from ethyl alcohol and stearic acid *(see both)*. Used as a wax and plasticizer.

1,2,6-HEXANETRIOL • An alcohol used as a solvent. No known skin toxicity.

HEXOCHLOROBENZENE • A fungicide. *See* Benzene.

HEXYL ALCOHOL • **1-Hexanol.** A colorless liquid derived from ethyl caproate or from olefins, and used as a solvent and plasticizer for textile and leather finishing agents. *See* Hexylene Glycol.

HEXYLENE GLYCOL • A colorless, odorless liquid used in hydraulic brake fluids, printers' inks, as a coupling agent and penetrant for textiles, a fuel and lubricant additive, an emulsifying agent, and as antifreeze for carburetors. Toxic by ingestion and inhalation, and irritating to the skin, eyes, and mucous membranes. *See* Glycols.

HINOSAN • *See* Organophosphates.

HOUSE DUST • A mixture of lint, mites, insect parts, fibers, bacteria, food particles, bits of plants, and other particulate matter such as hair and danders from pets, believed to be the most common cause of year-round hay fever. Other important components of house dust may be disintegrated stuffing materials from pillows, mattresses, toys, and furniture, as well as disintegrated fibers from draperies, furniture coverings, blankets, and carpets. The breakdown of these materials, from use and aging, seems to enhance their ability to sensitize susceptible persons. Geography also plays a part in the composition of house dust. Allergists are not quite sure about the allergens in house dust, but they believe the most allergenic component is probably related to mites, those microscopic, spiderlike insects found in many house dust samples. Both live and dead mites appear to contribute to allergic reactions, though dead mites seem to be more aggravating. Mites flourish during the summer, but symptoms of allergic patients are often worse in the colder months. This is thought to be due to the fact that the summer mites die and disintegrate into fragments, which can reach the respiratory tract more easily than intact mites.

Dust is hard to avoid, but it can be reduced. If an allergic person cleans, he or she should wear a disposable surgical mask that covers the nose and mouth. Leaving the house immediately after cleaning for an hour or so is advisable to avoid stirred-up dust. The most practical program is to make at least one room as dust-free as possible. Since most adults spend at least a third of their time in the bedroom and children spend half of theirs in the bedroom, sleeping quarters should be dust-free target areas.

• In the bedroom furnishings, avoid ornate and upholstered furniture, carpeting, venetian blinds, shelves filled with books or knickknacks, stuffed animals, and wall hangings. Instead, use simple metal or wood furniture with washable cotton or synthetic shades, and cotton or fiberglass curtains. Scatter rugs may be used if washed weekly.

• Walls should be painted or covered with washable wallpaper.

• Closet doors should be kept closed.

• Beds can be prime sources of dust. Bunk beds and canopy beds, in particular, should not be used. Mattresses, box springs, and pillows should be completely enclosed with allergen-proof coverings. Dacron or synthetic pillows are recommended over those made of kapok *(see)* or feathers. Blankets and bedspreads should be cotton or synthetic—not fuzzy wools or chenille.

• The room should be wet-dusted daily; the floor damp-mopped, and the baseboards oil-mopped. The complete bedroom, including walls, ceilings, closet, and backs of furniture should be cleaned thoroughly once a week. Vacuum cleaners can redistribute dust, so use a tank type. The tank should be left outside the room during vacuuming, or another hose can be attached to the air outlet and vented outside the room.

• Dust-seal compounds are available for application to furniture and fabrics, but may be of limited use.

• A central humidifier to add moisture to the air during the heating season will prevent nose and throat mucous membranes from becoming dry and irritated.

• Central air conditioning can filter out pollens, molds, and some dust from the entire home if the windows and doors are kept closed.

• Various types of air purifiers can be attached to the central air return to decrease the amount of dust in the air.

HOUSEHOLD AMMONIA • The ammonium hydroxide concentration ranges from 3 to 10 percent. The 3 percent solution can be irritating to the skin and eyes, but higher concentrations may be corrosive. Inhalation of ammonia fumes can irritate and injure the lungs. A mixture of half water and half household ammonia cleans as well as the more expensive, perfumed products in fancy bottles, but, of course, does not smell as nice. *See* Ammonia.

HUMECTANT • A substance used to preserve the moisture content of materials, especially in hand creams and lotions. The humectant of glycerin and rose water, in equal amounts, is the earliest known hand lotion. Glycerin, propylene glycol, and sorbitol *(see all)* are widely used humectants in hand creams and lotions. *See* individual substances for toxicity.

HYDANTOIN • Derived from methanol *(see),* and used as an intermediate in the synthesis of textile lubricants and resins. Also used in swimming pool sanitizers and algicides. It caused cancer when injected into the abdomens of rats in doses of 1,370 mg per kilogram of body weight and when given orally to rats in doses of 1,500 mg per kilogram.

HYDRATED • Combined with water.

HYDRATED ALUMINA • *See* Aluminum Hydroxide.

HYDRATED SILICA • An anticaking agent to keep loose powders free-flowing. *See* Silica and Hydrated.

HYDROCARBONS • A large class of organic compounds containing only carbon and hydrogen. Derived principally from petroleum, coal tar, and plant sources. *Aliphatic hydrocarbons*—so named because they have an open chain of carbon atoms, are used as solvents and for many other purposes. Pentane and hexane are used in thermometers, in place of mercury. Gasoline is used as fuel, in mixing paints, and in rubber cement. Naphtha is used in varnishes; and kerosene is used in lamps, flares, as a degreaser and cleaner, and in insecticides. *Aromatic hydrocarbons,* so called because they have a benzene ring, include benzene, aniline, xylene, styrene, and naphtha. They are used for artificial leather, linoleum, oilcloth, airplane dopes, varnishes and lacquers, and as solvents for waxes, resins, and oils. The *aromatics* may be absorbed through the skin and are a common cause of skin rash. *Chlorinated hydrocarbons,* which contain chlorine, include carbon tetrachloride, perchlorethylene, and chloroform *(see all).* They may cause skin irritation and other health problems. Hydrocarbon ingestions account for about 5 percent of all calls reported to poison control centers in the United States. In descending order of frequency, the most common hydrocarbons involved in such calls were gasoline, lacquer thinner, pine oil, furniture polish, kerosene, and charcoal lighter fluid. Many hydrocarbons are known or suspected cancer-causing agents. *See* individual compounds for further health information.

HYDROCARBONS, HALOGENATED • A hydrocarbon in which one or more of the hydrogen atoms has been replaced by fluorine, chlorine, bromine, or iodine. Among these are carbon tetrachloride, chloroform, methylene chloride, 1,1,1-trichloroethane, PCBs, the freons, tetrachloroethene, and trifluoromethane. Used in aerosol propellants, fumigants, pesticides, refrigerants, paints, paint strippers, deodorizers, insect repellents, typing correction fluids, and degreasing, dewaxing, and dry-cleaning solvents, and moth crystals. A number of the chlorinated types are used in insecticides. Many halogenated hydrocarbons are highly toxic and may cause cancer. Some are emitted during hot showers in the bathroom.

HYDROCHLORIC ACID • A clear, colorless, or slightly yellowish, corrosive liquid; a water solution of hydrogen chloride of varying concentrations. An acid used as a modifier for food starch, in the manufacture of sodium glutamate *(see)* and gelatin, for the conversion of cornstarch to syrup (0.012 percent), and to adjust the pH (acid-alkalinity balance) in the brewing industry (0.02 percent). Also used as a solvent and in metal cleaning, general cleaning, as an alcohol denaturant, and in hair bleaches to speed up oxidation in rinses and remove color. Inhalation of the fumes causes choking, and inflammation of the respiratory tract. Ingestion may corrode the mucous membranes, esophagus, and stomach, and cause diarrhea. Circulatory collapse and death can occur. *See* Bleaches.

HYDROCHLOROFLUOROCARBON, 22, 142b, 152a • Propellants and refrigerants derived from chlorofluorocarbon, any of several compounds comprised of carbon, fluorine, chlorine, and hydrogen. Though safer than many propellant gases, their use has diminished because of suspected effects on stratospheric ozone. *See* Hydrocarbons, Halogenated.

HYDROFLUORIC ACID • A colorless, fuming liquid. Derived from hydrogen fluoride in water, it will attack glass and any silicon-containing compound *(see* Silicon). It is found in many aluminum cleaners, in products to etch glass, and in some rust removers. It is toxic by ingestion and inhalation, and highly corrosive to skin and mucous membranes. The pain from the burns may be delayed for several hours, during which time the acid will burn deep into the skin. Burns may not become apparent for up to twenty-four hours, and may appear as reddened, pasty white, blistered, or charred skin.

HYDROGEN PEROXIDE • A bleaching and oxidizing agent, detergent, and antiseptic. An unstable compound readily broken down into water and oxygen, it is made from barium peroxide and diluted phosphoric acid. Used in bleaching and deodorizing textiles, paper wood pulp, and fur. It is used as a plasticizer, in rocket fuel, foam rubber, the manufacture of glycerol, in electroplating, and for cleaning metals. Also used as a substitute for chlorine in water and sewage treatment, and as a neutralizing agent in wine. Solutions that may be found around the home usually contain 3 percent hydrogen peroxide in water. Generally recognized as safe as a preservative and germicide in cosmetics, as well as in milk and cheese. A 3 percent solution is used medicinally as an antiseptic and germicide. A strong oxidizer, undiluted it can cause burns of the skin and mucous membranes. In 1980, the Japanese notified the World

Health Organization that hydrogen peroxide was a suspected cancer-causing agent. (It was widely used in Japanese fish cakes.) No systemic effects are caused upon ingestion of diluted hydrogen peroxide because it decomposed in the bowel before absorption. Strong solutions, however, are dangerous fire and explosion risks, and can be highly toxic and strongly irritating.

HYDROGENATION • The process of adding hydrogen gas under high pressure to liquid oils; the most widely used chemical process in the edible fat industry. Used in the manufacture of petrol from coal. Used primarily, however, in the cosmetics and food industries to convert liquid oils to semisolid fats at room temperature, as in the manufacture of margarine and shortening. Reduces the amount of acid in the compound and improves color. Hydrogenation usually increases the saturation in the fat but decreases the loss of flavor and spoilage due to oxidation. Hydrogenated oils still contain some unsaturated components that are susceptible to rancidity. Therefore, the addition of antioxidants is still necessary.

HYDROLYZED • Subject to hydrolysis or turned partly into water. "Hydrolysis" is derived from the Greek *hydro,* meaning "water," and from *lysis,* meaning "a setting free." It occurs as a chemical process in which the decomposition of a compound is brought about by water, resolving into a simpler compound. Hydrolysis also occurs in the digestion of foods.

HYDROQUINONE • White crystals, soluble in water, derived from aniline *(see).* It is used in black-and-white developer for photography, as an inhibitor that slows the rate of reactions, as a stabilizer in paints, varnishes, motor fuels, and oils, and as an antioxidant for fats. Poisonous when ingested, it is an active allergen and a strong irritant. Absorption through the skin and other tissues can cause symptoms that include ringing in the ears, nausea, dizziness, a sensation of suffocation, an increased rate of respiration, vomiting, pallor, muscular twitching, headache, cyanosis, delirium, and collapse. Contact can cause a skin rash and discoloration of the cornea of the eye.

HYDROQUINONE BENZOYL PEROXIDE • *See* Benzoyl Peroxide.

HYDROQUINONE DIBENZYL ETHER • A tan powder, insoluble in water. Used as a solvent, and in perfumes, soaps, plastics, and pharmaceuticals. See Hydroquinone.

HYDROXY ETHYL CELLULOSE • A white, free-flowing powder derived from wood or vegetable fiber, it is grease and oil resistant.

Used as a thickening and suspending agent; as a stabilizer for vinyls, to retard water evaporation in cements, as a binder in ceramic glazes, films, and in paper and textile sizing.

HYDROXY PROPYLMETHYL CELLULOSE CARBONATE • Prepared from wood pulp or cotton by treatment with methyl chloride. Used as a substitute for water-soluble gums, to render paper grease proof, as a thickener, and in paint-stripping preparations.

HYDROXYACETIC ACID • Colorless crystals that absorb water and smell like burnt sugar, occurring naturally in sugar cane syrup. Used for leather dyeing and tanning, textile dyeing, and cleaning, polishing, and soldering compounds, in adhesives, electroplating, wallpaper removers, and pH control.

p-HYDROXYBENZOIC ACID • Prepared from p-bromophenol. Used as a preservative and fungicide. See Benzoic Acid for toxicity.

HYDROXYLAMINE SULFATE • A hair-waving component in permanent wave solutions, it is a crystalline ammonium sulfate compound. Used for dehairing hides, in photography, as a chemical reducing agent, and to purify aldehydes (see) and ketones (see). Also used for making paints and varnishes, in rust proofing, and in the manufacture of synthetic rubbers. An irritant to the skin.

HYDROXYLATE • The process in which an atom of hydrogen and an atom of oxygen are introduced into a compound to make the compound more soluble.

HYDROXYQUINOLINE • See Oxyquinoline Sulfate.

HYDROXYQUINOLINE SULFATE • Pale yellow powder with a slight saffron odor and burning taste. It is used as an antiseptic, antiperspirant, deodorant, and fungicide.

HYPERSENSITIVITY • The condition in persons previously exposed to an antigen, in which tissue damage results from an immune reaction to a further dose of the antigen. Classically, four types of hypersensitivity are recognized, but the term is often used to mean the type of allergy associated with hay fever and asthma.

HYPO- • Prefix from the Greek, meaning "under" or "below," as in hypoacidity—acidity in a lesser degree than is usual or normal.

HYPOCHLORITE • A solution of a metallic salt of hypochlorous acid, which is formed by the action of water on chlorine. A strong oxidizing agent, used in the bleaching of textiles, as an antiseptic agent, and as a swimming pool sanitizer. An irritant to skin and eyes.

IAQ • The abbreviation for Indoor Air Quality.

IDLH • **Immediately Dangerous to Life or Health**. A term that is used to describe an environment that is very hazardous due to high concentrations of toxic chemical(s), insufficient oxygen, or both.

IMIDAZOLE • Made from ammonia and glyoxal, it is very soluble in water. Used to control insects, especially fabric-feeding bugs. Less toxic than organophosphates.

IMIDAZOLIDINYL UREA • A germ killer and preservative widely used in cosmetics. Has low oral toxicity but allergic reactions have been reported.

INCOMPATIBLE • A term used describe materials that could cause dangerous reactions from direct contact with one another.

INDANTHRENE® • **Indanthrene Blue R.** A blue dye or pigment derived from aminoanthroquinone. Used in dyeing cotton, and as a pigment in quality paints and enamels. *See* Coal Tar.

INDELIBLE INKS • Contain nigrosine dyes, a class of dark blue or black dyes and solvents. May also contain carbon or lamp black, naphthas, toluene, or xylene *(see all)*. Toxic if swallowed.

INDIGO • Probably the oldest known dye. Dark blue powder with a coppery luster. Prepared from various indigofera plants native to Bengal, Java, and Guatemala, or made synthetically from aniline *(see)*. Used in textile dyeing, printers' inks, and paints. No known skin irritation.

INERT INGREDIENT • A component of a compound (such as a solvent or carrier) that is not active against the job specified, such as cleaning up dirt or killing pests. Unlike the active ingredient, the inert is not toxic to target pests in pesticides but, nonetheless, may cause health effects in humans. For example, while methylene chloride *(see)* is used as an inert ingredient in some pesticides, CPSC (the Consumer Product Safety Commission) is issuing special labeling requirements for some consumer products containing this chemical due to its potential to cause a variety of health effects. In 1987, the EPA identified fifty-seven inerts that have known toxic effects, or which are structurally similar to other compounds with known toxicity. The EPA is in the process of requesting additional health and environmental effects data about inerts from pesticide producers. As of now, the majority of inerts, whether toxic or not, do not have to be listed on the label.

INGESTION • Taking in or swallowing a substance through the mouth.

INHALATION • Breathing in a substance.

INITIATOR • A substance or agent that can start the process of cancer.

INK ERADICATOR • Active agents are tin, sodium bisulfite, sodium hypochlorite, and sodium chloride *(see all)*. The eradicator can cause contact dermatitis. Corrosive if swallowed. The ink removers for ballpoint pens contain alcohols, glycol ethers, surfactants, naphthas, chlorinated hydrocarbons, and emulsifiers. Hair spray followed by soap and water can often remove ink stains.

INK-STAIN REMOVER • *See* Stain Remover.

INKS • **Marking Pens. Newsprint.** May contain acid and basic dyes, iron salts, tannic acid, gallates, phenol, silver nitrate, alkalies, castor oil *(see all)*. May also contain toluene, naphtha and xylene, which are subject to inhalation abuse and may cause brain and nerve damage. The odor of inks can trigger allergic respiratory reactions, and touching them can cause allergic contact dermatitis. Many people who are allergic to flaxseed are also allergic to inks. *See* Acacia Gum, Printing Inks, Indelible Ink, and Ballpoint Ink.

INSECT REPELLENTS • Used to prevent gnats and other insects from biting and annoying people. Common active ingredients include diethyl toluamide, dimethyl phthalate, ethyl hexanediol, indalone, di *n*-propylisocinchoronate, bicycloheptane dicarboximide, and tetrahydro furaldehyde. Diethyl toluamide (DEET) is present in most repellents, ranging in concentration from 7 to 100 percent. It is listed on the labels as *N*,*N*-Diethyl-*m*-toluamide. Some products are 100 percent DEET. In 1991, New York State health officials warned consumers not to use insect repellents with high levels of the chemical because of health risks. They also proposed that such products be banned. DEET-related health problems include skin rashes and scarring in adults, and in a few cases produced neurological problems in children, such as loss of coordination and mental confusion. The officials claimed that products with lower concentrations of DEET were just as effective as those with high concentrations. Major producers of DEET answered, at the time, that DEET formulas have been used since the 1950s and are safe and effective when used as directed. Another ingredient in insect repellents, indalone, has caused liver and kidney damage in animals. Ethyl hexanediol may also cause liver and kidney damage. Ingestion of large amounts of insect repellents can cause loss of coordination, central nervous system depression, and coma. If you must use products containing DEET, indalone, or ethyl hexanediol, use a minimum amount, do not put on irritated or sunburned skin, and do not put on a child's hands. Keep all insect repellents out of reach of children. A safer alternative may be products containing citronella oil as the active ingredient. You may also try rubbing some bath oil on the skin. Some people have found that it works as an insect repellent.

INSECTICIDAL SOAP • Contains potassium salts of fatty acids *(see)*. Used to control aphids, mealybugs, white fly, scales, and spider mites on houseplants. Harmful if swallowed and should not be used where food may be contaminated but it is less toxic than most other insecticides.

INSECTICIDES • Pesticides aimed at killing bugs. The inorganic type of product may contain arsenic, lead, and copper, but is not used very much anymore because it is highly toxic to humans. The natural organic compounds such as rotenone and pyrethrins *(see both)* are relatively harmless since they quickly decompose to nontoxic compounds. Also among these natural compounds are nicotine, copper naphthenate, and petroleum derivatives. Synthetic organic compounds include chlorinated hydrocarbons such as chlordane, dichlorobenzene, and the parathions. Among newer insecticides are insect-growth regulators and natural predators such as beetle-eating wasps, and insect-killing bacteria that is harmless to humans. The chemical insecticides, with the exceptions of the pyrethrins and rotenones, are toxic in varying degrees. Most of the organophosphorous types, such as parathion, are highly toxic. Deaths have occurred by wearing clothes that were contaminated with the insecticide and then laundered. *See also* Pesticides, Fumigants, Herbicides, and Rodenticides.

INSOLUBLE METALWORKING FLUID • A type of liquid used in machine processes such as cutting or grinding. The insoluble type may be oily, amber to brown, and is usually found in extreme-pressure agents. The insolubles may cause skin rash, cancer, and pneumonia if precautions are not taken against exposure, according to the Hazard Evaluation System and Information Service of California. *See* Metalworking Fluids.

INSULATION • Generally refers to materials that are used to insulate temperature, such as mineral fibers, aluminum silicate, cellulose, and glass fibers. Other materials include plastic foams and cellular rubber.

INTERMEDIATE • A chemical substance found as part of a necessary step between one organic compound and other, as in the production of dyes, pharmaceuticals, or other artificial products that develop properties only upon oxidation. An intermediate is used, for instance, in hair-dye bases that have dyeing action only when exposed to oxygen.

IODINE • Discovered in 1811, and classed among the rarer earth elements, it is found in the earth's crust as bluish black scales. Nearly two hundred products contain this chemical. They are prescription and over-the-counter medications. Iodine compounds are used as expectorants and thinners, particularly in the treatment of asthma, and in contrast media for X rays and fluroscopy. Iodine is also used in dyes, germicides, photographic film, water treatment, and medicinal soaps. It can produce a diffuse, red, pimply rash, hives, asthma, and, sometimes, anaphylactic shock.

IPECAC • Used as a denaturant in alcohol. From the dried rhizome and roots of *Cephaelis ipecacuanha*, a creeping South American plant with drooping flowers. Used to induce vomiting in poisonings. Fatal dose in humans is as low as 20 milligrams per kilogram of body weight. Irritating when taken internally, but no known toxicity on the skin.

IPRODIONE • Colorless crystals from methane; used as a fungicide.

IRRITANT • A substance that can cause an inflammatory response or reaction of the eye, skin, or respiratory system.

IRRITATION • Unlike allergic contact dermatitis, irritant contact dermatitis a more common type—is a nonallergic inflammatory skin reaction caused by exposure to irritating substances that actually damage the skin. Not everyone is allergic but everyone's skin can become irritated. Contact with strong irritants such as acid or lye can result in blisters, erosion, and ulcers within minutes or hours. For weaker irritants, such as soaps or detergents, exposure over days or weeks may be necessary before symptoms occur.

ISO- • Greek for "equal." In chemistry, *iso-* is a prefix added to the name of one compound to denote another composed of the same kinds and numbers of atoms, but different in structural arrangement.

ISOAMYL ACETATE • *See* Amyl Acetate.

ISOAMYL ALCOHOL • A clear liquid with a pungent odor and replusive taste, used in photographic chemicals, as a solvent, and in pharmaceutical products. A skin and eye irritant, a suspected cancer-causing agent, and moderately toxic when ingested.

ISOBUTANE • A constituent of natural gas and illuminating gas, colorless and insoluble in water, and used in refrigeration plants, synthetic rubber, and motor fuels. Also used as a propellant for aerosols. Highly flammable. *See* Paraffin and Propellant.

ISOBUTYL STEARATE • The ester of isobutyl alcohol and stearic acid. Used in waterproof coatings, polishes, face creams, rouges, ointments, soaps, dyes, and lubricants. No known toxicity.

ISOBUTYLENE/ISOPRENE COPOLYMER • *See* Butyl Rubber.

ISOBUTYLENE/MALEIC ANHYDRIDE COPOLYMER • A copolymer of isobutylene and maleic anhydride monomers derived from petroleum and used as a resin. A strong irritant.

ISOCYANATES • **Toluene Diisocyanate (TDI). Methylene bis-Phenylisocyanate (MDI). Hexamethylene Diisocyanate (HDI). Naphthalene Diisocyanate (NDI). Methylene bis-Cyclohexyl-isocyanate (HMDI). Isophorone Diisocyanate (IPDI). Centari®. Imron®. Nacconate®. Rubinate®. Desmodur®. Isonate®. Niax®. Hylene®. Mondur®. PAPI®.** Isocyanates are the raw materials from which all polyurethane products are made. Jobs that may involve exposure to isocyanates include painting, foam-blowing, and the manufacture of many products, such as chemicals, polyurethane foam and rubber, insulation products, surface coatings, car seats, furniture, foam mattresses, undercarpet padding, packaging materials, shoes, laminated fabrics, adhesives, and other polyurethane products. The most commonly used isocyanates are TDI and MDI. TDI is used mainly to make soft, flexible foams for padding or insulation. MDI is used mainly to make hard, rigid foams for insulation in buildings, vehicles, and refrigeration and industrial equipment. Isocyanates are also widely used in surface coatings such as paints, sealants, and finishes, and in the manufacture of rubbery plastics such as those used to coat wires. Isocyanates chemically react to form a solid polyurethane foam or a plastic coating. The finished product is almost nontoxic, unless it is burned or caused to generate dust. The isocyanates in single-component coating products are already chemically reacted, so that very little of the raw isocyanate remains. Two-component coating products contain unreacted isocyanates and are usually much more hazardous with which to work. Isocyanates that evaporate into the air can affect the lungs, particularly causing asthma. According to California's Hazard Evaluation System and Information Service, about one out of twenty people becomes sensitized to them and has asthma attacks any time isocyanates are present in the air. Isocyanates can cause severe skin rashes upon contact or even inhalation. They are very irritating to the eyes, nose, and throat. TDA is known to cause cancer in laboratory animals. Most other isocyanates have not been tested. The California/OSHA *(see)* limit for worker exposure to isocyanates is that it not exceed 0.005 ppm over an eight-hour period.

ISOPENTANE • A volatile, flammable, liquid hydrocarbon found in petroleum, and used as a solvent in cosmetics, and the manufacture of chlorine-containing compounds. A skin irritant. Narcotic in high doses. Highly flammable.

ISOPHORONE • A watery liquid used as a solvent for vinyl mixtures, nitrocellulose resins, pesticides, and lacquers. Irritant to skin and eyes. *See* Grease Removers.

ISOPRENE • A component of natural rubber, insoluble in water but soluble in alcohol, ether, and solvents. It is derived from petroleum and is used in the manufacture of butyl rubber and synthetic rubber compounds. Irritating to the skin and mucous membranes, and narcotic in high doses. Highly flammable.

ISOPROPANOL • *See* Isopropyl Alcohol.

ISOPROPANOLAMINE • An emulsifying agent with a light ammonia odor, soluble in water. Used as a plasticizer and in insecticides, as well as in cosmetic creams. A strong irritant, it is moderately toxic by ingestion, inhalation, and skin absorption. Occasionally causes sensitization. Narcotic in high concentrations. A fire hazard when exposed to heat or flame.

ISOPROPYL ACETATE • The ester of isopropyl alcohol and acetic acid, a colorless liquid with a strong odor, it is used as a solvent for resin, gums, inks, cellulose, and lacquers. Flammable.

ISOPROPYL ALCOHOL • **Isopropanol.** An antibacterial, solvent, and denaturant *(see)*. It is prepared from propylene, which is obtained in the cracking of petroleum. Used in antifreeze compositions, and as a solvent for gums, shellac, and essential oils. Also used in many cosmetics. Rubbing alcohol contains 70 percent isopropyl alcohol. Ingestion or inhalation of large quantities of the vapor may cause flushing, headache, dizziness, mental depression, nausea, vomiting, narcosis, anesthesia, and coma. The fatal ingested dose is around a fluid ounce. Has low skin toxicity, but alcohol baths for fever have caused toxicity through skin absorption, or inhalation. Workers exposed to it show an excess of sinus and throat cancers. A fire hazard.

ISOPROPYL CREOSOLS • *See* Cresol.

ISOPROPYL ESTER OF PVM/MA COPOLYMER • A polymer *(see)* used as a resin. See Polyvinyl Alcohol.

ISOPROPYL ETHER • A colorless, volatile liquid derived from propane *(see)*, and used as a solvent for a wide variety of products. It is found in small amounts of alcohol, paint and varnish removers, and rubber cements. Toxic by inhalation, and a strong irritant. A fire hazard when exposed to heat or flame.

ISOPROPYLAMINE DODECYLBENZENESULFONATE • *See* Quaternary Ammonium Compounds.

IVORY SNOW™, LIQUID • A nonionic detergent containing sodium alkyl ethoxylate sulfate *(see)*.

J

JAPAN WAX • **Japan Tallow. Sumac Wax. Vegetable Wax.** A fat squeezed from the fruit of a tree grown in Japan and China. Pale yellow, flat cakes, disks or squares, with a fatlike, rancid odor and taste. Used as a substitute for beeswax in cosmetic ointments; also in floor waxes and polishes. It is related to poison ivy and may cause allergic contact dermatitis.

JAPANESE WHITE OIL • *See* Camphor Oil.

JEWELRY CLEANERS • Usually contains a fatty acid, ammonia, isopropanol *(see all)*, dye, perfume, and water. May also contain cyanide or thiourea, sulfuric acid and/or polyethylene glycols *(see all)*. For those who work professionally making or cleaning jewelry, the California Occupational Health Program maintains there is no need to use cyanide-containing products anymore since special alloys are now available that are bright and need no stripping. At home, you can use baking soda or toothpaste to clean your gold jewelry. For silver pieces, you can use two tablespoons of cream of tartar and a sheet of aluminum foil placed in a bowl of hot water. Let the silver jewelry sit in the solution for an hour and then rinse off with plain water.

JOINT COMPOUNDS • Fillers for pipes, wall boards, and other building materials that are "joined" together. Contain casein, ammonium oxalate, ammonium borate or sodium pentachlorophenate, asbestos, mica, and calcium carbonate *(see all)*.

JOY® DISHWASHING DETERGENT • Contains ammonium alkyl ethoxylate sulfate, ammonium alkyl sulfate, ethanol, alkylamine oxide, ammonium xylene sulfonate, and minor ingredients. Another formula for Joy® also contains magnesium alkyl ethoxylate sulfate. *See* Detergents and Dishwashing Detergents (Hand).

JUTE • An East Indian plant belonging to the genus *Corchorus* from which strong, glossy fibers are obtained. It is of great commercial importance because, next to cotton, it is the most widely used natural fiber. Used in sacks, twine, mats, and furniture. May cause contact dermatitis, and may mix with house dust *(see)* and cause respiratory allergies.

K

KAOLIN • **China Clay.** Essentially a hydrated aluminum silicate *(see)*, it is a white or yellowish white mass or powder, insoluble in water, and absorbent. Originally obtained from Kaoling, a hill in Kiangsi province, southeast China. Used in the manufacture of porcelain, pottery, bricks, and colors. Also used in baby powder, bath powder, face masks, foundation cake makeup, and other cosmetics. Aids in the covering ability of face powder, and absorbing oils secreted by the skin. Used medicinally to treat intestinal disorders, but in large doses may cause obstructions, perforations, or granuloma (tumor) formation. No known toxicity for the skin.

KAPOK • Cottonlike fibers obtained from the seedpods of various species of bombax and ceiba trees grown in Ecuador, the Philippines, and Indonesia. Light and resilient, it is used in life jackets, insulation, pillows, and upholstery. Flammable.

KARAYA GUM • *See* Gum Karaya.

KELP • Recovered from the giant Pacific marine plant *Macrocystis pyriferae,* it is used as a fertilizer and in plastics. No known toxicity.

KEROSENE • A white, oily liquid with a strong odor derived from petroleum. Used in rocket, jet engine diesel and tractor fuels, for domestic heating, as a solvent, in insecticidal sprays, in lamps and flares, and as a degreaser and cleaner. Also used in waterless hand cleaners. Researchers at John B. Pierce Foundation Laboratories in New Haven, Conn., have found that the use of kerosene heaters is associated with chronic upper- and lower-respiratory symptoms in infants age six to twenty-four months, a particularly sensitive group, and causes cough, phlegm, wheezing, and runny/stuffy nose symptoms. At this writing, the researchers were also testing mothers exposed to kerosene heaters. Kerosene is a moderate fire risk, potentially explosive, toxic by inhalation, and causes headache, drowsiness, and coma. Also has a defatting action on the skin that can lead to irritation and infection. Swallowing can cause diarrhea and vomiting, but vomiting should not be induced. Aspiration of vomitus can cause pneumonia.

KETONES • Acetone, Methyl, or Ethyl. Aromatic substances obtained by the oxidation of secondary alcohols. Ethereal or aromatic odor, generally insoluble in water, but soluble in alcohol or ether. Solvents are used for fats, oils, waxes, resins, rubber, plastics, lacquers, varnishes, rubber cements, nail polish, and nail polish removers. Reportedly not skin sensitizers. *See* Acetone for skin toxicity. *See also* Clothing.

Kg • Abbreviation for kilogram *(see)*.

KIESELGUHR • *See* Silica.

KILOGRAM • Kg. A metric unit of mass equaling 1,000 grams *(see)*, or about 2.2046 pounds.

KRAZY GLUE® • *See* Cyanoacrylate.

KWELL® • *See* Lindane.

L

LABELS • May contain rosins and/or corn. May cause allergic-contact dermatitis.

LACQUER • A decorative or protective coating. May contain nitrocellulose, ester gum, cottonseed oil, synthetic resins from cotton or soya beans, pigments, nitric acid, lead oxide, or magnesium oxide. A Japanese lacquer tree contains a lacquer related to poison ivy that is used on some furniture. Most lacquers are highly flammable. *See* Shellac.

LACQUER THINNER • May contain toluene *(see)*, which can be abused by inhalation and cause nerve and brain damage, hallucinations, lethargy, and coma. May also contain ethyl alcohol, ethyl acetate, butyl alcohol, butyl acetate, aliphatic hydrocarbons plus amyl acetate, isopropyl acetate, isopropyl alcohol, pigment, and xylene *(see all)*. *See also* Solvents.

LACTIC ACID • Butyl Lactate. Ethyl Lactate. Odorless, colorless, usually a syrupy product normally present in blood and muscle tissue as a product of the metabolism of glucose and glycogen. Present in sour milk, beer, sauerkraut, pickles, and other food products made by bacterial fermentation. Also an acidulant. It is produced commercially by fermentation of whey, cornstarch, potatoes, and molasses. Used as an acidulant in beverages, candy, olives, dried egg whites, cottage cheese, confections, bread, rolls, buns, cheese products, frozen desserts, sherbets, ices, fruit jelly, butter, preserves, jams (sufficient amounts may be added to compensate for the deficiency of fruit acidity), and in the brewing industry. Also used in infant-feeding formulas. Used in blackberry, butter, butterscotch, lime, chocolate, fruit, walnut, spice, and cheese flavorings for beverages, ice cream, ices, candy, baked goods, gelatins, puddings, chewing gum, toppings, pickles, and olives (24,000 ppm). Also used in skin fresheners. It is caustic in concentrated solutions when taken internally or applied to the skin. In cosmetic products, it may cause stinging in sensitive people, particularly in fair-skinned women. The final report to the FDA of The Select Committee on GRAS Substances stated in 1980 that it should continue its GRAS status with no limitations other than good manufacturing practices.

LAMPBLACK • A bluish black, fine soot deposited on a surface by burning liquid hydrocarbons *(see)* such as oil. Duller and less intense in color than other carbon blacks, and has a blue undertone. Used in pigments for paints, enamels, and printing inks. *See* Carbon Black for toxicity.

LANETH-5 THROUGH -40 • Emulsifiers. *See* Lanolin Alcohols.

LANETH-9 AND -10 ACETATE • Emulsifiers. *See* Lanolin Alcohols.

LANOLIN • **Wool Fat. Wool Wax.** A product of the oil glands of sheep. Widely used in cosmetics, leather finishing, soaps, and facial tissues. Lanolin has been found to be a common skin sensitizer causing allergic contact skin rashes. It is not used in pure form today because of its allergy-causing potential. Products derived from it are less likely to cause allergic reactions.

LANOLIN ALCOHOLS • **Sterols, triterpene, alcohols. Aliphatic alcohols.** Derived from lanolin *(see)*, lanolin alcohols are available commercially as solid waxy materials that are yellow to amber in color or as pale to golden yellow liquids. They are widely used as emulsifiers and emollients in hand creams and lotions and while less likely to cause an allergic reaction than lanolin, still may do so in the sensitive.

LATENCY • The time between exposure and the first appearance of an effect.

LATEX • **Synthetic Rubber.** The milky, usually white juice or exudate of fig, and rubber trees, and other plants, obtained by tapping. Used in beauty masks for its coating ability, and in balloons, condoms, and gloves. Any of various gums, resins, fats, or waxes in an emulsion of water and synthetic rubber of plastic are now considered latex. Ingredients of latex compounds can be poisonous, depending upon which plant products are used. Can cause skin rash. In May 1991, the FDA cautioned doctors and manufacturers about potential allergic reactions to latex products. Allergic reactions caused the deaths of four patients undergoing medical procedures involving an inflatable latex cuff. The FDA also reported fifty cases of life-threatening allergic reactions involving latex gloves and, in other instances, caused by contact with rubber dental devices, balloons, and racquetball handles.

LATHER • Produced by action of air bubbles in a soap solution.

LAURALKONIUM BROMIDE • *See* Quaternary Ammonium Compounds.

LAURALKONIUM CHLORIDE • *See* Quaternary Ammonium Compounds.

LAURAMIDE DEA • A mixture of ethanolamides of lauric acid, the principal fatty acid of coconut oil. Used widely in cosmetic soaps and detergents as a softener and foam inhibitor. *See* Lauric Acid.

LAURAMIDE MEA • *See* Lauric Acid.

LAURAMIDE MIPA • A mixture of isopropanolamides of lauric acid used widely as a wetting agent in soaps and detergents. *See* Lauric Acid.

LAURAMIDOPROPYL DIMETHYLAMINE • *See* Lauric Acid and Dimethylamine.

LAURAMINE OXIDE • *See* Lauric Acid.

LAURAMINOPROPIONIC ACID • *See* Propionic Acid.

LAURETH-1, -23 • *See* Lauryl Alcohol.

LAURIC ACID • *n*-**Dodecanoic Acid.** A common constituent of vegetable fats, especially coconut oil and laurel oil. Its derivatives are used widely as a base in the manufacture of soaps, detergents, and lauryl alcohol *(see)* because of their foaming properties. Has a slight odor of bay and makes large, copious bubbles when in soap. A mild irritant, but not a sensitizer.

LAURIC ALDEHYDE • *See* Lauric Acid.

LAUROAMPHOACETATE • A preservative. *See* Imidazolidinyl Urea.

LAUROAMPHODIACETATE • A preservative. *See* Imidazolidinyl Urea.

LAUROAMPHODIPROPIONATE • *See* Lauric Acid and Propionic Acid.

LAUROAMPHODIPROPIONIC ACID • A preservative. *See* Lauric Acid and Propionic Acid.

LAUROAMPHODROXYPROPYLSULFONATE • *See* Imidazolidinyl Urea.

LAUROAMPHOPROPINOATE • *See* Lauric Acid and Propionic Acid.

LAUROYL HYDROLYZED ANIMAL PROTEIN • A condensation product of lauric acid chloride and hydrolyzed animal protein *(see)*, used in soaps.

LAURTRIMONIUM CHLORIDE • *See* Quaternary Ammonium Compounds.

LAURYL ALCOHOL • **1-Dodecanol.** A colorless, crystalline compound that is produced commercially from coconut oil. Used to make detergents because of its sudsing ability. Has a characteristic fatty odor. Soluble in most oils, but insoluble in glycerin. Used in perfumery. *See* Lauric Acid for toxicity.

LAURYL AMINE • *See* Lauric Acid.

LAURYL AMINOPROPYLGLYCINE • *See* Lauryl Alcohol and Glyceric Acid.

LAURYL BETAINE • *See* Lauric Acid.

LAURYL DIETHLENDIAMINEGLYCINE • *See* Lauryl Alcohol.

LAURYL DIMETHLAMINE ACRYLINOLATE • *See* Lauric Acid and Dimethylamine.

LAURYL DIMETHYLAMINE ACRYLINOLATE • *See* Acylic Acid.

LAURYL GLYCOL • *See* Lauryl Alcohol and Glycol.

LAURYL HYDROXYETHYL IMIDAZOLINE • *See* Imidazole.

LAURYL ISOQUINOLINIUM BROMIDE • A quaternary ammonium compound *(see)*. Used as an agricultural fungicide.

LAURYL ISOSTEARATE • The ester of lauryl alcohol and isostearic acid *(see both)*.

LAURYL LACTATE • *See* Lauric Acid and Lactic Acid.

LAURYL METHACRYLATE • *See* Lauric Acid and Acrylates.

LAURYL PALMITATE • The ester *(see)* of lauryl alcohol and palmitic acid *(see both)*.

LAURYL PYRIDINIUM CHLORIDE • *See* Quaternary Ammonium Compounds.

LAURYL STEARATE • The ester of lauryl alcohol and stearic acid *(see both)*.

LAURYL SULFATE • Derived from lauryl alcohol *(see)*. Its potassium, zinc, magnesium, sodium, calcium, and ammonium salts are used in shampoos for their foaming properties. *See* Sodium Lauryl Sulfate.

LAURYL SULTAINE • *See* Lauryl Alcohol and Betaine.

LAVANDIN OIL • The essential oil of a hybrid related to the lavender plant. Fragrant, yellowish, with a camphor-lavender scent. Used in soaps and perfumes.

LAWN-CARE CHEMICALS • A great deal of concern was expressed in 1991 by legislators and environmentalists about the chemicals used to create and maintain green lawns. Synthetic products usually release their nutrients all at once, provide green, weedless lawns quickly, and are less expensive than organic products. They can run off into streams, may be highly toxic, and children and pets must be kept off the lawn for a period of time after application to avoid exposure. The synthetics can soak down into underground water supplies, kill earthworms, beneficial bugs and bacteria, and overstimulate the grass. Organic products such as manure and bone meal usually act more slowly, and there is less runoff than with synthetics. As the organic products decompose, they condition the soil, and there is less danger involved in handling them, however, they are more expensive than synthetic and sometimes not as effective.

To cut down on the use of all lawn chemicals:

• test your soil to determine lime and fertilizer needs before treating.

• grow the appropriate grass for your yard.

• read and follow label instructions.

• treat specific problems instead of using general weed or insect killers.

• do not apply chemicals on a windy day.

• do not cut more than one-third of grass blade height at one time.

• use organic alternatives whenever possible.

• wear long sleeves, pants, hat, dust mask, and gloves and shoes of the most impermeable material (plastic or rubber is better than canvas or leather).

• if clothing comes in contact with pesticides, change immediately and wash it separately. Wash gloves thoroughly before removing them.

• keep children and pets aways from treated areas for 24 hours if possible.

• when your lawn or your neighbor's lawn is being treated, close house and car windows, turn off air conditioners, and remove or cover lawn furniture, toys, swimming pools, fish ponds, hoses, pets' bowls, and bird feeders.

• before choosing a lawn-care company, check to see if the service is licensed by your state and ask what specific training employees have. If treatment is recommended, ask what specific problems exist and what chemical the service plans to use before you sign an agreement.

The General Accounting Office, the investigative arm of Congress, criticized the EPA's failure to complete reviewing two of the most popular home pesticides: Diazinon™, an insecticide that is the most widely used lawn pesticide and is linked with bird kills, and 2,4-D, a common weed killer with possible links to cancer *(see both)*. The EPA has banned use of Diazinon™ on golf courses and sod farms. The National Academy of Sciences has reported that homeowners use four to eight times as many chemical pesticides per acre as farmers. *See* Cadmium, Pesticides, Insecticides, Pyrethrins, Siduron, Tempo2®, and Insecticidal Soap.

LC50 • **Lethal Concentration-50 Percent.** A concentration of chemical in air that will kill 50 percent of the test animals inhaling it.

LD50 • **Lethal Dose-50 Percent.** The dose of a chemical that will kill 50 percent of the test animals receiving it. The chemical may be given by mouth, applied to the skin, or injected. A given chemical will generally show different LD50 values depending on how it is given to the animals. A coarse measure of acute toxicity.

LEAD ACETATE • **Sugar of Lead.** Colorless, white crystals or grains with an acetic odor. Bubbles slowly. Has been used as a topical astringent but is absorbed through the skin and, therefore, might lead to lead poisoning. Also used in hair dyeing and printing colors. Still used to treat bruises and skin irritations in animals. Not recommended for use in humans because of the possibility of lead buildup in the body. Permission was given in 1981 by the FDA to use this in progressive hair dyes, although it is a proven carcinogen. Permanently listed in 1969 as a color component of hair dye, with a caution required on the package that it "should not be used on cut or abraded scalp." *See* Lead Compounds.

LEAD-BASED PAINT • A major source of lead poisoning, particularly for young children. Lead was used as a pigment and drying agent in oil-based paint. Latex water-based paints generally do not contain lead. About 75 percent of the homes built before 1940 and 50 percent of the homes built from 1940 to 1960 contain heavily leaded paints. Some homes built after 1960 may also contain heavily leaded paints. It may be on any interior or exterior surface, particularly on woodwork, doors, and windows. In 1978, the U.S. Consumer Product Safety Commission lowered the legal maximum lead content in most kinds of paint to 0.6 percent. Exposure occurs when lead-based paint "chalks," chips, or peels from deteriorated surfaces. Walking on small paint chips on the floor, or opening and closing a painted frame window, can also create lead dust.

If you have lead-based paint, you should take steps to reduce your exposure by:

• having the painted items replaced. (Doors or windows are easily removed but other items may have to be replaced by professionals who will control lead dust.)

• covering lead-based paint with a sealant or gypsum wallboard. However, painting over lead-based paint with nonlead-based paint is not a long-term solution because the lead will still be released as the new paint begins to deteriorate.

• having the lead-based paint removed by a professional trained in the process.

• reducing lead dust exposure by frequently wet mopping and wiping surfaces and floors with a high-phosphorous (at least 5 percent) cleaning solution. Wear waterproof gloves to prevent skin irritations.

LEAD COMPOUNDS • Workers in more than 120 occupations are exposed to lead. Automotive and industrial batteries now account for about 80 percent of all lead consumed in the United States. Other important current uses of lead include X ray and radiation shielding, cable sheathing, acoustical damping, and numerous applications in the electronics and computer industries. Lead also is being evaluated as a protective barrier against radon exposure in homes. A few industries where significant lead exposure is common, in addition to battery manufacture, are construction and demolition; radiator repair; lead smelting; and in foundries, in the casting of lead, brass, or bronze. Lead also is used in ointments and hair dye pigments.

Lead can enter your body in two ways: inhalation and ingestion.

You can inhale lead when lead dust, mist, or fumes are present in the air you breathe. Particles of lead can be swallowed if lead gets on your hands, face, or clothing, or into your food or drink. Other sources of lead include deposits that may be present in and around homes after years of using leaded gasoline, and from industrial sources such as smelting. You also can generate lead dust by sanding, scraping or heating lead-based paint *(see)*. Lead dust can settle on floors, walls, and furniture. Sweeping or vacuuming, or movement of people through a house can cause lead to be inhaled. Lead paint-chips can also be a source of ingestion. Once lead gets into your body, it stays there for a long time. Lead can build up in your body if you are exposed to even small amounts for a long time. In general, the more lead in your body, the more likely that harm will occur. Lead may cause contact dermatitis. It is poisonous in all forms. It is one of the most hazardous of toxic metals because its poison is cumulative, and its toxic effects are many and severe. Among these are leg cramps, muscle weakness, numbness, depression, brain damage, coma, and death. Ingestion and inhalation of lead cause these most severe symptoms. The amount of lead in your blood can be measured to find out if you have been overexposed. Obvious symptoms of lead toxicity may occur in some people with levels as low as 40 micrograms of lead per deciliter of blood. In other people, symptoms may not begin until the blood lead level reaches 100 micrograms. *See also* Lead-Based Paint, and Lead Crystal.

LEAD CRYSTAL • The U.S. Food and Drug Administration advised in 1991 that consumers be cautious about lead crystal containers for foods, and beverages because large amounts of lead had been found in wine stored in crystal bottles. It recommended that lead crystal glasses not be used every day, and that foods or beverages not be stored in crystal, especially acidic juices, vinegar, or alcoholic beverages. Women of childbearing age should not use crystal ware and children should not be fed from crystal bottles or tumblers.

LEATHER DRESSING • Usually contains a vegetable wax, turpentine, a soap, a solvent, and one or several of the following: alcohol, natural resins, neat's-foot oil, plasticizers, soya bean oil, sperm oil, methyl polysiloxane, xylene, and a propellant. Tanneries have been looking for ways to replace solvents that could subject workers and the public to potentially harmful vapors. U.S. Agricultural Research Service scientists have found a way to use solvent-free formulations that can be applied to leather and cured by ultraviolet light. This produces attractive and durable products, while reducing health and environmental concerns. The process also saves energy costs for tanneries. It is, at this writing, being test-marketed.

LEATHER DYES • These contain methyl, ethyl or isopropyl alcohol, xylene, and aniline. May also contain nitrobenzene, dichlorobenzene, and trichloromethane *(see all)*. Toxic.

LEATHER GLUE • The rubber-type contains, in addition to 25 percent rubber, resins, toluene, hexane, and ethyl acetate. The polyvinyl acetate-type contains water, 50 percent polyvinyl acetate emulsion in water. Other leather glues are nitrocellulose cements or polystyrene-based adhesives. *See* Nitrocellulose and Polystyrene.

LEATHER POLISH • Usually contains carnauba wax and animal or vegetable oils with triethanolamine *(see)*. You can make your own with ¼ cup lanolin and ¼ cup food-grade linseed oil. Mix well and rub into leather with a soft cloth.

LECITHIN • From the Greek *lekithos,* meaning "egg yolk." A natural antioxidant and emollient found in all living tissue. Used as a surfactant, and in treating leather and textiles.

LEMON OIL • **Cedro Oil. Citrus Peel Oil.** The volatile oil expressed from the fresh peel; a pale yellow to deep yellow, with the characteristic odor and taste of the outer part of fresh lemon peel. Used in furniture polish, perfumes, and food flavorings. Can cause allergic reaction, and has been suspected of being a cancer-causing agent.

LEMONGRASS OIL • **Indian Oil of Verbena.** The volatile oil distilled from the leaves of lemongrasses. A yellowish or reddish brown liquid, it has a strong odor of verbena. Used in perfumes, especially those added to soap. Also used in insect repellents, and in fruit flavorings for foods and beverages. Death was reported when taken internally, and autopsy showed lining of the intestines was severely damaged. Skin toxicity unknown.

LENS CLEANER • Usually contains a surfactant *(see),* water, and alcohol or phosphate *(see).*

LESION • Any destructive change in the structure of organs or tissues.

LEUKEMIA • Cancer of the blood-forming organs.

LIGHTER FLUID • May contain naphtha *(see),* which can cause a narcotic-like syndrome, and is subject to inhalation abuse. May instead contain kerosene *(see).*

LIGNOCERIC ACID • Obtained from beechwood tar or by distillation of rotten oakwood. Occurs in most natural fats. Used in shampoos, soaps, and plastics. No known toxicity.

LIGNOL • *See* Lignoceric Acid.

LIME • *See* Calcium Oxide.

LIMONENE • **D,L and DL forms.** A synthetic flavoring agent that occurs naturally in star anise, buchu leaves, caraway, celery, oranges, coriander, cumin, cardamom, sweet fennel, common fennel, mace, marigold, oil of lavandin, oil of lemon, oil of mandarin, peppermint, petigrain oil, pimento oil, orange leaf (absolute), orange peel (sweet oil), origanum oil, black pepper, peels of citrus, macrocarpa bunge, and hops oil. Used in lime, fruit, and spice flavorings for beverages, ice cream, ices, candy, baked goods, gelatin desserts, and chewing gum. A skin irritant and sensitizer.

LINDANE • A pesticide that is poisonous by ingestion, inhalation, or skin absorption. In acute poisoning it causes dizziness, convulsions, shortness of breath, vomiting, diarrhea, tremors, weakness, and circulatory collapse. In chronic exposure, liver damage and sensitivity reactions may occur. Vapors may irritate the eyes, nose, and throat. Also a cancer-causing agent. Lindane was formerly used as a general-purpose insecticide against indoor pests. Because of concern over the potential long-term risks of cancer, the EPA, in 1986, canceled the registration of all indoor fumigating devices containing lindane. Check to see whether you have products still containing lindane around your home. *See* Pesticides.

LINOLEAMIDE DEA • Alkyl amides produced by a diethanolamine *(see)* condensation of linoleic acid *(see)*. Used as a foaming agent in soaps and shampoos.

LINOLEIC ACID • Used as an emulsifier. An essential fatty acid *(see)* prepared from edible fats and oils. Component of vitamin E and a major constituent of many vegetable oils, as, for example, cottonseed and soybean. Used in emulsifiers, vitamins, soaps, and protective coatings. Large doses can cause nausea and vomiting. No known skin toxicity and, in fact, may have emollient properties.

LINOLEYL ALCOHOL • A colorless, solid, fatty alcohol derived from linoleic acid, and used in paints, paper, surface-active agents, resins, and leathers. *See* Linoleic Acid.

LINOLEUM CEMENT • *See* Tile Adhesives.

LINOLEUM FLOOR CLEANER OR WAX • Mop with one cup of white vinegar mixed with two gallons of water to remove dull, greasy film. Polish with club soda. *See* Floor Polish.

LINSEED OIL • A yellowish oil that gradually thickens when exposed to air, expressed or extracted from flaxseed. It has a peculiar odor and a bland taste. Used in shaving creams, emollients, and medicinal soaps. Soothing to the skin. Also used in paint, varnish, oilcloth, putty, printing inks, packings, and linoleum. Can cause allergic reaction.

LIPSTICK-STAIN REMOVER • *See* Stain Remover.

LIQUID FURNITURE POLISH • Mineral seal oil *(see)*, and an alcohol. May be toxic on inhalation. *See also* Furniture Polish.

LIQUID PETROLEUM GAS • *See* LPG.

LIQUID SHOE POLISH • *See* Shoe Polish.

LITER • A metric unit of volume. One U.S. quart is about 0.9 liter. One liter equals 1,000 cubic centimeters.

LITHIUM CHLORIDE • A crystalline salt of the alkali metal, used as a scavenger in purifying metals, to remove oxygen, and in soaps and lubricant bases. The crystals absorb water and then become neutral or slighly alkaline. Also used in the manufacture of mineral waters, in soldering, and in refrigerating machines. Formerly used as a salt substitute. Prolonged absorption may cause disturbed electrolyte balance in humans, impair kidney function, and cause central nervous system problems.

LITHIUM HYDROXIDE • A granular, free-flowing, acrid, and strongly alkaline powder, the salt of the alkaline metal that absorbs water from the air, and is soluble in water. Used in making cosmetic resins and esters *(see both)*. Also used in photo developers and in batteries. Very irritating to the skin, and flammable in contact with the air.

LITHOPONE • **Pigment White. Griffith's Zinc White.** A white pigment consisting of zinc sulfate, barium sulfate, and some zinc oxide. Used in water and oil paints to improve gloss and flow. *See* Zinc and Barium Sulfate for toxicity.

LPG • **Liquid Petroleum Gas.** A colorless, odorless gas with a foul odor added commercially as a warning. A compressed gas obtained from by-products in petroleum refining or natural gasoline manufacture. Used as a fuel, in welding, and metal cutting. Impurities may cause narcosis or asphyxiation. Hazardous, with risk of fire and explosion when exposed to heat or flame.

LUBE OIL ADDITIVE • A chemical added to lubricating oils to impart special qualities. Some additives are butene polymers, stearate soaps, and silicones.

LUBRICANT, SYNTHETIC • Organic fluids that have properties not in petroleum-derived lubricants. More expensive than natural lubricants, they each have a special action. The major types are polyglycols (hydraulic and brake fluids), phosphate esters (fire resistant), and polyphenyl ethers (excellent heat and oxygen resistance).

LUBRICATING GREASE • A mixture of mineral oil or oils with one or more soaps. Greases range in consistency from thin liquids to solid blocks. Among the ingredients other than petroleum oils and soaps may contain barium, chromate, dye, graphite, lead compounds, talc, or zinc.

LUBRICATING OIL • **Lube Oil.** Mixtures of hydrocarbons that vary in chemical composition. All are derived from crude petroleum, together with low concentrations of nonpetroleum additives. Made from mineral oil, they are designed to lubricate moving surfaces. Frequent and prolonged contact may cause acnelike lesions. *See also* Motor Oil, Cutting Fluid, and Transmission Fluid.

LYCRA • *See* Spandex.

LYE • *See* Sodium Hydroxide, Potassium Hydroxide, and Calcium Hydroxide.

LYMPHOMA • A cancer that arises in lymph tissue.

LYSOL® BRAND DISINFECTANT (Regular) • An active ingredient, *o*-phenylphenol *(see)*, was cited among the top pesticides in the household environment, according to the nonoccupational personal-exposure study published by the EPA. The other ingredients are soap, *o*-benzyl-*p*-chlorophenol, alcohol, xylenols, isopropyl alcohol, and tetrasodium ethylenediamine tetraacetate *(see all)*.

LYSOL® BRAND PINE ACTION • Contains *N*-alkyl dimethyl ammonium chloride, and octyl decyl dimethyl ammonium chloride. *See* Ammonium Chloride.

LYSOL BRAND® TOILET BOWL CLEANER • Contains hydrochloric acid *(see)*.

M

MAGNESIUM • A silver-white, light, malleable metal that occurs abundantly in nature and is used widely as a powder in combination with various chemicals. Used in white and dry batteries. It was reevaluated by the FDA in 1976 and found not harmful at presently used levels. The World Health Organization recommended further studies because of kidney damage found in dogs that ingested it.

MAGNESIUM ACETATE • Made from the interaction of magnesium carbonate and acetic acid *(see both)*, and used as a dye fixative in textile printing, deodorants, disinfectants, and antiseptics.

MAGNESIUM ARSENATE • An insecticide made from magnesium carbonate and arsenic acid *(see both)*. Toxic by ingestion and inhalation.

MAGNESIUM BORATE • Derived from heating magnesium *(see)* and boric anhydride. Used as a preservative, antiseptic, and fungicide. *See also* Boron Oxide.

MAGNESIUM CARBONATE • A silver-white, very crystalline salt that occurs in nature as magnetite or dolomite *(see)*. Can be prepared artificially and is used in paint, printing ink, table salt, and as an antacid. Also a perfume carrier, anticaking agent, and coloring agent used in baby powder and cosmetics. Nontoxic to the intact skin, but may cause irritation when applied to abraded skin.

MAGNESIUM CHLORIDE • Derived from the action of hydrochloric acid on magnesium *(see both)*, it is used in disinfectants, fire extinguishers, for fireproofing wood, in refrigerating brines, in ceramics, sizing and filling of cotton and wool fabrics, thread lubricant, paper manufacture, and floor-sweeping compounds. Toxic by ingestion.

MAGNESIUM FLUOSILICATE • A white, crystalline powder derived by heating magnesium hydroxide with hydrofluosilicic acid. Used in ceramics, concrete hardeners, waterproofing, mothproofing, and some laundry products. A strong irritant.

MAGNESIUM LAURYL SULFATE • *See* Surfactants.

MAGNESIUM OXIDE • A white powder prepared by heating magnesium carbonate *(see),* and used in ceramics, electrical insulation, paper manufacture, fertilizers, as an inorganic rubber-accelerator, and as a food and feed additive. Toxic by inhalation of fumes.

MAGNESIUM PALMITATE • Used as a varnish drier, and as a lubricant for plastic. *See* Magnesium.

MAGNESIUM PHOSPHATE, MONOBASIC • Derived from magnesium hydroxide, it is used for fireproofing wood, and as a stabilizer for plastics. *See* Magnesium.

MAGNESIUM SILICATE • Derived from magnesium salt and silicate, it is used in rubber filler, paper filler, ceramics, glass, varnishes, and as an anticaking agent in foods. Toxic by inhalation.

MAGNESIUM SULFATE • Colorless crystals derived from the action of sulfuric acid on magnesium *(see both)*, and used in fireproofing, textiles, mineral waters, ceramics, fertilizers, paper, and cosmetic lotions.

MALATHION • A yellow liquid derived from diethyl maleate and dimethyldithiophosphoric acid, it is an insecticide against such pests as aphids, and leaf cutter bees. Also has been used against the Mediterranean fruit fly. Toxic when absorbed through the skin and can damage transmission of nerve signals. *See* Pesticides.

MALEIC ACID • Colorless crystals with a faint odor, derived from benzene. Used in dyeing and finishing cotton, wool, and silk, and as a preservative for oils and fats. Toxic by ingestion.

MALEIC ANHYDRIDE • Colorless needles derived from benzene, and used in polyester resins, pesticides, as a preservative for oils and fats, and in permanent-press resins. Irritating to tissue. *See* Benzene.

MALEIC HYDRAZIDE • Regulates the growth of unwanted "suckers" on about 90 percent of the U.S. tobacco crop It is also applied to 10 to 15 percent of domestic potatoes and onions to prevent sprouting after harvest. It is highly toxic to humans and has produced central nervous system disturbances and liver damage in experimental animals. It has led to liver and other tumors in some mice. It has produced genetic damage in plant and animal systems, a fact that often signals a cancer-causing effect.

MANCOZEB • **Fore (80W). Dithane M-45 (80W).** A fungicide derived from zinc, and used on fruits and vegetables and turfgrass. A suspected human carcinogen.

MANGANESE • Widely distributed, abundant steel gray element that constitutes .085 percent of the earth's crust. It occurs in minerals and in minute quantities in water, plants, and animals. Used in the manufacture of steel, for rock crushers, and in alloys. Toxic by inhalation of dust or fumes. Causes central nervous system disturbances.

MANGANESE ACETATE • Pale, red crystals derived from the action on manganese hydroxide. Used in textile dyeing, paint and varnish, fertilizers, food packaging, and feed additive. May cause central nervous system damage and pneumonia. One unusual reaction, according to an FDA article to overexposure, can be inappropriate laughter.

MANGANESE CARBONYL • Used in antiknock gasoline. Toxic. *See* Manganese.

MANGANESE NAPHTHENATE • A paint and varnish drier. *See* Manganese.

MANGANESE OCTOATE • A drier for paints, enamels, varnishes, and printing inks. *See* Manganese.

MANGANESE OLEATE • Used as a paint and varnish drier. *See* Manganese.

MANGANESE SULFATE • The salt of the element manganese, a metal ore. Usually prepared by dissolving dolomite *(see)* or magnetite in acid. Its pale, red crystals are used in red hair dye and to make red glazes on porcelain. Also used medicinally as a purgative, and as a dressing. No known toxicity to the skin but very small doses injected into mice are lethal.

MANGANOUS CHLORIDE • Pink crystals that absorb water. Used in paints, dyeing, and fertilizers. Toxic by inhalation.

MANGANOUS OXIDE • A green powder derived by heating carbonate, and used in textile printing, ceramics, paints, colored glass, bleaching tallow, fertilizers, and dietary supplements.

MARKING PENS • *See* Inks and Art Materials.

MARTIN'S RAT STOP LIQUID™ • A rat killer. *See* Thallium.

MATCHES • *See* Chromium.

MAVRIK AQUAFLOW® • An insecticide for use on indoor and outdoor ornamental plants, turf, trees, shrubs, and flowers. Contains fluvalinate *(see)*. May cause allergic reactions in people and pets. For indoor applications, a respirator should be worn and no one other than the person applying it should be present. Causes mild eye irritation. Harmful if absorbed through the skin. Rubber gloves should be worn.

MAXFORCE™ • **Hydramethylnon.** A pesticide *(see)*.

MBTE • The abbreviation for methyl-tert-butyl ether *(see)*. *See* also Gasoline.

MCPA • A herbicide. *See* Chlorophenoxy Derivatives.

MCPB • A herbicide. *See* Chlorophenoxy Derivatives.

MCPP • A herbicide. *See* Chlorophenoxy Derivatives.

MCS • Multiple Chemical Sensitivity *(see)*.

MEA • *See* Acetamide.

MEK • **Methyl Ethyl Ketone. 2-Butanone.** A flammable, colorless, liquid compound resembling acetone and most often made by taking the hydrogen out of butyl alcohol. It is a widely used solvent. Similar to, but more irritating than acetone, its vapor is irritating to mucous membranes and eyes. Central nervous system depression in experimental animals has been reported, but the irritating odor usually discourages further inhalation in humans. No serious poisonings reported in humans, except for skin irritation when nail polish was applied with MEK as a solvent. It enhances neurotoxicity of other solvents such as hexane and methyl *n*-butyl ketone. Large doses inhaled by rats are lethal.

MELAMINE • A white, free-flowing, powdered resin. Used in nail enamel. First introduced into industry in 1939, it is now used in a wide variety of products including boil-proof adhesives and scratch-resistant enamel finishes. Combined with urea resins, it forms the heat-resistant amino plastics. May cause skin rash, but this is believed to be caused by the formaldehyde component rather than the melamine. See Urea-Formaldehyde Resin.

MELTING POINT • The temperature at which a solid substance changes to the liquid state.

MENTHOL • Used in perfumes, emollient creams, hair tonics, mouthwashes, shaving creams, preshave lotions, after-shave lotions, body rubs, liniments, and skin fresheners. It gives that "cool" feeling to the skin after use. It can be obtained naturally from peppermint or other mint oils and can be made synthetically by hydrogenation (see) of thymol (see). It is a local anesthetic. It is nontoxic in low doses, but in high concentrations it exerts an irritant action that can, if continued long, induce changes in all layers of the mucous membranes.

MERCAPTAN • See Thiol.

MERCAPTOBENZOTHIAZOLE • Rubber-compound accelerator and anticorrosion agent. Can cause allergic contact dermatitis.

MERCERIZING • See Clothing.

MERCURIC CHLORIDE • White, odorless crystals or powder, derived by combining chlorine with mercury (see both). Used in tanning, as a sterilant for seed potatoes, a fungicide, insecticide and wood preservative, in embalming fluids, textile printings, dry batteries, photography, engraving, and lithography. Toxic by ingestion and inhalation.

MERCURIC NAPHTHENATE • A dark, amber liquid derived from mercury and naphtha (see both), and used as a mildew preventative in paints.

MERCURIC OXIDE, RED • Derived from mercury (see), the orange-red powder is used in paint pigment, ceramics, dry batteries, polishing compounds, fungicides, and antiseptics. Highly toxic.

MERCURY • **Quicksilver.** Elemental mercury, unlike other metals, is liquid. Commonly used in dentistry, for the preparation of fillings; in laboratories and hospitals, as a reagent and fixative; and in medical instruments, electrical equipment, thermometers, barometers, pharmaceuticals, and some fluorescent light bulbs. Also used in the manufacture of glassware and jewelry, and the processing of gold and silver. Potential sources of elemental mercury in the home include mercury switches and mercury-containing devices such as thermostats, thermometers, and barometers. Spilled mercury gravitates to cracks in the floor and into carpeting. Even though it may not be visible, the mercury can slowly volatilize indoors, and may lead to chronic mercury poisoning through inhalation exposure. Vacuuming a contaminated area may facilitate the spread of mercury vapor throughout the house. The potential for indoor mercury exposure is increased when indoor air exchange is reduced—when doors and windows are kept closed. Warm air from heating ducts and vents may enhance vaporization when circulated over spilled mercury. Mercury vapor concentration is likely to be higher near the floor, and children may be exposed to higher concentrations than adults. A Detroit youngster suffered mercury poisoning after his apartment was painted with latex paint, and toxic mercury lingered at high levels. The EPA has banned mercury-containing fungicides from interior latex paint. You do not have to cover old latex paint since emission levels fall once the paint has dried. However, there are many household products that contain mercury to retard the growth of fungus, but do not say so on the label. Among these are adhesives, joint compounds, and cleaning solutions.

Toxic effects of mercury have been recognized since at least the sixteenth century, yet occupational and residential exposures to mercury remain a source of poisoning. Liquid mercury easily changes into vapor, and exposure is most likely to be through inhalation rather than through the skin. Most effects of mercury exposure develop slowly over time. Symptoms may occur only after repeated overexposure. These effects include insomnia, loss of appetite, nausea, weakness, and muscle tremors. Brief exposure to very high levels of mercury vapors can affect the lungs. Long-term overexposure to the vapors can cause a number of symptoms. Initial symptoms may be loss of appetite, fatigue, insomnia, and changes in behavior or personality (nervousness, excitability, and shyness). Later, more serious symptoms may include nausea, abdominal cramps, diarrhea, weight loss, weakness, and muscle tremors. Some of these symptoms have been reported after years of exposure to mercury at air levels slightly above the legal limit (0.05 milligrams of mercury per cubic meter of air over eight hours). When overexposure stops, these symptoms will usually go away. Severe mercury poisoning can permanently damage the nervous system. Such damage may be accompanied by hallucinations, whole-body tremors, a tingling "pins and needles" sensation, pain, tenderness, numbness, and weakness. Long-term exposure to mercury can damage the kidney, lungs, eyes, nose, and throat. It also can cause increased salivation, and discolor the lenses of the eyes, even without any other symptoms of overexposure. Prolonged skin contact with liquid mercury can irritate the skin and cause a rash that allows increased absorption through the skin. The effects of metallic mercury on human pregnancy and reproduction have not been studied thoroughly. Animal studies have shown that mercury caused growth retardation, birth defects, and the death of the fetus. The amount of mercury in the body can be estimated by measuring mercury in urine or blood.

Mercury must not be poured down the sink. Mercury waste must be disposed of as hazardous waste according to state and local regulations.

MERPAN™ • *See* Captan.

MERTECT™ • *See* Thiabendazole.

METAL CEMENTS • Contains vinyl plastic, ketone solvents, diethyl phthalate, and butyl acid phosphate. May also contain epoxy resins and iron. *See all*.

METAL CLEANERS AND ANTI-RUST COMPOUNDS • Phosphoric acid, oxalic acid, hydrochloric acid, sulfuric acid, chromic acid *(see all)*. The alkaline type contains caustic soda or potash (alkali), trisodium phosphate, sodium metasilicate, and a soap or detergent. The solvent type contains perchloroethylene, trichloroethylene, and trichlorethane. Another type of solvent cleaner contains kerosene, potassium soap of oleic acid, glycol ether, and a surfactant. The acid type contains hydrochloric acid plus sulfuric acid or chromic acid, or phosphoric acid and a surfactant. All metal cleaners are toxic by ingestion, skin irritants, and some are also lung irritants.

METAL FUME FEVER • A flulike syndrome of fever, muscle pain, and respiratory complaints associated with the inhalation of fumes from metal, particularly zinc oxide.

METAL POLISHES • Usually contain a petroleum solvent such as naphtha, an acid such as citric, abrasives, triethanolamine oleate, and ammonium hydroxide. Also may contain oxalic acid, fatty acids, ammonia, pine oil, alkyl sodium sulfates, bentonite, dye, perfume, kerosene, nitric acid, paraffin oil or wax, phenolic derivative, phosphoric acid, plasticizer, soap, sulfuric acid, and trisodium phosphate *(see all)*.

METALAXYL • **Subdue**™. *See* Fungicides.

METALLIC FIBER • A manufactured decorative fiber composed of metal, plastic-coated metal, metal-coated plastic, or some other core completed covered by metal. Used in household draperies, shoelaces, table linens, bathing suits, ribbons, braids, and as packing material for gifts and perfumes. Aluminum foil is coated on both sides with adhesives to which the desired color has been added. A sheet of transparent plastic film is applied to each side of the adhesive-coated foil. In well-produced fibers, salt water, chlorinated water in swimming pools, or climatic conditions do not affect them.

METALWORKING FLUIDS • These fluids reduce friction and carry away heat, thereby acting as lubricants and coolants. They are also used to wash away waste metal chips. Almost all machinists who do cutting, grinding, milling, turning, lapping, boring, broaching, or honing are exposed to these fluids. Metalworking fluids, and the additives they contain, may cause a variety of health problems according to California's Hazard Evaluation System and Information Service (HESIS). Skin exposure to metalworking fluids can cause rashes. Inhalation may cause bronchitis. Some of the additives in metalworking fluids are suspected of causing cancer. The health hazards of metalworking fluids, according to HESIS, depend upon the type of fluid used, as well as the additives and contaminants that may be present. Therefore, it is important for you to know the type of fluid you are using. See Insoluble Metalworking Fluid, Insoluble Oils, Water-Soluble Oils, and Semisynthetic Soluble Metalworking Oil. See also Cresol, Formaldehyde, 2-Ethoxyethanol, 2-Methoxyethanol, Pentachlorophenol, Phosphorus, Diethanolamine, and Iodine, all of which may be used in metalworking fluids.

METALWORKING OIL • See Semisynthetic Soluble Metalworking Oil.

METHALDEHYDE • See Formaldehyde.

METHAM • **Vapam.** A herbicide. See Carbamate.

METHAMIDOPHOS • **Monitor**™. Crystals from ether. Extremely toxic pesticide and acaracide (see) used on fruits and vegetables. Causes reproductive effects and interferes with the transmission of nerve signals. See Lindane.

METHANAL • See Formaldehyde.

METHANOL • **Methyl Alcohol. Wood Alcohol. Wood Spirit.** A solvent and denaturant obtained by the distillation of wood. Flammable, poisonous liquid with a nauseating odor. Better solvent than ethyl alcohol. Used primarily in antifreeze compounds, paints, cements, inks, varnishes, shellacs, wood strippers, windshield wiper solvents, and as a solvent for dyes. Also used in the fuel, Sterno®, and home heating oil extenders, as an octane booster in gasoline, and as a fuel for soldering torches. It is a softening agent for plastics, and the raw material for making formaldehyde. Methanol is highly toxic and readily absorbed from all routes of exposure. It possesses narcotic properties. Toxic effects are primarily on the nervous system; symptoms include headache, dizziness, confusion, abdominal pain, lung problems, weakness, and coma. Ingestion can cause blindness and death. Lesser exposure causes blurring of vision, headache, and gastrointestinal disturbances. It is also a fire hazard. If you must use a product containing methanol, make sure you do so either outdoors or in a well-ventilated area. Use gloves.

METHENAMINE • **Hexamethylene tetramine.** An odorless, white, crystalline powder made from formaldehyde and ammonia. Used as an antiseptic and bactericide cosmetics, a corrosion inhibitor, rubber accelerator, and a fungicide. It is also used in explosives. A source of skin irritations, which are believed to be caused by formic acid that forms through the action of perspiration on the formaldehyde. It is omitted from hypoallergenic cosmetics. One of the most frequent causes of skin rash in the rubber industry.

METHICONE • **4-Methoxy-*m*-Phenylenediamine Sulfate.** *See* Phenylenediamine and Silicones.

METHIDATHION • **Supracide™. Somonil™.** Crystals from methanol *(see)* used as an insecticide and acaracide *(see)* on fruits and vegetables. *See* Pesticides.

METHOXYCHLOR • A white, crystalline solid derived from ether and chloral hydrate. Dissolves in alcohol, but not in water. An insecticide effective against flying insects. Also used in deodorant sprays *(see)*. Moderately toxic by ingestion, and skin absorption, it is an irritant, an allergen, and a suspected cancer-causing agent and mutagen. Prolonged exposure may cause kidney injury. Emits highly toxic fumes when heated.

2-METHOXYETHANOL • **Ethylene Glycol Monomethyl Ether.** A widely used solvent in industrial products such as surface coatings, inks, dyes, cleaning fluids, degreasing agents, metalworking and hydraulic brake fluids. The permissible human exposure levels of this ethylene glycol ether are 25 to 5 ppm, and a further reduction has been proposed. It is both a reproductive and developmental toxicant. May cause birth defects. *See* Glycol Ethers and Metalworking Fluids.

METHYL ACETATE • **Acetic Acid.** A colorless liquid that occurs naturally in coffee, with a pleasant apple odor. Used in perfume to emphasize floral notes *(see)*, especially that of rose, and in toilet waters having a lavender odor. Also naturally occurs in peppermint oil. Used as a solvent for many resins and oils. May be irritating to the respiratory tract and, in high concentrations, may be narcotic. Since it has an effective fat solvent-drying effect on skin, it may cause skin problems such as chafing and cracking.

METHYL ACRYLATE • 2-Propanoic Acid. Methyl Ester. Derived from ethylene chlorohydrin, it is transparent and elastic. Used to coat paper and plastic film. Can be highly irritating to the eyes, skin, and mucous membranes. Convulsions occur if vapors are inhaled in high concentrations.

METHYL ALCOHOL • Wood Alcohol. *See* Methanol.

METHYL ALDEHYDE • *See* Formaldehyde.

METHYL BENZENE • *See* Toluene.

METHYL BROMIDE • Bromo-O-Gas®. Brom-O-Sol®. Brozone®. Celfume®. Dowfume®. Embafume®. Haltox®. Isobrome®. Kayafume®. Mebr®. Metafume®. Metho-O-Gas® Profume®. Rotox®. Terabol®. Terr-O-Gas.®. Zytox®. An inexpensive insect fumigant for soil, grain, fruits, and warehouses, and other buildings. It is a practically odorless gas, which adds to its danger. Fatalities have occurred during the application process, after cleanup operations, and after premature entry into fumigated buildings. At greatest risk are fumigators, but tilling the soil as long as four to nine days after methyl bromide has been applied can lead to air concentrations up to 15 ppm. The OSHA *(see)* permissible exposure limit (*see* PEL) is 5 ppm. Mild, systemic poisoning is characterized by headache, nausea, vomiting, visual changes, confusion, malaise, dizziness, weakness, numbness, and breathlessness. Avoid use. If you must have methyl bromide applied, make sure that you do not reenter a building until the gas has completely dissipated. Toxic effects may lead to long-term disability. An eye, skin, and mucous membrane irritant that produces fluid in the lungs, convulsions, and in high doses, coma.

METHYL CELLOSOLVE® • An additive in metalworking fluids. May cause birth defects. *See* Glycol Ethers and Metalworking Fluids.

METHYL ETHYL KETONE • *See* MEK and Enamel Paint.

METHYL HYDROXYMETHYL OLEYL OXAZOLINE • A synthetic wax. *See* Oxazoline.

2-METHYL-4-HYDROXYPYRROLINE • A plasticizer derived from acetylene and formaldehyde *(see both)*.

METHYL ISOBUTYL KETONE • **MIBK.** A colorless liquid with a pleasant odor that is used as a solvent for paints, varnishes, and nitrocellulose lacquers, and as a denaturant for alcohol. A synthetic fruit-flavoring agent. It is similar in toxicity to methyl ethyl ketone, which is irritating to the eyes and mucous membranes, but likely more toxic. Causes intestinal upsets and central nervous system depression. Hazardous by either ingestion or inhalation. *See* Enamel Paint.

METHYL LAURATE • The ester of methyl alcohol and lauric acid; derived from coconut oil. Used in detergents, emulsifiers, wetting agents, stabilizers, resins, lubricants, plasticizers, and flavorings. No known toxicity.

METHYL LINOLEATE • The ester of methyl alcohol and linoleic acid; a colorless oil derived from safflower oil. Used in detergents, emulsifiers, wetting agents, stabilizers, resins, lubricants, and plasticizers. No known toxicity.

METHYL METHACRYLATE • **MMA. Methylacrylic Acid. Methyl Methylacrylate. Diakon®. Osteobond®. Lucite®. Plexiglas®.** A clear liquid with a distinctive, sharp, fruity odor. Used in glues, adhesives, orthopedic cement, polyester resins, synthetic fibers, and dental prostheses. The main hazard to health comes from breathing the vapors of liquid MMA. The most common effect of overexposure is irritation of skin, eyes, nose, throat, or lungs. MMA can affect the nervous system, causing symptoms similar to drunkenness. Most people can smell MMA when the level in the air is considerably below the level hazardous to health. The permissible level for workers is 100 parts of MMA per million parts of air. *See* Clothing.

METHYL NONYL KETONE • An oily liquid with a strong odor; derived from oil of rue, or made synthetically. Used in perfumery, in flavorings, and as an animal repellent.

METHYL PALMITATE • The ester of methyl alcohol and palmitic acid; a colorless liquid derived from palm oil. Used in detergents, emulsifiers, wetting agents, stabilizers, resins, lubricants, and plasticizers. Low toxicity.

METHYL PARABEN • One of the most widely used preservatives in cosmetics, it has a broad spectrum of antimicrobial activity and is relatively nonirritating, nonsensitizing, and nonpoisonous. It is stable over the acid-alkalinity range of most cosmetics and is sufficiently soluble in water to produce the effective concentration in the water phase. Can cause allergic reactions.

METHYL PARATHION • An extremely toxic pesticide. *See* Parathion and Organophosphates.

METHYL RICINOLEATE • The ester of methyl alcohol and ricinoleic acid. A colorless liquid used as a plasticizer, lubricant, cutting oil, and wetting agent. *See* Castor Oil.

METHYL SALICYLATE • **Oil of Wintergreen.** A counterirritant, local anesthetic, and disinfectant used in perfumes, toothpaste, tooth powder, and mouthwash. The volatile oil obtained by maceration and subsequent. Used as a flavor in foods, beverages, and pharmaceutical and used as an odorant, in perfumery and in sunburn lotions as an ultraviolet absorber. Toxic by ingestion. Use in foods restricted by the FDA. Lethal dose 30 cc in adults, 10 cc in children.

METHYL SILICONE • Prepared by hydrolyzing *(see)* dimethyldichlorosilane or its esters, it is used to help compounds resist oxidation. No known toxicity. *See* Silicones.

METHYL SULFIDE • **Rail.** A synthetic flavoring agent is obtained from distilling potassium methyl sulfate. It has a disagreeable odor. It is also used as a solvent for minerals. No known toxicity.

METHYLAMINE • A colorless gas with a strong ammonia odor, derived from methanol and ammonia *(see both)*. Used in dyes, insecticides, fungicides, surface-active agents, tanning, dyeing of acetate textiles, as a fuel additive, in paint removers, as a solvent, and in photographic developer. An intense skin irritant, it is a fire hazard and, when heated, decomposes and emits toxic fumes.

p-**METHYLAMINOPHENOL** • *See* *p*-Methylaminophenol Sulfate and Phenol.

p-**METHYLAMINOPHENOL SULFATE** • Crystals that discolor in air and are soluble in water. They are used in photographic developers, for dyeing furs, and for hair dyes. May cause skin irritation, allergic reactions, and a shortage of oxygen in the blood. In solution applied to the skin, restlessness and convulsions have been produced in humans.

METHYLBENZETHONIUM CHLORIDE • **Diaparine Chloride.** A quaternary ammonium compound used as a germicide and topical disinfectant. *See* Quaternary Ammonium Compounds for toxicity.

METHYLCELLULOSE • **Cellulose, Methyl Ether.** Prepared from wood pulp or chemical cotton by treatment with alcohol. Swells in water. Soluble in cold water and insoluble in hot. A binder, thickener, dispersing and emulsifying agent used in cosmetics, in water-based paints, film and sheeting, and as a sizing agent. See also Carboxymethyl Cellulose. Nontoxic on the skin.

METHYLCHLOROISOTHIAZOLINONE • A preservative used in shampoos, taken from industry, to replace formaldehyde. It has been shown to be a sensitizer in animals, but has not been shown to be one in humans.

METHYLENE CHLORIDE • Dichloromethane. Methane Dichloride. Methylene Dichloride. Aerothene NM®. Solaestine®. Freon 30®. Somethine®. F-30®. A colorless gas that compresses into colorless liquid of pleasant odor and sweet taste. It is used widely as a degreaser, as a solvent for waxes, oils, paint and varnish thinner, and as cleansers in many industries and work settings, in aerosols, including pesticides. It is also used in refrigeration and air-conditioning equipment, in coffee decaffeination and spice extraction processes, and in paint and varnish removers. It is considered the best liquid paint remover and is a component in aerosol propellants in many formulations including cosmetics, pesticides, paints, and lubricants. Methylene chloride is nonflammable and a good grease remover, and therefore products may contain very high percentages of the chemical. For instance, paint strippers are usually 40 to 80 percent methylene chloride. Some which may be labeled "nonflammable" are almost 100 percent. Spray paints may contain up to 33 percent of the chemical. High concentrations are narcotic. Methylene chloride enters your body when you breathe it in the air. Once it enters the body, methylene chloride generates carbon monoxide, which interferes with the blood's ability to pick up and deliver oxygen. The body responds to lack of oxygen by driving the heart to work harder. People with angina (chest pains) from coronary artery disease are extremely sensitive to carbon monoxide and may have increased chest pains from exposure to methylene chloride, even below the legal exposure limit (100 parts per million over an eight-hour workshift). There is no one watching how consumers use the products. The use of a paint remover in a poorly ventilated setting has been implicated in a fatalities, according to a report in the November 8, 1990, issue of *American Journal of Emergency Medicine*. Since smoking increases the carbon monoxide level in the blood, smokers are doubly affected. Small amounts can also be absorbed through the skin. Damage to the liver, kidney, and central nervous system can occur, and persistent symptoms after inhalation include headache, nervousness, insomnia, and tremor. It is also a skin irritant. Methylene chloride is considered to have poor warning properties, since most people cannot smell it until it reaches a hazardous level (100–500 ppm). If you can smell it, you may be overexposed. Methylene chloride causes cancer in animals, and is considered a potential cancer-causing agent in humans. If you must use a product containing methylene chloride, use the product only with good ventilation, preferably out of doors in the shade. Paint stripper, which may be almost all methylene chloride, is usually applied with a brush. For convenience in dipping the brush, people usually pour some paint stripper from the big stock can (which usually has a small mouth) into a small, wide can or jar. There can be significant escape of methylene chloride from such containers left open during the time (often one to two hours) that paint stripping is being done, so containers should aways be kept covered when not actually in use. Keep children away from the area where this product is in use. Avoid breathing vapors or contact with the skin. Leave the area immediately after applying this product. Proper cleanup is important after using methylene chloride–containing products, such as paint strippers or degreasers. Brushes that are to be kept after being used should be stored well away from people, preferably in an open can. *See also* Oven Cleaners and Paint Strippers.

METHYLENE GLYCOL • *See* Formaldehyde.

METHYLENE OXIDE • *See* Formaldehyde.

METHYLISOTHIOCYANATE • Derived from methylamine and carbon disulfide, it is an insecticide and its use by the military as a poison gas has been suggested. Toxic by ingestion. A strong irritant to eyes and skin.

METHYLSTYRENE/VINYLTOLUENE COPOLYMER • The polymer of methylstyrene and vinlytoluene monomers. Used as a wax. *See* Styrene.

METHYL-TERT-BUTYL ETHER • **MBTE.** Made from methanol *(see)* and t-butyl alcohol, it is used to boost octane in gasoline. Has been considered to break up gallstones and cholesterol in humans. *See* Gasoline.

METHYLTIN • *See* Tin Compounds and Organotin Compounds.

MEVINPHOS • *See* Organophosphates.

mg/kg • A way of expressing dose: milligrams of a substance (mg) per kilogram (kg) of body weight.

MIBK • *See* Methyl Isobutyl Ketone.

MICA • Any of a group of minerals that are found in crystallized, thin, elastic sheets that can be separated easily. They vary in color from pale green, brown, or black to colorless. Ground and used as a lubricant and coloring in cosmetics. Also used in electrical equipment, vacuum tubes, dusting agents, lubricant, windows, paints, glass, roofing, rubber, special paper for insulation, wallpaper, and wallboard joint cement. Irritant by inhalation, may be damaging to the lungs. Nontoxic to the skin. Coloring permanently listed for cosmetic use in 1977.

MICE DOOM PELLETS • *See* Strychnine.

MICROCRYSTALLINE CELLULOSE • The colloid crystalline portion of cellulose fibers. *See* Cellulose Gums.

MICROCRYSTALLINE WAX • Any of various plastic materials that are obtained from petroleum. They are different from paraffin waxes *(see)* in that they have a higher melting point, higher viscosity, and much finer crystals, which can be seen only under a microscope. No known toxicity.

MILDEW • A minute parasitic fungus that frequently appears on the leaves, stems, and various other parts of plants or other decaying organic substances as a white, frostlike down, or with spots or various discolorations. The mildews are among the most destructive fungi known and can cause respiratory allergies. For clothes, brush off what you can and then, depending on the fabric, launder the article with a half cup of chlorine bleach, peroxide, or sodium perborate *(see all)*. To remove mildew from walls, try salt with lemon juice or white vinegar. *See also* Fungi.

MILDEW REMOVERS • *See* Calcium Hypochlorite.

MILLIGRAM • **mg.** A metric unit of mass. One gram equals 1,000 mg. One U.S. ounce equals 28,375 mg.

MINERAL OIL • **White Oil.** A mixture of refined liquid hydrocarbons *(see)* derived from petroleum. Colorless, transparent, odorless, and tasteless. When heated, it smells like petroleum. It stays on top of the skin and leaves a shiny protective surface. Nontoxic.

MINERAL SEAL OIL • **Signal Oil.** Used in furniture polish. May cause lung injury.

MINERAL SPIRITS • **Ligroin. Painter's Naphtha. Stoddard Solvent. White Spirits. Varsol. Mineral Turpentine. Petroleum Spirits.** A refined solvent of naphtha, it contains naphthenes and paraffin *(see)*. Used as a solvent in cosmetic oils, fats, and waxes, in dry cleaning, and as a paint thinner. May cause central nervous system depression and lung injury. *See* Stoddard Solvent.

MINERAL TURPENTINE • *See* Mineral Spirits.

MINERAL WAX • *See* Ceresin.

MINERAL WOOL • **Rock Wool.** Fibers made by blowing air or steam through slag, the residue from smelters or gasification processes. Can be harmful to the lungs if inhaled.

MINUTE MILDEW REMOVER™ • *See* Mildew and Bleaches.

MIPAFOX • *See* Organophosphates.

MIST • *See* page 13, Introduction.

MITES • Microscopic, spiderlike insects found in many house dust samples. Both live and dead mites contribute to allergic reactions, though dead mites may be more aggravating. Mites flourish during the summer, but symptoms of allergic patients are often worse in the colder months. This may be because after the summer the mites die and disintegrate into fragments, which can more easily reach the respiratory tract. *See* House Dust.

MITICIDE • A pesticide that kills mites, small animals of the spider class. *See* Acaracides and Pesticides.

MIXED TERPENES • A class of organic compounds widely distributed in nature. They are components of volatile or essential oils and are found in substantial amounts in cedarwood oil, camphor, thymol, eucalyptol, menthol and turpentine. Used as wetting agents and surfactants. Can cause local irritation.

MODACRYLIC • Fibers made from resins that are combinations of acrylonitrile and other materials such as vinyl chloride, vinylidene chloride or vinylidene dicyanide. The fibers, which can be stretched, embossed, and modeled into special shapes, are used for fake furs, fleece fabrics, flame-resistant draperies, scatter rugs, stuffed toys, paint rollers, knits, carpets, hair pieces, men's lightweight summer hats, and awnings. Dry cleaning or fur cleaning is recommended for deep-pile garments. For washable items, a low dryer setting is recommended and a hot iron is not.

MODEL CEMENT • May contain nitrocellulose, acetone, cellulose acetate, isopropanol, dibutyl phthalate, hexane, ethyl (isopropyl, amyl, butyl) acetate, toluol, naphtha, ethanol, and camphor. May also contain polystyrene *(see all)*.

MO-GO™ • Rat and mouse killer. *See* Strychnine.

MOLD • Primitive organisms that cannot make their own food, and so steal it from living plants and animals, from decaying matter that was once alive, and from various substances such as paint, paste, and human tissue. There are thousands of different fungi, but most can be placed into two categories—yeasts and molds. Yeasts are single cells that divide to form clusters. Molds consist of many cells that grow as branching threads. Although both groups can cause allergic reactions, only a small number of molds are widely recognized as offenders. The seeds or reproductive particles of fungi are called "spores," and they multiply, each being capable of producing millions of spores. When inhaled, spores or fragments of spores may cause allergic rhinitis. This means sneezing, runny nose, congestion, and itching in the nose or eyes. Because they are so small, mold spores may evade the protective mechanisms of the nose and upper respiratory tract to reach the lungs and bring on allergic asthma. Less frequently, spores may lead to a lung disease known as "hypersensitivity pneumonitis." Molds grow almost anywhere. They may be found wherever there is moisture, oxygen, and a source of the few other chemicals they need. In the forest they grow on rotting logs and fallen leaves. They also grow on grains, in humidifiers, air conditioners, garbage pails, mattresses, upholstered furniture, and old foam-rubber pillows. Bakeries, breweries, barns, dairies, and greenhouses are all good places for mold production. *See* Mildew.

MOLE NOTS™ • Mole killer. *See* Strychnine.

MONOCROTOPHOS • *See* Organophosphates.

MONOMER • A molecule that by repetition builds up a long chain or large structure called a polymer *(see)*. Ethylene, the gas, for instance, is the monomer of polyethylene *(see)*.

MONTAN WAX • A clay forming the main ingredient of bentonite and fuller's earth *(see both)*. Used in the petroleum industry as a carrier. Inhalation of the dust can cause respiratory irritation.

MOP AND GLOW WAX® • A nonionic detergent floor wax containing acrylic copolymer and alkyl phenyl ethoxylate *(see both)*.

MORDANTS • Chemicals that are insoluble compounds that serve to fix a dye, usually a weak dye, to hasten the development of the desired shade or to modify it in hair colorings. Toxicity depends upon specific ingredients.

MORESTAN™ 4 • A pesticide that controls mites and whiteflies attacking flowers, shrubs, and trees. It contains 6-methyl-1,3-dithiolo[4,5-b] quinoxalin-2-one. Harmful if swallowed, or absorbed through the skin. Causes mild to moderate eye irritation. Prolonged or frequently repeated skin contact may cause allergic reactions. Residues on the skin may cause an increased sensitivity to sunlight.

MORPHOLINE • A salty fatty acid used as a surface-active agent *(see)* and an emulsifier in cosmetics. Prepared by taking the water out of diethanolamine *(see)*. A mobile, water-absorbing liquid that mixes with water, and has a strong ammonia odor. A cheap solvent for resins, waxes, and dyes. Also used as a corrosion inhibitor, antioxidant, plasticizer, viscosity improver, insecticide, fungicide, local anesthetic, and antiseptic. May cause kidney and liver injury, and can produce sloughing of the skin. Irritating to the eyes and mucous membranes.

MORPHOLINE STEARATE • A coating and preservative. *See* Morpholine.

MOTHBALLS • Contain naphthalene and/or *p*-Dichlorobenzene *(see both)*. In one year, according to the Children's Medical Center of Brooklyn, 4918 children under the age of six ingested mothballs in the United States. Children can develop severe anemia when exposed to such repellants.* Less toxic alternatives include: brushing clothes, because fragile moth eggs are easily destroyed; placing cedar chips, newspapers, or lavender flowers with clothing; sealing in airtight containers or placing in deep freeze to kill larvae. A recipe used by weavers includes placing a half pound of rosemary, a half pound of mint, a quarter pound of thyme, two tablespoons of cloves, and a quarter pound of ginseng in cheesecloth bags.

MOTH-KILLING PRODUCTS • *See* Mothballs and *p*-Dichlorobenzene.

MOTOR CLEANERS • *See* Engine and Motor Cleaners.

MOTOR OIL • **Lubricating Oil.** Contains mineral oils, oxidation inhibitors, detergents, zinc dialkyl dithiophosphate, phosphorus, barium and calcium petroleum sulfonate, and barium and calcium phenolates. They may also contain polymethacrylate esters, polyisobutylene, alkyl stryene polymers, and naphthalene products with polysiloxanes. Used motor oil can be harmful through skin contact, skin absorption, inhalation, or ingestion. Toxicity depends upon ingredients. Many of the problems linked to it are due to exposure to heavy metals. Health problems can be cumulative because with each exposure to heavy metals, the toxins accumulate in the body. Some of the hydrocarbons may be carcinogenic over a long period of time. Wear protective gloves when handling motor oil. Do not dispose of used motor oil in the trash or pour it into the ground or down storm sewers. Do not burn it. Take the used oil to a disposal facility. Ask your local gas station operator or your local trash collection agency for the address. *See* Phenols and Naphthalenes.

MOUSE LURE • Mouse killer. *See* Strychnine.

MOUSE NOTS • Mouse killer. *See* Strychnine.

MOUSE SEED • Mouse killer. *See* Strychnine.

MR. CLEAN™ LIQUID HOUSEHOLD CLEANER • A nonionic detergent containing sodium alkyl ethoxylate sulfate.

---

*New England Journal of Medicine (December 5, 1991), p. 1660.

MR. MUSCLE™ OVEN CLEANER • A caustic containing sodium hydroxide.

MSDS • **Material Safety Data Sheet.** A form that lists the properties and hazards of a product or substance.

MSMA • **Monosodium Methanearsonate.** A herbicide. *See* Arsenic.

M-TRAK • A new biological pesticide made by Mycogen. It contains bacteria that kill pests.

MUCILAGE • A solution in water of the sticky principles of vegetable substances. Used as a soothing application to the mucous membranes. *See* Glue.

MULTIPLE CHEMICAL SENSITIVITY • **MCS.** People with a wide array of symptoms—such as headaches, rashes, watery eyes, fatigue, asthma, nasal congestion, and depression—to very low synthetic chemical exposure are being diagnosed as MCS suffers. *Chemical Sensitivity: A Report to the New Jersey State Department of Health* (by Nicholas A. Ashford Ph.D., J. D., and Claudia Miller, M. D., M. S.), December 1989, identified four populations at the greatest risk of toxic exposure that may induce chemical sensitivity:

• Industrial workers, primarily men between 20 to 65 years of age.

• Occupants of "tight buildings," including office workers and schoolchildren.

• Residents of communities with contaminated air or water.

• Individuals with significant personal exposures to chemicals in the air, water, consumer products, foods, or drugs.

MURIATIC ACID • *See* Hydrochloric Acid and Acids.

MUTAGEN • A chemical or physical agent able to change the genetic material in cells.

MUTAGENIC • Having the power to cause mutations. A "mutation" is a sudden change in the character of a gene that is perpetuated in subsequent divisions of the cells in which it occurs. It can be induced by the application of such stimuli as radiation, certain food chemicals, or pesticides. Certain food additives such as caffeine have been found to "break" chromosomes.

MVP • A new biological pesticide made by Mycogen. It contains bacteria that kill pests.

MYRISTALKONIUM CHLORIDE • *See* Quaternary Ammonium Compounds.

MYRISTAMIDOPROPYL BETAINE • *See* Surfactants.
MYRISTAMIDOPROPYL DIETHYLAMINE • *See* Quaternary Ammonium Compounds.
MYRISTAMIDOPROPYLAMINE OXIDE • *See* Quaternary Ammonium Compounds.
MYRISTIC ACID • Used in shampoos, shaving soaps, and creams. A solid organic acid that occurs naturally in butter acids (such as nutmeg, butter to the extent of 80 percent), oil of lovage, coconut oil, mace oil, cire d'abeille in palm seed fats, and in most animal and vegetable fats. Also used in food flavorings. When combined with potassium, myristic acid soap gives a very good copious lather. No known toxicity.

N

NABAM • **Disodium Ethylenebisdithiocarbamate.** Crystals from alcohol. Used as a fungicide and a starting material for many carbamate pesticides. Irritating to the skin and mucous membranes, and in high doses is narcotic. Can cause violent vomiting if alcohol is ingested after exposure.
NALED • **Bromex. Dibrom. 1,2-Dibromo-2,2-Dichloroethyl Dimethyl Phosphate.** A solid or liquid that is derived from bromic acid and used as an insecticide and acaricide. Poisonous by ingestion, inhalation, and skin, it interferes with nerve signals. Use may be restricted. *See* Parathion and Organophosphates.
NAPHTHALENE • A coal tar *(see)* derivative. Used to manufacture dyes, solvents, fungicides, smokeless powder, lubricants, as a moth repellent, and a topical and internal antiseptic. It has been used as a dusting powder to combat insects on animals. Naphthalene can enter your body through inhalation, skin absorption, ingestion, and eye and skin contact. It may produce damage to the eyes, liver, kidneys, skin, red blood cells, and the central nervous system. Has reportedly caused anemia in infants exposed to clothing and blankets stored in naphthalene mothballs. Can cause allergic contact dermatitis in adults and children.
NAPHTHAS • **VM & P Naphthas.** Obtained from the distillation of petroleum, coal tar, and shale oil. It is a common diluent *(see)* found in nail lacquer. "Naphtha" is an imprecise term because it may also be used for various derivatives of petroleum. Among the common naphthas that are used as solvents are coal tar/naphtha and

petroleum/naphtha. Naphthas are used as solvents for asphalts, road tars, pitches, paints, dry-cleaning fluids, in cleansing compounds, engraving and lithography, rubber cements, and naphtha soaps. Causes upper-respiratory-tract irritation. *See* Kerosene for toxicity.

NAPHTHOL • A coal tar *(see)* derivative. Used as an antiseptic, in hair dyes, and to treat eczema, ringworm, and psoriasis. Also used in dyes, pigments, antioxidants, fungicides, and insecticides. Toxic by ingestion and skin absorption. May cause allergic contact dermatitis.

B-NAPHTHYL ETHYL ETHER. • **Nerolin.** White crystals with an orange-blossom odor. Used in perfumes, soaps, and flavoring.

B-NAPHTHYL METHYL ETHER. • White crystals with a menthol odor. Used to perfume soaps. *See* Naphthol.

***p-b*-NAPHTHYLAMINE.** • An antioxidant in rubber compounds. Can cause contact allergic dermatitis.

NAVADEL • *See* Dioxathion.

NEAT'S-FOOT OIL • A lubricant used in creams and lotions. A pale yellow, fatty oil made by boiling the feet and shinbones of cattle. Used chiefly as a leather dressing and waterproofing. Can cause allergic reactions in the hypersensitive.

NEODECANOIC ACID • A colorless liquid used in plasticizers, lubricants, and paint driers. *See* Decanoic Acid.

NETTLES • Used in hair tonics and shampoos. Obtained from the troublesome weed with stingers, it has a long history, and is used in folk medicine. Its flesh is rich in minerals and plant hormones that supposedly stimulate hair growth, and shines and softens hair. Also used to make tomatoes resistant to spoilage, to encourage the growth of strawberries, and to stimulate the fermentation of humus. No known toxicity.

NEWSPAPERS • Can cause such allergic symptoms as contact dermatitis, allergic rhinitis, and asthma, because of their ink or odor. It is sometimes helpful to dry newspapers in the oven on "warm" before reading, or to wear gloves when handling them.

NEWSPRINT • *See* Ink.

NFPA • **National Fire Protection Association.** The NFPA has developed a scale for rating the severity of fire risk, reactivity, and health hazards of substances.

NICKEL • A lustrous, white, hard metal that occurs in the earth. Among the products that contain it are coins, keys, doorknobs, water faucets, bathroom fixtures, kitchen utensils, vacuum cleaners, washing machines, dishwashers, sewing utensils, safety pins, writing materials, fountain pen caps, razors, electric razors, metal parts of shoes, bicycle handlebars, false teeth, eyeglass frames, fashion jewelry, hair clips, lipstick holders, underwear fasteners, zippers and garters, instruments, telephone dials, automobile fittings, nickel salts used in fat refining, nickel alloys, ceramics, and artificial fertilizers used in potted plants. Nickel is one of the most common skin allergens. The location of the contact dermatitis usually gives the physician a clue as to what the offending nickel product may be. Those allergic to nickel also may be allergic to chromium and cobalt *(see both)*. Ingestion of large amounts of the soluble salts of nickel may cause nausea, vomiting, and diarrhea. Nickel poisoning can cause central nervous system damage and respiratory diseases, including cancer.

NICKEL SULFATE • Used in hair dyes and astringents. Occurs in the earth's crust as a salt of nickel. Obtained as green or blue crystals, and used chiefly in nickel plating. Also used in dyes, printing textiles, coatings, and ceramics. It has a sweet, astringent taste and acts as an irritant, causing vomiting when swallowed. Its systemic effects include blood vessel, brain, and kidney damage, and nervous depression. Frequently causes skin rash when used in cosmetics. *See* Nickel.

NICOTINE SULFATE. • The salt of the distillation product of tobacco, used as an agricultural spray and insecticide. May cause dermatitis.

NIGROSINE • A class of dark blue or black dyes, soluble in water, alcohol, or oil. Used to manufacture indelible inks and shoe polish, and in dyeing leather, wood, and textiles. Also used as a shark repellent.

NIOSH • **National Institute of Occupational Safety and Health.** Congress set up this institute in 1970 to play a key role in helping to protect the health of workers on the job. The agency was to conduct occupational-health research; to inspect manufacturer's plants at the request of employers and workers, and for its own studies; and to recommend standards for safe exposure to hazardous substances. NIOSH is supposed to work closely with OSHA *(see),* the organization responsible for setting the legally permitted exposure levels *(see* PFL) to hazards in the workplace. NIOSH, through its investigations into plant conditions and studies of already available data, provides OSHA with the scientific background needed to determine these rules. When a workplace crisis arises, the two agencies often work in tandem to find out how the workers were harmed and to help the industry correct the problem. Under the law, NIOSH documents, summarizing its findings about a hazard, should be used by OSHA to help set health and safety regulations for the industry. (*See* Further Information for address.)

NITRIC ACID • Used as an oxidizer in hair dyes and as a stabilizer in cosmetics. A corrosive, colorless, inorganic acid made by the action of ammonia on sulfuric acid and nitrate. Used chiefly as an oxidizing agent in the manufacture of fertilizers, explosives, and nitroparaffin. Also used in metallurgy, photoengraving, etching steel, urethanes, and rubber chemicals. In moist air, its fumes give off a choking odor. Ingestion can cause burning and corrosion of the mouth, esophagus, and stomach, and can result in death. Chronic inhalation of vapors can cause bronchitis. Can be irritating to the skin.

NITRILOTRIACETIC ACID • NTA. A chelating and sequestering agent. Used in detergents. Can be irritating. *See* Nitric and Acetic Acids.

NITRO- • A prefix denoting one atom of nitrogen and two of oxygen. "Nitro-" also denotes a class of dyes derived from coal tars. Nitro dyes can be absorbed through the skin. When absorbed or ingested they can cause a lack of oxygen in the blood. Chronic exposure may cause liver damage. *See* Colors.

NITROBENZENE • Greenish yellow crystals, or yellow, oily liquid derived from benzene *(see)* and used in the manufacture of aniline, as a solvent for cellulose, as an ingredient of metal polishes and shoe polishes, and in lubricating oils and soaps. A skin and eye irritant; rapidly absorbed by the skin. Moderately toxic by skin absorption and ingestion, it causes a lack of oxygen in the blood. It is a common air contaminant. The vapor is hazardous. Do not get into eyes or on skin or clothing. Avoid breathing vapor. Use adequate ventilation. May cause headache, drowsiness, nausea, vomiting, and oxygen starvation. In case of contact, immediately remove all contaminated clothing, including shoes. Flush skin and eyes with copious amounts of water for at least fifteen minutes while awaiting medical help. Nitrobenzene is particularly hazardous to pregnant women and products containing it should be avoided by them. It is also more hazardous for persons who ingest alcohol.

NITROCELLULOSE • Any of several esters *(see)* obtained as white, fibrous, flammable solids by adding nitrate to cellulose, the cell walls of plants. Used in skin protective creams, nail enamels, and lacquers. Also used in fast-drying automobile lacquers, high explosives, rocket propellant, printing inks, in coating bookbinding cloth, leather finishing, and the manufacture of celluloid. No known toxicity.

NITROFEN • An agricultural pesticide used as a selective contact herbicide for pre- and postemergent control of annual grasses and broadleaf weeds on a variety of food crops. Agricultural workers and manufacturers are exposed through skin absorption and by inhalation. The general public is exposed through ingestion due to possible persistent residual quantities of nitrofen on food crops. Adverse effects on agricultural workers following excessive exposure over prolonged periods included reduction of hemoglobin and white blood cell counts, inhibition of cholinesterase (an enzyme necessary for transmission of nerve signals), and abnormalities in red blood cell and serum-enzyme levels. The chemical was given to rats and mice for 78 weeks. It proved to be a liver carcinogen in mice of both sexes and in female rats.

NITROGEN • A gas that is, by volume, 78 percent of the atmosphere, and essential to all living things. Odorless. Used as a preservative for cosmetics, in the production of ammonia and cyanides, in fertilizers, in food refrigeration and freeze drying, and for inflating tires. In high concentrations, it can asphyxiate. Toxic concentration in humans is 90 ppm.

NITROGEN DIOXIDE • NO_2. A slightly yellow to reddish gas that is heavier than air, with a faint, chlorine-bleachlike odor. It is produced by combustion, gas stoves, water heaters, dryers, and cigarettes, as well as from industrial, manufacturing, or agricultural sources. Health effects depend upon concentration in the air and duration of exposure. Initially, there may be mild irritation of the throat and nose, a cough, red eyes, shortness of breath, headache, dizziness, nausea and, less commonly, a stuffy nose, sleepiness, and loss of consciousness. The severity of initial symptoms does not correlate well with subsequent lung problems, although patients with mild nitrogen dioxide exposure often do not develop later complications. After a latent period of three to thirty hours, patients may develop fluid in the lungs, fever, irregular heartbeat, wheezing, may turn blue, and may even have complete respiratory failure.

NITROPARAFFIN • Colorless liquids with a pleasant odor, derived from propane and paraffin *(see both)*. Used as a solvent for dyes, waxes, resins, and gums. Also used in inks, propellants, and fuel additives. Toxic by inhalation.

NITROUS OXIDE • Laughing Gas. A whipping agent for whipped cosmetic creams, and a propellant in aerosols. Has a slightly sweetish odor and taste. Colorless. Used in rocket fuel. Less irritating than other nitrogen oxides, but narcotic in high concentrations, and can asphyxiate.

NONANAL • Pelargonaldehyde. A colorless liquid with an orange-rose scent. Used as an odorant and flavoring agent. *See* Aldehydes.

NONIONIC • A group of emulsifiers used in detergents, paper manufacture, grease removal, and hand creams. Resist freezing and shrinkage. Toxicity depends upon specific ingredients. *See* Detergents.

NONOXYNOL-2 • Polyoxyethylene(2) Nonylphenyl Ether. Used as a nonionic *(see)* surface-active agent, antifoaming agent, dispersing agent, spermicide, and in detergents. No known toxicity. See Polyethylene Glycol and Phenols.

NYLON • The commonly known synthetic material used as a fiber in eyelash lengtheners and mascaras, and as a molding compound to shape cosmetics. Comes in clear or white opaque plastic for use in making resins. Resistant to organic chemicals, but is dissolved by phenol, cresol *(see both),* and strong acids. Nylon clothing, including stockings, particularly when wet, can cause allergic contact dermatitis. No known toxicity.

NYTRIL • A soft, resilient synthetic fabric that is easy to clean, does not pill, resists wrinkling, and retains its shape after pressing. Used for coats, suits, sweaters, yarns, and imitation furs. *See* Polymers.

O

OCHER • Any of the yellow, brown, or red earthy powders consisting of iron mixed with clay or sand. Used in paint pigments.

1-OCTADECONOL • *See* Stearyl Alcohol.

OCTAFLUOROCYCLOBUTANE • A nonflammable gas. A refrigerant, propellant, and aerating agent in foamed or sprayed food products. Used alone or in combination with carbon dioxide or nitrous oxide *(see both).* Nontoxic when used alone.

OCTANE • A number indicating the antiknock properties of automobile fuel. Pure heptane is a very high-knocking fuel and is rated as zero, while 2,2,4-trimethylpentane is assigned 100. Premium leaded gasolines have an octane rating of about 100 but unleaded gasolines are from 85 to 90. The addition of methyl-tert-butyl ether *(see)* raises the rating. Airplane fuel is 100.

1-OCTANOL • **Caprylic Alcohol.** Used in the manufacture of perfumes. Colorless, viscous liquid, soluble in water, insoluble in oil. Occurs naturally in oil of lavender, oil of lemon, oil of lime, oil of lovage, orange peel, and coconut oil. It has a penetrating, aromatic scent. May cause skin rash.

2-OCTANOL • **Caprylic Alcohol.** An oily, aromatic liquid, with a somewhat unpleasant odor. Used in the manufacture of perfumes and disinfectant soaps. *See* 1-Octanol.

OCTOCRYLENE • An absorbent. *See* Phenol.

OCTODODECYL MYRISTATE • *See* Myristic Acid.

OCTODODECYL NEODECANOATE • The ester of octyldodeca-nol and neodecanoic acid *(see both)*.

OCTOXYNOL-1, -3, -10, -13, -40 • Waxlike emulsifiers, dispers-ing agents, and detergents used in hand creams, lotions, and lip-sticks. Derived from phenol *(see)* and used as a surfactant.

OCTRIZOLE • An absorbent derived from phenol *(see)*.

OCTYL AMMONIUM METHARSONATE • A herbicide in con-sumer products, it is toxic, and autopsies of animals poisoned with it showed kidney damage and irritation of the lining of the stom-ach.

n-OCTYL BICYCLOHEPTENE DICARBOXIMIDE • A liquid that is miscible with most organic solvents and oils, it is derived from maleic anhydride. Used in insecticides, pesticides, and pet sham-poos. Toxic by ingestion and skin absorption.

OCTYL PHENOL • White flakes derived from phenol and used in nonionic surfactants *(see)*, fuel oils, resins, fungicides, bactericides, dyes, adhesives, and in rubber compounds. *See* Phenol.

OCTYLACRYLAMIDE/ACRYLATES/BUTAMINOETHYL METHACRY-LATE COPOLYMERS. • See Acrylates.

OCTYLDODECETH-20, -25. • Polyethylene ethers of octyldode-canol *(see)*.

ODOR THRESHOLD • The lowest concentration of a substance in air that can be smelled. For given chemicals, individuals usually have very different odor thresholds.

OIL OF MUSTARD • The oil expressed from mustard seeds. It contains oleic acid and other fatty acids including arachidic. The straw-colored or brownish yellow liquid is used in the manufacture of oleomargarine and soap, and as a lubricant.

OIL OF VITRIOL • *See* Sulfuric Acid.

OIL RED • *See* Sudan III.

OIL SCARLET • *See* Sudan III.

OIL-STAIN REMOVER • Rub garments with white chalk before washing. *See also* Stain Removers.

OLEAMIDOPROPYL DIETHYLAMINE GLYCOLATE • *See* Quaternary Ammonium Compounds.

OLEFIN • Made from petroleum (propylene and ethylene gases), it produces a very lightweight carpeting, knitwear that is able to give good bulk and cover, and sportswear and carpeting that is abrasion and stain resistant, and quick drying. Very sensitive to heat. Should be machine-washed in lukewarm water and dried on a very low setting. Stains on carpeting containing olefin fibers will usually blot away with an absorbent tissue.

OLEIC ACID • Obtained from various animal and vegetable fats and oils. Colorless. On exposure to air, it turns a yellow to brown color and develops a rancid odor. Used in preparations of Turkey-red oil *(see)*, soft soap, permanent wave solutions, vanishing creams, polishing compounds, lubricants, surface coatings, and food additives. Possesses better skin-penetrating properties than vegetable oils. Also employed in liquid makeup. Low oral toxicity, but is mildly irritating to the skin.

OLEOYL SARCOSINE • The condensation product of oleic acid with N-methylglycine, widely used in polishing compounds, soaps, and in lubricating oils. Can be mildly irritating to the skin.

OLETH-20 • An oily liquid derived from fatty alcohols. Used as a surface-active agent *(see)*. No known toxicity.

OLEYL ALCOHOL • Ocenol®. Found in fish oils. Oily and usually pale yellow. Gives off an offensive burning odor when heated. Chiefly used in the manufacture of detergents and wetting agents, and as an antifoam agent. Also used as a plasticizer for softening and lubricating fabrics, and as a carrier for medications. No known toxicity.

OPIDN • *See* Organophosphates.

OPTICAL BLEACHES • **Optical Brightener.** A colorless, fluorescent, organic compound that absorbs ultraviolet light and emits it as visible blue light. The blue light masks the yellow of textiles, paper, detergents, and plastics. "Brighteners" used in "whiter-than-white" detergents can be photosensitizers.

OPTICAL BRIGHTENER • *See* Optical Bleaches.

ORGANIC • There are no federal standards for the term, but it usually refers to produce grown without pesticides, herbicides, or synthetic fertilizers on land that has been free of such chemicals for from one to seven years.

ORGANIC COMPOUNDS • Chemicals that contain carbon. Volatile organic compounds vaporize at room temperature and pressure. They are found in many indoor sources, including many common household products and building materials.

ORGANOPHOSPHATES • Compounds containing phosphorus that belong to several groups including:

• phospholipids or phosphatides, which are widely distributed in plants and animals. Lecithin is an example.

• esters of phosphinic and phosphonic acids, which are used as plasticizers, insecticides, resin modifiers, and flame retardants such as Fyrol FR-2™ *(see)*.

• pyrophosphates, which are the basis for many insecticides that inhibit cholinesterase, an enzyme necessary for nerve transmission. Tetraethyl pyrophosphate (TEPP), which is highly toxic, was developed during World War II.

• the phosphoric esters of glycerol, glycol, and other fatty alcohols that are used in fertilizers.

Organophosphates, pesticides, and insecticides can be extremely toxic. They can kill quickly or slowly depending on the amount of exposure. Most are easily absorbed through the skin, eyes, stomach, and lungs. Among the organophosphate pesticides in use are azinphosmethyl, carobphenothion, demeton, diazinon, dichlorvos, dicrotophos, dimethoate, endothion, EPN, fensulfothion, fenthion, Hinosan, methyl demeton, methyl parathion, mevinphos, mipafox, monocrotophos, naled, parathion, phorate, phosphamidon, Phostex, tetraethyl pyrophosphate (TEPP), thiometon, and trichlorfon. If you must use products containing organophosphates, use extreme caution and follow the directions precisely.

Organophosphorous compounds are now being studied for delayed neurotoxicity (OPIDN). It can occur in factory workers exposed during the production of organophosphorous chemicals, which are used as plasticizers, lubricants, fire-retardants, and pesticides.

ORGANOPHOSPHOROUS COMPOUNDS • *See* Organophosphates.

ORGANOTIN COMPOUNDS • A family of alkyl tin compounds widely used as stabilizers for plastics, especially for piping. They are both liquids and solids. All are highly toxic and regulated by OSHA *(see)*. Organotins may cause eye, skin, liver, nervous system, and heart effects. *See* Tin Compounds.

ORLON • The trademark for acrylic fiber *(see)* from E. I. du Pont. It is a light, bulky fiber that imparts wash-and-wear and wrinkle-resistant properties to fabrics with which it is constructed. It is versatile and can be blended with other fibers such as wool for coats, sweaters, and socks.

ORTHENE® TURF, TREE, & ORNAMENTAL SPRAY • An insect spray for grass, trees, shrubs, and greenhouse plants, it contains acephate *(see)*. Harmful if swallowed; causes eye and skin irritation. Avoid breathing dust or spray mist. Wash hands thoroughly after handling. Children or pets should not come into contact with treated areas until sprays have dried.

ORTHO- • A prefix meaning "straight ahead." In organic chemistry, it designates the most highly water-saturated version of a chemical.

ORTHOCIDE™ • *See* Captan.

ORTHO-TOLUIDINE • A light yellow liquid that becomes reddish brown on exposure to air. It is derived from *o*-nitrotoluene and is used in textile printing, and as a rubber accelerator. A study of 1,749 workers at the Goodyear Tire and Rubber plant in Niagara Falls, N.Y., found that workers exposed directly to ortho-toluidine and aniline had 6.5 times the rate of bladder cancer than the average citizen of the state. Toxic by inhalation and ingestion, and is absorbed by the skin.

ORTHO WEED-B-GON® JET WEEDER FORMULA II • Kills dandelion, plantain, chickweed, wild onion, and broadleaf weeds, roots and all. Active ingredients: Diethanolamine salt of (2,4-Dichlorophenoxy)acetic acid; Diethanolamine salt of 2-(2-Methyl-f-chlorophenoxy)propionic acid. Carries the usual cautions, including do not apply to water.

ORYZALIN • **Surflan.** *See* Herbicides and Aniline.

OSHA • **Occupational Safety and Health Administration.** An agency in the U.S. Department of Labor that establishes workplace safety and health regulations. Many states have their own OSHA programs. This organization has been able to enact human-exposure standards for a relatively small number of chemicals in use in the workplace. It has been criticized for not policing U.S. agencies, and for cracking down only on businesses, especially small businesses. The Supreme Court ruled that OSHA inspectors cannot conduct surprise health and safety checks at workplaces without a warrant. *See* PEL.

OURICURY WAX • The wax exuded from the leaves of the Brazilian palm tree. The hard brown wax has the same properties and uses as carnauba wax *(see)*.

OUTGASSING • Usually meant the release of gas from a metal by heating but has come to mean the liberation of vapors from furniture, carpet, walls, and other objects and equipment into room air. Outgassing of toxic molecules has been cited as a cause of Sick Building Syndrome and Indoor Pollution *(see both)*.

OVEN CLEANERS • Most contain sodium or potassium hydroxide *(see both)* along with starch glue and detergents. They may also contain n-acetyl ethanolamine, butyl cellosolve, glycols, methylene chloride, oleic acid, petroleum distillates, pine oil, silica, sodium orthosilicates, sodium xylene sulfonate and whiting. The spray type contains amines, detergents, ether-type solvents, sodium hydroxide, and thickeners. Many spray types are highly irritating to the skin and lungs, particularly those with sodium and potassium hydroxide (lye), methylene chloride, and petroleum distillates. A less toxic alternative is to wipe the oven while it is still warm; use baking soda/water paste and steel wool to scrub. Another alternative is to sprinkle salt on the spill while the oven is still warm. If the spill is dry, wet it lightly. When the oven cools down, scrape away the spill and wash the area clean with soap and water. *See* Methylene Chloride, Potassium Hydroxide, and Pine Oil.

OXALATE • A salt or ester of oxalic acid *(see)*.

OXALIC ACID • Occurs naturally in many plants and vegetables, particularly in the *Oxalis* family; also in many molds. Used in freckle and bleaching cosmetic preparations, blueprints, tanning, cleaning iron, and leather. Used industrially to remove paint, varnish, rust, and ink stains, and as a bleach. Also used in dentistry to harden plastic models. Fingernails exposed to it have turned blue, become brittle, and fallen off. Caustic and corrosive to the skin and mucous membranes; may cause severe intestinal upsets and kidney damage if ingested.

OXAZOLINE • A series of synthetic waxes that are versatile and miscible with most natural waxes and can be applied to the same uses.

OXIDATION • Reaction in which oxygen combines chemically with another substance. It also means the loss of electrons by a substance.

OXIDIZER • A substance that causes oxygen to combine with another substance. Oxygen and hydrogen peroxide are examples of oxidizers.

OXYDOL • An anionic detergent containing sodium alkyl benzene sulfonate and sodium perborate. *See* Anionic Surfactant.

OXYQUINOLINE • **8-Hydroxyquinoline** • A white, crystalline powder made from phenol, it is almost insoluble in water. Used as a fungistat, and for reddish orange colors when combined with bismuth. Used internally as a disinfectant. Has caused cancer in animals both orally and when injected. *See* Oxyquinoline Sulfate.

OXYQUINOLINE BENZOATE • **8-Quinolinol Benzoate. Benzoxiquinine.** The salt of benzoic acid and oxyquinoline *(see both).* Used as a disinfectant.

OXYQUINOLINE SULFATE • Made from phenols; composed of either white crystals or powder, almost insoluble in water and ether but soluble in alcohol, acetone, and benzene. Used as a preservative in cosmetics for its ability to prevent fungus growth and to disinfect. *See* Phenol for toxicity.

OXYSTEARIN • A mixture of the glycerides *(see)* of partially oxidized stearic acids *(see)* and other fatty acids *(see).* Tan; waxy. Occurs in animal fat and is used chiefly in manufacture of soaps, candles, cosmetics, suppositories, and pill coatings. Also used as a crystallization inhibitor in cottonseed and soybean cooking, in salad oils up to .125 percent, and as a defoamer in the production of beet sugar and yeast.

OZOKERITE • **Ceresin.** A naturally occurring waxlike mineral; a mixture of hydrocarbons. Colorless or white when pure, with a horrid odor. Upon refining, it yields a hard, white, microcrystalline wax known as ceresin *(see).* An emulsifier and thickening agent used in lipstick, cream rouge, and in candles and waxes. It is also used for grease crayons, sizings, printing inks, waxed cloth, waxed paper, and carbon paper. No known toxicity.

OZONE • A blue gas with a pungent odor, formed in air from lightning, by ultraviolet (UV) radiation, from automobile engines, and by electrolysis of alkaline perchlorate solutions. It may also be produced by photocopying machines, laser printers, and by electrostatic air cleaners in homes. Commercial mixtures containing up to 2 percent ozone are produced by electronic irradiation of air. Used for purification of drinking water, industrial waste treatment, deodorization of air and sewer gases, bleaching of waxes, oils, paper and textiles, and as a bactericide.

Although the concentration of ozone in the stratosphere is only a few parts per million, it plays an important role in the life cycle on earth by absorbing nearly all the remaining shortwave solar ultraviolet radiation, as well as most of the longer UV rays. Thus the ozone layer shields the earth from most of the harmful UV radiation. A depletion of the ozone layer would allow increasing amounts of harmful radiation to reach the earth's surface, adversely affecting plant, animal, and human life, as well as causing changes in the climate. It has been theorized that the release of various chemical compounds into the environment such as halogens, nitrogen fertilizers, and emissions from subsonic and supersonic aircraft, deplete the ozone. Estimates of the amount of stratospheric ozone destroyed by release of gases—used as refrigerants and as propellants in some aerosol sprays—has been reported to be depleting the ozone more rapidly than estimated. The use of chlorofluorocarbon propellants has been banned since 1979 by the FDA and EPA except for a few specialized products. In fact, a recent increase in melanoma, a deadly skin cancer, has been blamed on the decrease in the ozone layer. The concentrated gas is highly irritating to lungs and eyes. Inhalation of ozone gas has produced tumors in mice.

P

PABA • **4-Aminobenzoic Acid.** **p-Aminobenzoic Acid.** *See* Para-Aminobenzoic Acid.

PAHs • *See* Polycyclic Aromatic Hydrocarbons.

PAINT CLEANERS • **Varnish Cleaners.** One type contains just soap and detergents. Another type contains ammonia and a fatty alcohol. Still another formulation contains borax *(see)*, kerosene, colloidal clay, isopropyl alcohol, and tetrasodium pyrophosphate. Among other ingredients that may be in these products are silica, kaolin, sodium carbonate, dichloromethane, paraffin, resin, rubber, and acetophenol *(see all)*. To remove fresh paint from your skin, try shampoo or shaving cream. You can also try these on the brushes.

PAINT REMOVERS • **Varnish Removers.** A paste or liquid product containing solvents and ingredients that retard evaporation of the solvents. Among the solvents used are methanol, phenol, cresol, denatured alcohol, methylene chloride, toluene, benzene, and ethyl acetate. Paraffin is often used to slow evaporation. Caustic strippers may contain concentrated alkalies such as sodium phosphate, sodium silicate, and caustic soda. Other ingredients that may be in a product are naphthalene, trichloroethane, resin, borax, mineral spirits, and potassium oleate. Those that contain benzene, toluene, trichloroethane, ethylene chloride, or a strong alkali are the most toxic. *See* Paint Cleaners.

PAINT STRIPPERS • Contain phenols, cresols, methylene chloride, and a salt such as acetate plus a strong alkali. *See* Paint Removers.

PAINT THINNERS AND TURPENTINE • May contain butyl alcohol, acetone, methyl isobutyl ketone, and petroleum distillates *(see all)*. A less toxic alternative is to use water with water-based paints.

PAINTBRUSH CLEANERS • Usually contain acetone, benzene, ammonia and alcohol, methyl alcohol, and naphtha, stoddard solution or kerosene *(see all)*.

PAINTING (HOUSE) • Among the compounds to which painters are exposed include acetone, acids, alkalies, aniline, arsenic, barium, benzene, carbon disulfide, carbon tetrachloride, chromates, lead, manganese, mercury, methanol, methylene chloride, nitrogen oxides, and solvents such as trichloroethylene and turpentine *(see all)*. *See also* Paints, Paint Cleaners, Paint Removers, and Lead-Based Paint.

PAINTS • There are many varieties of paints. Anti-algae paints may contain copper, arsenic, mercury, and phenol, most of which are poisonous. Anti-rust paints contain pigments such as zinc or lead chromate, rosin or pine oil, and ingredients such as ammonium hydroxide, arsenic, copper, ethyl alcohol, kerosene, mercuric oxides, metallic soap, methylene chloride, and paraffin. Acrylates in paint include butyl and epoxy acrylates. Pigments include alizarin, chromates, nickel, rhodamine. Vehicles include linseed oil, rosin, or synthetic resins. Antifoam agents such as dibutyl phthalate and pine oil may be in them as well as antioxidants such as hydroquinone. Cobalt may be used to make the paint dry faster. Preservatives may include chloracetamide and mercuric oxide. The newer water-based paints include merthiolate, phenyl mercuric nitrate, and chloracetamide, which are used as preservatives and may produce allergic reactions. Latex- or water-based paints are the least toxic. See individual chemicals. *See also* Enamels, Latex, and Lead-Based Paint.

PALM CHRISTI OIL • *See* Castor Oil.

PALM-KERNEL OIL • **Palm Nut.** The oil from palms, particularly the African palm oil tree. White to yellowish edible fat; it resembles coconut oil more than palm oil. Used chiefly in making soaps and ointments. No known toxicity.

PALM OIL • **Palm Butter. Palm Tallow.** Oil used in baby soaps, ordinary soaps, liniments, and ointments. Obtained from the fruit or seed of the palm tree. A reddish yellow to dark dirty red. A fatty mass with a faint violet odor. Also used to make candles and lubricants. No known toxicity.

PAPER • More than six hundred ingredients are used to create paper from the cellulose fibers of trees. These include fillers, preservatives, plasticizers, whitening agents, adhesives, dispersing agents, corrosion inhibitors, and solvents and other chemicals such as ammonia, hydrogen sulfide, sulfuric acid, carbon monoxide, sodium hydroxide, chlorine, and formaldehyde. Formaldehyde *(see)* and its derivatives are used in paper to make the product stronger and water resistant. It also serves as a disinfectant and preservative. Paper towels may contain melamine formaldehyde resin to increase resistance to water, and paper money may contain formaldehyde and its resins to prevent mildew. Reactions to formaldehyde may occur more often with wrapping paper, inexpensive paper, and newsprint, which all contain unbound formaldehyde. Glossy table paper contains a formaldehyde resin. The shiny, heavy, more expensive table paper is much more likely to contain formaldehyde than the thinner, less expensive, duller, more fragile type of paper. Reading most newspapers, magazines, and books often produces skin rash in formaldehyde-sensitive people. The formaldehyde-sensitive person can have a skin reaction to many types of paper including tissues, paper towels, and paper plates and cups. Marcal products, according to Alexander A. Fisher, M.D., in his book, *Contact Dermatitis,* does not contain formaldehyde. Formaldehyde-sensitive people cannot tolerate any art paper used for acrylic paint or water colors, except for paper with the Grumbacher label, according to Dr. Fisher. Paper may also contain perfume, particularly facial tissue, toilet paper, and sanitary napkins. These perfumes can cause a skin rash, particularly if they contain cinnamic aldehyde or cinnamic alcohol. Clays may also be used as fillers for paper. *See also* Carbon Paper, Carbonless Copy Paper, and Typing Paper.

PARA-AMINOBENZOIC ACID • The colorless or yellowish acid found in vitamin B complex. In an alcohol-and-water solution plus a little light perfume, it is sold under a wide variety of names as a sunscreen lotion to prevent skin damage from the sun. It is also used as a local anesthetic in sunburn products. It is used medicinally to treat arthritis. However, it can cause allergic eczema *(see)* and a sensitivity to light in susceptible people whose skin may react to sunlight by erupting with a rash, sloughing, and/or swelling.

PARABENS • The parabens, methylparaben, and propylparaben, and parahydroxybenzoate, are the most commonly used preservatives in the United States. In 1977, about 30 percent of the cosmetic products registered with the Food and Drug Administration contained parabens.* Water is the only ingredient used more frequently in cosmetics. The parabens have a broad spectrum of antimicrobial activity, are safe to use—relatively nonirritating, nonsensitizing, and nonpoisonous—are stable over the pH *(see)* range in cosmetics, and are sufficiently soluble in water to be effective in liquids. The typical paraben preservative system contains 0.2 percent methylparaben and 0.1 percent propylparaben. *See* Methylparaben and Butylparaben.

PARACIDE • *See* Para-dichlorobenzene.

PARA-DICHLOROBENZENE • *p*-Dichlorobenzene. Paracide. PDB. Crystals made from chlorine and benzene that have a penetrating odor, are almost insoluble in water, and are noncorrosive and nonstaining. A solvent for many organic materials, PDB is employed in degreasing hides and wool, in metal polishes, and in moth repellents, general insecticides, germicides, spray deodorants and fumigants. PDB is commonly found in room deodorizers and moth-killing products. Vapors may cause irritation to the skin, throat, and eyes, and prolonged exposure to high concentrations may cause weakness, dizziness, loss of weight, and liver damage. A well-known animal cancer-causing agent, the chemical can linger in the home for months or even years after use. Toxic by ingestion and inhalation, and irritating to mucous membranes. You can lessen your exposure to PDB by reading product labels and avoiding preparations that contain it (although not all labels list it). A simple way to freshen the air is to place cloves and cinnamon in a cheesecloth bag, or put a few drops of vanilla in water, and boil them gently on the stove. Another way is to put a drop of perfume on a light bulb. Moths can be thwarted by cleaning all clothes before storing them, and then placing herbal sachets (containing rosemary and mint, for example) in closets and drawers. Moth eggs can be destroyed by running garments through a warm dryer. The eggs are

---

*E. I. Richardson. "Preservatives: Frequency of Use in Cosmetic Formulas as Disclosed to the FDA." *Cosmetic Toiletry* (1977), 92:85.

so delicate that just brushing the clothes sometimes can destroy them.

PARAFFIN • Obtained from the distillate of wood, coal, petroleum, or shale oil. Colorless or white, odorless, greasy, and not digestible, or absorbable in the intestines. Easily melts over boiling water and is used to cover food products. Used in cosmetics, as a floor treatment, in lubricants, as flame retardants, sealant, and in detergents. Pure paraffin is harmless to the skin, but the presence of impurities may give rise to irritations and eczema.

PARAFFIN WAX • Obtained from the distillate of wood, coal, petroleum or shale oil, it easily melts over boiling water. Cleared for use by the FDA as a synthetic masticatory substance in chewing gum. A colorless, somewhat translucent, odorless mass with a greasy feel, it is used to make candles, as a paper coating, in glass-cleaning preparations, for matches, crayons, photography, and to protect rubber from sun damage. Pure paraffin is harmless to the skin but the presence of impurities may give rise to irritations and eczema.

PARAFFINIC OILS • Used as lubricant in metalworking, in floor treatments, and as plant spray. Can cause skin rash, and skin and scrotal cancer. *See* Paraffin and Rockland® Horticultural Spray Oil.

PARAFORMALDEHYDE • A white solid derived from formaldehyde, and having the same odor. Used as a fungicide, a bactericide, and in disinfectants. Also used in adhesives and as a waterproofing agent. Toxic by ingestion. *See* Formaldehyde.

PARATHION • Deep brown to yellow liquid, it is an organophosphate *(see)* insecticide and acaracide. Highly toxic by skin contact, inhalation, or ingestion, it interferes with the transmission of nerve signals. Repeated exposure may, without warning, be increasingly hazardous. *See* Organophosphates.

PARZATE™ • A series of fungicides containing zineb. *See* Fungicides and Zineb.

PASTE, LIBRARY • Corn, wheat, or potato dextrin with glucose, phenol, or sodium *o*-phenylphenate; oil of wintergreen, glycerine, and water. May also contain borax or trisodium phosphate. The starch gum paste may, in addition to starch, contain glycerin, defoamer, formaldehyde, phenol, and water. Also may contain Dowicide™, sodium nitrate, mineral spirits, sodium pentachlorphenate, animal glue, sodium bicarbonate, aluminum sulfate, benzoate, bentonite, and sodium fluosilicate *(see all)*.

PATCHING CEMENT • Contains mostly sand with portland cement, resin, and stabilizers. Patching plaster may contain limestone, plaster of paris, mica, ground marble, and glue. Plastic putty contains plaster of paris, limestone, polyvinyl alcohol, methyl cellulose polymer, wood flour, thickeners, and pigments.

PCA • 2-Pyrrolidone-5-Carboxylic Acid. Employed in the manufacture of polyvinylpyrrolidone *(see)*, which goes into hair sprays. Also a high-boiling solvent in petroleum processing, and a plasticizer and coalescing agent for floor polishes. No known skin toxicity.

PCBs • Polychlorinated Biphenyls. Aroclor®. Askarel®. Eucarel®. Pyranol®. Dykanol®. Clorphen®. Clorinol®. Chlorextol®. Diaclor®. Hyvol®. Asbestol®. Inerteen®. Elemex®. Saf-T-Kuhl®. No-Flanol®. Nepolin®. EEC-18® and others. Clear, amber-colored, or dark, oily liquids. They may have a faint smell like motor oil, and some contain chlorobenzenes, which make them smell like mothballs. Widely used since the 1930s because of their excellent electrical and insulating abilities, PCBs were banned in 1978 by the Environmental Protection Agency. Their toxic effects were first noted when over twelve hundred people in Japan were poisoned by eating food cooked in oil heavily contaminated with PCBs. Soon afterward, studies showed that PCBs cause cancer in test animals and it was, therefore, considered likely that they could cause cancer in humans.

PCBs remain in the environment for a long time because they do not break down. Equipment manufactured after 1979 usually does not contain PCBs. Most pre-1979 capacitors do contain PCBs, while many pre-1979 transformers do not. Transformers within buildings or vaults are more likely to contain PCBs. Fluorescent light ballasts may contain about an ounce of PCBs. What usually leaks from a burned-out light ballast are not PCBs, but a black, tarry material that is used to muffle noise from the capacitor. However, it is safest to assume that anything that leaks from a pre-1979 transformer, capacitor, or light ballast contains PCBs unless there is a "no PCBs" label on the equipment. PCBs are easily absorbed through the skin, and by inhalation of their vapors from overheated equipment. There is no way to remove PCBs once they have entered the body. If you suspect equipment in your home, office, or yard is leaking PCBs, rope off the area and call your regional EPA for further instructions. *See* Environmental Protection Agencies for listings.

PEAR OIL • *See* Amyl Acetate.

PEG • The abbreviation for polyethylene glycol/polyethylene, used in making nonionic surfactants. The low molecular polyethylene glycols from 200 to 400 may cause hives and eczema. The higher polyethylenes are not sensitizers. *See* Surfactants and Nonionic.

PEG-4, -6, -8, -9, -10, -12, -14, -16, -18, -32, -40, -150, -200, -350 • Polymers *(see)* of ethylene oxide. Usually, a waxy compound. The number refers to the liquidity: the higher the number, the harder the composition.

PEG-7 BETA-NAPHTHOL • The polyethylene glycol ether of 2-naphthol. *See* Polyethylene Glycol and Beta-Naphthol.

PEG-8 CAPRATE • The polyethylene glycol ester of capric acid. *See* Capric Acid and Polyethylene Glycol.

PEG-9 CAPRYLATE • The polyethylene glycol ester of caprylic acid *(see)*.

PEG-8 CAPRYLATE/CAPRATE • The polyethylene glycol ester of a mixture of caprylic and capric acids *(see all)*.

PEG-6 CAPRYLIC/CAPRIC GLYCERIDES • The ethoxylated glycerides of caprylic and capric acid derivatives. *See* Caprylic and Capric Acids and Glycerides.

PEG-3 TO -200 CASTOR OIL • The polyethylene glycol derivatives of castor oil *(see)*. The higher the number after the listing, the more solid the compound. *See* Polyethylene Glycol.

PEG-3 TO -11 COCAMIDE • The polyethylene glycol amides of coconut acid. The higher the number, the more solid the compound. Used as emulsifiers. *See* Polyethylene Glycol and Coconut Oil.

PEG-2 TO -15 COCAMINE • The polyethylene glycol amines of coconut acid. The higher the number, the harder the compound.

PEG-5, -8, or -15 COCOATE • The polyethylene glycol esters of coconut acid. The lower the number, the more liquid the compound. *See* Polyethylene Glycols and Coconut Oil.

PEG-2 OR -15 COCOMONIUM CHLORIDE • *See* Quaternary Ammonium Compounds.

PEG-15 COCOPOLYAMINE • The polyethylene glycol polyamine and coconut acid. *See* Polyethylene Glycol and Coconut Oil.

PEG-4 THROUGH -150 DILAURATE • The polyethylene glycol diesters of lauric acid *(see)*. The higher the number, the more solid the compound. *See also* Polyethylene Glycol.

PEG-6 TO -150 DIOLEATE • The polyethylene glycol diester of oleic acid *(see)*. The lower the number, the more liquid the compound. *See* Polyethylene Glycol.

PEG-3 DIPALMITATE • The polyethylene glycol diester of palmitic acid *(see)*.

PEG-2 THROUGH -175 DISTEARATE • The polyethylene glycol diesters of stearic acid. The higher the number, the more solid the compound. *See* Stearic Acid and Polyethylene Glycol.

PEG-8 OR -12 DITALLATE • The polyethylene glycol diesters of tall oil *(see)*.

PEG-8 DITRIRICONOLEATE • *See* Ricinoleic Acid and Polyethylene Glycol.

PEG-22 OR -45 DODECYL GLYCOL COPOLYMERS • *See* Polyethylene Glycol.

PEG-7 OR -30 GLYCERYL COCOATE • The polyethylene glycol ethers of glyceryl cocoate. *See* Coconut Oil.

PEG-15 OR -20 GLYCERYL RICINOLEATE • The polyethylene glycol ethers of glyceryl ricinoleate. The lower the number, the more liquid the compound. *See* Polyethylene Glycol and Castor Oil.

PEG-5 THROUGH -120 GLYCERYL STEARATE • *See* Polyethylene Glycol and Stearic Acid.

PEG-28 GLYCERYL TALLOWATE • *See* Tallow Glyceride and Polyethylene Glycol.

PEG-25 GLYCERYL TRIOLEATE • *See* Oleic Acid and Polyethylene Glycol.

PEG-5 THROUGH -200 HYDROGENATED CASTOR OIL • *See* Polyethylene Glycol and Castor Oil.

PEG-2 THROUGH -150 LAURATE • The polyethylene glycol esters of lauric acid. The number signifies liquidity. Yellow, oily liquid insoluble in water. Widely used in soaps and detergents. Emulsifier in cosmetic creams and lotions. Gives an oil-in-water emulsion. No known toxicity other than allergic reactions in some persons sensitive to laurates. *See* Lauric Acid.

PEI • The abbreviation for polyethylenimine.

PEI-7 • **Polyethylenimine 7.** A highly viscous liquid used as an adhesive or anchoring agent for cellophane and as a disinfectant for the skin. Also used in water purification.

PEI-15 THROUGH -2500 • *See* PEI-7.

PEL • **Permissible Exposure Level.** A maximum allowable exposure level under OSHA *(see)* regulations.

PELARGONIC ACID • **Nonanoic Acid.** A synthetic flavoring agent that occurs naturally in cocoa and oil of lavender. Used in berry, fruit, nut, and spice flavorings. A strong irritant.

PENDIMETHALIN • **Pre-M**™. Orange crystals derived from benzene and aniline. It is a preemergent crabgrass and weed killer. *See* Benzene, Lawn Chemicals, and Pesticides.

PENETRANT • Any substance that increases the speed and ease with which a bath or liquid permeates a material being processed.

PENTACHLOROETHANE • A dense, colorless liquid derived from trichloroethylene. Used as a solvent for oil and grease in metal cleaning. *See* Tetrachloroethane.

PENTACHLOROPHENOL • A biocide in metalworking fluids *(see)*, and a fungicide, bactericide, algicide, herbicide, and wood preservative for telephone poles and pilings. This additive has been shown to cause decreased birth weights in the offspring of test animals. According to the California Hazard Evaluation System and Information Service, although it is not known whether this will occur in humans, metalworking liquids containing pentachlorophenol should be used with caution, and impervious gloves worn whenever possible.

PENTAERYTHRITOL • Prepared from acetaldehyde and formaldehyde *(see both)*. It is used in synthetic resins.

PENTAERYTHRITOL ROSINATE • The ester of acids derived from rosin *(see)* mixed with pentaerythritol *(see)*.

PENTANAL • **N-Valderdehyde. Valeral.** An aldehyde *(see)* derived from amyl alcohol. Used as a flavoring agent, in resin chemistry, and as a rubber accelerator. A fire hazard. A mild irritant. *See* Aldehydes.

PENTANE • The aliphatic hydrocarbon derived from petroleum. Used as a solvent, in artificial ice manufacture, in the manufacture of plastics, and in pesticides. Narcotic in high doses.

2-PENTANOL • **Pentyl Alcohol. n-Amyl Alcohol.** A liquid with a mild odor, slightly soluble in water. Used as a solvent for paints and lacquers. Irritating to the eyes and respiratory passages. Absorption may cause a lack of oxygen in the blood.

1-PENTANOL ACETATE • *See* Amyl Acetate.

PER- • A prefix from the Latin *per*, or "through," indicating that a compound has the ultimate amount of oxygen it can carry.

PERCHLOROETHYLENE • **Perc. Perchlor. Tetrachloroethylene. Tetrachloroethane. Ethylene Tetrachloride. 1,1,2,2,-Tetrachloroethylene. Carbon Dichloride.** A clear, colorless, nonflammable liquid with an etherlike smell, it is the main solvent used in the dry-cleaning process. Also used in metal degreasing, during the production of fluorocarbons, and in some adhesives, aerosols, paints, and coatings. Perc enters your body when you breathe its vapors. Liquid perc can be absorbed through the skin, to a limited extent. The most common effects of overexposure are irritation of the eyes, nose, throat, or skin. Like most organic solvents, perc affects the brain the same way as drinking alcohol does. The symptoms of short-term overexposure usually clear up within hours after exposure stops. The mildest effects may start occurring at exposure levels of about 1,090 ppm. Effects occur more quickly and become more noticeable and serious as the exposure levels increases. Effects of perc on the nervous system include feeling "high," dizziness, headache, nausea, vomiting, fatigue, weakness, confusion, slurred speech, loss of balance, and poor coordination. At very high exposure (above 5,000 to 10,000 ppm) it can cause loss of consciousness and even death. According to the California Hazard Evaluation System and Information Service, some studies show that overexposure to organic solvents over months or years may have long-lasting and possibly permanent effects on the nervous system. The symptoms of these long-term effects include fatigue, poor muscle coordination, difficulty in concentrating, loss of short-term memory, and personality changes such as increased anxiety, nervousness, and irritability. Perc causes cancer in laboratory animals at exposure levels close to the level legally allowed in the workplace. Contamination of drinking water with perc in Massachusetts and New Jersey has been implicated in clusters of leukemia and birth defects among residents. In any case, do not use perc around an open flame or intense ultraviolet light. Do not smoke where perc is being used. As with most solvents containing chlorine, perc can break down into very hazardous compounds such as phosgene, hydrochloric acid, and chlorine.

PERLITE • Natural, volcanic glass, an amorphous mineral consisting of sodium potassium aluminum silicate and quartz. Expands when finely ground and heated. Used in gardening and in the manufacture of steel. The dust may be irritating to the lungs, throat, and eyes.

PERMAFRESH™ • A series of commercial resins used in the textile industry for wash-and-wear fabrics, crease resistance, shrinkage control, durable finishes, and bodying agents. These include certain cellulose reactants, melamine derivatives, and carbamide resins. *See* Permanent Press and Clothing.

PERMANENT PRESS • **Durable Press.** Garments labeled "durable" or "permanent press" are designed to need no ironing. This is achieved through the pre-curing of fabrics, where a special resin finish is applied to them before garments are made, and then permanently pressed in with a heat process after garments are completed. In the post-cured method, resin-impregnated garments are pressed in the conventional method and a no-iron finish baked in by placing finished garments in the open and subjecting them to heat. *See* Wrinkleproof Finishes.

PERMETHRIN • Ambush™. Pounce™. Synthetic pyrethroid insecticide. As active as pyrethrins. Mild irritant to the skin and eyes, but of low toxicity. *See* Safrotin™.

PEROXIDE • Used in bleaches and to add oxygen to compounds. A strong oxidant and irritant that can injure the skin and eyes, and may cause hair breakage. Chemists are cautioned to wear rubber gloves and goggles when handling it. *See* Hydrogen Peroxide.

PEST • An insect, rodent, nematode, fungus, weed, virus, bacterium, or other microorganism or form of plant or animal life considered to be an annoyance, and which may be injurious to health or the environment.

PESTICIDES • Compounds that are used to kill pests. Inorganic and organometallic pesticides include arsenic trioxide, barium carbonate, copper sulfate, lead arsenate, mercuric chloride, phosphorus, sodium arsenate, sodium chlorate, sodium fluoride, thallium sulfate, zinc phosphide, and mercury compounds. Natural pesticides include anabasine, nicotine, pyrethrum, rotenone, sabadilla, and strychnine. Solvents, propellants, and oil insecticides include dichlorodifluoromethane, kerosene, Tetralin™, and xylene. Phenolic and nitrophenolic pesticides include dinitrobutylphenol, 2,4-dinitrophenol, dinocap, dinitrocresol (DNOC) and pentachlorophenol. Chlorinated hydrocarbon insecticides include aldrin, chlordane, DDT, dieldrin, p,p'-dichlorodiphenylmethyl carbinol (DMC), endosulfan, endrin, isobenzan, hexachlorocyclohexane, lindane, methoxychlor, tetrachlorodiphenylethane (TDE), and toxaphene. *See* Fumigants, Organophosphates, Insecticides, and Carbamates.

The potential for a pesticide to cause injury is determined by several factors.

• Toxicity of the active ingredient. "Toxicity" is a measure of the inherent ability of a chemical to produce injury. Some pesticides, such as pyrethrins, have low human toxicity, while others, such as sodium fluoroacetate, are extremely toxic.

• Dose. The greater the dose of pesticide, i.e., the amount absorbed, the greater the risk of injury. Dose is dependent upon the absolute amount of the pesticide absorbed relative to the weight of the person. Therefore, small amounts of pesticide might produce illness in a small child while the same dose in an adult might be relatively harmless.

• Route of absorption. Swallowing a pesticide usually creates the most serious problem. In practice, however, pesticides are absorbed through the skin, and the more toxic pesticides have caused fatalities through this route.

• Duration of exposure. The longer a person is exposed to pesticides, the higher the level in the body. However, there is a point at which an equilibrium will develop between the intake and the output. When this occurs, the level will no longer continue to increase. This point may be either above or below the known toxic level.

• Physical and chemical properties. The distribution and the rates of breakdown of pesticides in the environment significantly alter the likelihood that injury might occur.

• Population at risk. Persons who run the greatest danger of poisoning are those whose exposure is highest, such as workers who mix, load, or apply pesticides. However, the general public also faces the possibility of exposure, and children, because of their small size, are more vulnerable than adults to pesticide poisoning.

• Risk identified on the label. There is a key word on the label that tells you into which one of the four toxicity categories the pesticide product falls. Category I is the most toxic and the label will read, "Danger Poison." A moderately toxic one will carry "Warning." The slightly toxic category carries the word "Caution," and the nontoxic products do not have any of these warnings.

FIRST AID FOR PESTICIDE POISONING

First aid is the first step in treating a pesticide poisoning. Study the "Statement of Treatment" on a product's label before you use a pesticide. When you realize a pesticide poisoning is occurring, before calling for emergency help, make sure the victim is not being further exposed to the poison. An unconscious victim will have to be dragged into fresh air. Caution: do not become poisoned yourself while trying to help. You may have to put on breathing equipment or protective clothing to avoid becoming the second victim.

After giving initial first aid, get medical help immediately. This advice cannot be repeated too often. Bring the product's container with its label to the doctor's office or emergency room where the victim will be treated. Keep the container out of the passenger space of your vehicle to avoid further contamination (best to transport the container in your trunk). The doctor will need to know the hazardous chemical contents of the pesticide before prescribing treatment (information that is also on the label). Sometimes the label even includes a telephone number to call for additional treatment information.

A good resource in a pesticide emergency is the National Pesticide Telecommunications Network (NPTN), a toll-free telephone service. NPTN operators are on call 24 hours a day, 365 days a year, to provide information on pesticides, and on recognizing and responding to pesticide poisonings, for animals as well as humans. If necessary, they can transfer inquiries directly to affiliated poison control centers.

To contact the NPTN you may call the toll-free number: (800) 858-7378.

To keep your pets from being poisoned, follow label directions on flea and tick products carefully, and keep pets off lawns that have been newly treated with weed killers and insecticides.

The EPA is interested in receiving information on any adverse effects associated with pesticide exposure. If you have such information, contact the Pesticide Incident Response Officer, Field Operations Division (H-7506C), Office of Pesticide Programs, EPA, 401 M Street, SW, Washington, D.C. 20460. You should provide as much information as possible, including any official investigation report of the incident and medical records concerning adverse health effects. Medical records will be held in confidence.

To sterilize pesticide-contaminated clothing, the following tips are suggested.

TIPS FOR LAUNDERING PESTICIDE-CONTAMINATED CLOTHING*

AIR

• Hang garment outdoors to air. Sunshine and ventilation aid the breakdown of certain pesticides. Do not hang contaminated garments with uncontaminated garments. Do not hang contaminated garments close to residences or in areas frequented by people or pets.

*Prepared by Charlotte W. Coffman, Department of Textiles and Apparel, Cornell Cooperative Extension. Printed with permission.

PRE-RINSE

- Use one of three methods:

1. Hose off garments outdoors in an area away from people and pets.

2. Rinse in separate tub or pail kept for that purpose.

3. Agitate in automatic washer.

PRE-TREAT (heavily soiled garments)

- Use a heavy-duty liquid.

WASHER LOAD

- Wash garments separately from family wash. Pesticides can migrate from contaminated clothing to other clothing, to equipment, or to the unprotected hands of the person doing the laundry.

- Wash garments contaminated with the same pesticide together.

LOAD SIZE

- Wash only a few garments at once.

WATER LEVEL

- Use full water level.

WATER TEMPERATURE

- Use hot water, 140°F or higher.

WASH CYCLE

- Use normal 12-minute wash cycle.

LAUNDRY DETERGENT

- Use a built heavy-duty laundry detergent. Heavy-duty detergents include built and unbuilt formulations in either powdered or liquid form. Built detergents contain additional cleaning agents that control water hardness, increase and maintain alkalinity of wash water, react with oily soils, and suspend particulate soil. Built detergents are preferred for pesticide-contaminated clothing because the pesticide is often mixed with other natural soils. Polyphosphates are the preferred builder because they clean well without forming a precipate that adheres to the clothing. Where use of phosphates in detergents is prohibited, as in New York State, sodium carbonate, sodium aluminosilicate, and sodium nitrilotriacetate may be used as builders.

- Use amount recommended on package or more for heavy soil/ hard water.

- Remember to dissolve powdered detergent before adding the clothing to the washing machine.

RINSE

- Use two full warm rinses.

REWASH

- Wash contaminated garments two or three times before reuse for more complete pesticide removal.

DRY

- Dry outdoors to avoid contaminating dryer and to encourage further dissipation of the chemical.

CLEAN WASHER

- Run complete, but empty, cycle. Use hot water and detergent.

Other Tips

- Read the labels on the pesticide container for protective clothing recommendations.

- Avoid leather garments such as shoes, belts, or wristbands. Leather soiled with pesticides cannot be decontaminated.

- Save clothing worn while handling pesticides for that use only. Keep separate from other clothing before, during, and after laundering.

- Wear a disposable coverall over work clothes. The coveralls must be intended for pesticide use, free of tears, and disposed of properly.

- Consider clothing worn under disposable coveralls to be contaminated and treat them accordingly.

- Remove contaminated clothing before entering enclosed tractor cabs.

• Synthetic rubber is a good choice for gloves and boots because it protects against dry and wet formulations. Natural rubber products are only effective for dry formulations.

• Wear waterproof gloves when handling contaminated clothing. Replace gloves periodically.

• Wash contaminated clothing after each use. When applying pesticides daily, wash clothing daily.

• Dry cleaning is not recommended for pesticide-contaminated clothing.

• Bury shoes and garments that were saturated with highly toxic/concentrated pesticides.

• Wash hands frequently, especially before eating, smoking, or toileting.

• Shower immediately after using pesticides. Remember to shampoo your hair and clean your nails.

PET • **Polyethylene Terephthalate**. A plastic used to make soda containers. About 20 percent is being recycled today. Its primary uses as recycled products include carpet backing and fiberfill for sleeping bags and clothing, and nonfood bottles. It is also used in automobile bumpers, furniture, bathtubs, awnings, and swimming pools. *See* Polyethylenes.

PET CARE PRODUCTS • Many products are available for the health and grooming needs of cats, dogs, birds, and other small animals. They include powders, soaps, and shampoos, breath fresheners, colognes, deodorants, coat conditioners, and medications sold for treatment of mange, eczema, diarrhea, carsickness, worms, and vitamin deficiencies. Most are not toxic except for the pesticides and some of the medications. Wormers may include piperazine adipate, hydrochloride, phosphate, and citrate. Some contain tetrachloroethylene *(see),* mineral oil, and butyl chloride. Another may contain toluene and quinacrine hydrochloride plus benzocaine. *See* Pet Pesticides and Dog and Cat Shampoos.

PET PESTICIDES • The products that can kill fleas, ticks, mites and other pests on your pet, if not carefully handled, can also kill your pets and family members. Some are more dangerous than others. The most toxic one, according to Gosselin, Smith, and Hodge—authors of *Clinical Toxicology of Commercial Products,* 5th ed. (Baltimore: Williams & Wilkins, 1984)—is sodium arsenite *(see* Arsenics). Others that are very toxic include BHC, boric acid, carbaryl, DDVP *(see)*, dichlorophene, benzethonium chloride, lindane, malathion, naphthalene, oil of anise, para-cymene (xylene), pine tar, rotenone™, sodium cresylate, and toxaphene. Others that are not as toxic but still dangerous include allethrin, benzene hexachloride, chloranil, DDD, dimethyl phthalate, dipentene, menthols, methoxychlor, and pyrethrins. Bird sprays for lice and mites include pyrethrins, piperonyl butoxide, petroleum distillates, and glycols. Sprays for hamsters also include the same substances in slightly larger amounts. Less toxic alternatives are herbal collars or ointments with eucalyptus or rosemary, a flea comb, or brewer's yeast (call your veterinarian for the amount).

PET STAIN REMOVERS • Usually contain an enzyme and detergent. Products such as Ultra Fresh Pet Stain and Odor Remover™ claim to be harmless to children. For a do-it-yourself alternative, blot stain thoroughly. Saturate with club soda. Blot again, then apply white vinegar and blot till dry.

PETROLATUM • **Vaseline. Petroleum Jelly. Paraffin Jelly.** Used in cold creams, emollient creams, conditioning creams, wax depilatories, eyebrow pencils, eyeshadows, liquefying creams, liquid powders, nail whites, lipsticks, protective creams, baby creams, and rouge. It is a purified mixture of semisolid hydrocarbons from petroleum. Yellowish to light amber or white, semisolid, unctuous mass, practically odorless and tasteless, almost insoluble in water. As a lubricant in lipsticks, it gives them a shine and in creams it makes them smoother. Helps to soften and smooth the skin in the same way as any other emollient and is less expensive. The oily film helps prevent evaporation of moisture from the skin and protects the skin from irritation. However, petroleum does cause allergic skin reactions in the hypersensitive. It is generally nontoxic.

PETROLEUM • **Crude Oil. Mineral Oil. Rock Oil. Paraffin Oil.** A highly complex mixture of paraffinic, naphthahenic, and aromatic hydrocarbons containing some sulfur and trace amounts of nitrogen and oxygen compounds. Believed to have originated from both plant and animal sources millions of years ago. By cracking petroleum into fractions, the gases butane, ethane, and propane are obtained, as well as naphtha, gasoline, kerosene, fuel oils, gas oil, lubricating oils, paraffin wax, and asphalt. From the hydrocarbon gases, ethylene, butylene, and propylene are obtained; these are used to obtain alcohols, ethylene glycols, and a wide range of plastics. Benzene, phenol, toluene, and xylene can be made from petroleum, as well as hundreds of other products. Petroleum is flammable, toxic by ingestion and inhalation, and is a local skin irritant. Many of its products are reported to be cancer-causing agents. *See also* Aliphatic Hydrocarbons.

PETROLEUM DISTILLATES • Clear, colorless, highly flammable distillates from petroleum used as a solvent for fats, oils, and detergents. They are found in a wide variety of consumer products including lip gloss, liquid gas, fertilizer, furniture polish, pesticides, plastics, paint thinners, motor oil, and fuels. Petroleum jelly (Vaseline®) is considered harmless, but naphthalene *(see)* is not, yet they are both petroleum distillates. Armomatic compounds (they easily vaporize) are the most toxic and are linked to cancer, with long-term use. Aromatic compounds are found in all crude oils and most petroleum products. Many have a pleasant odor and include such substances as naphthalene, xylene, toluene, and benzene *(see all)*. Petroleum distillates are harmful if ingested and vomited. When swallowed, the lighter, more volatile distillate products can be sucked into the lungs, causing a chemical pneumonia. Aspiration of fluid into the lungs can occur both during swallowing and vomiting of the product. Upon skin contact, petroleum distillates can produce local skin irritation. Products that contain petroleum distillates should be used carefully. Wear gloves and do not mix different petroleum distillate products. *See* Kerosene.

PETROLEUM NAPHTHA • **VM & P Naphtha. Petroleum Ether. Petroleum Benzin.** A clear colorless, highly flammable liquid, used as a solvent. May contain benzene. *See* Petroleum and Solvents.

PGME • *See* Glycol Ethers.

PGMEA • *See* Glycol Ethers.

pH • The scale used to measure acidity and alkalinity. pH is the hydrogen (H) ion concentration of a solution. The "p" stands for the power of hydrogen ion. The pH of a solution is measured on a scale of 14. A truly neutral solution, neither acidic nor alkaline, such as water, is 7. The pH of blood is 7.3; vinegar is 2.3; lemon juice is 8.2; and lye is 13. Skin and hair are naturally acidic. Soap and detergents are alkaline.

PHENOL • **Carbolic Acid.** Used in shaving creams and hand lotions. Obtained from coal tar. Occurs in urine and has the characteristic odor present in coal tar and wood. A general disinfectant and anesthetic for the skin. Used in phenol resins, epoxy resins, 2,4-D, solvents, germicidal paints, slimicides, dyes, and rubber. Ingestion of even small amounts may cause nausea, vomiting and circulatory collapse, paralysis, convulsions, coma, and greenish urine as well as necrosis of the mouth and gastrointestinal tract. Death results from respiratory failure. Fatalities have been reported from ingestion of as little as 1.5 grams (30 grams to the ounce). Fatal poisoning can occur through skin absorption. Although there have been many poisonings from phenolic solutions, it continues to be used in commercial products. A concentration of 1 percent used to prevent itching from insect bites and sunburn, applied for several hours, caused gangrene resulting from spasms of small blood vessels under the skin. Swelling, pimples, hives, and other skin rashes following application to the skin have been widely reported. A concentration of 2 percent causes gangrene, burning, and numbness. Phenol, which is also used in metalworking fluids *(see)* may act as a cancer promoter, according to California's Hazard Evaluation System and Information Service (HESIS). HESIS reports that if you use a metalworking fluid containing mineral oil and phenol, your risk of developing skin cancer is likely to be greater than if you were exposed to the mineral oil alone.

PHENOL METHYLCARBAMATE • *See* Baygon™ and Pesticides.

PHENOXY ACID COMPOUNDS • *See* 2,4-D and TCDD.

PHENOXYETHANOL • **2-Phenoxyethanol.** An oily liquid with a faint, aromatic odor and a burning taste. Derived from treating phenol with ethylene oxide in an alkaline medium. Used as a fixative for perfumes, as a bactericide, insect repellent, and topical antiseptic. *See* Phenol.

PHENOXYISOPROPANOL • **1-Phenoxy-2-Propanol.** *See* Phenol.

PHENYL • Means "derived from benzene" *(see)*.

PHENYL ANTHRANILATES • *See* Coal Tar.

PHENYL MERCAPTAN • Used to kill mosquito eggs. Toxic. *See* Phenol and Mercury.

PHENYL METHYL PYRAZOLONE • A white powder made from phenylhydrazine with ethylacetoacetate used as an intermediate in dyes and plastics. *See* Pyrazole.

PHENYL PELARGONATE • A liquid, insoluble in water. Used in flavors, perfumes, bactericides, and fungicides. *See* Phenol.

PHENYL SALICYLATE • A white, crystalline powder made from salicylic acid and phenol. Used to protect plastics, waxes, and polishes from sun damage.

PHENYL TRIMETHICONE • **Methyl Phenyl Polysiloxane.** Silicone oil used as a skin protectant and to give it gloss. It is treated to make it water-repellent. *See* Silicones.

PHENYLENEDIAMINE m-, o-, p- • Used in black, blue, or brown clothing as well as in hair dye and fur dye. Most permanent home and beauty parlor dyes contain this chemical or a related one such as 4-nitro-o-phenylenediamine. Also called "oxidation," "amino," "para," or "peroxide" dyes. PPD was first introduced in 1890 for dyeing furs and feathers. It comes in about thirty shades and is used as an intermediate in coal tar dyes. May produce eczema, bronchial asthma, gastritis, skin rash, and death. Can cross-react with many other chemicals, including azo dyes used for temporary hair colorings. Can also produce photosensitization. Has been found to cause cancer in animals and is a cancer suspect in humans.

PHENYLETHENE • *See* Styrene.

PHENYLETHYLENE • *See* Styrene.

PHENYLMERCURIC ACETATE • White, creamy prisms that are derived from benzene and mercuric acetate. Used as a fungicide, herbicide, mildewcide for paints and to keep swimming pool water free of slime. Toxic by ingestion, inhalation, and skin absorption. Strongly irritating.

PHENYLMERCURIC BENZOATE, BORATE, AND CHLORIDE • Used as fungicides and bactericides. Toxic. *See* Mercury, Benzene, and Borate.

PHENYLMERCURITRIETHANOLAMMONIUM LACTATE • Derived from phenylmercuric acetate with triethanolamine and lactic acid. It is a fungicide for turf and for fruit trees. Toxic by ingestion, inhalation, and skin absorption. *See* Mercury.

o-PHENYLPHENOL • **Orthoxenol. Dowicide 1™.** Prepared from phenol, it consists of white, flaky crystals with a mild odor. Used in the rubber industry, in agriculture fungicides, disinfectants such as Lysol®, and in spray deodorants. *See* Phenol for toxicity.

PHORATE • *See* Organophosphates.

PHOSKIL™ • *See* Parathion.

PHOSMET • **Imidan™.** White crystals used as a pesticide on fruits and vegetables. Insecticide and acaracide. Toxic by ingestion and may interfere with nerve signals. *See* Organophosphates.

PHOSOPHAMIDON • *See* Organophosphates.

PHOSPHATE • A salt of phosphoric acid *(see)*. Used as an emulsifier, texturizer, and sequestrant in cosmetics and foods. Also, used as a corrosion inhibitor in metalworking fluids. Can cause skin, ear, nose, and throat irritation.

PHOSPHINE, GAS AND SOLID • **Hydrogen Phosphate.** A colorless gas with a garliclike or fishy odor, derived by the action of hydrogen, or potash on phosphorus. It is also found in small amounts in decaying organic matter containing phosphorus. Used as a doping agent, as a catalyst, and as a fumigant *(see)*. A poisonous gas, it is spontaneously flammable, and is a strong irritant. *See* Fumigants.

PHOSPHORIC ACID • Made from phosphate rock from deposits in Tennessee and the western United States. Used in metal cleaning, rust-proofing, and as a disinfectant. Also used to make fertilizers and in engraving. In concentrated solutions, it is irritating to skin and mucous membranes.

PHOSPHORUS • **White, Yellow, Red, and Black.** The white, also called "yellow," phosphorus is very toxic. The red and black forms are practically insoluble in water and single doses are considered essentially harmless. Chronic doses, however, may cause poisoning. Modern matches that can be struck on any rough surface contain either red phosphorus or phosphorous sesquisulfide, together with potassium chlorate and glue. Safety matches that must be ignited on a prepared surface have tips containing potassium chlorate and antimony sulfide, but the striking surface contains red phosphorus, sand, and glue. Acute phosphorus poisonings frequently occur because of accidental ingestion of rat poisons or roach powders where yellow phosphorus may be present in concentrations of up to 5 percent. Ingestion affects the liver, causes vomiting and marked weakness, and can cause destruction of the jawbone. Skin contact with phosphorous solutions produces painful second- and third-degree burns as a result of both chemical and thermal damage. Very dangerous fire hazard and explosive risk from spontaneous chemical reaction with air.

PHOSTEX • *See* Organophosphates.

PHOTOGRAPHIC CHEMICALS • There are many products in various combinations. Among the chemicals that may be used in the "developers" are monomethyl-*p*-amino phenol sulfate (*see* Phenol), hydroquinone, sodium sulfite, paraformaldehyde, sulfuric acid, borax, boric acid, citric acid, glycine, potassium iodine, sulfuric acid, and sodium metaborate. "Film cleaners" may contain ammonium hydroxide, chlorinated solvents, alcohol, chloroform, benzine, trichloroethane, and wax. "Fixing baths" may contain sodium thiosulfate, sodium sulfite, acetic acid, boric acid, borax, potassium aluminum sulfate, potassium metabisulfite, and potassium thiocyanate. "Hardeners" usually contain formaldehyde as well as aluminum chloride, boric acid, and sulfites. "Hypo eliminators" contain hydrogen peroxide, and ammonium hydroxide. "Hypo test solutions" may contain silver nitrate, iodine, potassium permanganate, sodium hydroxide, hydrochloric acid, and mercuric chloride. "Intensifiers" and "reducers" may contain a whole host of various chemicals including the bleaches, potassium dichromate, hydrochloric acid, and "redevelopers," which may include silver nitrate, potassium dichromate, sulfuric acid, sodium bisulfate, hydroquinone, lead nitrate, potassium ferricyanide, and potassium permanganate. Stain removers may contain thiourea, potassium permanganate, and sulfuric acid. "Stop baths" usually contain acetic acid, sodium sulfate, or potassium chromium sulfate. "Toners" contain an even wider variety of chemicals, but usually have a potassium solution, an iron solution, and other chemicals such as silver nitrate, oxalic acid, and salt. Many of the photographic products, particularly the intensifier and reducing formulas, contain extremely toxic materials. An increasing number of communities have special disposal procedures for them, so check with your local authority.

PHTHALIC ACID • Obtained by the oxidation of various benzene derivatives, it can be isolated from the fungus *Gibberella fujikuroi*. When rapidly heated, it forms phthalic anhydride *(see)* and water. It is used chiefly in the manufacture of cosmetic esters, dyes, and nail polishes. Moderately irritating to the skin and mucous membranes.

PHTHALIC ACID ESTERS • Derived from *o*-toluic acid and xylene, these esters *(see)* are used widely as plasticizers and also are dispersed widely in the environment. They have been linked to liver cancer.

PHTHALIC ANHYDRIDE • White, crystalline needles derived from naphthalene *(see)*. Used as a hardener for resins and a plasticizer. Also used in many dyes, chlorinated products, insecticides, and polyesters. A skin irritant. *See* Clothing.

PHTHALIMIDES • A class of fungicides with low acute toxicity; used widely. Some cause a poison-ivylike rash. They cause birth defects in animals, and pregnant women are advised to avoid exposure to them. Included in this group are captan, captafol, and folpet.

PHYTIC ACID • Occurs in nature in the seeds of cereal grains and is derived commercially from corn. It is used to chelate heavy metals, as a rust inhibitor, in metal cleaning, and in the treatment of hard water. Nontoxic although those allergic to corn may have a reaction.

PICLORAM • Crystalline solid made from picolinic acid, it is used as a herbicide and defoliant. It is toxic by ingestion and inhalation. Its use has been restricted in the United States.

PICRIC ACID • Yellow crystals or yellow liquid, very bitter; derived from phenol and sulfuric acid. Used in explosives, textile dye, matches, electric batteries, and for etching copper. Poisonous by ingestion. Skin exposure causes local and systemic allergic reactions. Symptoms of systemic poisoning are nausea, vomiting, diarrhea, inability to urinate, and yellow discoloration of the skin. There may also be convulsions and stupor. Highly explosive and very dangerous, it can explode on decomposition and yields very toxic fumes.

PIGMENT • Any substance, usually a dry powder, that colors another substance. Pigments differ from dyes in that they have no affinity for fiber. When used in fabric printing, they are held to the fabric with a resin such as albumin or phenol.

PINE OIL • The extract from a variety of pine trees. As a pine tar it is used in hair tonics; also a solvent, disinfectant, and deodorant. As an oil from twigs and needles, it is used in pine bath oil emulsions, as a preservative, to scent products, and as a disinfectant. Irritating to the skin and mucous membranes. It can cause nausea, vomiting, convulsions, and dizziness if ingested. In general, pine oil in concentrated form is an irritant to human skin and may cause allergic reactions. The reported adult lethal dose of pine oil is 60 to 120 grams, although survival without ill effects after an ingestion of 400 to 500 grams has been noted. Pine oil products primarily cause gastrointestinal irritation, bleeding, chest pain, nausea, vomiting, and diarrhea. It may also cause nervous system depression, weakness, respiratory failure, sleepiness, delirium, and headache. Kidney failure may occur.

PINE RESIN • *See* Pine Oil.

PINE SOL™ **DISINFECTANT** • Contains pine oil and isopropyl alcohol *(see both)*.

PINE TAR OIL • The extract from a variety of pine tree. A synthetic flavoring obtained from a species of pinewood. Used in licorice flavorings for ice cream, ices, and candy. Also used as a solvent, disinfectant, and deodorant. As a pine tar it is used in hair tonics; also a solvent, disinfectant, and deodorant. *See* Pine Oil.

PINENE • A synthetic flavoring agent that occurs naturally in angelica root oil, anise, star anise, asafoetida oil, coriander, cumin, fennel, grapefruit, juniper berries, oils of lavender and lime, mandarin orange leaf, black pepper, peppermint, pimenta, and yarrow. It is the principal ingredient of turpentine *(see)*. Used chiefly in the manufacture of camphor. Used in lemon and nutmeg flavorings for beverages, ice cream, ices, candy, baked goods, and condiments. Also used as a chewing gum base. Readily absorbed from the gastrointestinal tract, the skin, and respiratory tract. It is a local irritant, central nervous system depressant, and an irritant to the bladder and kidney. Has caused benign skin tumors from chronic contact. The fatal dose is estimated at 180 grams orally as turpentine.

PIPE JOINT CEMENTS • One type contains linseed oil, lithophone, and slate filler. Another type may contain blackstrap molasses, amorphous graphite, vermiculite, bentonite, lithophone, sodium pentachlorophenate, and, possibly, slate and titanium dioxide.

PIPERONYL BUTOXIDE • A light brown liquid with a mild odor. Used in insecticides in combination with pyrethrins *(see)*, in oil solutions, emulsions, powders, or aerosols. Large doses have caused vomiting and diarrhea.

PITCH • A sticky residue from the distillation of coal tar, petroleum, pine tar, and fatty acids. Some are natural. Used as sealants, roofing compounds, and wood preservatives. *See* Coal Tar.

PLASTER OF PARIS • *See* Calcium Sulfate.

PLASTIC CEMENT • **Styrene.** The polyvinyl acetate type contains clay, polyvinyl alcohol, sodium *o*-phenylphenate, and colloid. Nitrocellulose cement, which contains 20 percent nitrocellulose, also contains acetone, methyl acetate, and camphor. Rubber cement contains hexane and rubber. Polystyrene cement contains benzene, toluene, acetone, and naphtha *(see all)*. May be subject to inhalation abuse, and may cause sudden death.

PLASTICIZERS • Chemicals added to natural and synthetic resins and rubbers to impart flexibility, workability, or distensibility without changing the chemical nature of the material. Dibutyl phthalate *(see)* is a plasticizer for nitrocellulose used in lacquers.

PLASTICS • The hard plastics, such as those used on counters, are rarely allergens because their molecules are not airborne. However, the soft plastics or plasticizers used to make substances soft, flexible, or stretchable may cause problems. Among the plastics that may be trouble markers for the sensitive are foam rubber, polyurethane, polyethylene food or garment bags, polyester clothing, and Naugahyde™.

PLATINUM • A silvery white, malleable metal that occurs in Canada, South Africa, Russia, and Alaska. It is used as a catalyst, in jewelry, electrical contacts, electroplating, and magnets, among many other uses. Exposure to complex platinum salts has been shown to cause allergic reactions, including wheezing, coughing, runny nose, tightness of the chest, shortness of breath, and oxygen starvation. Exposure to the pure dust of platinum does not have the same effect.

PLAY-DOH™ • Contains water, wheat flour, salt; calcium chloride, mineral spirits, titanium dioxide, aluminum sulfate, borax *(see all);* coloring, and perfume.

PM ACETATE • See Enamel Paint and Acetate.

POLISHES • A general-purpose polish may have turpentine, mineral spirits, waxes *(see all),* and any of several other ingredients such as a perfume, coloring, detergent, zinc stearate *(see),* and a wood preservative *(see). See also* Furniture Polish, Floor Polish, Leather Polish, Metal Polishes, Porcelain Polish, and Automobile Polishes.

POLOXAMER 188 • **Poloxalene.** A liquid, nonionic *(see)* surfactant polymer. If chain lengths of polyoxyethylene and polyoxypropylene are increased, the product changes from liquid to paste to solid. No known toxicity. *See* Polymer and Surfactants.

POLY- • A prefix from Greek meaning "many."

POLYACRYLAMIDE • The polymer of acrylamide monomers, it is a white solid, water soluble, used as a thickening agent, suspending agent, and as an additive to adhesives. Also used in tanning creams, and in the manufacture of plastics used in nail polishes. A skin irritant that can be absorbed through unbroken skin. Causes central nervous system paralysis. Highly toxic.

POLYACRYLIC ACID • *See* Acrylic Resins.

POLYBUTENE • **Indopol. Polybutylene.** A plasticizer. A polymer *(see)* of one or more butylenes, obtained from petroleum oils. Used in lubricating oil, adhesives, sealing tape, cable insulation, films, and coatings. May cause asphyxiation.

POLYBUTYLENE • *See* Polybutene.

POLYCHLOROTRIFLUOROETHYLENE • Colorless, impervious to corrosive chemicals, it resists most organic solvents and heat. Nonflammable. Used as a transparent film.

POLYCYCLIC AROMATIC HYDROCARBONS • **PAHs.** These are members of a broad class of chemicals produced by incomplete combustion of organic matter. Cigarette smoke, vehicle exhaust, and even charcoal-broiled meat have been shown to contain substantial quantities of these potent carcinogens. The original discovery of their cancer-causing potential was made in the late 1700s, when Sir Percivall Pott made his correlation between cancer and chimney sweeping in England. The EPA considers PAHs to be one of the major indoor air quality hazards.

POLYESTER • A manufactured fiber derived from coal, air, water, and petroleum. Used to make permanent (durable) press merchandise, suits, shirts, slacks, underwear, dresses, blouses, lingerie, children's wear, curtains, draperies, thread, carpeting, sails, fire hose, rope, tire cord, fishnets, power belting, pillow and other stuffing, and knits. Most items made from polyester can be machine-washed and ironed with a moderately warm iron if desired.

POLYETHYLENE • A polymer *(see)* of ethylene; a product of petroleum gas or dehydration of alcohol. One of a group of light-weight thermoplastics with good resistance to chemicals, low moisture absorption, and good insulating properties. Used as a chewing gum-base ingredient, and as a film-former, as sheets for packaging, trash bags, flexible ice trays, dishes, tumblers, food storage bags, plastic wraps, children's toys, and plumber's pipe. Used in hand lotions, liquid polishes, and textile-finishing agents. No known skin toxicity, but implants of large amounts in rats have caused cancer. Ingestion of large oral doses has produced kidney and liver damage.

POLYETHYLENE 6000 OR MORE • An excellent barrier to water vapor and moisture, it resists solvents and corrosive solutions. It is combustible but nontoxic.

POLYETHYLENE GLYCOL • **PEG.** A binder, plasticizing agent, solvent, and softener that improves resistance to moisture and oxidation. Widely used for cosmetic cream bases and pharmaceutical ointments. Used in hair straighteners and tonics, antiperspirants, baby products, fragrances, polish removers, and lipsticks. Also used in metalworking as a lubricant. No known toxicity.

POLYETHYLENE TEREPHTHALATE • *See* PET and Polyethylene.

POLYGLYCEROL • One of several mixtures of ethers of glycerol *(see)*. Thick liquids to solids, they act as humectants much like glycerol. Used as surface-active agents, emulsifiers, plasticizers, adhesives, lubricants, and in other compounds. *See* Glycerol.

POLYGLYCEROL ESTER • One of several partial or complete esters of saturated and unsaturated fatty acids with a variety of derivatives of polyglycerols. Used as lubricants, plasticizers, paint and varnish vehicles, gelling agents, humectants, surface-active agents, dispersants, and emulsifiers in foods and cosmetic preparations.

POLYISOPRENE • The major component of natural rubber, but also made synthetically. Nontoxic.

POLYMER • A substance or product formed by combining many small molecules (monomers). The result essentially is recurring long-chain structural units that have tensile strength, elasticity, and hardness. Examples of polymers (literally, "having many parts") are plastics, fibers, rubber, and human tissue. Polymers provide much of the physical structure of the world in which we live. Natural polymers include wool, silk, cotton, and protein. Synthetic polymers are usually mixtures such as polyesters and polyamides.

POLYNAPH THALENE SULFONATE • Used as a solvent. *See* Naphthalene.

POLYOLS • Alcohol compounds that absorb moisture. They have a low molecular weight: polyols with a target weight above 1,000 are solids, and less toxic than those with a weight of 600 or below. The latter are liquids and, although higher in toxicity, are fatal to animals only in very large doses. Such deaths in animals have been found to be due to kidney damage. *See* Propylene Glycol and Polyetheylene Glycol.

POLYOXYETHYLENE COMPOUNDS • The nonionic emulsifiers. *See* Polyethylene Glycol.

POLYPROPYLENE • A synthetic, translucent or white, crystalline, plastic solid derived from propylene. It is resistant to acids. Used for blankets, protective clothing, fabrics, carpets, and filter cloths. *See* Propylene.

POLYSTYRENE • A colorless to yellowish, oily liquid with a penetrating odor. Obtained from ethylbenzene by removing the hydrogen, or by chlorination. Sparingly soluble in water; soluble in alcohol. Used in the manufacture of cosmetic resins, foam coffee cups, plates, and fast-food carry-out containers. Reported to be an unintentional additive when tea and coffee are served in polystyrene cups. May be irritating to the eyes, mucous membranes, and, in high concentrations, may be narcotic. In 1991, a Stanford University pediatrics professor, Dr. Ron Ariagno*, issued a warning against use for infants of pillows containing polystyrene. He said several deaths had occurred when babies ran out of fresh air and oxygen while on the pillows. Their exhaled air became trapped in the polystyrene and was reinhaled instead of fresh, oxygen-rich air. *See* Clothing.

POLYSTYRENE LATEX • A white, plastic solid derived from petroleum. It has outstanding moisture resistance. No known toxicity. *See* Latex.

---

*"Babies Don't Need Pillows, and Cushions Stuffed with Polystyrene Can Even Be Deadly, Pediatrician Says," *Stanford University Medical Center Health Tips*. August 1991.

POLYURETHANE • A synthetic polymer that is elastic and resistant to moisture. It is used in spandex fibers for girdles and other fabrics requiring elasticity and for brush bristles. It has many other uses, including coatings, weatherproofing, sealants, caulking agents, adhesives, films, shoe heels, for "foam" pillows and mattresses, and for furniture, insulation, and flooring. It is combustible and produces toxic fumes when burned.

POLYVINYL ACETATE • *See* Polyvinylpyrrolidone.

POLYVINYL ALCOHOL • Synthetic resins used in lipsticks, thickeners, ceramics, cements, imitation sponges, printing inks, photosensitive films, leather, and paper coatings. Dry, unplasticized polyvinyl alcohol powders are white to cream colored and have different viscosities. Solvent in hot and cold water, but some require alcohol-water mixtures. No known toxicity.

POLYVINYL BUTYRAL • The condensation of polyvinyl alcohol and butyraldehyde *(see both)*. It is a synthetic flavoring found naturally in coffee and strawberry. Used in the manufacture of rubber, synthetic resins, and plasticizers. May be an irritant and narcotic.

POLYVINYL CHLORIDE • **PVC. Chloroethylene Polymer.** Derived from vinyl chloride *(see)*, it consists of a white powder or colorless granules resistant to weather, moisture, acids, fats, petroleum products, and fungus. It is used widely for everything from plumbing to raincoats: in flooring, wall covering, siding, plumbing pipe, windows, doors, furniture, and plastic bottles; in cosmetic and toiletries in containers, nail enamels, and creams. PVC has caused tumors when injected under the skins of rats in doses of 100 milligrams per kilogram of body weight. The use of PVC as a plastic wrap for food, including meats, and for human blood transfusions has alarmed some scientists. Human and animal blood can extract potentially harmful chemicals from the plastic. The chemicals are added to polyvinyl chloride to make it flexible, and they migrate from the plastic into bloodstream and meats in an amount directly proportional to the length of time of storage. The result can be contamination of the bloodstream, causing lung shock, a condition in which the patient's blood circulation to lungs is impeded.

POLYVINYLIDENE CHLORIDE • **Saran.** A tasteless, odorless plastic that is resistant to moisture, chemicals, and abrasion. It is derived from vinylidene chloride and used for food packages, insecticide-impregnated paper bags, pipes, seat covers, upholstery, bristles, coatings, and fibers.

POLYVINYLPYRROLIDONE • **PVP.** A faintly yellow, solid, plastic resin resembling albumin. Used to give a softer set in shampoos, hair sprays, and lacquers. Also used to detoxify chemicals such as dyes, iodine, and phenol, and to make tablets, photographic emulsions, textile finishes, detergents, and adhesives. Ingestion of PVP may produce gas, and fecal impaction of damage to lungs and kidneys. It may survive in the system for up to a year. Strong circumstantial evidence indicates thesaurosis—foreign substances in the body—may be produced in the lungs of susceptible individuals from concentrated exposure to PVP in hair sprays. Modest intravenous doses in rats caused them to develop tumors.

POOL CHEMICALS • A swimming pool is most comfortable when it is maintained at a pH between 7.2–7.6. (The pH scale that measures acid-alkalinity is measured on a scale of from 1 to 14 with 7 being neutral.) The pH is adjusted by adding either acid such as muriatic or hydrochloric acid or sodium bisulfate to lower the pH. The pH is raised with an alkali such as sodium carbonate (soda ash) or sodium bicarbonate. Sanitizers include sodium or calcium hypochlorite, cyanuric acid, and hydantoins *(see all)*. The algae-fighter type contains alkyl *(see)* compounds such as alkyl aryl ammonium chloride. The algicides may also contain copper EDTA, sodium carbonate or sodium tripolyphosphate, phenylmercuric acetate, isopropanol, and a hydantoin compound *(see all)*.

Pool chemicals are often in concentrated form so handle with care and read the labels thoroughly. Do not use your bare hands or get them on your skin or clothing or in your eyes. Never mix the chemicals together and always use separate scoops for each. Even mixing different chlorine products can cause a severe reaction or explosion. Always add the chemical to the water, never add water to dry or concentrated chemicals. When adding chlorine into the pool, pour it as far from the pool edge as possible so it will disperse quickly into the water. Pool chemicals should be added gently, without splashing and always only one at a time. Add chemicals while the filter pump is running and *never* add chemicals when people are swimming in the pool. Do not allow swimmers to enter the water until you are sure the chemicals are thoroughly dispersed. Pool chemicals are considered hazardous waste and many communities have special arrangements for disposal. Check with your authority.

PORCELAIN ENAMEL • Various blends of clays, feldspars, and other silicates ground up and sprayed onto a metal surface, to which they bond after firing, giving a shiny, polished surface. Used in light reflectors, storage tanks, and other equipment such as marine engine tanks subjected to high temperatures.

PORCELAIN POLISH • Contains an abrasive, soap, pine oil, ammonium hydroxide, and oxalates *(see all)*.

PORTLAND CEMENT • An odorless, gray powder that is made up of lime, alumina, silica, and iron oxide. The cement may be modified with plastics and resins.

POTASH • *See* Potassium Silicate.

POTASSIUM ARSENATE • *See* Arsenate, Potassium.

POTASSIUM BINOXALATE • **Potassium Acid Oxalate. Salt of Sorrel.** White, odorless crystals, which are poisonous, used in nail bleaches and wood cleaners, as an ink-stain remover, in scouring metals, and in photography.

POTASSIUM BIPHTHALATE • **Phthalic Acid. Potassium Acid Salt.** A buffer used to affect alkalinity/acidity ratios. *See* Phthalic Acid.

POTASSIUM BITARTRATE • *See* Cream of Tartar.

POTASSIUM BORATE • A crystalline salt used as an oxidizing agent and preservative. *See* Borates for toxicity.

POTASSIUM BROMATE • Antiseptic and astringent in toothpaste, mouthwashes, and gargles as 3 to 5 percent solution. Colorless or white crystals. Very toxic when taken internally. Burns and skin irritation have been reported from its industrial uses. In toothpaste it has been reported to have caused inflammation and bleeding of gums.

POTASSIUM CARBONATE • **Salt of Tartar. Pearl Ash.** Inorganic salt of potassium. Odorless, white powder, soluble in water but practically insoluble in alcohol. Used in freckle lotions, in the manufacture of soap, glass, printing inks *(see)* and pottery and to finish leather. Irritating and caustic to human skin and may cause dermatitis of the scalp, forehead, and hands.

POTASSIUM CHLORATE • A colorless or white powder that dissolves slowly in water. Used in bleach, freckle lotions, and in disinfectants; also used in explosives, fireworks, matches, and in printing and in dyeing cotton and wool black. May be absorbed through the skin. Irritating to the intestines and kidneys. Can cause dermatitis of the scalp, forehead, and hands.

POTASSIUM CHLORIDE • A colorless, crystalline, odorless powder with a salty taste, derived from sylvite deposits in New Mexico and Canada. It is used as a fertilizer, a source of potassium salts, a plant food, salt substitute, buffer solution, and in photography. Large doses ingested can cause gastrointestinal irritation, purging, weakness, and circulatory collapse.

POTASSIUM CHROMATE • Yellow crystals derived from chromite. Used as a dye, and in enamels and inks. Toxic by ingestion. *See* Chromate Salts.

POTASSIUM DICHROMATE • Derived from potassium chloride and sodium dichromate, it is a bright yellowish red. Used in adhesives, blueprinting, detergents, bleaches, matches, spackle compounds, in tanning and the fur industries, photography, photoengraving lithography, electroplating, yellow and orange paints, ink manufacture, chrome plating, stainless steel, steel polishing, welding, cement, rubber, glass, linoleum, wood stains, poisoned flypaper, and anti-rust compounds. It is a skin sensitizer and also an irritant. Toxic by ingestion.

POTASSIUM FLUOSILICATE • White, odorless potassium made from silica and fluorine. Used as an insecticide and in ceramics. Toxic by ingestion and inhalation, and strongly irritating to tissue.

POTASSIUM HYDROXIDE • **Caustic Potash.** Used as an emulsifier in hand lotions, as a cuticle softener, and as an alkali in liquid soaps, protective creams, bleaches, dyes, liquid fertilizers, herbicides, and paint removers. Prepared industrially by electrolysis of potassium chloride *(see)*. White or slightly yellow lumps. Extremely corrosive, and ingestion may cause violent pain, bleeding, collapse, and death. When applied to the skins of mice, moderate dosages cause tumors. May cause skin rash and burning. Concentrations above 5 percent can destroy fingernails as well.

POTASSIUM IODIDE • **Potassium Salt.** A dye remover and an antiseptic. Used in table salt as a source of dietary iodine. It is also in some drinking water. May cause allergic reactions.

POTASSIUM NITRATE • **Niter. Saltpeter.** Transparent, colorless or white crystals that are used in fireworks, explosives, matches, fertilizers, and glass manufacture. Can catch fire or explode when shocked, heated, or in contact with a strong oxidizing agent.

POTASSIUM PERMANGANATE • Dark purple crystals derived from manganate. It is a disinfectant, deodorizer, bleach, and dye. Used in tanning and water purification. A fire hazard and explosion risk.

POTASSIUM PERSULFATE • Colorless or white, odorless crystals. A powerful oxidant. Soluble in water. The solution is acidic, and is used in the manufacture of soaps and as a germicidal preparation for the bathroom. It is also used in bleaches, in photography, in pharmaceuticals, and in textile processing. Aqueous solutions of 2.5 to 3 percent are not irritating to humans, but may cause a skin rash.

POTASSIUM PHOSPHATE • Monobasic, Dibasic, and Tribasic. A colorless to white powder used as a yeast food in the production of champagne and other sparkling wines. Also used in fertilizers, as a buffering agent in shampoos and cuticle removers, and a buffer in antifreeze. Has been used medicinally as a urinary acidifier. No known toxicity.

POTASSIUM SALTS OF FATTY ACIDS • The reaction of potassium salts *(see all)* on fatty acids *(see)* creates liquid soap.

POTASSIUM SILICATE • Soluble Potash Glass. Colorless or yellowish, translucent to transparent, glasslike particles derived from potassium carbonate and silica. Used in the manufacture of glass, soap, welding rods, mortars, adhesives, and plant feeders. Also used for inorganic protective coatings and phosphorus on television tubes. Usually very slowly soluble in cold water. No known toxicity.

POTASSIUM SODIUM TARTRATE • **Rochelle Salt.** Derived from potassium acid tartrate, it is used in the manufacture of baking powder and in the silvering of mirrors. Translucent crystals or white, crystalline powder with cooling saline taste. Slight efflorescence in warm air. No known toxicity.

POTASSIUM SULFATE • Does not occur freely in nature, but is combined with sodium sulfate. Colorless or white, crystalline powder, with a bitter taste. Used as a reagent *(see)* in cosmetics and as a salt substitute; also a water corrective in brewing, a fertilizer, and a cathartic. Large doses can cause severe gastrointestinal bleeding. No known toxicity to the skin.

POTASSIUM SULFOCARBONATE • A soil fumigant. Toxic by ingestion and a strong irritant. *See* Fumigants.

POUNCE™ **•** *See* Permethrin.

***p*-PHENYLENEDIAMINE •** *See* Phenylenediamine.

ppb • The abbreviation for parts per billion, a measure of concentration, such as parts of a chemical per billion parts of air or water. One thousand times smaller than ppm.

ppm • The abbreviation for parts per million, a measure of concentration, such as parts of a substance per million parts of air.

PRECURSOR. • Forerunner; sign or indication that precedes.

PRE-M™ **•** A herbicide for crabgrass. *See* Pendimethalin.

PRESSED-WOOD PRODUCTS • A group of materials used in building and furniture construction that are made of wood veneers, particles, or fibers bonded together with an adhesive under heat and pressure. *See* Wood.

PRINTING INKS • Printing inks are made up of coloring or pigment, and a liquid containing oils, resins, and solvents. Black inks are 75 to 80 percent oil. Other colors have a lower oil content because of the amount of pigments needed to produce hues. Soybean inks are rapidly replacing standard petroleum-based inks in books. *See* Inks.

PRISTANE • A liquid hydrocarbon obtained from the liver oil of sharks, and from ambergris *(see both)*. Used as a lubricant and anticorrosive agent.

PROMECARB • **Banol.** A carbamate *(see)* pesticide used on turf-grass and plants. It is a organophosphate *(see)*, and must be used with great caution.

PROMOTER • A substance or agent that completes the cancer process after initiation. *See* Carcinogen.

PROPANE • A gas heavier than air; odorless when pure. Cleared for use as a propellant and aerating agent for foamed and sprayed cosmetics and foods. Also used as a household and industrial fuel, and a refrigerant. May be narcotic in high concentrations. *See* Aerosols, Enamel Paint, and Propellant.

2-PROPANONE • *See* Acetone.

PROPELLANT • A compressed gas used to expel the contents of containers in the form of aerosols. Chlorofluorocarbons were used widely because of their nonflammability. The strong possibility that they contribute to the depletion of the ozone layer of the upper atmosphere has resulted in prohibition of their use for this purpose. Other propellants used are hydrocarbon gases, such as butane and propane, carbon dioxide, and nitrous oxide.

PROPELLANT 11 • **Trichlorofluoromethane. Freon 11**®. A low-pressure, odorous propellant used for hair sprays, shaving lathers, and other products with alcohol. Less toxic than carbon dioxide *(see)*, but decomposes into harmful materials when exposed to flames or high heat. May be narcotic in high concentrations.

PROPELLANT 12 • **Dichlorodifluoromethane. Freon 12**®. A high-pressure propellant used in aerosols, particularly for foam products such as hair coloring. Frequently used for perfumes because it has no odor of its own. *See* Aerosols for toxicity.

PROPELLANT 114 • **Dichlorotetrafluoroethane. Freon 114**®. Most frequently used propellant. It is a low-pressure one. *See* Aerosols for toxicity.

PROPELLANT 142B • **Chlorodifluoroethane. Freon 142**®. A propellant not frequently used because of its high pressure. *See* Aerosols for toxicity.

PROPELLANT 152A • **Difluoroethane.** A propellant used in glass, plastic, and aluminum containers. *See* Aerosols for toxicity.

PROPETAMPHOS • A pesticide. *See* Safrotin™ and Pesticides.

PROPIONIC ACID • Occurs naturally in apples, strawberries, tea, and violet leaves. An oily liquid with a slightly pungent, rancid odor. Can be obtained from wood pulp, waste liquor, and by fermentation. Used in perfume bases, and as a mold inhibitor, antioxidant, and preservative in cosmetics. Its salts are used as antifungal agents to treat skin mold, and in weed killers. It is also used as a fungicide, herbicide, and preservative for grains and wood chips, in nickel-plating, and in the manufacture of plastics. Large oral dose in rats is lethal. A strong irritant.

PROPOXUR • *See* Baygon™

PROPYL ALCOHOL • Obtained from crude fusel oil. Alcoholic and slightly overpowering odor. Occurs naturally in cognac green oil, cognac white oil, and onion oil A synthetic fruit flavoring. Used instead of ethyl alcohol as a solvent for shellac, gums, resins, oils; as a denaturant *(see)* for alcohol in perfumery. Also used in brake fluids, and as a grease solvent. Not a primary irritant, but because it dissolves fat, it has a drying effect on the skin and may lead to cracking, fissuring, and infections. No adverse effects have been reported from local application as a lotion, liniment, mouthwash, gargle, or sponge bath.

PROPYLENE DICHLORIDE • A colorless liquid with a chloroformlike odor; derived from the action of chlorine on propylene. It is used as a lead scavenger for antiknock fluids; in solvents for fats, oils, waxes, gums, and resins; in scouring compounds, metaldegreasing agents, and as a soil fumigant for worms. It is highly flammable and potentially explosive. Toxic by ingestion and inhalation. *See* Fumigants.

PROPYLENE GLYCOL • **1,2-Propanediol.** A clear, colorless, viscous liquid, slightly bitter tasting, derived from propylene oxide. It is the most common moisture-carrying vehicle in cosmetics, other than water. It has better permeation through the skin than glycerin and is less expensive, although it has been linked to more sensitivity reactions. Absorbs moisture, acts as a solvent, and a wetting agent. Used in liquid makeup as a solvent for fats and oils, waxes and resins; in cellophane, antifreeze solution, brake fluids, humectants, and preservatives. It is being reduced in use, or replaced by safer glycols such as butylene and polyethylene.

PROPYLENE OXIDE • A colorless, sweet-smelling liquid used as a food additive and insecticidal fumigant. It is also used for urethane foams, in detergents, lubricating oils, synthetic elastomers, and as a solvent. A skin and eye irritant, and a possible cancer-causing agent. It is moderately poisonous if ingested, inhaled, or if it touches the skin. A very dangerous explosive and fire hazard.

PT 3-6-10 AERO-CIDE • A pesticide containing pyrethrins, piperonylbutoxide, and petroleum distillate *(see all)*.

PT 565 PYRETHRUM • A pesticide containing pyrethrins, piperonylbutoxide, and petroleum distillates. *See* Pesticides.

PULMONARY EDEMA • Filling of the lungs with fluid, which produces coughing and difficulty breathing.

PULPS • From wood, straw, bagasse, or other natural sources; a source of cellulose in food. The wood is treated with a mixture containing mainly sodium hydroxide *(see)*. Treatment removes the fibrous lignin—the resinous substance that binds the fiber lining the cells of wood.

PUREX™ FABRIC SOFTENER • A quaternary ammonium compound *(see)*. *See* Bleaches.

PUTTY • A mixture of chalk containing 12 to 18 percent linseed oil, with or without white lead or other pigment. Containers must be airtight. Glazing compounds may contain fish oil, soybean oil, linseed oil, fatty acid, mineral spirits, asbestos, titanium dioxide, polybutene, and marble dust. Wood putties contain calcium sulfate, dextrin, and wood flour. Used as a sealant and caulking agent.

PVC • *See* Polyvinyl Chloride.

PVP • **1-Vinyl-2-Pyrrolidone.** Abbreviation for polyvinylpyrrolidone.

PYDRIN™ • *See* Fernvalerate.

PYRAZOLE • A crystalline compound used to overcome acidity of aluminum chloride in antiperspirants. Soluble in water, alcohol, ether, and benzene. No known toxicity when used externally. A modest injection into the abdomens of mice is lethal.

PYRETHRINS • Thick esters that are the most potent insecticidal ingredients of the chrysanthemum. Used in household insecticidal sprays and powders, and deodorant sprays. Also used in paper bags for shipping cereals. Insecticides labeled nontoxic to human beings and pets usually contain pyrethrins. Pyrethrin I is more toxic than Pyrethrin II. *See* Pyrethrum.

PYRETHRUM • The natural insecticide obtained by extraction of chrysanthemum flowers. Can cause severe allergic dermatitis and systemic allergic reactions. Large amounts may cause nausea, vomiting, ringing in the ears, headache, and other central nervous system disturbances. Very toxic if ingested, and a dose of a half an ounce was fatal to a child. It is, however, rapidly detoxified in the intestinal tract. Prolonged exposure causes slight but definite liver damage.

PYRIDINE • A slightly yellow or colorless liquid with a terrible odor and burning taste, derived from coal or coke. It is used as a fungicide, a solvent in waterproofing, a denaturant for alcohol, and in antifreeze mixtures. A skin and eye irritant, it is moderately toxic by inhalation. It can cause central nervous system depression, kidney and liver damage, and gastrointestinal upset. A very dangerous explosive and a fire hazard.

PYRIDIUM COMPOUND • A toxic, water-soluble, flammable liquid with a disagreeable odor that is obtained by distillation of bone oil or as a by-product of coal tar. Used as a modifier and preservative in shaving creams, soaps, hand creams, and lotions; also a solvent, a denaturant in alcohol, and an industrial waterproofing agent. No known toxicity when used externally. The lethal dose injected into the abdomens of rats is only 3.2 milligrams per kilogram of body weight.

PYROCATECHOL • Colorless leaflets, soluble in water; prepared by treating salicylaldehyde with hydrogen peroxide. Used in blond-type dyes, as an oxidizing agent, as an antiseptic, and for dyeing furs; also in inks, and photography. It can cause eczema and systemic effects similar to phenol *(see)*.

PYROPHYLLITE • A natural aluminum silicate found in rocks; a white to greenish gray powder similar to chalk. Used in ceramics, insecticides, slate pencils, paints, and wallboard.

PYRROLIDINE • A colorless to pale yellow liquid, used in fungicides, insecticides, and epoxy resins. Toxic by ingestion and inhalation.

Q

QUARTZ • White to red silica *(see)*, used for electronic components, radio and TV components, and abrasives. Chronic inhalation of the dust is damaging to the lungs and may cause fibrosis, which causes shortness of breath, decreased chest expansion, and lessened capacity for work.

QUASSIN • **Extract of Jamaica Bitter Wood.** A bitter alkaloid obtained from the yellowish white to bright yellow wood shavings of the quassia *(Quassia amara),* a tree found in Jamaica and the Caribbean islands. Chiefly used as a denaturant for ethyl alcohol. Also used to poison flies, in paper, lacquers, and waterproofing. Toxic to humans.

QUATERNARIUM 1 THROUGH 6 • *See* Quaternarium-7.

QUATERNARIUM-7 • A surfactant and germicide derived from lauric acid *(see).* Positively charged with a low irritation potential, it is effective against a wide range of organisms.

QUATERNARY-8 THROUGH -14 • *See* Quaternarium-15.

QUATERNARIUM-15 • A water-soluble antimicrobial agent that is active against bacteria but not very active against yeast. It is a formaldehyde *(see)* releaser, and is the number one cause of dermatitis from preservatives, according to the American Academy of Dermatology's Testing Tray results. *See* Allergy Testing Tray.

QUATERNARIUM-16 THROUGH -29 • *See* Quaternarium-18.

QUATERNARIUM-18, -19, -20, -23 • Derived from cellulose *(see),* it is a film-former and binding agent used in products to give hair a sheen.

QUATERNARIUM-28 DODECYLBENZYL TRIMETHYLAMMONIUM CHLORIDE • *See* Quaternary Ammonium Compounds.

QUATERNARIUM-29 DODECYLXYLYL BIS • *See* Quaternary Ammonium Compounds.

QUATERNARIUM-18 HECTORITE • *See* Quaternary Ammonium Compounds.

QUATERNARY AMMONIUM COMPOUNDS • A wide variety of preservatives, surfactants, germicides, sanitizers, antiseptics, and deodorants used in cosmetics. Benzalkonium chloride *(see)* is one of the most popular. Quaternary ammonium compounds are synthetic derivatives of ammonium chloride *(see),* and are used in aerosol deodorants, fungicides, mildew control, in dyes for film in photography, paints, antistatic products, and biocides. Diluted solutions are used in medicine to sterilize the skin and mucous membranes. All quaternary ammonium compounds can be toxic, depending upon the dose and concentration. Concentrated solutions irritate the skin and can cause necrosis of the mucous membranes. Concentrations as low as 0.1 percent are irritating to the eye and mucous membranes except benzalkonium chloride, which is well tolerated at such low concentrations. Ingestion can be fatal.

QUICKLIME • *See* Calcium Oxide.

QUICKSILVER • *See* Mercury.

QUINOLINE • A coal tar derivative used in the manufacture of cosmetic dyes. Also a solvent for resins. Made either by the distillation of coal tar, bones, and alkaloids, or by the interaction of aniline *(see)* with acetaldehyde and formaldehyde *(see both)*. Absorbs water; has a weak base. Soluble in hot water. Also used as a preservative for anatomical specimens. A suspected human carcinogen. See Coal Tar for toxicity. *See also* Colors.

8-QUINOLINOL • **Bioquin. Oxin. Oxychinolin. 8-Oxyquinoline. Tumex.** Derived from phenol, it is a white, crystalline powder used as a fungistat (inhibits the growth of fungi without destroying them). Causes cancer when given orally to rats.

QUINOMETHIONATE • Yellow crystals used as a fungicide and acaracide *(see both)*.

QUINSOL • See Fungicides.

QUINTOZENE • **PCNB. Terraclor. Nor-Am.** Prepared from benzene *(see)*, it is used as a fungicide on turfgrass and seed. *See* Fungicides.

R

® • Signifies registration of a trademark, which means the trademark has been approved by the U.S. Patent and Trademark Office. ™ means the trademark is pending.

RABBIT HAIR • Found in gloves, clothing, and imitation fur. Can cause contact dermatitis.

RADON • A naturally occurring radioactive gas that cannot be seen, smelled, or tasted. Radon seeps into homes from the surrounding soil through cracks and other openings in the foundation. The EPA estimates that 10 percent of all U.S. homes have radon levels high enough to require corrective action. And in some areas such as Iowa, 71 percent of the homes tested had unacceptable estimates. Radon can also enter homes when it is released from well water while showering, washing clothes, and performing other household activities. State surveys to date show that about one out of five homes has elevated screening levels. Once inside, Radon is completely invisible to sight, smell, or taste. The only way to know if a home has elevated levels of radon is to test it. Testing is simple and easy. A short-term testing (a few days to several months) is the fastest way to determine if a potential problem exists. Charcoal canisters and alpha track detectors are currently the most common short-term devices. Short-term testing should be conducted in the lowest livable level of your home, with the doors and windows shut, during the cooler months of the year. Long-term testing—up to one year—is the most accurate way to test for radon. To obtain information on testing for Radon, you can call a 24-hour toll-free number 1-800-SOS-RADON.

Your risk of developing lung cancer from radon depends on the average annual level of radon in your home, and the amount of time you are exposed to it. Obviously, the longer your exposure, or the higher the level of radon in your home, the greater the risk. The annual level of 100 pCI/L reading (equal to having 2,000 chest X rays a year), according to the EPA, in a community of 100 people exposed to it, about 35 may die from radon. Those 100 exposed to 2 pCi/L (equal to having 100 chest X rays each year) will cause the death of about one person in the community. Radon-decay products attach to particles that are inhaled and become lodged in the lungs. Once lodged, they can radiate and penetrate lung tissue initiating the process of cancer growth. Smoking increases the risk of exposure to radon. Children may be more sensitive and at higher risk to radiation exposure. The American Medical Association and the EPA maintain that thousands of lung cancer deaths each year are attributed to radon and that the risk of developing lung cancer depends upon the concentration of radon and the length of exposure. In 1991, however, a report by the Research Council of the National Academy of Sciences funded by the EPA said that the radon risk estimates for the risk of developing lung cancer from household exposure may have been overestimated by as much as 30 percent because the original estimates were based on exposure of underground miners. The committee cautioned, however, that its findings do not imply that radon is less carcinogenic than previously believed. It stressed that there is still much remaining uncertainty in estimating the risk of lung cancer from radon exposure in domestic environments.

Homes with high radon levels can be fixed for about $500 to $2,000.

RAID® HOUSE & GARDEN FORMULA 11 • A product of Johnson Wax, it contains as active ingredients the synthetic pyrethrins, piperonyl butoxide, and Tetramethrin [(Cyclohexene-1,2,Dibarboximide) Methyl 2,2-Dimethyl-3-(2 Methylpropenyl) Cyclopropanecarboxylate]. The product also contains sodium nitrite and "inert ingredients." The label warns that the product is hazardous to humans and domestic animals and says that it is a violation of federal law to use the product in a manner inconsistent with labeling. The label gives specific directions for use against crawling and flying bugs and how to dispose of the aerosol container. It is a good label and contains a phone number for further information. *See* Pyrethrins.

RAPESEED AMIDOPROPYL BENZYLDIMONIUM CHLORIDE • *See* Rapeseed Oil and Quaternary Ammonium Compounds.

RAPESEED AMIDOPROPYL ETHYLDIMONIUM ETHOSULFATE • *See* Rapeseed Oil and Quaternary Ammonium Compounds.

RAPESEED OIL • Brownish yellow oil from a turniplike annual herb of European origin. Widely grown as a forage crop for sheep in the United States. Has a distinctly unpleasant odor. Used chiefly as a lubricant, an illuminant, and in rubber substitutes; also used in soft soaps and margarine. Can cause acnelike skin eruptions.

RAT AND MOUSE CONTROLLER PASTE • *See* Thallium.

RAT AND MOUSE POISONS • Include brodifacoum, coumarins, and strychnine *(see all)*. If you remove the food supply and/or use live traps, you would be using a less toxic alternative.

RAYON • Regenerated cellulose. Man-made textile fibers of yarn and regenerated cellulose, produced from wood pulp. Similar in appearance to silk. There are several types of rayon fibers sold today, and named according to the process by which the cellulose is treated. "Viscose" rayon is produced by converting purified cellulose to xanthanate, dissolving the xanthanate in dilute caustic soda, and then regenerating the cellulose. Most rayon today is made by this viscose process. "Cuprammonium" rayon is made with copper and ammonia. It is used for lightweight summer dresses and blouses, and combined with cotton to make textured fabrics with slubbed, uneven surfaces. "Saponified" rayon is synthesized by reconverting cellulose acetate to cellulose. In cosmetics, rayon is used to give shine and body to face powders and in eyelash extenders in mascaras. Rayon also is used to make suits, coats, rainwear, lingerie, accessories, hats, work clothes, draperies, slip covers, upholstery, tablecloths, sheets, bedspreads, and blankets; floor coverings, medical/surgical products, and industrial products such as tire cord. Most rayon fabrics wash well, but some garments require dry cleaning for best results. Some finishes are also sensitive to chlorine bleach. No known toxicity.

REACTION • A chemical transformation or change.

REACTIVITY • The ability of a substance to undergo a chemical reaction, such as combining with another substance. Substances that are highly reactive are often hazardous.

REAGENT • A chemical that reacts or participates in a reaction; a substance that is used for the detection or determination of another substance by chemical or microscopical means. The various categories of reagents are "colorimetric"—to produce color-soluble compounds; "fluxes"—used to lower melting point; "oxidizers"—used in oxidation; "precipitants"—to produce insoluble compounds; "reducers"—used in reduction *(see);* and "solvents"—used to dissolve water-insoluble compounds.

REAL KILL® ANT & ROACH KILLER • Contains chlorpyrifos, d-trans allethrin, and related ingredients. *See* Chlorpyrifos.

RED PETROLATUM • A minimally refined variety of petrolatum *(see)*.

REDUCING AGENT • A substance that decreases, deoxidizes, or concentrates the volume of another substance (as when used to convert a metal oxide to the metal itself). Also, a substance that adds hydrogen agents to another (as when acetaldehyde is converted to alcohol in the final step of fermentation).

REDUCTION • The process of removing oxygen from a compound or adding hydrogen. This is the opposite of oxidation *(see)* and can be done chemically or electronically. Stannous chloride is a common chemical reducing agent.

REDWOOD • A red color in dyeing manufacture, red inks, and woodworking. Can cause contact dermatitis.

REENTRY INTERVAL • The period of time immediately following the application of a pesticide to an area, during which unprotected workers or consumers should not enter the area.

REFRIGERANTS • Any compounds that lower temperature. Most commercial refrigerants are liquids that cool when vaporizing. Ammonia, sulfur dioxide, and ethyl or methyl chloride were once popular, but were found to be flammable and toxic. The fluorocarbons were then widely used as refrigerants, but with the concern for their effects on the ozone level *(see* Ozone), their use is in question.

REFRIGERATOR DEODORANTS • Activated charcoal or baking soda.

REGISTRANT • Any manufacturer or formulator who obtains registration for a pesticide, active ingredient, or product.

REGISTRATION • Under the Federal Insecticide, Fungicide, and

Rodenticide Act (as amended), the formal listing with the EPA of a new pesticidal active ingredient prior to its marketing.

REL • Abbreviation for Recommended Exposure Limit (NIOSH).

RELATIVE RISK • A measure of risk of disease in an exposed population, compared with the risk in an unexposed group. A relative risk of 1.0 means risks in the two groups are the same. If, for example, risk is double for an exposed population, the relative risk is 2.

RESIDUE • The pesticide remaining after natural or technological processes have taken place.

RESINS • The brittle substance, usually translucent or transparent, formed from the hardened secretions of plants. Among the natural resins are dammar, elemi, and sandarac. Synthetic resins include polyvinyl acetate, various polyester resins, and sulfonamide resins. Resins have many uses in cosmetics. They contribute depth, gloss, flow adhesion, and water resistance. Toxicity depends upon ingredients used.

RESORCINOL • Obtained from various resins, resorcinol's white crystals become pink on exposure to air. A preservative, antiseptic, antifungal agent, astringent, and antiitching agent, particularly in dandruff shampoos. It has a sweetish taste. Also used in tanning, explosives, printing textiles, and the manufacture of resins. Irritating to the skin and mucous membranes. May cause allergic reactions, particularly of the skin.

RESPIRATOR • A device worn to prevent inhalation of hazardous substances. It must be properly fitted and maintained to be effective.

RESTRICTED USE • When a pesticide is registered, some or all of its uses may be classified under the Federal Insecticide, Fungicide, and Rodenticide Act (FIFRA) for restricted use if the pesticide requires special handling due to its toxicity. Restricted-use pesticides may be applied only by trained, certified applications, or those under their direct supervision.

RETROSPECTIVE • Describing a study that tries to ascertain data based on past events.

RHODAMINE B • A red dye related to xanthene *(see)*. It is used for dyeing paper, wool, and silk, where a bright fluorescent effect is desired. Caused cancer when injected under the skins of rats. *See* Phenol.

RICINOLEATE • Salt of ricinoleic acid found in castor oil. Used in the manufacture of soaps. No known toxicity.

RICINOLEIC ACID • A mixture of fatty oils found in the seeds of castor beans. Castor oil contains 80 to 85 percent ricinoleic acid. The oily liquid is used in soaps, added to Turkey-red oil *(see)*, and in contraceptive jellies. It is believed to be the active laxative in castor oil. Also used externally as an emollient. No known toxicity.

RISK/BENEFIT • The relation between the risks and benefits of a given treatment or procedure.

ROACH AND ANT KILLERS • Many contain organophosphates, carbamates, and pyrethrins. Sometimes you can handle a small problem by using full-strength ammonia on and around where the roaches traipse. Another homemade compound for roaches is a mixture of one part boric acid and one part powdered sugar. Chili powders sprinkled around where ants enter the home may discourage them. However, boric acid *(see)* may be toxic to children and pets. Prevent their exposure to it. *See* Insecticides.

ROCHELLE SALT • **Potassium Sodium Tartrate.** Used in the manufacture of baking powder and the silvering of mirrors. Translucent crystals or white, crystalline powder with a cooling saline taste. Slight efflorescence in warm air. Probably used in mouthwashes, but use not identified in cosmetics. No known toxicity.

ROCK SALT CRYSTALS • *See* Sodium Chloride.

ROCKLAND® HORTICULTURAL SPRAY OIL • Used on fruit trees and other trees to kill insect pests in the egg stage such as spider mites and mealybugs. It is hazardous to humans, domestic animals, and fish. Harmful if swallowed or inhaled. Irritating to mucous membranes. May contaminate water during cleaning of equipment or disposal of waste.

ROCKLAND® SEVIN SL • *See* Carbaryl.

RODENTICIDE • Compounds used to kill rats, mice, moles, and other rodents. Warfarin, a coumarin derivative *(see)* is one of the most widely used rodenticides, and has a good safety record. Rodents must eat the bait for several days before dying, which means that children and pets require repeated doses before toxicity develops. Warfarin can cause hemorrhaging. Because rodents developed resistance to warfarin, new potent warfarin compounds were developed—difenacoum and brodifacoum, which inhibit blood from clotting. Other rodenticides are d-Con®, Prolin™, and Couma Furyl™, all anticoagulants. Other products include thallium, sodium monofluoracetate, strychnine, zinc phosphate, elemental yellow phosphorus, and arsenic, all highly toxic. Moderately toxic products include naphthylthiourea (ANTU), and low-toxicity products contain red squill *(Urginea maritima)*, indandiones, and norbormide.

ROGON™ • A pesticide used on fruit and vegetables. *See* Dimethoate.

RONNEL • Powder or granules used as an insecticide. Toxic by ingestion and inhalation. *See* Parathion.

ROOFING CEMENT • Contains petroleum asphalt, petroleum solvents, asbestos fiber, and limestone, clay, or other fillers *See* Asphalt, Asbestos, and Solvents.

ROSIN • The pale yellow residue left after distilling off the volatile oil from the oleoresin obtained from various species of pine trees grown chiefly in the United States. Used in soaps, hair lacquers, wax depilatories, adhesives, sealants, varnishes, paper sizing, printers' inks, polyesters, fireworks, and ointments. It can cause contact dermatitis. *See* Clothing.

ROTENONE • White, odorless crystals derived from derris and cube root. Used as an insecticide, flea powder, fly spray, mothproofing agent, and fish poison. Toxic by ingestion; can be fatal because it paralyzes respiration. It is a skin irritant. Chronic exposure injures liver and kidneys. Supposedly leaves no harmful residues on vegetable crops. *See* Insecticides.

ROTTENSTONE • A soft aluminum silicate (*see* Silicates) used as a polishing agent.

ROVRAL™ • A pesticide. *See* Iprodione.

ROZOL TRACKING POWDER™ • **Indandion.** A pesticide.

RUBBER • Rubber and rubber-based adhesives are common causes of contact dermatitis. The natural gum obtained from the rubber tree is not allergenic; the offenders are the chemicals added to natural rubber gum to make it a useful product. Such chemicals are accelerators, antioxidants, stabilizers, and vulcanizers, many of which can cause allergies. Mercaptobenzothiazole and tetramethylthiuram are the most frequent, but certainly not the only sensitizers. Rubber is used in vehicle tires, hose, conveyor belt covers, footwear, foam rubber, electric insulation, and many other products.

RUBBER CEMENT • Contains hexane, rubber, and solvents such as toluene, benzene, hexane, ketone, and trichloroethane. May also contain rosin, ester gum, and antioxidants. The butadiene styrene latex-type contains, in addition to butadiene at 50 percent, rosin gum, water, ammonium hydroxide, 2,2-methylenebis (4-methyl-6-tertiary-butylphenol)sodium *o*-phenylphenate, sodium pentachlorophenate, and colloid. The latex type contains, in addition to latex from 50 to 70 percent, carbon, ethylene glycol, sulfur, trisodium phosphate, creosote, stabilizer, ammonium, and earths or flour. May be abused by inhalation. Some of the ingredients such as hexane and toluene may cause nerve and brain damage, and can lead to sudden death by disrupting the rhythm of the heart. *See also* Contact Cement.

RUBBER GLOVES • Rubber gloves should be worn for those allergic to chemicals in solutions, most commonly housewives and janitors, who use cleaning products. However, even cotton-lined rubber gloves themselves may cause allergic contact dermatitis, so allergists recommend wearing cotton gloves under the rubber gloves and, whenever possible, using long-handled brushes to keep hands out of solutions.

RUBBER SOLVENT • *See* Naphtha.

RUBBING ALCOHOLS • Isopropyl alcohol *(see),* probably the most common rubbing alcohol, is used in astringents, skin fresheners, colognes, and perfumes. It can be irritating to the skin. Ethanol *(see)* is used in perfumes, and as a solvent for oils. It also can be an irritant. Rubbing alcohols are denatured with chemicals to make them poisonous so they will not be ingested as alcoholic beverages.

RUG AND UPHOLSTERY CLEANERS • Most contain synthetic detergents, fatty alcohol, and trisodium phosphates. Another type contains sodium, carbonate (washing soda), borax, naphthalene, and perfume. A soap-solvent type contains Butyl Cellosolve®, ethylene dichloride, oleic acid, triethanolamine, and alcohol. An absorbent type may contain sawdust or wood flour plus trichloroethylene, and a petroleum distillate. Other ingredients may be diethylene glycol or oxalic acid *(see all).* Less toxic alternatives include a fast application with soda water or baking soda paste. Then vacuum when dry.

RUST-PREVENTING PAINTS • Most contain methylene chloride, petroleum distillates, and toluene *(see all).* They are flammable and toxic. *See also* paints.

RUST-STAIN REMOVER • *See* Stain Remover.

RYANIA • Extracted from the wood of tropical South American shrubs, *Ryania speciosa,* it is ground up and used in certain insecticide products. Moderately toxic.

S

SAFER™ INSECTICIDAL SOAP • *See* Insecticidal Soap.
SAFER™ INSECTICIDE CONCENTRATE • An insecticide for foliage plants, flowers, shrubs, trees, vegetables, fruits, and nuts, for use in and around buildings, homes, greenhouses, orchards, and

nurseries. It is made from the potassium salts of natural fatty acids. Harmful if swallowed, and irritating to the eyes, it should be kept out of lakes, streams, and pools.

SAFROTIN™ • **Proteamphos.** A yellowish liquid made from butanoic acid, used as an insecticide.

SALICYLANILIDE • Usually made from salicylic acid with aniline. Odorless leaflets, slightly soluble in water, freely soluble in alcohol. Fungicide, slimicide, antimildew agent, and an ingredient in bacterial soaps. Toxic by ingestion. In concentrated form may cause irritation of the skin and mucous membranes. When exposed to sunlight, it can cause swelling, reddening, and/or rash of the skin.

SALICYLIC ACID • Occurs naturally in wintergreen leaves, sweet birch, and other plants. Synthetically prepared by heating phenol with carbon dioxide. It has a sweetish taste and is used as a preservative and antimicrobial at 0.1 to 0.5 percent in skin softeners, face masks, hair tonics, deodorants, dandruff preparations, protective creams, hair dye removers, and suntan lotions and oils. It is antipruritic (antiitch) and antiseptic. In fact, in medicine, it is used as an antimicrobial at 2 to 20 percent concentration in lotions, ointments, powders, and plasters. It is also used in making aspirin. It can be absorbed through the skin. Absorption of large amounts may cause vomiting, abdominal pain, increased respiration, acidosis, mental disturbances, and skin rashes in sensitive individuals.

SALTPETER • *See* Potassium Nitrate.

SANDALWOOD OIL • The pale yellow, somewhat viscous, volatile oil obtained by steam distillation from the dried, ground roots and wood of the sandalwood tree. It is soluble in most fixed oils, and has a strong, warm, persistent odor. Used for incense, as a fumigant, and in perfume. May produce skin rash in the hypersensitive, especially if present in high concentrations.

SANDARAC GUM • Resin from the sandarac tree, which is found in Morocco. Light yellow, brittle, insoluble in water. Used in tooth cements, varnishes, and for gloss and adhesion in nail lacquers. Also used as an incense. No known toxicity.

SANFORIZING • *See* Clothing.

SANGUINARIA • **Bloodroot.** Derived from the dried roots and rhizome of the North American herb. The resin is used to soothe the skin, and its reddish juice stanches blood when used in styptic pencils. No known toxicity.

SANI-FLUSH® **TOILET BOWL CLEANER** • Contains an acid and sodium bisulfate *(see)*.

SANITIZERS • Disinfectants used on food-processing equipment, dishes and glassware, surfaces, floors, and room air. There are several types. General-use liquid products include quaternary ammonium compounds *(see)*, and chlorine compounds with sodium or calcium hypochlorite *(see both)*. There are also the iodine-detergent mixtures, and the acid type, which may contain cresylic and phosphoric acids *(see both)*. Air sanitizers usually have an alkyl ammonium compound plus versene, and an alcohol such as isopropanol, a propellant, and glycols *(see all)*. All sanitizers should be considered toxic by ingestion.

SAPONIFICATION • The making of soap, usually by adding alkalies to fat, with glycerol. To saponify is to convert to soap.

SAPONIN • Any of numerous natural glycosides—natural or synthetic compounds derived from sugars—that occur in many plants such as soapbark, soapwort, or sarsaparilla. Characterized by their ability to foam in water. Yellowish to white, acrid, hygroscopic. Extracted from soapbark or soapwort, and used chiefly as a foaming and emulsifying agent, and detergent; also to reduce surface tension, and produce fine bubble lather in shaving creams and shampoos. It is used as a foaming agent in fire extinguishers and in sizing. No known skin toxicity. In powder form can cause sneezing.

SARAN • *See* Polyvinylidene Chloride and Saran Fiber.

SARAN FIBER • Manufactured fibers composed mostly of polyvinylidene chloride, highly resistant to most chemicals and solvents, and to weather, moths, and mildew. Used in screens, upholstery, curtain and drapery fabrics, rugs, carpets, awnings, and filter cloth. *See* Polyvinylidene Chloride.

SARCOMA • A cancer that arises in connective and skeletal tissue such as muscle or bone.

SASSAFRAS OIL • The yellow to reddish yellow, volatile oil obtained from the roots of the sassafras tree. It is 80 percent safrole, and has the characteristic odor and taste of sassafras. Applied to insect bites and stings to relieve symptoms; also a topical antiseptic, and used medicinally to break up intestinal gas. Used in dentifrices, perfumes, soaps, and powders to correct disagreeable odors. May produce dermatitis in hypersensitive individuals.

SCOURING POWDER • Most contain chlorine bleach *(see)*. Do not use cleansers containing bleach with cleaning products, that contain ammonia, such as toilet bowl cleaner, oven cleaner, or all-purpose cleansers. The combination produces chloramine gas, which can be fatal. Baking soda or salt can be an alternative to commerical scouring powder. You can let pots and pans soak in a baking soda solution before washing. Bon Ami™ does not contain chlorine.

SD ALCOHOLS 3-A; 23-H; 38-B; 38-F; 39-B; 39-C; 40; 40-A; 40-B; 40-Cl46 • All ethyl alcohols denatured *(see)* in accordance with government regulations. Used as thickeners, solidifiers, and liquefiers.

SEALANTS • Substances that are soft enough to pour or smear, and then harden to form a permanent seal. Most products today contain synthetic polymers such as silicones, urethanes, acrylics, or polychloroprene. Natural sealants include putty, asphalt, and waxes *(see all)*. See also Adhesives.

SEER • The National Cancer Institute's Surveillance, Epidemiology, and End Results program, established in 1973. It monitors annual cancer incidence and survival in the United States. The original registries made up of a 10 percent nonrandom sample of the population, representing diverse groups. In 1983, SEER was expanded to represent 12 percent of the population in six states, four metropolitan areas, and Puerto Rico.

SEMISYNTHETIC SOLUBLE METALWORKING OIL • Metalworking fluids are liquids used in machining processes, such as cutting or grinding. The semisynthetic type contains a large amount of water, is transparent, and often tinted green or other colors. These oils are found in lubrication aids, corrosion inhibitors, biocides, and antifoaming agents. According to California's Hazards Evaluation System and Information Service, they can cause eye, nose, and throat irritation upon exposure. *See* Metalworking Fluids.

SENSITIVITY • **Hypersensitivity.** An increased reaction to a substance or substances that may be quite harmless to nonallergic persons.

SENSITIZE • To administer or expose to an antigen provoking an immune response so that, on later exposure to that antigen, a more vigorous secondary response will occur.

SEPTIC TANK AND CESSPOOL CLEANERS • Most common ingredient is strong sodium hydroxide *(see)*. Compounds may also contain trichlorobenzene, kerosene, urea, lime, yeast, enzymes *(see all)*, and copper sulfate. Products containing sodium or potassium hydroxide (lye) are highly caustic. They also change the acidity of water and speed soil clogging. Septic tank cleaners containing solvents such as trichloroethylene should not be used because they take a long time to break down, often contaminate water, and have been linked to cancer. Avoid putting items down your toilet or sink that bacteria cannot digest, or that disrupt the environment. Substances difficult for bacteria to digest include grease, fat, hair, cigar and cigarette butts, filters, facial tissues, paper towels, napkins, sanitary napkins, and adhesive bandages. *See also* Copper and Calcium Oxide.

SEQUESTERING AGENT • A preservative that prevents physical or chemical changes affecting color, flavor, texture, or appearance of a product. Ethylenediamine tetraacetic acid (EDTA) is an example. It prevents adverse effects of metals in solutions.

SERPENTARIA EXTRACT • **Snakeroot. Snakeweed.** Extracted from the roots of *Rauwolfia serpentina*, its yellow rods turn red upon drying. Used in the manufacture of resins, and as a bitter tonic. No known toxicity when applied to the skin, but can affect heart and blood pressure when ingested.

SESAME OIL • An East Indian herb with a rosy or white flower. It yields a pale yellow, bland-tasting, almost odorless oil used in the manufacture of margarine. The oil has been used as a laxative and skin softener, and contains elements active against lice. May cause allergic reactions, primarily contact dermatitis.

SEVIN™ • A surface and below-ground insecticide. *See* Carbaryl.

SHEA BUTTER • The natural fat obtained from the fruit of the karite tree, *Butyrosperum parkii*. Also called "karite butter," it is used chiefly as a food, but in soaps and candles, as well. No known toxicity.

SHELLAC • A resinous excretion of certain insects feeding on appropriate host trees, usually in India. As processed for marketing, the *lacca*, which is formed by the insects, may be mixed with small amounts of arsenic trisulfide for color, and with rosin. White shellac is free of arsenic. Shellac is used as a sealer coat under varnish, to finish floors, furniture and carvings, and on jewelry and accessories. May cause allergic contact dermatitis. *See* Clothing.

SHELLAC WAX • Bleached refined shellac. *See* Shellac.

SHOE CEMENT • May contain hexane, rubber, rosin, ester gum, antioxidants, nitrocellulose, acetone, butadiene styrene latex, casein, ammonium hydroxide, sodium *o*-phenylphenate, sodium pentachlorophenate, titanium dioxide, clay, and alcohol *(see all)*.

SHOE POLISH • The liquid type contains toluene and chlorinated hydrocarbons *(see both)*, dye, phenylmercuric acetate, and possibly, borax and lanolin. The liquid type may be subject to inhalation abuse. May cause brain and nerve damage. The paste-type polishes contain animal, petroleum and vegetable waxes, mineral spirits, turpentine, dye, silicones, and may also contain lanolin and nitrobenzene. Suede polish contains alcohol, aniline dye, silicones, and solvents such as trichloroethane. White shoe polish contains titanium dioxide, clay, and waxes, plus other ingredients such as lanolin, perfume, preservatives, and bentonite *(see all)*.

SICK BUILDING SYNDROME (SBS) • Term that refers to a set of symptoms that affect a number of building occupants during the time they spend in the building, and diminish or go away during periods when they are not in the building. Cannot be traced to specific pollutants or sources within the building. *See also* Building-Related Illness.

SIDURON • **Tupersan.** Derived from urea, it is a starter fertilizer with crab grass control. *See* Urea.

SILICA • **Crystalline Quartz. Diatomaceous Earth. Diatomite. Kieselguhr. Colloidal Silica Gels.** A white powder, slightly soluble in water, that occurs abundantly in nature; present in 12 percent of all rocks. Sand is a silica. Upon drying and heating in a vacuum, hard, transparent, porous granules are formed that are used in absorbent and adsorbent material in toilet preparations, particularly skin protectant creams. Also used as a coloring agent and in the manufacture of glass, ceramics, abrasives, water filtration, concrete, paper, insecticides, silicone rubber, and in paints and insulation. Chemically and biologically inert when ingested in any of its many forms. Chronic inhalation of crystalline quartz, however, may cause lung damage. *See* Silicones.

SILICA GEL • **Silicic Acid.** A white, gelatinous substance obtained by the action of acids on sodium silicate *(see)*. Odorless, tasteless, inert, white fluffy powder when dried. Insoluble in water and acids. Absorbs water readily. It is a dehumidifying and dehydrating agent, and is used in refrigerants, cosmetics, and waxes. No known toxicity. *See* Silicates.

SILICATES • Salts or esters derived from silicic acid *(see)*. Any of the numerous, insoluble, complex metal salts containing silicon and oxygen that constitute the largest groups of minerals and, with quartz, make up of the greater part of the earth's crust (as rocks, soils, and clays). Contained in building materials such as cement, concrete, bricks, and glass. Also used in plastics, rubber, paper coatings, and anticaking agents. Silica dust is toxic by inhalation.

SILICIC ACID • *See* Silica Gel.

SILICONES • Any of a large group of fluid oils, rubbers, resins, and compounds derived from silica *(see)*, and which are water repellent, skin adherent, and stable over a wide range of temperatures. Used in cosmetics, adhesives, protective coatings, coolants, in flexible windows, as bonding agents, and as laminates. Also used in waterproofing and lubrication. No known toxicity when used externally.

SILICON CARBIDE • **Carborundum**™. Blue-black, shiny crystals derived from heating carbon and silica at high temperature. A good conductor of heat and electricity, it is used as an abrasive for cutting and grinding metals, in the ceramics industry, for heat-resistant structures, and in nonslip tiles and threads.

SILICON DIOXIDE • *See* Silica.

SILOXANE • **Oxosilane.** A hydrocarbon *(see)* compound containing silicon and oxygen. *See also* Silicones.

SILVER • A white metal not affected by water or atmospheric oxygen. Used as a catalyst *(see),* and as a germicide and coloring in cosmetics. Prolonged absorption of silver compounds can lead to grayish blue discoloration of the skin. May be irritating to the skin and mucuous membranes.

SILVER BROMIDE • A yellowish, odorless powder that darkens on exposure to light. Used in photography, as a topical antiinfective agent and astringent, and in the production of mirror finishing. May cause contact dermatitis.

SILVER POLISH • May contain ammonia, petroleum solvent, citric acid, water, pine oil, oxalic acid, or soaps. To polish silver, you may try a solution of soapy water and baking soda, or mix one teaspoon of cream of tartar or sodium bicarbonate in one quart of warm water. Use an aluminum pan, or put a piece of aluminum foil into the solution. Let the silver soak in the solution until shiny.

SILVER CYANIDE • A white, odorless, tasteless powder derived from adding sodium cyanide or potassium cyanide to a solution of silver nitrate. Used for silver plating. Toxic by ingestion or inhalation.

SILVER NITRATE • Silver is dissolved in nitric acid, the solution is evaporated, and the residue heated. Odorless, colorless, and transparent, it darkens with exposure to light in the presence of organic matter. Silver combines readily with protein and turns brown. A germicide, antiseptic, and astringent in cosmetics, and a coloring agent in metallic hair dyes, it is also used for photographic film, indelible inks, silver plating, and silvering mirrors. On the skin, it may be caustic and irritating. If swallowed, it may cause severe gastrointestinal symptoms and, frequently, death.

SILVER SULFATE • *See* Silver Nitrate.

SIZING • A substance such as starch, gelatin, casein, gums, oils, waxes, silicones, rosin, and polymers applied to yarns, fabrics, paper, leather, and other products to improve or increase their stiffness, strength, smoothness, or weight. *See* Clothing.

SLAKED LIME • *See* Calcium Hydroxide.

SLIMICIDE • A substance, such as chlorine or phenol, that kills the types of bacteria and fungi that contaminate water and other liquids.

SMOKE DETECTOR • There are two types: photoelectric, which detects only visible products of combustion; and ionizing, which detects both the visible and invisible products of combustion. Ionizing smoke detectors contain a minute amount of radioactive material, Americium-241 (Am-241). Am-241 has a half-life of nearly 500 years and emits alpha particles. The ionizing smoke detector is constructed so that to gain access to the radioactive sections would require the complete destruction of the smoke detector. If possible, when you want to dispose of it, you should return the ionizing smoke detector to the manufacturer. The photoelectric smoke detector can be disposed of in the trash.

SMOKING • *See* Tobacco.

SNO BOL® • Toilet bowl cleaner by Staley Manufacturing Company of Decatur, Ill. It contains 15 percent hydrochloric acid *(see)*.

SOAP • The oldest cleanser, usually a mixture of sodium salts of various fatty acids. In liquid soaps, potassium is used instead of sodium salts. Bar soaps vary in contents from brand to brand, depending on the fats or oils used. Sodium hydroxide makes a strong soap; fatty acids, a mild soap. So-called neutral soaps actually are alkaline, whith a pH of about 10 when dissolved in water (compared to skin, which is 5 to 6.5 pH). Soaps are usually present in toothpastes, tooth powders, and shaving creams. Soap is usually made by the saponification of a vegetable oil with caustic soda. Hard soaps consist largely of sodium oleate or sodium palmitate and are used medicinally as antiseptics, detergents, or suppositories. Many people are allergic to soaps. They may also be drying to the skin, irritate the eyes, and cause rashes, depending upon ingredients.

SOAPSTONE • **Silicate Soapstone.** Odorless solid, noncombustible, containing about 1 percent crystalline silica. *See* Talc.

SODA ASH • *See* Sodium Carbonate.

SODA LYE • *See* Sodium Hydroxide.

SODIUM ACETATE • **Sodium Salt of Acetic Acid.** Transparent crystals highly soluble in water. A preservative and alkalizer in cosmetics; also used in photography, and dyeing processes, and in foot warmers because of its heat-retention ability. Medicinally, it is used as an alkalizer and diuretic. No known toxicity.

SODIUM ACID SULFATE • Acid used in toilet bowl cleaners. *See* Sodium Bisulfate.

SODIUM ACRYLATE/VINYL ALCOHOL • **Acrylic Acid, Polymer with Vinyl Alcohol Sodium Salt.** *See* Polyvinyls.

SODIUM ALKYL BENZENE • Colorless, almost odorless liquid made from benzene, sulfur, and ammonia. Used in detergents. Can be irritating to the skin, eyes, and mucous membranes.

SODIUM ALKLYL BENZENESULFONATE • Manufactured from benzene and sulfonic acid, it is used in detergents. The sulfonates are less soluble in hard water than the sulfates. Alkyl sodium sulfonates have been shown to irritate the skin and eyes of rabbits but have low toxicity.

SODIUM ALKLYL ETHOXYLATE SULFATE • Nonionic surfactant prepared by treating fatty acids with ethylene oxide. Used in liquid Ivory Snow®. *See* Detergents.

SODIUM ARSENATE • Very poisonous white or grayish powder used in the manufacture of arsenical soap for use on skin, for treating vines against certain scale diseases, and as a topical insecticide for animals. May cause contact dermatitis. *See* Arsenate, Sodium.

SODIUM BICARBONATE • **Bicarbonate of Soda. Baking Soda.** An alkali prepared by the reaction of soda ash with carbon dioxide. Its white crystals or powder are used in baking powder, as a gastric antacid, as an alkaline wash, and to treat burns. Used also as a neutralizer for butter, cream, milk, and ice cream. It is used in the manufacture of sponge rubber, in gold and platinum plating, treating wool and silk, fire extinguishers, prevention of wood mold, and cleaning preparations. Essentially harmless to the skin, but when used on very dry skin in preparations that evaporate, leaves an alkaline residue that may cause irritation.

SODIUM BISULFATE • **Sodium Acid Sulfite. Sodium Hydrogen Sulfite.** Colorless or white crystals with a disagreeable taste, fused in water. Used as a disinfectant in the manufacture of soaps, and in perfumes, foods, and pickling compounds. Also used as a bleach and antioxidant. Concentrated solutions are irritating to the skin. Ingestion causes restlessness, irritability, convulsions, and breathlessness, and death can result in thirty to forty-five minutes. *See* Sodium Bisulfite.

SODIUM BORATE • Borax Glass. Hard, odorless crystals, the salt of boric acid *(see)*. Used as a preservative, it penetrates dry wood and provides protection from termites, carpenter ants, and wood borers. Also used in soldering metals, the manufacture of glazes and enamels, tanning, in cleaning compounds, to artificially age wood, and in fireproofing fabrics and wood. Ingestion of 5 to 10 grams by children can cause severe vomiting, diarrhea, and death.

SODIUM BROMATE • Derived from bromine and sodium carbonate, the colorless, odorless crystals liberate oxygen. Used as a solvent. *See* Potassium bromate for toxicity.

SODIUM CARBONATE • Soda Ash. Small, odorless crystals or powder occurring in nature in ores and found in lake brines or seawater. Absorbs water from the air. Has an alkaline taste. Used in dishwasher detergents (automatic) to soften water, and as a suds-control agent. Also used in photography, cleaning compounds, pH control of water, the manufacture of glass, cleaning and bleaching textiles, in cosmetics, and in vaginal douches. It is the cause of scalp, forehead, and hand rash when hypersensitive individuals use cosmetics containing it. *See* Dishwasher Detergents (Automatic) and Bleaches.

SODIUM CETEARYL SULFATE • The sodium salt of a blend of cetyl and stearyl alcohol *(see both)* and sulfuric acid ester. A wax used as a surface-active agent *(see)*. No known toxicity. *See* Fatty Alcohols.

SODIUM CETYL SULFATE • Marketed in the form of a paste. Contains alcohol, sodium sulfate *(see)*, and water. A surface-active agent *(see)*. No known toxicity.

SODIUM CHLORATE • Colorless, odorless crystals derived from heating sodium chloride. It is used as an oxidizing agent and bleach for paper pulps, as a herbicide and defoliant, in matches, explosives, flares, and for leather tanning. Highly flammable when in contact with organic materials.

SODIUM CHLORIDE • Common Table Salt. Opaque, white, water-absorbing crystals. Odorless, with a characteristic salty taste. Used as a seasoning and, topically, to treat inflamed lesions. Also used in ceramic glazes, metallurgy, soap manufacture, home water softeners, highway deicing, herbicides, fire extinguishers, resins, and supercooled solutions. Diluted solutions are not considered irritating, but upon drying, water is drawn from the skin and may produce irritation. Salt workers have a great many skin rashes.

SODIUM CHLORITE • A powerful oxidizer prepared commercially and used as a bleaching agent for textiles and paper pulp, and in water purification. Toxicity depends on concentration. Highly flammable and easily explosive.

SODIUM CHLOROACETATE • A white, odorless powder used in weed killers and dyes. *See* Sodium Chlorite.

SODIUM CHROMATE • Yellow, translucent crystals derived from chrome iron ore melted with lime and soda. It is used for inks, dyeing, paint pigment, leather tanning, anticorrosives for iron, and as a wood preservative. Toxic. *See* Chromium Compounds and Chromate Salts.

SODIUM CITRATE • White, odorless crystals, granules, or powder with a cool, salty taste. Stable in air. Used as a sequestering agent *(see)* to remove trace metals in solutions, and as an alkalizer and water softener. Also used in photography, detergents, and food products. It attaches itself to trace metals present in water and inhibits them from entering living cells. Proposed as a replacement for phosphates in detergents, but also causes algal growth, and removes the necessary trace metals from water, in addition to the toxic ones.

SODIUM CYANIDE • White, water-absorbing crystals made from cyanide and sodium hydroxide. It is used for insecticides, cleaning metals, fumigation, the manufacture of dyes and pigments, and as a chelating agent. Toxic by ingestion and inhalation.

SODIUM DIACETATE • White crystals with an acetic acid odor, used as a buffer, mold inhibitor, varnish hardener, antitarnishing agent, and as a sequestrant. *See* Acetic Acid.

SODIUM DICHLOROISOCYANURIC ACID • A white, slightly water-absorbing powder that is the active ingredient in dry bleaches, dishwashing compounds, scouring powders, sanitizers, and swimming pool disinfectants. Strong oxidizing material and a fire risk. Toxic by ingestion.

SODIUM 2,4-DICHLOROPHENOXYACETATE • A crystalline solid, used as a herbicide. Inhalation irritant. *See* 2,4-D.

SODIUM DODECYLBENZENESULFONATE • An anionic detergent *(see),* it may irritate the skin. Will cause vomiting if swallowed. *See* Sodium Lauryl Sulfate.

SODIUM-2-ETHYHEXYLSULFOACETATE • Light, cream-colored flakes; water-soluble, a good foam-maker, and good in hard water. Used as a solubilizing agent, particularly for soapless shampoo compositions. *See* Quaternary Ammonium Detergents.

SODIUM FLUORIDE • Used in toothpastes to prevent tooth decay and as an insecticide (not to be used on living plants), disinfectant, and preservative. It is used to fluoridate municipal water, as a wood preservative, rodenticide, for chemical cleaning, electroplating, glass manufacture, as a preservative for adhesives, and in infrared detection systems. Can cause nausea and vomiting when ingested, and even death, depending upon the dose. Strong irritant to tissue. Fluorides, including sodium fluoride, have been added to public drinking water supplies (1 ppm) to reduce the incidence of dental caries. The concentration used has been established to be far below the permissible level of toxicity (*see* PEL) of fluorine-containing compounds in the human body. The program has been in existence for more than thirty years, yet there are still some scientists and citizens who worry about its adverse effects. There is little doubt that it has helped children grow up with fewer cavities. Chronic endemic fluorosis due to high concentrations of natural fluoride in local water supplics involves mottling of the teeth, bone changes, and, rarely, brain and nerve involvement. Acute fluoride poisoning can cause heart, brain, nerve, and gastrointestinal damage. *See* Fluorides.

SODIUM FLUOROACETATE • A fine, white, odorless powder soluble in water. Derived from fluoride, it is one of the best rodenticides. It is rapidly absorbed by the gastrointestinal tract, but is slowly absorbed by the skin unless the skin is broken. It affects both the cardiovascular and the nervous systems in all species. In humans, it produces convulsive seizures and depression, then nausea and anxiety, heart irregularities, and death. Its use is now limited by law to licensed pest control operators due to its high toxicity for birds and mammals, including humans.

SODIUM FLUOROSILICATE • Derived from fluosilicic acid and sodium carbonate, it is used in fluoridation, for enamel and glass, in insecticides and rodenticides, as a moth repellent, and in glue, leather, and wood preservatives. Toxic by ingestion, and inhalation, and a strong skin irritant.

SODIUM GLUCONATE • Made from glucose by fermentation, a white to yellowish powder, used in metal cleaners, paint strippers, bottle-washing preparations, metal plating, and rust removers. Nontoxic.

SODIUM GOLD CHLORIDE • **Gold Salts.** Yellow crystals soluble in water, derived by neutralizing chloroauric acid with sodium carbonate. Used in photography, glass staining, and for decorating porcelain. *See* Art Materials.

SODIUM HEXAMETAPHOSPHATE • Calgon™. Derived from phosphoric acid, it is used in potable water to prevent scale formation and corrosion. Because it keeps calcium, magnesium, and iron salts in solution, it is an excellent water softener and detergent. It is a glass cleaner. No known toxicity to the skin in dilute solutions. *See* Sodium Metaphosphate.

SODIUM HYDROXIDE • Caustic Soda. Soda Lye. White or nearly white pellets, flakes, or sticks derived from brine. Readily absorbs water. An alkali and emulsifier in cosmetics, modifier for food starch, glazing agent for pretzels, and peeling agent for tubers and fruits. Also used for etching and electroplating. The FDA banned use of more than 10 percent in household liquid drain cleaners. Its ingestion causes vomiting, prostration, and collapse. Inhalation causes lung damage. Prolonged contact with dilute solutions has a destructive effect upon tissue. Reacts violently with acids. *See* Bleaches.

SODIUM HYPOCHLORITE • Made by the addition of chlorine to sodium hydroxide, it is used for bleaching paper pulp and textiles, in water purification, in fungicides, as a swimming pool disinfectant, in laundry products, and as a germicide. Liquid household bleaches such as Purex™ and Clorox™ are approximately 5 percent sodium hypochlorite solutions. Also used as a preservative in the washing of cottage cheese curd, and an antiseptic for wounds. Ingestion may cause corrosion of mucous membranes, and esophageal or gastric perforation. Among other popular bleaches containing sodium hypochlorite are Eau de Javelle and Dazzle®. Do not mix bleach with acids such as vinegar, ammonia, toilet bowl cleaners, or drain cleaners. This could produce a gas that is toxic and even fatal. If you use "fresh scented" bleach, be aware that it may prevent ability to recognize overexposure to the bleach product. *See* Bleaches.

SODIUM LACTATE • A plasticizer substitute for glycerin; colorless, thick, odorless liquid miscible with water, alcohol, and glycerin. Solution is neutral. Used in antifreeze as a corrosion inhibitor. No known toxicity.

SODIUM LAURETH SULFATE • The sodium salt of sulfated ethoxylated lauryl alcohol, widely used as a water softener, and in baby and other nonirritating shampoos as wetting and cleansing agents. *See* Surfactants.

SODIUM LAUROYL ISETHIONATE • Sodium Lauryl Isethionate. A mild synthetic soap, one of the main ingredients in Dove®. *See* Surfactants.

SODIUM LAURYL SULFATE • A widely used detergent, wetting agent, and emulsifier, prepared by sulfation of lauryl alcohol followed by neutralization with sodium carbonate. Faint fatty odor; also emulsifies fats. A skin irritant. May cause drying of the skin because of its degreasing ability.

SODIUM LIGNOSULFONATE • The sodium salt of polysulfonated lignin, derived from wood. A tan, free-flowing powder used as a dispersing agent, an emulsifier, stabilizer, and cleaning agent. No known toxicity.

SODIUM MAGNESIUM FLUOROSILICATE • An inorganic salt used in enamel as an insecticide, and as a rat poison. Used in shampoos, to kill lice. *See* Silicates and Sodium Fluorosilicate.

SODIUM MAGNESIUM SILICATES • *See* Silicates.

SODIUM METAPHOSPHATE • **Graham's Salts.** Derived from sodium phosphates, used in dental polishing agents, detergents, water softeners, sequestrants, emulsifiers, food additives, and textile laundering. *See* Sodium Hexametaphosphate.

SODIUM METASILICATE • An alkali usually prepared from sand and soda ash. Used in detergents, for floor cleaning, bleaches, and deinking paper. Caustic substance, corrosive to the skin, harmful if swallowed, and cause of severe eye irritations. *See* Dishwasher Detergents (Automatic).

SODIUM METHANEARSONATE • White solid used as a herbicide for grassy weeds. Toxic. *See* Arsenic Compounds.

SODIUM-*n*-METHYLDITHIOCARBAMATE   DIHYDRATE • A white, crystalline solid used as a fungicide, worm killer, weed killer, insecticide, and soil fumigant. Irritating to human tissue and toxic to plants. *See* Carbamates and Pesticides.

SODIUM NAPHTHALENE • A white paste used in detergents, emulsifiers, disinfectants, and the manufacture of paint driers. *See* Naphthas.

SODIUM NITRATE • **Soda Niter. Chile Saltpeter.** Colorless, transparent, odorless crystals, derived from nitric acid and sodium carbonate, and from Chile saltpeter. Used in fertilizers, refrigerants, matches, dynamite, dyes, pottery enamels, and meat preservative. Toxic by ingestion. A fire hazard.

SODIUM NITRITE • Slightly yellowish or white crystals made from sodium nitrate, used as a preservative in cured meats, in photography, and as an antidote for cyanide poisoning. A cancer-causing agent, and explosive when heated.

SODIUM OLETH-7 OR -8 PHOSPHATE • The sodium salts of the phosphate esters of oleth, used in mild cleansers such as baby shampoos. No known toxicity.

SODIUM ORTHOSILICATE • Dustless, white flakes used in commercial laundries, metal cleaning, and heavy-duty cleaning. *See* Cleaning Compounds.

SODIUM OXALATE • **Sodium Salt of Oxalic Acid.** A white, odorless, crystalline powder used as an intermediate *(see)*, in hair dyes, as a texturizer, in leather finishing, and blueprinting. Toxic when ingested. May be irritating to the skin.

SODIUM PENTACHLOROPHENATE • A white or tan powder soluble in water. It is used in joint compounds, fungicides, herbicides, and as a disinfectant in finishes and papers. Toxic by ingestion and inhalation. A skin irritant.

SODIUM PERBORATE • White crystals soluble in water, used as an antiseptic and as a bleaching agent in laundry products. Strong solutions that are very alkaline are irritating to the skin.

SODIUM PERCARBONATE • A stable, crystalline powder derived from sodium carbonate and hydrogen peroxide *(see both)*. Used as a denture cleaner, mild antiseptic, and bleaching agent. Toxic by ingestion. *See also* Peroxide.

SODIUM PEROXIDE • A yellowish white powder that absorbs hydrogen and carbon dioxide from air. Derived from carbon dioxide heated in aluminum trays. A strong oxidizing agent, it is used to bleach many materials, including paper and textiles. Also used in deodorants, antiseptics, water purification products, in textile dyeing and printing, and in germicidal soaps. It is a dangerous fire and explosion risk in contact with water, alcohols, and organic material. An irritant.

SODIUM PERSULFATE • An oxidizing agent that promotes emulsion. Used as a bleaching agent for fats, oils, and fabrics. An inorganic salt; a white crystalline powder that decomposes in moisture and warmth. Can cause allergic reactions in the hypersensitive. Toxic when ingested. A fire hazard.

SODIUM PHENOXIDE • *See* Phenol.

SODIUM *o*-PHENYLPHENATE • **Sodium *o*-Phenylphenolate. Sodium Salt of *o*-Phenylphenol.** An antiseptic, germicide, fungicide, and mold inhibitor. Yellow flakes or powder with a slight soap odor. Soluble in water, alcohol, and acetone. A skin irritant. Regarded as more effective than phenol and cresol *(see both)* because it has greater germ-killing power, may be used in smaller concentrations, and is less irritating to the skin, although it is often considered toxic by some cosmetics companies for use in products.

SODIUM PHOSPHATE • Colorless, translucent crystals or white powder, derived from phosphoric acid. It is used in fertilizers, for fireproofing wood and paper, in soldering enamels, tanning, ceramic glazes, detergents, water softeners, paint removers, industrial cleaners, photographic developers, metal cleaners, and as a dietary supplement. Stable in air. Without water, it can be irritating to the skin, and some forms are toxic by ingestion.

SODIUM PROPIONATE • Colorless or transparent, odorless crystals that gather water in moist air. Used as a preservative in cosmetics and foodstuffs to prevent mold and fungus. It has been used to treat fungal infections of the skin, but can cause allergic reactions.

SODIUM PYRITHIONE • **Sodium Omadine®. Sodium Salt of Pyrithione Zinc Derivative.** Used as a fungicide and bacteria killer. Used in dandruff shampoos to control dandruff, and as an antibacterial in soaps and detergents. No known toxicity.

SODIUM PYROPHOSPHATE PEROXIDE • A white powder, water soluble, used as a denture cleanser, in dentifrices, household laundry detergents, and as an antiseptic. *See* Hydrogen Peroxide.

SODIUM SALICYLATE • Shiny white crystals made from salicylic acid, and used as a preservative for paste, mucilage, glue, and hides. *See* Salicylic Acid.

SODIUM SELENATE • White crystals used as an insecticide for nonedible plants. Toxic by ingestion. *See* Pesticides.

SODIUM SESQUICARBONATE • White crystals, flakes, or powder produced from sodium carbonate. Soluble in water. Used as an alkalizer in bath salts and for leather tanning, and as a detergent, a soap builder, a mild soap for general cleaning, and a water softener. Irritating to the skin and mucous membranes. May cause allergic reaction in the hypersensitive.

SODIUM SILICATE • **Water Glass.** Consists of colorless to white, or grayish white crystallike pieces or lumps. These silicates are almost insoluble in cold water. Strongly alkaline. Used as a detergent in soaps, depilatories, and protective creams. Also used in silica gels, adhesives, paperboard, water treatment, bleaching and sizing of textiles, as a flame retardant, and in glass foam. As a topical antiseptic can be irritating and caustic to the skin and mucous membranes. If swallowed it causes vomiting and diarrhea. *See* Dishwasher Detergents (Automatic).

SODIUM SILICOALUMINATE • *See* Silicates.

SODIUM SOAP • *See* Sodium Stearate.

SODIUM STEARATE • A fatty acid that is 92.82 percent stearic acid *(see)*. A white powder with a waterlike odor, a soapy feel, and a slightly tallowlike odor. It is used in deodorant sticks, stick perfumes, waterproofing, gelling agent, and as a stabilizer in plastics. Slowly soluble in cold water or cold alcohol. One of the least allergy causing of the sodium salts of fatty acids. Nonirritating to the skin.

SODIUM SULFATE • **Salt Cake.** Occurs in nature as the minerals mirabilite and thenardite. Used chiefly in the manufacture of dyes, soaps, and detergents. Also used as a chewing gum base and, medicinally, to reduce body water. It is a reagent *(see)* and a precipitant; mildly saline in taste. Usually harmless when applied in toilet preparations. May prove irritating in concentrated solutions if applied to the skin, permitted to dry and then remain. May also enhance the irritant action of certain detergents.

SODIUM SULFIDE • Crystals or granules prepared from ammonia that easily absorb water; used in chewing gum bases, dehairing hides and wool pulling, dyes, paper pulp, engraving, and cotton printing. Fire and explosive hazard.

SODIUM SULFITE • An antiseptic, preservative, and antioxidant used in hair dyes. White to tan or pink, odorless or nearly odorless powder having a cooling, salty, sulfurlike taste. It is used as a bacterial inhibitor in wine brewing, and distilled-beverage industries; to bleach straw, silk and wool; and as a developer in photography. Products containing sulfites may release sulfur dioxide. If this is inhaled by people who suffer from asthma it can trigger an asthmatic attack. Sulfites are known to cause stomach irritation, nausea, diarrhea, skin rash, or swelling in sulfite-sensitive people. People whose kidneys or livers are impaired may not be able to produce the enzymes that break down sulfites in the body. Sulfites may destroy thiamine and, consequently, are not added to foods that are sources of this B vitamin.

SODIUM SULFONATE • A bubble bath-clarifying agent and a dispersing agent used to make shampoos clear. Also used as a solvent and in oils for textiles and metalworking. *See* Sulfonated Oils.

SODIUM TALLOW SULFATE • A defoamer, emollient, intermediate *(see),* and surface-active agent. A mixture of sodium alkyl sulfates. *See* Tallow.

SODIUM TALLOWATE • The sodium salt of tallow *(see)*. Used in soaps and detergents.

SODIUM TETRADECYL SULFATE • *See* Detergents.

SODIUM THIOSULFATE • An antioxidant used to protect raw, sliced potatoes and french fries from overbrowning, and as a stabilizer for potassium iodide in iodized salt. Also used to neutralize chlorine and to bleach bone, as a fixing agent in photography, and in the dechlorination of water. It is an antidote for cyanide poisoning, and has been used in the past to combat blood clots, and treat ringworms and mange in animals. Poorly absorbed by the bowel.

SODIUM *p*-TOLUENESULFOCHLORAMINE • Chloramine-T. A water-purifying agent and deodorant used to remove unwanted odor in cheese. Suspected of causing rapid allergic reactions in the hypersensitive. Poisoning by chloramine-T is characterized by pain, vomiting, sudden loss of consciousness, circulatory and respiratory collapse, and death.

SODIUM TOLUENESULFONATE • Methylbenzenesulfonic Acid. Sodium Salt. An aromatic compound that is used as a solvent. *See* Benzene.

SODIUM TRIDECYLBENZENESULFONATE • A mixture of alkyl benzene sulfonates used as a synthetic detergent. *See* Sodium Dodecylbenzenesulfonate.

SODIUM TRIPOLYPHOSPHATE • STPP. A crystalline salt used in bubble baths and as a texturizer in soaps. Moderately irritating to the skin and mucous membranes. Ingestion can cause violent purging. *See* Sodium Phosphate and Dishwasher Detergents (Automatic).

SODIUM XYLENESULFONATE • An isolate from wood and coal tar. Used as a solvent in detergents. No known toxicity. *See* Xylene, Solvent, and Solubility.

SOFTENERS • *See* Fabric Softeners.

SOLDERING FLUX • A low-melting alloy usually of the lead-tin type, used for joining metals. The solder acts as an adhesive. Usually contains zinc chloride and hydrochloric acid *(see both)*. May also contain rosin, silver, urea, boric acid, and alcohol *(see all)*.

SOLUBILITY • The degree to which a chemical can dissolve in a solvent, forming a solution.

SOLUBILIZATION • The process of dissolving in water such substances as fats and liquids that are not readily soluble under standard conditions by the action of a detergent or similar agent. Technically, a "solubilized" product is clear because the particle side of an emulsion is so small that light is not bounced off the particle. Solubilization is used in colognes and clear lotions. Sodium sulfonates *(see)* are common solubilzing agents.

SOLUBILIZED VAT DYES • The sodium salts of vat dyes. They are comparatively expensive, but give excellent penetration and fastness. *See* Vat Dyes.

SOLUBLE METALWORKING FLUIDS • Metalworking fluids are liquids used in machining processes such as cutting or grinding. The soluble, oil base-type emulsifiers are milky white. They commonly are found in emulsifiers, high-pressure additives, corrosion inhibitors, antifoaming agents, lubrication aids, pH stabilizers, coupling agents, and biocides. They can cause skin rash and eye, nose, and throat irritation upon exposure, according to California's Hazard Evaluation System and Information Service. *See* Metalworking Fluids.

SOLUBLE METALWORKING OIL • Oil based with emulsifiers. Usually milky white. May contain corrosion inhibitors, antifoaming agents, pH stabilizers, and biocides. Can cause dermatitis, eye, nose, and throat irritation.

SOLUBLE POTASH • A plant food. *See* Potassium Silicate.

SOLUTION • A mixture in which the components are uniformly dispersed. All solutions consist of some kind of solvent, such as water or alcohol, which dissolves another substance, usually a solid.

SOLVENT • A liquid capable of dissolving or dispersing one or more substances. Methyl ethyl ketone is an example of a solvent. A substance is defined as a solvent by how it is used rather than by its chemical composition. Water, for example, is a solvent when it is used to dissolve salt. Water-based solvents are relatively nontoxic, but are not effective in dissolving organic or carbon-based sustances commonly used in industry. Solvents are used to thin paints, clean, degrease, and manufacture many chemicals. There are hundreds of solvents used to produce over thirty thousand blends of solvents. Most solvents can be hazardous if you use them without adequate controls and protection. How hazardous a solvent is depends not only on the toxicity of its ingredients, but also on its chemical concentration, its ability to vaporize, how long you are exposed to it, and how much of it is absorbed by your body. Your sensitivity to a particular solvent, and its combination with other chemicals in your environment are also important.

Among the toxic organic solvents common to household products are: aromatic hydrocarbons (benzene, toluene, xylene); chlorinated hydrocarbons (ethylene dichloride, methylene chloride, perchloroethylene, trichloroethylene, trichloroethane); isopropyl alcohol; methanol; naphthas; petroleum solvents (kerosene, gasoline, mineral spirits); turpentine; and acetone. To protect yourself from the ill effects of solvents, work outdoors or in a well-ventilated area. Wear goggles and gloves, and clothing that covers exposed skin. After handling solvents, always wash your hands and any exposed skin, particularly before eating or smoking. Do not drink alcoholic beverages while using solvents because they increase toxicity. Solvents should be stored in well-ventilated areas away from flames or sparks.

SOLVENT DYE • Generally insoluble in water, but dissolves to varying degrees in liquid, molten, and solid forms of organic media, including alcohols, oils, fats, and waxes. These dyes are used in plastics, printing ink, polyester, and other synthetic fibers. Can be irritating to the skin.

SOLVENT RED 23 • *See* Sudan III.

SOMONIL™ • *See* Methidathion.

SORBIC ACID • A white, free-flowing powder obtained from the berries of the mountain ash. Used in cosmetics as a preservative and humectant. Also used as a mold and yeast inhibitor, and a replacement for glycerin in emulsions, ointments, embalming fluid, mouthwashes, dental creams, and various cosmetic creams. A binder for toilet preparations and plasticizers. Produces a velvetlike feel when rubbed on skin. In large amounts, sticky. Practically nontoxic, but may cause skin irritation in susceptible people. *See* Sorbitol.

SORBITAN OLEATE • **Sorbitan Monooleate.** An emulsifying agent, defoaming agent, and plasticizer. No known toxicity.

SORBITOL • First found in the ripe berries of the mountain ash, it also occurs in other berries (except grapes), and in cherries, plums, pears, apples, seaweed, and algae. Consists of white hygroscopic powder, flakes, or granules, with a sweet taste. A humectant, texturizing agent, and sequestrant. Gives a velvety feel to skin. Used as a replacement for glycerin in emulsions, ointments, embalming fluid, mouthwashes, dental creams, and various cosmetic creams. Also used in antifreeze, as a sugar substitute, in writing inks to ensure a smooth flow from the point of the pen, and to increase the absorption of vitamins in pharmaceutical preparations. Used medicinally to reduce body water, and for intravenous feedings. No known toxicity if taken externally. However, if ingested in excess, it can cause diarrhea and gastrointestinal disturbances; also it may alter the absorption of other drugs, making them less effective or more toxic. *See* Sorbic Acid.

SOYBEAN OIL • Extracted from the seeds of plants grown in eastern Asia, especially Manchuria, and the midwestern United States. Used in the manufacture of soaps, shampoos, and bath oils, printing inks, nylon, plasticizers, paints, and varnishes. Pale yellow to brownish yellow. About 300 million bushels of soybeans are grown yearly in the United States, a third more than in China. May cause allergic reactions.

SPANDEX • The generic name for fiber in which there is a long chain of polyurethane molecules. Imparts elasticity to garments such as bras, girdles, bathing suits, and special hosiery.

SPECTROCIDE™ • *See* Diazinon.

SPERMACETI • **Cetyl Palmitate.** Used as a base of ointments and creams, and as an emollient in cleansing creams. Also in shampoos, cold creams, and other creams to improve their gloss and increase their viscosity. Derived as a wax from the head of the sperm whale. Generally nontoxic but may become rancid and cause irritations.

SPIC & SPAN® HOUSEHOLD CLEANER • Contains sodium sesquicarbonate *(see)*.

SPIC & SPAN ® ALL-PURPOSE LIQUID CLEANER • Contains anionic detergent *(see)*, butyldiglycol, sodium citrate, and tetrasodium EDTA as water-softening agents, and sodium cumene sulfonate as a "quality control agent," which, according to Procter and Gamble, keeps sodium "mixed and the same for as long as you use it." The informations specialist who answers questions could not supply the derivative of sodium cumene sulfonate, when asked. (Cumene is used as a solvent and sulfonate is usually used as a germicide.) Also contains color and perfume but no phosphorus. The label on this cleaner is one of the best found on any cleaning products; it includes a telephone number, for questions and comments.

SPIC & SPAN® PINE CLEANER • Contains anionic surfactant and pine oil *(see both)*, sodium citrate to soften water, color, perfume, and water.

SPIKE LAVENDER OIL • **French Lavender.** Used in perfumes. A pale yellow, stable oil with a lavenderlike odor, obtained from the European mint *Lavandula latifolea*, grown in the Mediterranean region. Used in flavorings for beverages and confections, and in perfumes, blended with lavender oil, soaps, and varnishes. Used also for fumigating to keep moths from clothes. No known toxicity.

SPOT REMOVERS • *See* Cleaning Fluids and Stain Removers.

SQUALENE • Obtained from shark-liver oil. Occurs in smaller amounts in olive oil, wheat germ oil, and rice bran oil. A faint agreeable odor, tasteless; miscible with vegetable and mineral oils, organic solvents, and fatty substances. Insoluble in water. A bactericide, it is used in surface-active agents. No known toxicity.

STABILIZER • A substance added to a product to give it body and maintain a desired texture, as, for instance, the stabilizer, alginic acid.

STAIN REMOVER • The bleach type usually contains sodium hypochlorite or sodium perborate. The solvent type may contain perchloroethylene or trichloroethane, naphtha, alcohol, and acetic acid *(see all)*. The general type includes amyl, butyl and ethyl acetate, benzene, perfume, oxalic acid, *p*-hydroxybenzoic acid, soap, sodium sulfate, tetrapotassium pyrophosphate, and toluene *(see all)*. Lipstick removers usually include alcohol, isoamylacetate, petroleum hydrocarbons, butyl cellosolve, and chloroform *(see all)*. Rust- and ink-stain removers contain phosphoric acid, alcohol, oxalic acid, and erosion inhibitors *(see all)*.

STAINLESS STEEL CLEANERS • Usually contain an acid such as citric, salt, an abrasive such as silica, and an anionic detergent *(see)*. You can make your own polish by using vinegar to remove spots and baking soda or mineral oil for shining.

STAINLESS STEEL POLISH • *See* Stainless Steel Cleaners.

STAINS/FINISHES • Contain one or several of the following: acetone, methyl ethyl ketone, alcohols, xylene, toluene, or methyl chloride *(see all)*. All solvents must be handled with care and used in well-ventilated areas or outdoors. *See* Solvents.

STANNIC CHLORIDE • Tin Tetrachloride. A thin, colorless, fuming, caustic liquid, soluble in water, used as a mordant *(see)* in metallic hair dyes and as a reagent *(see)* in perfumes and soaps. May be highly irritating to the eyes and mucous membranes.

STANNOUS CHLORIDE • Tin Dichloride. An antioxidant, soluble in water, and a powerful reducing agent, particularly in the manufacture of dyes. May be irritating to the skin and mucous membranes.

STARCH • Acid Modified. Pregelatinized and Unmodified. Starch is stored by plants and is found in wheat, potatoes, rice, corn, beans, and many other vegetable foods. Insoluble in cold water or alcohol, but soluble in boiling water. It is used in adhesives— gummed paper and tapes, cartons and bags—machine-coated paper, textile filer, sizing agent, gelling agent, and as a polymer base. Allergic reaction to starch in toilet goods includes stuffy nose and other symptoms due to inhalation. Absorbs moisture and swells, causing blocking and distension of the pores leading to mechanical irritation. Particles remain in pores and putrefy, accelerated by sweat.

STARCH/ACRYLATES/ACRYLAMIDE COPOLYMER • *See* Starch and Acrylic Acid.

STAY-PUF FABRIC SOFTENER™ • A cationic *(see)* detergent. *See also* Quaternary Ammonium Compounds.

STEARETH-2 • A polyoxyethyl *(see)* ether of fatty alcohol. The oily liquid is used as a surfactant and emulsifier *(see both)*. No known toxicity.

STEARETH-4 THROUGH -100 • The polyethylene glycol ethers of stearyl alcohol. The number indicates the degree of liquidity; the higher, the more solid. *See* Steareth-2.

STEARIC ACID • Occurs naturally in butter acids, tallow, cascarilla bark, and other animal fats and oils. A white, waxy, natural fatty acid, it is the major ingredient used in making bar soap and lubricants. A large percentage of all cosmetic creams on the market contains stearic acid. It is a possible sensitizer for allergic people. *See* Fatty Acids.

STEARYL ALCOHOL • **Stenol.** A mixture of solid alcohols prepared from sperm whale oil. Unctuous white flakes, insoluble in water, soluble in alcohol and ether. Can be prepared from sperm whale oil. A substitute for cetyl alcohol *(see)* to obtain a firmer product at ordinary temperatures. Used in pharmaceuticals, cosmetic creams, for emulsions, as an antifoam agent, and lubricant; also in resins. No known toxicity.

STEL • **Short-Term Exposure Limit.** A term used to indicate the maximum average concentration allowed for a continuous fifteen-minute exposure period.

STEROL • Any class of solid, complex alcohols from animals and plants. Cholesterol is a sterol.

STIFFENERS FOR RAYON • *See* Stiffening Agent.

STIFFENING AGENT • An ingredient to add body to cosmetics or fabrics. Many of the gums, such as karaya and carrageenan *(see)*, are used for this purpose.

STODDARD SOLVENT • **High Flash Naphtha. Mineral Spirits. White Spirits.** A widely used dry cleaner and spot remover derived from petroleum. Sometimes used as a paint thinner. Contains paraffins and, usually, some benzene *(see)*. Toxic by ingestion.

STPP • *See* Sodium Tripolyphosphate.

STRYCHNINE • A powerful poison from the seeds of nux vomica. It is toxic by ingestion and inhalation.

STYRENE • **Vinylbenzene. Vinylbenzol. Styrol. Cinnamene. Cinnamol. Styrolene. Phenylethene. Phenylethylene. Ethenylbenzene.** Obtained from ethylbenzene by taking out the hydrogen. Colorless to yellowish, oily liquid with a penetrating odor. Most people can smell styrene at levels below those that cause significant health effects. Its odor is sweet at low concentrations but becomes sharp and disagreeable at higher concentrations, which still may be well below the legal limits for exposure. Styrene is used in the production of polystyrene plastics, fiberglass-reinforced plastics, synthetic rubber, resins, styrenated polyesters, protective coatings, cosmetic resins, and plastics. May be irritating to the eyes and mucous membranes, and in high concentrations is narcotic. Styrene enters the body when you breathe its vapors. In the air, styrene at levels above 100 ppm can irritate the eyes, nose, throat, and lungs. It should not be used in an enclosed space. The liquid form can be absorbed through the skin, particularly if it is in contact with the skin for a long time. Skin contact with styrene can remove the natural protective oils from the skin. Frequent or prolonged skin contact can cause irritation and rash, with dryness, redness, flaking, and cracking. As with most organic solvents, styrene, according to California's Hazard Evaluation System and Information Service (HESIS), can affect the brain the same way drinking alcohol does. In fact, drinking alcohol within a few hours of exposure to styrene increases and prolongs the effects. Some studies, according to HESIS, suggest that repeated, frequent overexposure of organic solvents over months or years can have long-lasting and possibly permanent effects on the nervous system. The symptoms of these long-term effects include fatigue, poor coordination, difficulty concentrating, loss of short term memory, and personality changes such as increased anxiety, nervousness, and irritability. In limited studies, exposure of pregnant animals to styrene at 250–300 ppm, moderately above the legal workplace level, did not cause birth defects, but did result in the death of some of the developing fetuses early in pregnancy. According to HESIS researchers, it is not known if styrene can affect human reproduction. However, styrene inhaled by a pregnant woman can reach her developing fetus, and can enter her breast milk. Researchers found styrene in the air of 80 percent of the homes tested in Bayonne, New Jersey. *See also* Shoe Cement.

STYROL • *See* Styrene.

STYROLENE • *See* Styrene.

SUCCINIC ACID • Occurs in fossils, fungi, and lichens. Prepared from acetic acid *(see)*. Odorless, with a very acidic taste. The acid is used as a plant-growth retardant. A germicide and mouthwash and used in perfumes and lacquers; also a buffer and neutralizing agent. Has been employed medicinally as a laxative. No known toxicity in cosmetic use, or on the skin.

SUCROSE OCTAACETATE • A preparation from sucrose *(see)*. A synthetic flavoring. Used in adhesives and nail lacquers; a denaturant for alcohol. No known toxicity.

SUDAN III • **Oil Red. Oil Scarlet. Solvent Red 23.** A reddish brown powder used in colorings for waxes, oils, stains, dyes, and resins. May cause contact dermatitis.

SULFAMIC ACID • A strong, white, crystalline acid used chiefly as a weed killer, in cleaning metals, and as a softening agent. Used as a plasticizer and fire retardant for paper and other cellulose products; as a stablizing agent for chlorine and hypochlorite in swimming pools, in bleaching paper pulp, and as a catalyst for urea-formaldehyde resin *(see)*. A cleansing agent in cosmetics. Moderately irritating to the skin and mucous membranes.

SULFATED OIL • **Sulphated Oil.** A compound to which a salt of sulfuric acid has been added to help control the acid-alkali balance.

SULFIDES • Inorganic sulfur compounds that occur freely or in combination with minerals; salts of weak acid. Used as hair-dissolving agents in depilatories. They are skin irritants, and may cause hair breakage.

SULFONATE • **Alkyl. Trisodium.** Sulfonation involves a reaction adding sulfonic acid molecules into an organic compound and producing a compound like benzenesulfonic. The alkyl sodium sulfonates are anionic *(see)* detergents that are more stable in water than the sulfates but are less soluble in hard water. They have been shown to be irritating to rabbit skin and eyes. They have low toxicity.

SULFONATED OILS • **Sulfated.** Prepared by reacting oils with sulfuric acid. Used in soapless shampoos and hair sprays as an emulsifier and wetting agent. Shampoos containing sulfonated oils were first manufactured in 1880 and were effective in hard or soft water. Sulfonated oils strip color from both natural and colored hair and can bring out streaks. Sulfated castor oil has been used to remove all types of dye. Applied to hair and heated, it is used as a hair treatment. Sulfonated oils are used in hair tonics that remain on the hair as hairdressings. May cause drying of the skin.

SULFUR • **Brimstone.** Occurs in the earth's crust in the free state and in combination; is mined in Texas and Louisiana. A mild antiseptic in antidandruff shampoos, it is also used in the manufacture of pulp and paper, rubber vulcanization, detergents, dyes, insecticides, rodent repellents, fungicides, explosives, coating for controlled-release fertilizers, and as a base material for mortars. May cause irritation of the skin. A fire hazard.

SULFURIC ACID • **Oil of Vitriol.** A clear, colorless, odorless, oily acid used to modify starch and regulate acid-alkalinity pH. It is very corrosive, and produces severe burns on contact with the skin and other body tissues. Used in batteries, toilet bowl cleaners, fertilizers, and as a topical caustic in cosmetic products. Diluted sulfuric acid has been used to stimulate appetite. If ingested undiluted, it can be fatal. *See* Batteries.

SUNFLOWER SEED OIL • Oil obtained by milling the seeds of the large flower produced in the USSR, India, Egypt, and Argentina. A bland, pale yellow oil, it contains amounts of vitamin E and forms a "skin" after drying. Used in food and salad oils, and in resin and soap manufacturing. No known toxicity.

SURFACE-ACTIVE AGENTS • **Surfactants.** Compounds that reduce surface tension when dissolved in solutions. There are three types: detergents, wetting agents, and emulsifiers *(see all)*. See also Surfactants.

SURFACTANTS • **Surface-Active Agents.** Lower water's surface tension, permitting water to spread out and penetrate more easily. Surface-active agents are classified by whether or not they ionize in solution, and by the nature of their electrical charges. There are four major categories: anionic, nonionic, cationic, and amphoteric. Anionic surfactants, which carry a negative charge, have excellent cleansing properties. They are used as stain and dirt removers in household detergents, powders, liquids, and toilet soaps. Nonionic surfactants have no electrical charge. Since they are resistant to hard water and dissolve in oil and grease, they are especially effective in spray-on oven cleaners. Cationic surfactants have a positive charge. These are primarily ammonia derivatives, and are antistatic and sanitizing agents used as friction reducers in hair rinses and fabric softeners. Amphoteric surfactants may be either negatively or positively charged, depending on the activity or alkalinity of the water. They are used for cosmetics where mildness is important such as in shampoos and lotions.

SWEET CLOVER EXTRACT • The extract of various species of

Melilotus, grown for hay and soil improvement. It contains coumarin *(see)* and is used as a scent to disguise bad odors.

SWIMMING POOL CHEMICALS • *See* Pool Chemicals.

SYNERGISM • Cooperative effects of two agents, giving a total
effect greater than the sum of the two effects taken independently.

SYNTHETIC • Made in a laboratory, not by nature. "Synthetic"
vanillin, for example, may be identical to vanilla extracted from the
vanilla bean, but synthetic vanillin cannot be called "natural."

SYNTHETIC BEESWAX • A mixture of alcohol esters.

SYNTHETIC GLYCERIN • *See* Glycerol.

SYNTHETIC METALWORKING FLUIDS • Metalworking fluids
are liquids used in machining processes such as cutting or grinding.
Water-based, with no hydrocarbons, the synthetic type is transparent, and often tinted green or other colors. Found in lubrication aids,
corrosion inhibitors, biocides, antifoaming agents, dyes, extreme-
pressure agents, water softeners, and perfumes. May cause eye,
nose, and throat irritation, according to California's Hazard Evaluation System and Information Service (HESIS). *See* Metalworking
Fluids.

SYNTHETIC WAX • A wax derived from various compounds,
such as petroleum, sorbitol, or naphthalene. Common properties are
water repellency, smooth texture, and low toxicity.

T

2, 4, 5-T • **(2, 4, 5-Trichlorophenoxy) acetic acid.** One of the
major components of Agent Orange, it has been removed from the
commercial market.

TALC • **French Chalk.** A finely powdered magnesium silicate, a
mineral. It usually contains small amounts of other powders such as
boric acid or zinc oxide added as a coloring agent. The main
ingredient of baby, bath, and face powders, it is used in many
cosmetics. It is also used as a pigment in paints; in varnishes;
rubber; as a filler for paper; in fireproof and cold-water paints for
wood, metal and stone, in lubricating molds and machinery, in
glove and shoe powders, and as an electrical insulation. Prolonged
inhalation can cause lung problems because it is similar in chemical
composition to asbestos, a known lung irritant and cancer-causing
agent.

TALL OIL • **Liquid Rosin.** Dark brown liquid; acrid odor, a by-product of the pinewood pulp industry. Used to scent shampoos, soaps, varnishes, and fruit sprays. "Tall" is Swedish for "pine." A fungicide and cutting oil. Also used in paints, as a source of rosin *(see)*, in soaps and greases. It may be a mild irritant and sensitizer.

TALL OIL BENZYL HYDROXYETHYL IMIDAZOLINIUM CHLORIDE • *See* Quaternary Ammonium Compounds and Tall Oil.

TALON G™ AND TALON WEATHER BLOCK BAIT™ • Pesticide that contains brodifacoum. *See* Pesticides.

TALLOW • The fat from the fatty tissue of cattle and sheep in North America. White, almost tasteless when pure, and generally harder than grease. Used in soaps, leather dressing, candles, greases, and tire molds. Also used in shaving creams, lipsticks, and shampoos. May cause eczema and blackheads.

TALLAMIDE DEA • *See* Tall Oil.

TALLAMPHOPROPIONATE • *See* Tall Oil.

TALLOW ACID • *See* Tallow.

TALLOW AMIDE • *See* Tallow.

TALLOW AMINE • *See* Tallow.

TALLOW AMINE OXIDE • *See* Tallow.

TALLOW GLYCERIDES • A mixture of triglycerides (fats) derived from tallow *(see)*.

TANNIC ACID • Occurs in the bark and fruit of many plants, notably in the bark of the oak and sumac, in cherry, coffee, and tea. Used in electroplating, as a clarification agent in wine, in writing inks, paper sizing for colored papers, and in photography. Also used in food flavorings and, medicinally, as a mild astringent; when applied may turn the skin brown. Tea contains tannic acid, which explains its folk use as an eye lotion. Excessive use in creams or lotions in hypersensitive persons may lead to irritation, blistering, and increased pigmentation. Pure tannic acid is toxic by ingestion and inhalation.

TAR OIL • The volatile oil distilled from wood tar, usually from the family *Pinaceae*. It is used in paints, waterproofing, paper, varnishes, stains, and insecticides. The principle toxic ingredients are phenols and other hydrocarbons such as naphthalenes. Toxicity estimates are hard to make because even the U.S. Pharmacopoeia does not specify the phenol content of official preparations. However, if ingested, it is estimated that one ounce would kill. *See* Creosote.

TARS • Any of the various dark brown or black, bituminous, usually odorous, viscous liquids or semiliquids distilled from wood, coal, peat, shale, and other organic materials. An antiseptic, deodorant, and insecticide. Used in hair tonics and shampoos, and as a licorice food flavoring. May cause allergic reactions.

TARTARIC ACID • Widely distributed in nature in many fruits, but usually obtained as a by-product in winemaking. Consists of colorless or translucent crystals, or a white, fine-to-granular, crystalline powder, which is odorless and has an acidic taste. This effervescent acid is used in bath salts, denture powders, nail bleaches, and many other cosmetics. Also used in ceramics, photography, textiles, for silvering mirrors, and coloring metals. In strong solutions it may be mildly irritating to the skin.

TBS • *See* Tribromsalan.

TBZ • *See* Thiabendazole.

TBTO • *See* Bis(tributyltin) Oxide.

TCC • *See* Triclocarban.

TCDD • **2,3,7,8-Tetrachlorodibenzo-*p*-Dioxin.** A halogenated, aromatic hydrocarbon; causes mutagenic and carcinogenic changes in animals. A by-product of Agent Orange (2,4-D and 2,4,5-T), it is the most toxic of chlorine-containing dioxin compounds. The long-term human consequences of exposure to this compound are controversial, but it certainly would be wise to avoid exposure to it. It is a suspected cancer-causing agent. *See* 2,4-D and 2,4,5-T.

TDI • The abbreviation for toluene diisocyanate. It is used in paint, and can cause an asthma attack in the susceptible.

TEA- • The abbreviation for triethanolamine.

TEFLON CLEANER • Usually contains sodium perborate, sodium metasilicate, and a detergent *(see all)*.

TEMPO2™ • An insecticide for ornamental plants and lawn care, it contains a synthetic pyrethrum *(see)* formula—cyano(4-fluoro-3-phenoxyphenyl)methyl 3-(2,2-dichloroethenyl)-2,2-dimethyl-cyclopropanecarboxylate—and xylene solvents. It may cause eye injury. Harmful if swallowed, inhaled, or absorbed through the skin. Do not get in eyes, or on clothing. Avoid breathing vapors, or spray mist. Goggles should be worn, and hands, arms, and face thoroughly washed with soap and warm water after handling. Clothing should be washed with soap and hot water after use. The pesticide is toxic to fish and should not be applied directly to water.

TEPP • **Tetraethylpyrophosphate.** A liquid with an agreeable odor, derived from phosphoric acid. It is an insecticide, a central nervous system poison. Absorption through the skin results in an irreversible inhibition of nerve signals. *See* Organophosphates.

TERATOGEN • A chemical or physical agent that can lead to malformation of the fetus, and birth defects.

TERATOGENIC • From the Greek *terat* (monster) and the Latin *genesis* (origin): the origin or cause of a "monster," or, defective fetus.

TERMITES • May be controlled by sodium borate, or liquid nitrogen, which freezes the bugs but leaves no toxic residue. May also be controlled by pesticides, but should be applied by a certified pest-control expert.

TERPENES • A class of unsaturated hydrocarbons *(see)* occurring in most essential oils and plant resins. Among terpene derivatives are camphor, menthol, borneol, pinene, and dipentene *(see all)*.

TERSAN • *See* Benomyl.

TERRACLOR • *See* Quintozene.

TERT • The abbreviation for tertiary.

TERTIARY • Containing three.

TERTIARY AMINES • *See* Amines and Petroleum.

TERTIARY BUTYLHYDROQUINONE • **TBHQ.** An antioxidant derived from butane *(see)*. Application to the skin may cause allergic reactions.

TESTING TRAY • *See* Allergy Standard Patch-Testing Screening Tray.

TETRA- • Containing four.

TETRABROMOPHTHALIC ANHYDRIDE • Pale yellow crystals used as flame retardant for plastics, paper, and textiles.

TETRABUTYLTIN • An organotin compound, colorless or slightly yellow, used as a stabilizer and rust-inhibiting agent for silicones, and as a lubricant, and fuel additive. *See* Organotin Compounds.

TETRACHLOROETHANE • A heavy, corrosive liquid with a chloroformlike odor, derived from acetylene and chlorine. Used as a solvent, for cleansing and degreasing metals, in paint removers, varnishes, lacquers, photographic film, resins and waxes, alcohol denaturant, insecticides, weed killers, and fumigants. It is highly toxic and can damage the liver, gastrointestinal tract, and nervous system; also a cancer-causing agent, and a skin and eye irritant. OSHA recommends industrial workers avoid skin contact with tetrachloroethane.

TETRACHLOROETHYLENE • **Perchloroethylene. PCE.** A colorless, nonflammable liquid with a pleasant odor, made from acetylene and chlorine. An excellent, nonflammable solvent. There are more than 500,000 workers who may be exposed to PCE, in the dry-cleaning and textile industries primarily, which use most of the domestically produced tetrachloroethylene. Consumers are exposed to PCE through paints, solvents, spot removers, household cleansers, and dry-cleaned clothes. Hanging your dry-cleaned clothes outside before storing or wearing them can reduce your exposure to the chemical by 20 to 30 percent, according to University of Texas researchers. They also suggest you read the warning labels on all paints, craft supplies, and other household products, and be sure to take all precautions concerning proper ventilation and use of gloves, goggles, and masks. OSHA standards allow a maximum eight-hour exposure to 100 ppm, with one five-minute peak exposure between 200 and 300 ppm permissible every three hours. Above 100 ppm, mucous membrane and upper respiratory tract irritation occurs. Exposures between 200 and 500 ppm can cause drunkenlike symptoms. Used medicinally against hookworms. Has a drying action on the skin, and can lead to adverse skin reactions. Easily absorbed through the lungs, is excreted in breast milk, and may also affect the rhythm of the heart. A cancer-causing agent.

TETRACHLORVINPHOS • a white powder that inhibits the transmission of nerve signals. Used as an organophosphate insecticide to control pests on animals and food crops. *See* Dichlorvos.

TETRAHYDROFURFURYL ALCOHOL • A liquid that absorbs water and is flammable in air. A solvent for vinyl resins, dyes for leather, and nylon. Mildly irritating to the skin and mucous membranes. See Furfural.

TETRAHYDROXYPROPYL ETHYLENEDIAMINE • A clear, colorless, thick liquid, a component of the bacteria-killing substance in sugarcane. It is strongly alkaline and is used as a solvent and preservative. May be irritating to the skin and mucous membranes; also may cause skin sensitization.

TETRAMETHYLTHIURAM • A seed disinfectant. Sprayed on some bananas. A fungicide; bacteriostat in soap. Also used as an insecticide. Can cause contact dermatitis. Irritating to mucous membranes.

TETRAPOTASSIUM PHOSPHATE • **TKPP.** An emulsifier. *See* Tetrasodium Pyrophosphate.

TETRAPOTASSIUM PYROPHOSPHATE • Colorless crystals or white powder that absorbs water from the air. It is used in soaps and detergents as a sequestering agent and as a dispersing agent.

TETRASODIUM EDTA • Sodium Edetate. A powdered sodium salt that reacts with metals. A sequestering and chelating agent *(see both)* used in solutions. Can deplete the body of calcium if taken internally. No known toxicity on the skin. *See* Ethylenediaminetetraacetic Acid.

TETRASODIUM ETHYLENEDIAMINE TETRAACETATE • See Tetrasodium EDTA.

TETRASODIUM PYROPHOSPHATE • TSPP. A sequestering, clarifying, and buffering agent, and a water softener. Produced by removing the water from dibasic sodium phosphate. Insoluble in alcohol. A water softener in bath preparations.

TETRASODIUM PYROPHOSPHATE SODIUM CARBONATE • Produced from sodium phosphate *(see),* and used in cleansing compounds, and in rust- and ink-stain removers. It is a strong irritant and potentially caustic. *See* Top Job®.

TEXTURIZER • A chemical used to improve the texture of various compounds. For instance, in creams that tend to become lumpy, calcium chloride *(see)* is added to keep them smooth.

THALLIUM • A bluish white, leadlike metal discovered in 1861, and originally used to treat venereal disease, ringworm, and gout. It is used now in paste jewelry pigments, low-temperature thermometers, optical lenses, and depilatories. It also is used widely in rat poison and insecticides. Thallium toxicity is cumulative in humans and has been used to commit murder. It is quickly absorbed from the gastrointestinal tract, and can be absorbed through the skin. It can cause toxic hair loss. Thallium can also affect the fetus if a pregnant woman is exposed to it. Forms toxic compounds on contact with air, and should not come in contact with skin. Among the trade names of rodenticides with thallium are: Gizmo Mouse Killer; GTA Rat Bait™; Martin's Rat Stop Liquid™; Rat & Mouse Controller Paste™; Senco Corn Mix™; and Zelio Paste™.

THERMOMETERS • See Mercury and Pentane.

THIABENDAZOLE • TBZ. Mertect. White to tan crystals. Used as a fungicide on citrus fruits, and to combat worms. See Phenylenediamine and Pesticides.

THICKENING AGENTS • Substances to add body to lotions and creams. Those usually employed include such natural gums as sodium alginate and pectins.

THIMEROSOL • Mercurochrome™. The metallo-organic compound also known as Merthiolate™. Used as a bacteriostat and fungistat. May cause allergic reaction from either the mercury or the salicylates in the compound. May be removed from the market because of its mercury content.

THIODAN™ • *See* Endosulfan.

THIODIPROPIONIC ACID • An acid freely soluble in hot water, alcohol, and acetone. An antioxidant in general food use. Used also for soap products and polymers *(see)* of ethylene.

THIOKOL • One of the first synthetic elastomers *(see),* used in the manufacture of rubbers and resins. No known toxicity.

THIOL • A group of organic compounds similar to alcohols, but with sulfur groups instead of those composed of hydrogen. Many have stinking odors and, therefore, are used in fuel gas lines as odor warnings to signal gas leaks. They are also used in sanitizers. Toxic by inhalation. *See* Mercaptan.

THIOLANEDIOL • An antibacterial. *See* Phenol.

THIOUREA • **Thiocarbamide.** A white, crystalline powder with a bitter taste, used in photography and photocopying papers, as a rubber accelerator, and a mold inhibitor. A cancer-causing agent and skin irritant.

THIRAM • **Thiuram.** A white, crystalline powder soluble in alcohol, benzine, and chloroform, but insoluble in water. Used as a rubber-compound accelerator, fungicide, an animal repellent, and wood preservative. An irritant to the skin and eyes, and can cause allergic skin reactions. Toxic by ingestion and inhalation. Thiram is closely related to Antabuse™, which is used to produce an adverse reaction when an alcoholic drinks alcohol. *See* Organophosphates.

THIURAM • See Thiram.

THYMOL • Obtained from the essential oil of lavender, origanum oil, and other volatile oils. It destroys mold, preserves anatomical specimens, and is a topical antifungal agent with a pleasant, aromatic odor. Used in mouthwashes, and to scent perfumes, after-shave lotions, and soap. It can cause allergic reactions.

TIDE® LAUNDRY DETERGENT • An anionic detergent containing sodium alkyl benzenesulfonate *(see)*.

TILE ADHESIVES • May contain rubber, resin, rosin, butadiene styrene latex, water, casein, ammonium hydroxide, sodium *o*-phenylphenate, sodium pentachlorophenate, 2,2-methylenebis(4-methyl-6-tertiary-butylphenol). May also contain asphalt *(see),* mineral fillers, and epoxy resins *(see)*.

TILE CLEANERS • One type usually contains an abrasive, sodium tripolyphosphate, an alkyl sodium sulfonate, and trisodium sulfonate. Another type may contain a solvent, morpholine, soap, a wetting agent, and silica, as well as trisodium sulfonate. See sulfonates.

TILEX® INSTANT MILDEW REMOVER • Contains sodium hypochlorite, sodium hydroxide, and no phosphates. Not recommended for use by persons with heart conditions or chronic respiratory problems such as asthma, bronchitis, emphysema, or obstructive lung disease. Should not be mixed with acids, ammonia, toilet bowl cleaners, rust removers, or other household chemicals, as dangerous fumes may result. Has an excellent label. *See* Bleaches.

TIN COMPOUNDS • A silver-white metal, tin is soluble in acids. Elemental tin has low toxicity, but most of its compounds are toxic. Rapidly increasing in industrial use as polyvinyl stabilizers, catalysts, wood preservatives, marine antifouling agents, agricultural fungicides, insecticides, and moth and other insect repellents for use on fabrics. Several preliminary investigations revealed that one tin compound, methyltin, may act, in the environment, the same as mercury, a known nerve toxin. Other tin compounds known to be potent nerve toxins in mammals and inhibitors of oxygen uptake are trimethyltin and triethyltin.

TIRE CLEANERS • May contain potassium hydroxide, metasilicates, alkyl aryl sulfonate, and water. May also contain isopropyl alcohol, glycol ethers, xylene, and monoethaolamine. Whitewall tire cleaner may contain an anionic detergent, phosphates, a solvent, and an aerosol propellant. Still another type of tire cleaner may contain trisodium phosphate, metasilicate, alkyl aryl sulfonate, butyl cellosolve, EDTA, and fluorescein. Most products are toxic upon ingestion.

TIRE PAINT • Black tire paint contains solvents, resins, and pigments. The white tire paint contains pigments such as titanium dioxide and calcium carbonate, as well as silicates. The white paint is more toxic than the black, but both should be handled with care.

TIRE REPAIR • Products contain a synthetic rubber, a solvent such as benzene or toluene, cements, ammonia, sulfur, and, possibly, trichloroethylene. The tubeless bonding compound contains toluene, which is very toxic. *See* individual ingredients for toxicity.

TITANIUM DIOXIDE • Occurs naturally in minerals. Used chiefly as an opacifier; also a white pigment for candy and gum. The greatest covering and tinting power of any white pigment, it is also used in paints, paper, rubber, plastics, cosmetics, floor covering, glassware, ceramics, and printing and marking inks. The amount of dioxide may not exceed 1 percent by weight of food. A pound has been ingested without apparent ill effects. High concentrations of the dust may cause lung damage.

TITANIUM HYDROXIDE • See Titanium Dioxide.

TLV • **Threshold Limit Value.** An exposure limit recommended by the American Conference of Governmental Industrial Hygienists for concentrations of airborne substances in workroom air.

TM • See Trademark.

TOBACCO • Since 1964, when the surgeon general issued the first report on smoking and health, research on the toxicity and cancer-causing properties of tobacco smoke has demonstrated that the health risk from inhaling it is not limited to smokers, but also includes nonsmokers, who may inhale environmental tobacco smoke (ETS). ETS contains many of the toxic agents and carcinogens that are present in mainstream smoke, but in diluted form. According to NIOSH (in its *Current Intelligence Bulletin 54: Environmental Tobacco Smoke in the Workplace; Lung Cancer and Other Health Effects,* June 28, 1991) recent epidemiologic studies support and reinforce earlier findings published in reviews by the surgeon general and the National Research Council demonstrating that exposure to ETS can cause lung cancer. In these reviews, the relative risk of lung cancer was estimated to be approximately 1.3 times higher for a nonsmoker living with a smoker, as compared to a nonsmoker living with another nonsmoker. In addition, recent evidence also suggests a possible association between exposure to ETS and an increased risk for heart disease in nonsmokers. Cancer and heart disease are long-term consequences of ETS, but immediate intolerance is usually caused by chemical or mechanical irritation of the respiratory tract. Occasionally, a certain type of cigarette causes allergic symptoms. Each type of cigarette may contain a different type of compound to provide aroma and flavor. Most of the allergic reactions to cigarette smoking involve asthmalike symptoms.

TOILET BOWL CLEANERS • Many contain an acid. SnoBol® Toilet Bowl Cleaner (liquid) contains 15 percent hydrochloric acid; Lysol Brand® Toilet Bowl Cleaner (liquid) contains 8.5 percent hydrochloric acid. Sani-Flush® Toilet Bowl Cleaner (granular) and Vanish® Toilet Bowl Cleaner (granular) both contain 75 percent sodium bisulfate *(see all).* Some also may contain oxalic acid, soda ash, silicates, versene, zinc chloride, kerosene, muriatic or oxalic acid, phenols, salt, iodine, and alkyl amyl sodium sulfate *(see all).* Avoid direct skin contact and breathing of fumes. For a less toxic alternative, use a toilet brush and baking soda or borax, or soak with white vinegar.

TOLERANCE • The ability to live with an allergen. Also the maximum amount of pesticide residue allowed by law to remain in or on a harvested crop. The EPA sets these levels so that the chemicals "do not pose an unreasonable risk to consumers."

TOLUENE • **Toluol. Methyl Benzene.** A solvent for paints (*see* Enamel Paint), nail polish, lacquers, thinners, coatings, shellacs, adhesives, metal cleaners, rust preservatives, fuel system anti-freezes, asphalt removers, flame retardants, high-octane gasoline blends, rotogravure printing processes, and glue, and is being used to replace more toxic benzene solvents in many products. Obtained from petroleum or by distilling balsam Tolu. Resembles benzene but is less volatile, flammable, or toxic. May cause mild anemia if ingested, and is narcotic in high concentrations. Being tested at the U.S. Frederick Cancer Research and Development Center (Frederick, Md.) for possible cancer-causing effects. It can cause liver damage, and is irritating to the skin, and the respiratory tract. Halogenated hydrocarbons such as toluene are assumed responsible for health risks, with long-term effects due to low-level exposure to them in the drinking water of at least twenty cities. There is concern about the role of toluene on the brain and nervous system, because symptoms have been observed in workers chronically exposed in jobs such as spray painting. The chronic high-dosage exposures seen in toluene abuse, as with glue sniffers, have been associated epidemiologically with sudden death, secondary to irregular heart-beat, and liver and neurologic disorders. The current U.S. standard is 200 ppm in eight hours, and maximum peaks up to 500 ppm for ten minutes. NIOSH (*see*) currently recommends that toluene exposures be limited to 100 ppm. Brief exposure to 100 ppm causes statistical impairment of reflexes and thinking. Exposure to 800 ppm causes severe fatigue, confusion, and staggering; effects that may persist for several days. Exposure to 10,000 ppm can cause loss of consciousness, and death.

TOLUENE-2,5-DIAMINE • *See* Toluene.

TOLUENE-3,4-DIAMINOTOLUENE • An intermediate chemical in the manufacture of polyurethanes, dyes for textiles, fur and leather, varnishes, pigments, and hair dyes. In a National Cancer Institute study, it caused liver cancer when fed to rats and mice, as well as breast cancer in female rats. *See* Toluene and Phenylenediamine.

TOLUENE DIISOCYANATE • *See* TDI.

o-**TOLUIDINE** • *See* Ortho-Toluidine.

TOLUOL. • *See* Toluene.

o-**TOLYL BIGUANIDE** • *See* Toluene.

TOP JOB® • Contains tetrapotassium pyrophosphate and sodium carbonate *(see both).*

TORPEDO® • A pesticide containing permethrin. *See* Pesticides.

TOXIC • Harmful to living organisms.

TOXICITY • The inherent capability of a substance to cause adverse effects on human, animal, or plant life.

TRADEMARK • ™. A word, symbol, or insignia registered with the government trademark agency, and designating one or more proprietary products, or the manufacture of such products. The trade name, on the other hand, is the name of the company under which a company does business. The trademark ownership, when approved by the U.S. Office of Patents and Trademarks, is designated by an "R" with a circle around it.

TRADE NAME • *See* Trademark.

TRANSMISSION FLUID • Usually contains mineral oils, detergents, zinc dialkyl dithiophosphate, phosphorus, barium, hydrocarbon wax, antifoam agents such as polysiloxanes, antiwear agents such as organic borates, and a sealant such as triarylphosphate. See lubricating oils.

TREFLAN™ • *See* Trifluralin.

TRIAMYLAMINE • A colorless liquid derived from ammonia, and used as a corrosion inhibitor, and in insecticides. An irritant.

TRIBROMSALAN • **TBS. 3,4',5-Tribromosalicylanilide.** Used in medicated cosmetics; an antiseptic and fungicide. Irritating to the skin and may cause allergic reaction when skin is exposed to the sun. Salicylanilide is an antifungal compound used to treat ringworm. TBS is in the most popular soaps to kill skin bacteria. Used as a germicide frequently replacing hexachlorophene *(see).*

TRIBUTYL CITRATE • The triester of butyl alcohol and citric acid *(see both),* it is a pale yellow, odorless liquid used as a plasticizer, antifoam agent, and solvent for nitrocellulose. Low toxicity.

TRIBUTYL PHOSPHATE • A colorless liquid prepared from butyl alcohol and used as a plasticizer for cellulose, lacquers, plastics, and vinyl resins. Irritating to mucous membranes.

TRIBUTYLCRESYLBUTANE • Used as a stabilizer. *See* Phenol.

TRICAMBA • A herbicide. *See* Dicamba.

TRICHLORFON • **Dylox.** A sub-surface organophosphate *(see)* insecticide. It is absorbed by the skin and is highly toxic.

TRICHLOROBENZENE • White or colorless crystals made from benzene *(see).* Used as a solvent and in insecticides. Hazardous by ingestion and inhalation.

TRICHLOROETHANE • **TCA.** **Methyl** **Chloroform.** **MC.**
Aerothene®. Chlorothene®. Inhibisol®. A widely used industrial
solvent; a hydrocarbon. It is employed as a degreaser and cleaner for
metals, plastics, silicon chips, and other electronic parts; as a dry
cleaner and spot remover; as a propellant in aerosol cans; as a
quick-drying agent for typewriter correction fluid; in cosmetics as a
solvent and degreasing agent. Nonflammable liquid. Insoluble in
and absorbs some water. Less toxic than carbon tetrachloride, which
is used in fire extinguishers. Trichloroethane solutions are irritating
to the eyes and mucous membranes, and in high concentrations can
be narcotic. Can be absorbed through the skin. As with other
organic solvents, TCA can dissolve your skin's natural protective
oils. Frequent or lengthy skin contact with TCA can cause dryness,
redness, flaking, cracking, and skin rash. Inhalation and ingestion
produce serious symptoms ranging from vomiting to death.

TRICHLOROETHYLENE • **TCE.** The residue in decaffeinated coffee powder. Used in metal degreasing, as a solvent for fats, waxes,
dyeing, dry cleaning, refrigerant and heat exchange liquid, fumigants, paint thinners, and as a solvent in adhesives and for spice
oleoresins. Moderate exposure can cause symptoms similar to
alcoholic inebriation, and its analgesic and anesthetic properties
make it useful for short operations. High concentrations have a
narcotic effect. Deaths have been attributed to irregular heart
rhythm. Tests conducted by the National Cancer Institute (NCI)
showed that this chlorinated hydrocarbon caused cancer of the liver
in mice. Rats failed to show significant response, a fact that may be
attributed to the cancer resistance of the strain of mice used. Despite
difference of the species in cancer response, the NCI concluded that
the TCE test clearly showed the compound caused liver cancer in
mice. The findings are considered definitive for animal studies and
serve as a warning of possible carcinogenicity in humans. However,
the extent of the possible human risk cannot be predicted reliably on
the basis of these studies alone. A related compound, vinyl chloride
(see), does cause liver cancer in humans. It is irritating to the skin.
A combination of alcohol ingestion with exposure to trichloroethylene can cause flushing of the skin, nausea, and vomiting. Among
the products using this compound at this writing are Du Pont® Dry
Cleaner, Glamorene® Rug Cleaner, TriClene® Dry Cleaner, Tread
Metal® Cleaner, and Triad® Metal Polish.

TRICHLOROISOCYANURIC ACID • An organic oxidant that releases chlorine gas. It is a white, slightly water-absorbing powder,

the active ingredient in household dry bleaches, dishwashing compounds, scouring powders, detergent sanitizers, commercial laundry bleaches, swimming pool disinfectant, bactericide, algicide, and deodorant. Explosive when heated; toxic by ingestion. In strong solutions, it causes the eyes to tear. In the presence of water, it is irritating to the skin, and upper respiratory tract.

TRICHLOROMETHANE • *See* Chloroform.

TRICHLOROMONOFLUOROMETHANE • A liquid with a faint, sweet odor. Used in refrigerants, fire extinguishers, and deodorant sprays. Less toxic than carbon dioxide but decomposes into harmful chemicals when exposed to heat or flame. May be narcotic in high concentrations.

TRICLOCARBAN • Prepared from aniline and chlorophenyl isocyanate, it is used as an antiseptic in soaps and other cleaning products. *See* Aniline and Phenol.

TRICLOPYR • A preemergent weed killer.

TRICLOSAN • A broad-spectrum antibacterial agent that is active primarily against some types of bacteria. It is used in deodorant soaps, vaginal deodorant sprays and other cosmetic products, as well as in drugs and household products. Its deodorant properties are due to the inhibition of bacterial growth. Can cause allergy contact dermatitis, particularly when used in products for the feet.

TRICRESYL PHOSPHATE • **TCP.** Colorless or pale yellow liquid; a plasticizer for nail polish, polyvinyl chloride, polystyrene, and nitrocellulose, it is also used as a fire retardant, a waterproofing agent, and in hydraulic fluids. Can cause paralysis many days after exposure. In 1960, approximately 10,000 Moroccans became ill after ingesting cooking oil adulterated with turbojet engine oil containing 3 percent TCP. Can be absorbed through the skin and mucous membranes, causing poisoning. Persons sensitive to the plasticizer in eyeglass frames may develop a skin rash from tricresyl. Toxic dose in humans is only 6 milligrams per kilogram of body weight.

TRIDECYL ALCOHOL • Derived from tridecane, a paraffin hydrocarbon obtained from petroleum. Used as an emulsifier in cosmetic creams, a lubricant, in detergents, and as an antifoam agent.

TRIETAZINE • **2-chloro-4-diethylamino-6-ethylamino-s-triazine.** Solid, practically insoluble in water, it is used as a herbicide and plant-growth regulator.

TRIETHANOLAMINES • A coating agent for fresh fruit and

vegetables and widely used in surfactants *(see)*, antifoam agents, corrosion inhibitors, and household detergents. It is also used as a dispersing agent and is found in shaving creams, soaps and shampoo, cements, and cutting oils. It is also used in waxes, polishes, and as a solvent for shellac, dyes, and to increase the penetration of liquids into wood, cloth, and paper. Its principal toxic effect in animals has been attributed to overalkalinity. Gross pathology has been found in the gastrointestinal tract in fatally poisoned guinea pigs. It can cause ear, nose, and throat irritations, and skin rashes in humans.

TRIETHYL BORATE • A colorless liquid derived from borate *(see)*, and used in disinfectants, and as an antiknock agent. Highly flammable.

TRIETHYL CITRATE • A colorless liquid with a bitter taste, derived from citric acid, and used as a solvent and plasticizer, and in paint removers. *See* Citric Acid.

TRIETHYLENE GLYCOL • Prepared from ethylene oxide and ethylene glycol *(see both)*, it is used as a solvent and plasticizer in vinyl, polyester, and polyurethane resins, to maintain water in printers' inks, and in solid perfumes. *See* Polyethylene Glycol for toxicity.

TRIFLURALIN • **Treflan**™. A preemergent herbicide used on fruits and vegetables. *See* Aniline and Herbicides.

TRIMEC 899® • A broadleaf-weed control. *See* 2,4-D, MCPP, and Dicamba.

2,2,4-TRIMETHYL-1,3-PENTANEDIOL • A white solid derived from pentane *(see)*, and used in the manufacture of plasticizers, surfactants, pesticides, and resins.

TRIMETHYL PHOSPHITE • Derived from phosphorus, it is used for controlling spark plug fouling, surface ignition, and rumble in gasoline engines. Toxic by ingestion and inhalation, and strongly irritating to the skin.

TRIMETHYLACETANILIDE • *See* Acetanilide.

TRIPALMITIN • A white, crystalline powder derived from glycerol and palmitic acid. Used for soap, and leather dressing. Nontoxic.

TRIPHENYL PHOSPHATE • A noncombustible substitute for camphor in celluloid. Colorless; insoluble in water. Used as a fire-retarding agent, and as a plasticizer in nail polish and nitrocellulose. Causes paralysis if ingested and skin rash in hypersensitive people. Inhalation of only 3.5 milligrams per kilogram of bodyweight is toxic to humans.

TRIPOLYPHOSPHATE • *See* Sodium Tripolyphosphate.

TRIS (HYDROXYMETHYL) AMINOMETHANE • **THAM. Tro-methamine.** A white crystalline solid, it is used as an emulsifying agent in oils, fats, creams, and waxes, and as a buffer. It is irritating to the skin and eyes.

TRIS (HYDROXYMETHYL) NITROMETHANE • Crystals from ethyl acetate and benzene *(see both)*. Soluble in alcohol. Inhibits bacterial growth in water systems, cutting oils, nonprotein glues, and sizings. Irritating to the skin and mucous membranes. May release formaldehyde *(see)*.

TRISODIUM EDTA • *See* Tetrasodium EDTA.

TRISODIUM HEDTA • Mineral-suspending agent. *See* Sequestering Agent.

TRISTEARIN • Present in many animal and vegetable fats, especially hard ones like tallow and cocoa butter, it is used in surfactants, quaternary ammonium compounds, and emollients. No known toxicity.

TRUE FIXATIVE • Holds back the evaporation of the other materials. Benzoin is an example. *See* Fixatives.

TUNG OIL • **China Wood Oil.** A yellow, drying oil derived from the seeds of the *Aleurites cordata,* a tree grown in China. It is used in exterior paints and varnishes. No known toxicity.

TUPERSAN • *See* Siduron.

TURFLON 11 AMINE • **2,4-D. MCPP. Dicamba.** Broadleaf-weed control. *See* 2,4-D and Triclopyr.

TURKEY-RED OIL • One of the first surface-active agents *(see)*. Contains sulfated castor oil. Used in shampoos. It also is used to obtain bright, clear colors in dyeing fabrics. *See* Sulfonated Oils.

TURPENTINE • **Gum and Steam Distilled.** Any of the various resins obtained from pine trees. A yellowish, viscous exudate with a characteristic smell, it is a natural solvent composed of pine oils, camphenes, and terpenes. It is used as a solvent for paints, varnishes, and lacquers, as a rubber solvent, in insecticides, and in wax-based polishes. The volatile components of turpentine, pinene, and carene may be hazardous to the lungs. Turpentine is readily absorbed through the skin, and is irritating to the skin and mucous membranes. In addition, it can cause allergic reactions, and is a central nervous system depressant. Death is usually due to respiratory failure. As little as 15 milliliters has killed children.

TURPENTINE GUM • *See* Turpentine.

TWA • **Time Weight Average.** The average concentration of a chemical in air over the total exposure time—usually an eight-hour workday.

TYPEWRITER CLEANER • *See* Trichloroethane.

TYPEWRITER CORRECTION PAPER • Contains a formaldehyde and phenol *(see both)* resin that is used as a binder for the powder coating the paper. *See also* Paper.

TYPING PAPER • Skin reactions due to typing paper are usually attributed to the "sizing" in the paper, a gum resin containing rosin *(see)*. Sensitivity can also be to abietic acid *(see)*, juniper tar, and styrax. *See also* Paper.

U

UNDECANE • Colorless liquid used in petroleum distillation. Combustible.

UNDECYLENIC ACID • Occurs in sweat. Obtained from ricinoleic acid *(see)*. A liquid or crystalline powder, with an odor suggestive of perspiration or citrus. Used as a fungicide, in perfumes, as a flavoring, and as a lubricant additive in cosmetics. Has been given orally, but causes dizziness, headaches, and stomach upset. No known toxicity for the skin.

UNREASONABLE RISK • Under FIFRA *(see)*, "unreasonable adverse effects on the environment" means any unreasonable risk to humans or the environment, taking into account the economic, social, and environmental costs and benefits of the use of any pesticide.

UNSLAKED LIME • *See* Calcium Oxide.

UPHOLSTERY CLEANERS • There are many varieties, but most contain perchloroethylene or trichloroethylene *(see both)*, a petroleum solvent, and a propellant. They may also contain ammonia, borax, ethylene dichloride, lanolin, dichlorobenzene, pine oil, sodium bicarbonate, and salt *(see all)*. Most products contain some toxic chemicals. The warning on the aerosols is not to use near heat, not to purchase or incinerate the container, to avoid eye and skin contact, and to keep out of reach of children.

UREA • **Carbamide.** A product of protein metabolism, excreted from human urine. It was the first organic compound to be synthesized. It is derived from ammonia and liquid carbon dioxide, and consists of colorless or white, odorless crystals that have a cool salty taste. Used in animal feed, plastics, adhesives, flame proofing, and paper coatings. Also used in yeast food and wine production up to 2 pounds per gallon, and to brown baked goods such as pretzels. An antiseptic and deodorizer used in liquid antiperspirants, ammoniated dentifrices, roll-on deodorants, mouthwashes, hair colorings, hand creams, lotions, and shampoos. Medicinally, urea is used as a topical antiseptic, and as a diuretic. Its largest use, however, is as a fertilizer; only a small part of its production goes into the manufacture of other urea products. No known toxicity.

UREA-FORMALDEHYDE RESIN • UFFI. A large class of resins, the mixture of urea and formaldehyde *(see both)*, were the first colored plastics made. They are used in dinnerware, interior plywood, flexible foams, and insulation. Urea-formaldehyde foam insulations may release formaldehyde during decomposition, and have been found to release free formaldehyde into the indoor air. The level of formaldehyde released by the foam reportedly decreases over one to three years. The adverse health effects of UFFI are hotly debated. People exposed to UFFI in buildings report shortness of breath, headache, stuffy nose, irritated eyes, cough, frequent colds, rash, fatigue, sore throat, and vomiting. *See* Formaldehyde.

UREASE • An enzyme that hydrolyzes urea *(see)* to ammonium carbonate *(see)*. *See also* Hydrolyzed.

URETHANE • Ethyl Carbamate. Colorless crystals or white powder derived by heating alcohol and urea nitrate. Used in pesticides and fungicides. Toxic by ingestion. It induces cancer in experimental animals, and was the first carcinogen demonstrated to pass through the placenta and affect the fetus. *See* Polyurethane.

V

VA • The abbreviation for vinyl acetate.

VALDET™ • Detergents derived from phenol that are used as wetting agents, emulsifiers, antistatic agents, and for dyeing, bleaching, scouring, and washing after printing.

VALERIC ACID • Colorless, with an unpleasant odor, it occurs naturally in apples, cocoa, coffee, oil of lavender, peaches, and strawberries. Usually distilled from valerian root. Used in flavorings, perfumes, lubricants, plasticizers, and vinyl plastics. No known toxicity.

VANICIDE 89™ • *See* Captan and Ferban.

VANISH® TOILET BOWL CLEANER • Contains the acid, sodium acid sulfate *(see)*. *See also* Toilet Bowl Cleaners.

VAPONA™ • The trade name for an insecticide that contains more than 93 percent dichlorvos. *See* Dichlorvos.

VAPOR • Molecules that are in a liquid or solid state at normal temperature and pressure but which disperse into the air when these factors change. Vapors of organic liquids are often referred to as fumes.

VAPOR PRESSURE • A measure of the tendency of a liquid to evaporate and become a gas. The pressure exerted by a saturated vapor above its own liquid in a closed container at given conditions of temperature and pressure. The higher the vapor pressure, the greater the tendency of the substance to evaporate.

VARNISH • A protective coating, similar to paint, except that it does not contain coloring. It may consist of a vegetable oil and a solvent, or a natural resin and a solvent.

VARNISH REMOVERS • *See* Paint Removers.

VAT DYES • Water-soluble, aromatic, organic compounds. They dissolve in water when vatted with an alkaline solution of the reducing *(see)* agent sodium hydrosulfite. Good fastness. Considered low in toxicity.

VDTs • *See* Video Display Terminals.

VEGETABLE GUMS • Include derivatives from quince seed, karaya, acacia, tragacanth, Irish moss, guar, and sodium, potassium, ammonium and propylene glycol alginates. All are subject to deterioration and always need a preservative. The gums function as liquid emulsions, that is, they thicken cosmetic products and make them creams. No known toxicity other than allergic reactions in hypersensitive persons.

VEGETABLE OILS • Peanut, sesame, olive, and cottonseed oils, obtained from plants and used in foods, cosmetics, and industrial compounds. No known toxicity.

VENTILATION RATE • The rate at which outside air enters and leaves a building. Expressed in one of two ways: the number of changes of outside air per unit of time—air changes per hour (ACH)—or the rate at which a volume of outside air enters per unit of time—cubic feet per minute (CFM).

VEREL™ • The registered trademark for a modacrylic staple fiber produced by Eastman Chemical Products, Inc. It is used extensively in knitted pile fabrics for sports and dress apparel to give a "furlike" appearance. Among its properties are softness, abrasion resistance, and ease of cleaning.

VERMICULITE • An ore with soft, resilient crystals; it can absorb large amount of liquids and remain free flowing. Used as a filler and packing material. Nontoxic.

VERSENE • A chelating agent derived from ethylenediaminetetra-acetic acid *(see).* Used in air sanitizers.

VESICOL™ • *See* Chlordane.

VIDEO DISPLAY TERMINALS • **VDTs.** In the early 1980s, anecdotal reports from pregnant women at offices in the United States, Canada, and England described clusters of miscarriages and birth defects among pregnant women who worked at VDTs. In the late 1980s, two Swedish studies reported radiation emissions from video display terminals affected developing mouse and chicken fetuses. Their findings added to a series to implicate VDT electromagnetic radiation as a risk to pregnant women. In a study reported in the August 1990 issue of the *American Industrial Hygiene Association Journal,* however, researchers who measured the electrostatic and very low-frequency fields at fifty-four work stations during normal work hours found no evidence of exposure to electric, magnetic, or ionizing radiation fields. The standard position surveyed was approximately twelve inches from the screen. Because no X rays were found from normally operating VDTs, failure conditions were studied under high-voltage circuits and deliberate failure of critical components. The exposure rate closest to the screen even under these circumstances, the industrial hygienists reported, was below the prescribed leakage limit. The study did find some physical discomforts associated with the use of VDTs, such as eyestrain, blurred vision, and aches in the neck and shoulders.

VINCLOZOLIN • **Ronilan™.** A crystalline solid used as a fungicide on fruits and vegetables. *See* Fungicides.

VINYL • Made from acetylene with various other substances to form plastics.

VINYL ACETATE • A starch modifier not to exceed 2.5 percent in modified starch *(see).* Vapors in high concentration may be narcotic; animal experiments show low toxicity.

VINYL CHLORIDE • Banned in aerosol cans for hair sprays and deodorants, in 1974. It is a proven carcinogen for liver cancer in those who work with the compound.

VINYL POLYMERS • Include resins used in false nails, and nail lacquer preparations. A major class of polymer *(see)* material widely used in plastics, synthetic fibers, and surface coatings. Such materials are derived from the polymerization of vinyl groups, which include vinyl acetate and vinyl chloride. Vinyls are made from the reaction between acetylene and certain compounds such as alcohol, phenol, and amines. Inhalation of 300 ppm is toxic in humans.

VINYL PYRROLIDONE • *See* Polyvinylpyrrolidone.
VINYL RESINS • *See* Clothing.
VINYLBENZENE • *See* Styrene.
VINYLBENZOL • *See* Styrene.
VINYLDIMETHICONE • *See* Siloxane and Vinyl Polymers.
VOCs • *See* Volatile Organic Compounds.
VOLATILE • Having a tendency to evaporate readily to form a vapor.
VOLATILE ORGANIC COMPOUNDS • **VOCs.** As the consuming public has demanded greater and greater conveniences, the use of VOCs in products has increased. VOCs are used for dry cleaning, and to make clothes wrinkle free, brighter, and softer; to clean and polish floors and furniture; to dry paints more quickly; to develop adhesives; to purify drinking water; to eliminate pests; to correct typing errors; to make carbonless copy paper, synthetic carpets, wallpapers, and pressed-wood products; to remove greasy films; to scent the air; and for many other uses. VOCs can be major contributors to occupant complaints within a building: VOC-related symptoms include eye and nose irritation, and unpleasant odors, and since VOCs can cross the blood-brain barrier, more severe, chronic health effects do occur. VOCs can depress the central nervous system, which can lead to lethargy, dizziness, headaches, nausea, confusion, unconsciousness, and other symptoms. It is very difficult to identify the primary source of VOC contaminants. Among common sources of VOCs are aliphatic hydrocarbons, halogenated hydrocarbons, aromatics, alcohols, ketones, esters, and aldehydes. Sources can emit at varying rates depending on source age, surrounding temperature and humidity, surrounding ventilation, and use. The products containing VOCs include germicides, permanent-press clothes, textiles, paper products, ink, aerosols, refrigerants, paints, varnishes, window cleaners, lacquers, cooking and heating fuels, lubricants, and cleaning compounds.
VOLATILITY • A measure of how quickly a substance forms vapors at ordinary temperatures. The more volatile the substance is, the faster it evaporates, and the higher the concentration of fumes (gas) in the air.

W

WALLPAPER CLEANERS • Carbon tetrachloride *(see)* is in many such products along with borax, kerosene, ethylene dichloride, ethyl ether, naphtha and trisodium phosphate, all of which may be toxic *(see all)*. Other ingredients may be clay, soda ash, wheat flour, ammonium alum, a dye, glycerin, a detergent, sawdust, soda ash, and coconut oil soap.

WALLPAPER PASTES • May contain dextrin, animal glue, sodium bicarbonate, aluminum sulfate, bentonite, and also methyl alcohol, or vinyl acetate *(see all)*. Also may contain fungicides and mildew killers, which can outgas into the room air and cause problems in the sensitive.

WALLPAPER REMOVERS • Products may contain ethylene glycol, soda ash, alkyl sodium sulfate, hydroxyacetic acid, an acid, and a penetrant such as kerosene.

WATER GLASS • *See* Sodium Silicate.

WATER REPELLENTS • Paraffin wax, and aluminum or zirconium salt emulsions are used as water repellents on fabrics. Fluorocarbon combined with stearomidomethyl pyridium chloride, melamine, stearamide, and organo-silicon compounds are also used. Melamine and urea formaldehyde resins in combination with any of the aforementioned substances can assist with water repellency.

WATER SOFTENERS • Used to increase water's sudsing ability. This saves on soap costs and makes cleaning easier. Hard water contains dissolved minerals. The most popular residential method of softening water involves the zeolite process *(see)*. Water softeners of this type utilize salt to cause an exchange between the calcium and magnesium ions in the water and sodium ions from the salt. With this method, hardness can be reduced substantially, and the water takes on a slippery feel. You can soften water in your washing machine by adding one-quarter cup vinegar to the final rinse. *See also* Complex Sodium Phosphates and Sodium Carbonate.

WATER-SOLUBLE OIL • Ammonia, potash, or sodium soaps of oleic, rosin, or naphthenic acids dissolved in mineral oil. Used as cutting oils, lubricants, and for textiles and polishes.

WATER SPOT PREVENTION AGENT; DISHWASHER AND CHINA PROTECTION AGENT • *See* Sodium Silicate.

WATERCOLOR PAINTS • Contain pigment, hydroxy ethyl cellulose, gums, wetting agents, and water. May also contain barium and calcium salts, phenol, preservative, polyethylene glycol, and a plasticizer. *See* individual ingredients.

WATERPROOF ADHESIVES • Rubber cement usually contains rubber and hexane as a solvent. The casein type, which is almost nontoxic, contains urea, zinc oxide, ammonium hydroxide, and sodium *o*-phenylphenate. The epoxy resin—the polyamide resin type has to be mixed just before use. The formaldehyde-resorcinol type is still another kind of waterproof cement. *See all.*

WATERPROOFING • Compounds include alum, benzene, benzine, carbon tetrachloride, chromates, formaldehyde, melamine, pitch, resins, solvents, and tar. *See* Waterproof Adhesives and Paraformaldehyde.

WAXES • Obtained from insects, animals, and plants. Waxes have a wide application in the manufacture of cosmetics. Beeswax, for instance, is a substance secreted by the bee's special glands on the underside of its abdomen. The wax is glossy and hard, but plastic when warm; insoluble in water, but partially soluble in boiling alcohol. Used in hair-grooming preparations, hair straighteners, as an epilatory (hair pull) to remove unwanted hair, and as the traditional stiffening agent *(see)* in lipsticks. Wax esters such as lanolin or spermaceti *(see both)* differ from fats in being less greasy, harder, and more brittle. Waxes made in the United States are vegetable, petroleum, or insect based. One of the most common vegetable waxes, carnauba *(see),* is made from a palm leaf. Waxes from petroleum are the same as those used as chewing gum bases. The shellac used on some products is made from the secretion *(lacca)* of the lac bug, native to Pakistan and India. More than twenty varieties of fruits and vegetables, including cantaloupes, eggplants, oranges, peaches, persimmons, squash, cucumbers, sweet potatoes, and tomatoes, are being waxed. Waxing reduces the loss of moisture, keeping produce from dehydration. Some waxes are cosmetic. General-purpose waxes contain either natural or synthetic waxes and/or resins plus fatty acid emulsifiers, morpholine, and petroleum solvents. They may also contain *o*-benzyl-*p*-chlorophenol. *See also* Floor Wax and Car Wax.

WAX REMOVER • You can stop wax buildup on your floors by using one cup of ammonia in one gallon of water. *See* Grease Remover.

WAXED PAPER • *See* Ozokerite.

WEED KILLER • **ORTHO WEED-B-GON® JET WEEDER FORMULA II.** Kills dandelion, plantain, chickweed, wild onion, broadleaf weeds, roots and all. Active ingredients include diethanolamine *(see)* salts of acetic or propionic acid *(see both).* Carries the usual cautions, including a warning not to apply weed killer to water. *See* Herbicides.

WELDING • Compounds used include arsenic, benzene, cadmium, chromates, fluoride, lead, manganese, mercury, nitrous fumes, ozone, phosphorus, selenium, and zinc.

WETTING AGENT • Any of numerous water-soluble agents that promote spreading of a liquid on a surface, or penetration into a material such as skin. It lowers surface tension for better contact and absorption. *See* Surfactants.

WHEAT FLOUR • Milled from the kernels of wheat, *Triciticum aestivum*. *See* Wallpaper Paste.

WHITE • Inorganic pigments are widely used to "color" cosmetics, white paper, inks, and many other products. The most widely used are zinc oxide and titanium dioxide. Also used are gloss white (aluminum hydrate), barium sulfate (blanc fixe), and alumina. *See* all.

WICK-TYPE DEODORANTS • Usually contain a perfume, essential oil, coloring, and formaldehyde *(see)*. *See also* Deodorants.

WINDEX™ WINDOW CLEANER • Isopropyl alcohol *(see)*.

WINDOW CLEANERS • *See* Glass Window Cleaners.

WINDSHIELD WASHER FLUID • The concentrated type usually contains methyl alcohol, a detergent, water, and a dye. The ready-to-use variety contains isopropyl alcohol and/or methanol, a dye, a detergent, and often a glycol such as ethylene glycol or propylene glycol. *See* all.

WISK™ NONPHOSPHATE LAUNDRY DETERGENT • An anionic surfactant *(see)*.

WITCH HAZEL • A skin freshener, local anesthetic, and astringent made from the leaves and/or twigs of *Hamamelis virginiana*. Collected in the autumn. Witch hazel has an ethanol content of 70 to 80 percent, and a tannin content of 2 to 9 percent. Witch hazel water, which is what you buy at the store, contains 15 percent ethanol. See Ethanol for toxicity.

WOOD • A mixture of cellulose, lignin with various amounts of resins, sugars, water, and potassium compounds. Used for fuel, paper, construction, furniture, turpentine, rosin, tall oil, pine oil, methanol, synthetic fibers, cellophane, medicines, and numerous other things.

WOOD ALCOHOL • *See* Methanol.

WOOD ASH • Ashes of burned wood used as fertilizer for its potash *(see)* content.

WOOD CLEANERS • Wash painted cabinets with one-half cup

ammonia in one gallon of water. Wash natural finishes with one-fourth cup pine oil cleaner in one gallon of water. To remove scratches and stains on wood gently rub with soapy steel wool; rub toothpaste in the same direction as the grain to remove water rings.

WOOD CREOSOTE • *See* Creosote and Wood Preservatives.

WOOD DUST • Chronic exposure to the dust from woodworking, sanding, and scraping is implicated in the formation of cancers of the nose and nasal passages. It is also an allergen. See Furniture Workers.

WOOD PRESERVATIVES • **Osmose K-33C®. Osmose Special K-33® (CCA).** It is estimated that nearly one billion board feet of timber is treated each year with preservatives. Preserved-wood products are used widely in the construction, railroad, and utilities industries. Those products that contain arsenic or chromates can cause effects similar to those caused by exposure to pure inorganic arsenic or chromate compounds *(see both),* which can irritate the eyes, nose, throat, lungs, and skin, and can cause lung cancer. Arsenic also can damage the nervous system, and cause skin cancer. the two most common arsenic-containing wood preservatives are chromated copper arsenate (CCA) and ammonium copper arsenate (ACA). Inorganic arsenic and chromates are used in wood preservatives to prevent rotting when wood is exposed to damp soil, standing water, or rain. Arsenic and chromate are also present in some paints used to cover the cut ends of treated wood. After wood is pressure-treated with wood preservative, residues of the preservative can collect on the surface. Although initial residues may wash off, new layers of treated wood are continuously exposed as the wood weathers. Thus, when treated wood is used, it may carry surface residues of arsenic and chromates, which may be harmful.

To prevent skin contamination when handling and sawing wood, it is a good work practice to wear gloves made of a material, such as rubber, which is resistant to inorganic arsenicals and chromates. After using treated wood products, wash thoroughly before eating, drinking, or smoking. If oily wood preservatives or sawdust accumulate on clothes, launder before reuse. Wash work clothes separately from other clothing. Arsenic-treated wood must be disposed of at a municipal refuse landfill. Water repellents may be an adequate substitute for wood preservatives in above-ground applications where there is less risk of rot. Polyurethane or epoxy sealers soak into the wood and slow down the process that allows the wood preservative to free itself from wood and accumulate on the surface. Copper-8-quinolinate and copper naphthenate are less-toxic wood preservatives than the arsenic-containing products, although their toxicity has not been well studied. Try to choose water-based wood preservatives, because they are known to be less toxic. Never burn treated wood in the fireplace; the fumes will be toxic. Wood preservatives that contain creosote, inorganic arsenic compounds, or pentachlorophenol need to be disposed of by a licensed hazardous waste handler or through a professional household hazardous waste collection. Check with your local government for referral. *See* Arsenic and Chromates.

WOOD PUTTIES • *See* Putty.

WOOD SPIRIT • *See* Methanol.

WOOD STAINS • May contain gilsonite or asphalt, aniline dyes, vegetable oil varnish, alkyd resin, mineral spirits, and some wood preservatives, usually pentachlorophenol. The mineral spirits *(see)* are the most toxic.

WOOD, TREATED • *See* Wood Preservatives.

WOODWORKING • Compounds used include acetone, arsenic, chlorophenols, chromates, copper compounds, creosote, cresols, dinitrophenols, mercury, pitch, resins, tar, zinc, benzine, bleaches, methanol, methylene chloride, solvents, and turpentine *(See all)*.

WOOL • Sewing, knitting, or making use of wool, mohair, or synthetic fibers may cause contact dermatitis or respiratory allergies. Blankets, clothing, and contact with other people's clothing while being held may cause a flare-up of wool allergy.

WOOL FAT • Crude lanolin *(see)*. *See also* Wool Wax Alcohols.

WOOL WAX ALCOHOLS • **Wool Fat.** Chemically more like a fat than a wax, it is the deposit sheep make on their wool. Used as emollients. *See* Lanolin Alcohols.

WOOLITE™ RUG CLEANER • Sodium lauryl sulfate *(see)*.

WRINKLE-PROOF FINISHES • The resins used to prevent clothes from creasing may cause allergic contact dermatitis. Among them are urea-formaldehyde, ester gums, acrylates, polystyrene, vinyl resins, glycol resins, ketone resins, alkyd melamine formaldehyde, coumarins and indene polymers, phthalic and maleic anhydride, and rosin. *See* Durable Press and Clothing.

WRITING INKS • Contain synthetic dyes, water and any of the following: alcohol, gallic acid, glycols, carbon black, iron salts, mineral acids, and oxalic, tartaric or citric acid. May also contain sodium hydroxide, surfactants, tannic acid, thymol, or phenol. Washable inks contain glycerol. Fountain pen inks are more watery than ballpoint pen inks, which are pastelike. *See* all.

X

XENOBIOTICS • Substances that are pharmacologically, endocrinologically, or toxicologically active, but foreign to an organism such as humans. In order for many xenobiotics to exert a toxic effect, they must undergo metabolic activation by another chemical. There is much research yet to be done to understand how this process takes place and produces disease conditions.

XYLENE • **Xylol. Dimethylbenzene. Mixed Xylenes.** Xylene is an aromatic hydrocarbon as is chlorine. A clear, light-colored or colorless, flammable liquid that evaporates quickly, its odor is strong and sweetish like that of other aromatic solvents. It is used in solvents for gums, resins, and rubber cleaners, degreasers, paints, lacquers, varnishes, adhesives, cements, epoxy resins, inks and dyes, and aviation gasolines. It also is used in the manufacture of other chemicals, including plastics and synthetic fibers, insecticides, pesticides, insect repellents, and leather goods. Xylene enters the body rapidly when you breathe in its vapors. It can also be absorbed through the skin. Overexposure most commonly depresses the central nervous system, producing headaches, nausea, dizziness, drowsiness, and irritation of the eyes, nose, throat, and skin. It can also damage the kidneys. Xylene inhaled by a pregnant woman can reach her developing fetus, and contaminate her breast milk. California's Hazard Evaluation System and Information Service (HESIS) recommends that pregnant and nursing women minimize their exposure to xylene. Xylene easily penetrates most ordinary clothing, and can become trapped in ordinary gloves and boots. Xylene trapped in clothing can cause burns and blistering. Exposure to xylene at levels of 200 ppm or greater can irritate the lungs, causing chest pain and shortness of breath. Extreme overexposure, for example, in a confined space, can result in pulmonary edema, a potentially life-threatening condition in which the lungs fill with fluid. Xylene warrants further investigation as a cancer-causing agent. There has been no definite association, but it is toxic by inhalation or ingestion. *See* Enamel Paint.

2-4-XYLENOL • **2-4-Dimethylphenol.** A white, crystalline solid derived from coal tar, and toxic by ingestion and skin absorption. Used as a disinfectant and as a solvent in pharmaceuticals, as a solvent in insecticides and rubber manufacture, and as a wetting agent for dyestuffs. It caused cancer when painted on the skins of mice.

Y

YEAST • A fungi that is a dietary source of folic acid. It produces enzymes that convert sugar to alcohol and carbon dioxide. No known toxicity.

Z

ZANZIBAR GUM • A gum found on the island of Zanzibar and used in varnishes. *See* Gums.

ZECTRAN • *See* Organophosphates.

ZEIN • The protein of corn. Contains seventeen amino acids. A by-product of corn processing, it is used to coat food, and in label varnishes and microencapsulation fibers. Also used in face masks, nail polishes, as a plasticizer, and to make textile fibers plastics, printers' inks, varnishes, and other coatings and adhesives. No known toxicity.

ZEOLITE PROCESS • Water softeners of this type utilize salt to cause an exchange between the calcium and magnesium ions in the water and sodium ions from the salt. With this method, hardness can be reduced substantially, and the water takes on a slippery feel.

ZINC • A white, brittle metal, insoluble in water and soluble in acids or hot solutions of alkalies. Used in brass and bronze, electroplating, metal spraying, auto parts, electrical fuses, dry cell batteries, fungicides, roofing, gutters, engravers' plates, cable wrappings, thread lubricants, and widely used as an astringent for mouthwashes, a reducing agent *(see)*, and a reagent *(see)*. Ingestion of the salts can cause nausea and vomiting. Can cause contact dermatitis. Poisoning can cause metal fume disease, a flulike illness, stomach and intestinal disorders, and liver dysfunctions.

ZINC ACETATE • The zinc salt of acetic acid *(see)*, used in medicine as a dietary supplement, as a cross-linking agent for polymers *(see)*, and to preserve wood. See Zinc Salts for toxicity.

ZINC BORATE • The inorganic salt of zinc oxide and boric oxide, it is used as a fungistat, for fireproofing textiles, and as a mildew inhibitor. *See* Zinc Salts.

ZINC CHLORIDE • **Butter of Zinc.** A zinc salt used as an antiseptic and astringent in shaving creams, dentifrices, and mouthwashes. Also used in fireproofing, soldering fluxes, burnishing and polishing compounds for steel, and for electroplating, mercerizing, and sizing; in adhesives, dental cements, glass etching, parchment, embalming antistatic products, and as a denaturant for alcohol. Odorless and water absorbing, it is employed as a deodorant and disinfectant. Can cause contact dermatitis, is mildly irritating to the skin, and can be absorbed through it.

ZINC DIMETHYLDITHIOCARBAMATECYCLOHEXYLAMINE COMPLEX • Zinc Dithioamine Complex. A white powder that is used as a fungicide, rodent poison, and deer and rabbit repellent. Toxic by ingestion. *See* Carbamates.

ZINC FLUORIDE • A white powder soluble in acids and somewhat soluble in water, used in ceramic glazes, wood preserving and electroplating. Toxic. *See* Fluoride.

ZINC FLUOROSILICATE • Made from the reaction of zinc oxide and fluorosilicic acid, and used as a concrete hardener, preservative, and moth-proofing agent. *See* Zinc and Fluoride.

ZINC HYDROSULFITE • A white solid that is soluble in water, and used to bleach textiles, vegetable oils, straw, and animal glue. *See* Zinc.

ZINC LAURATE • A white powder, soluble in water, a combination of coconut oil and zinc, used in paints, varnishes, and rubber compounding. *See* Zinc and Lauric Acid.

ZINC NAPHTHENATE • Thick amber liquid derived from zinc and naphthenic acid, and used as a drier and wetting agent in paints, varnishes, resins, insecticides, fungicides, and mildew preventatives. Also used as a wood preservative, a waterproofing agent for textiles, and in insulating materials. *See* Zinc and Naphtha.

ZINC OXIDE • A white or grayish, odorless powder made by adding oxygen to zinc. It is used as an accelerator, and as a reinforcing agent in rubber. Also used as a mold inhibitor in paints, an ultraviolet light-absorber in plastics, and in ceramics, floor tile, glass, and seed treatments. It is a photoconductor in copying machines, and a pigment in color photography and artists' paints. Toxic by inhalation. Freshly formed fumes, as from welding, may cause fume fever with chills, raised temperature, tightness in the chest, and cough. *See* Metal Fume Fever.

ZINC PHENATE • A white powder used as an insecticide. Toxic by ingestion. See Phenol.

ZINC PHENOSULFONATE • An odorless, crystal powder used in insecticides and astringents. It also has been used as an antiseptic, and to heal skin ulcers. Toxic by ingestion.

ZINC PHOSPHIDE • A dark gray powder derived from phosphine and zinc sulfate. A deadly poison, used to kill rodents.

ZINC PROPIONATE • Needlelike crystals made from zinc oxide and propionic acid. Used as a fungicide on adhesive tape. *See* Propionic Acid.

ZINC RESINATE • Clear, amber lumps or yellowish liquid made from zinc oxide and a rosin *(see both)*. Used as a wetting, dispersing, and hardening agent, and as a drier in paints, varnishes, and resins.

ZINC RICINOLEATE • The zinc salt of ricinoleate *(see)*. Used as a stabilizer, fungicide, and emulsifier, and in greases, lubricants, and waterproofing, and as a stabilizer in vinyl compounds. *See* Zinc.

ZINC ROSINATE • The zinc salt of rosin *(see)*.

ZINC SALTS • These salts, if ingested, can produce irritation or corrosion of the gastrointestinal system, with pain and vomiting. Zinc chloride appears to be more corrosive and toxic than zinc sulfate. A few grams of zinc chloride have killed an adult, although recovery has been reported after ingestion of 90 grams. *See* Zinc Sulfate, Zinc Ricinoleate, and Zinc Propionate.

ZINC STEARATE • **Zinc Soap.** A mixture of the zinc salts of stearic and palmitic acids *(see both)*. Widely used in cosmetic preparations because it contributes to adhesive properties. Also used as a coloring agent. Baby powders of 3 to 5 percent zinc are water repellent and prevent urine scale. Zinc soap is also used in bath preparations, deodorants, face powders, hair-grooming preparations, hand creams, lotions, and ointments. It is used in tablet manufacture and in pharmaceutical powders and ointments. Inhalation of powder may cause lung problems and produce death in infants from pneumonitis, with lesions resembling those caused by talc but more severe. No known toxicity on the skin.

ZINC SULFATE • **White Vitriol.** The reaction of sulfuric acid with zinc. Mild, crystalline zinc salt is used in shaving cream, eye lotion, astringent, and styptic, and as a gargle spray, skin tonic, and after-shave lotion. Used medicinally as an emetic. Also used in the manufacture of rayon, in animal feeds, and as a wood preservative. Irritating to the skin and mucous membranes. May cause allergic reaction. Injection of 2.5 milligrams per kilogram of body weight caused tumors in rabbits.

ZINC SULFIDE • An inorganic zinc salt used as a fungicide and as a white pigment, in white and opaque glass, luminous paints, and phosphore in television screens. It is also used in the manufacture of plastics. *See* Zinc Salts.

ZINC YELLOW • **Citron Yellow. Buttercup Yellow.** A greenish yellow pigment that is used in artists' paints and as a rust inhibitor.

ZINEB • An organophosphate, used as an insecticide and fungicide. Toxic by inhalation and ingestion. Irritating to the skin, eyes, and mucous membranes. *See* Organophosphates.

ZIPPER LUBRICANT • Usually contains a petroleum *(see)* wax with a perchloroethylene *(see)* base. May also contain other waxes such as carnauba, and solvents, trichloroethylene, and varnish *(see all)*. *See also* Waxes.

ZIRAM • An organophosphate that is used as a fungicide and rubber accelerator. A strong irritant to the eyes and mucous membranes. *See* Organophosphates.

ZIRCONIUM • Discovered in 1789; a bluish black powder, or grayish white flakes. Used as a bonding agent, an abrasive, and in the preparation of dyes. High-quality zirconium is used as a pigment toner and solvent, in photo flashbulbs, firecrackers, metal-to-glass seals, and welding fluxes. Mildly acidic, it also has been used in body deodorants and antiperspirants. Zirconium hydroxide is used in nail whiteners. Has low systemic toxicity, but a disease of the skin has been reported in users of a deodorant containing sodium zirconium lactate. Manufacturers voluntarily removed zirconium from spray antiperspirants in 1976 because the element was found harmful to the lungs of monkeys. The FDA has said that zirconium is safe in formulations other than sprays. Zirconium oxide and zirconium silicate are no longer authorized for use in cosmetic colorings. *See* Zirconium Oxide and Zirconium Silicate.

ZIRCONIUM OXIDE • A white powder made by heating zirconium hydroxide or zirconium carbonate, and used in colored ceramic glazes, special glasses, and for batteries. Toxic by inhalation. *See* Zirconium.

ZIRCONIUM SILICATE • *See* Zirconium.

ZIRCONYL ACETATE • A sticky mass derived from the addition of acetic acid to zirconium oxide *(see both)*. Used in waterproofing textiles, and for textile and paper coatings.

ZIRCONYL HYDROXYCHLORIDE • A colorless powder that absorbs moisture, used as a water repellent for textiles. *See* Zirconium.

ZP™ TRACKING POWDER • A pesticide. *See* Zinc Phosphide.

FURTHER
INFORMATION

American Academy of Allergy
and Immunology
611 East Wells Street
Milwaukee, WI 53202
(414) 272-6071; Fax (414)
276-3349
The largest professional medical specialty organization
representing allergists and
clinical immunologists. Provides physician referrals and
public education materials.
(800) 822-ASMA

American Academy of Environmental Medicine
P.O. Box 16106
Denver, CO 80216
(303) 622-9755; Fax (303)
622-4224
A multispecialty medical society involved with studying,
treating, and preventing illnesses related to the environment. Readers may
contact AAEM and request
a list of member physicians
in their regions. They may
also request a list of publications in the field of environmental medicine, and
referral to local patient support groups and national
educational organizations involved with issues such as
chemicals around the home
or office.

American Cancer Society
1599 Clifton Road, NE
Atlanta, GA 30329
(800) 227-2345
Provides information on known
carcinogens.

American College of Allergy
and Immunology
800 East Northwest Highway
Suite 1080
Palatine, IL 60067
(708) 359-2800; Fax (708)
359-7367
A medical specialty organization representing allergists
and immunologists. The college provides patient education materials on both
allergy and asthma.

American Gas Association
1515 Wilson Boulevard
Arlington, VA 22209

American Industrial Hygiene Association
P.O. Box 8390
345 White Pond Drive
Akron, OH 44320
(216) 873-AIHA
A professional society for those practicing industrial hygiene in industry, government, labor, academic institutions, and independent organizations. Their goal is to keep workers, their families, and the community healthy and safe. It is the industrial hygienist's job to help ensure that federal, state, and local laws and regulations are followed in the work environment.

American Lung Association
1740 Broadway
New York, NY 10019

American Society of Heating, Refrigerating, and Air Conditioning
Public Relations Office
Engineers (ASHRAE)
1791 Tullie Circle NE
Atlanta, GA 30329

Arts and Crafts Materials Institute
715 Boylston Street
Boston, MA 02116
Provides information of safety-approved, certified arts and crafts products.

Asthma and Allergy Foundation of America
1717 Massachusetts Avenue NW
Suite 305
Washington, DC 20036
(202) 265-0265; Fax (202) 462-2412
A national lay, voluntary health services organization that exists to help meet the needs of those who suffer from asthma, allergies, and related disorders of the immune system. Provides physician contacts and public education materials.

Bureau of Environmental Epidemiology
(800) 392-7245 (Missouri only)

Center for Safety in the Arts
5 Beekman Street
Suite 1030
New York, NY 10038
(212) 227-6220
Provides information on chemicals associated with visual and performing arts.

Chemical Referral Center
Chemical Manufacturers Association
2501 M Street, NW
Washington, DC 20037
(800) CMA-8200

Energy and the Environment,
Office of
U.S. Department of Housing
and Urban Development
875 Conneticut Avenue, NW
Washington, DC 20410
(202) 673-5876

Hazard Evaluation System
and Information Service
(HESIS)
Department of Health Services/
Department of Industrial Relations
2151 Berkeley Way, Room
504
Berkeley, CA 94704
(415) 540-3014
For the state of California, but
the organization is very
cooperative and has pro-
vided information to persons
out of state.

Human Ecology Action
League, Inc.
P.O. Box 49126
Atlanta, GA 30359
(404) 248-1898
The Human Ecology Action
League collects and pub-
lishes information on human
reactions to the environ-
ment. It is interested in
adverse reactions to factors
found in air, water, food,
drugs, and habitat resulting
in environmental illness
(EI). Its purpose is to serve
those whose health has been
adversely affected by en-
vironmental exposure; to
provide information to those
who are concerned about the
health effects of chemicals;
and to alert the general
public about the potential
dangers of chemicals.

Indoor Air Division
U.S. Environmental Protection
Agency
Mail Code ANR-445
401 M Street SW
Washington, DC 20460

National Allergy and Asthma
Network/Mothers of
Asthmatics, Inc.
3554 Chain Bridge Road
Suite 200
Fairfax, VA 22030
(703) 385-4403; (800) 878-
4403

National Center For Environmental Health Strategies
Mary Lamielle, Director
1100 Rural Avenue
Voorhees, NJ 08043
(609) 429-5358
Provides a clearinghouse, technical, referral, support, and advocacy services for the public and those with environmentally and occupationally induced illnessess. NCEHS is involved in the elimination or minimization of toxic exposures in the home, workplace, school, and outdoor environments. Membership includes a newsletter, "The Delicate Balance."

National Foundation for the Chemically Hypersensitive
P.O. Box 9
Wrightsville Beach, NC 28480
(517) 697-3989
A nonprofit organization devoted to research, education, and dissemination of information about chemical hypersensitivity.

National Institute of Allergy and Infectious Diseases
National Institutes of Health
Building 31, Room 7A32
Bethesda, MD 20892
(301) 496-5717; Fax (301) 402-0120
Conducts and supports research to study the causes of allergic, immunologic, and infectious diseases, and to develop better means of preventing, diagnosing, and treating those illnesses. Offers scientific articles for professionals and a wide variety of pamphlets for the general public about allergic diseases.

National Institute for Occupational Safety and Health (NIOSH)
Hazards Evaluations and Technical Assistance Branch (R-9)
U.S. Department of Health and Human Services
4676 Columbia Parkway
Cincinnati, OH 45226
(513) 533-8236

National Pesticide Telecommunications Network
(800) 858-7378
Provides information on the acute and chronic health effects of pesticides.

Occupational Safety and
Health Administration
U.S. Department of Labor
200 Constitution Avenue NW
Washington, DC 20210
(202) 523-8148

Safe Building Alliance
Metropolitan Square
655 15th Street NW
Suite 12
Washington, DC 20005

Smoking and Health, Office of
U.S. Department of Health
and Human Services
Rockville, MD 20857

United States Consumer Product Safety Commission
(CPSC)
Washington, DC 20207
CPSC Consumer Hotline:
(800) 638-CPSC
Teletypewriter number (TTY)
for the hearing impaired:
(800) 638-8270

In Maryland only for the hearing impaired: (TTY) (800)
492-8140
Recorded information is available 24 hours a day when
calling from a touch-tone
phone. Operators are on
duty Monday to Friday from
10:30 A.M. to 4:00 P.M.
EST to take complaints
about unsafe consumer products.

United States Environmental
Protection Agency
Public Information Center
Mail Code PM-211B
401 M Street SW
Washington, DC
For copies of "Fact Sheets on
Ventilation and Air Quality
in Offices."
Toxic Substances Hotline to
answer questions from the
public: (202) 554-1404; and
to fax questions: (202) 554-
5603

World Health Organization
Publications Center
49 Sheridan Avenue
Albany, NY 12210

A M E R I C A N
A S S O C I A T I O N
O F
P O I S O N
C O N T R O L   C E N T E R S

CERTIFIED REGIONAL POISON CENTERS

Alabama

Alabama Poison Control Systems, Inc.
809 University Boulevard East
Tuscaloosa, AL 35401
Emergency Numbers: (800)
  462-0800 (AL only); (205)
  345-0600

Children's Hospital of Alabama—Regional Poison Control Center
1600 Seventh Avenue, South
Birmingham, AL 35233-1711
  Fax (205) 939-9245
Emergency Numbers: (205)
  933-4050; (800) 292-6678

Arizona

Arizona Poison and Drug Information Center
Arizona Health Sciences Center, Room 3204–K
University of Arizona
1501 North Campbell Avenue
Tucson, AZ 85724
Emergency Numbers: (602)
  626-6016; (800) 362-0101
  (AZ only)

Samaritan Regional Poison Center
Good Samaritan Medical Center
1130 East McDowell Road,
  Suite A–5
Phoenix, AZ 85006
Emergency Number: (602)
  253-3334

California

Fresno Regional Poison Control Center of Fresno
Community Hospital and
  Medical Center
P.O. Box 1232
2832 Fresno and R Streets
Fresno, CA 93715
Emergency Numbers: (209)
  445-1222; (800) 346-5922
  (seven counties only: Fresno, Kern, Kings, Madera,
  Mariposa, Merced, and Tulare)

317

Los Angeles County Medical Association
Regional Poison Control Center
1925 Wilshire Boulevard
Los Angeles, CA 90057
Emergency Numbers: (213) 484-5151; (800) 77–POISN
(three counties only: LA, Santa Barbara, and Ventura)

San Diego Regional Poison Center
UCSD Medical Center
225 Dickinson Street
San Diego, CA 92103
Emergency Numbers: (619) 543-6000; (800) 876-4766
(two counties only: San Diego and Imperial)

San Francisco Bay Area Regional Poison Control Center
San Francisco General Hospital, Room 1 E 86
1001 Potrero Avenue
San Francisco, CA 94110
Emergency Numbers: (415) 476-6600; (800) 523-2222
(415, 707 only)

UCDMC Regional Poison Control Center
2315 Stockton Boulevard
Sacramento, CA 95817
Emergency Numbers: (916) 734-3692; (800) 342-9293
(only some counties)

Colorado
Rocky Mountain Poison and Drug Center
645 Bannock Street
Denver, CO 80204-4507
Emergency Numbers: (303) 629-1123; (800) 332-3073
(CO only)

District of Columbia
National Capital Poison Center
Georgetown University Hospital
3800 Reservoir Road NW
Washington, DC 20007
Emergency Numbers: (202) 625-3333; (TTY) (202) 784-4660

Florida
Florida Poison Information Center at the Tampa General Hospital
P.O. Box 1289
Tampa, FL 33601
Emergency Numbers: (813) 253-4444; (800) 282-3171
(FL only)

Georgia
Georgia Regional Poison Control Center
Grady Memorial Hospital
Box 26066
80 Butler Street SE
Atlanta, GA 30335-3801
Emergency Numbers: (404) 589-4400; (800) 282-5846
(GA only); (TTY) (404) 525-3323

Indiana

Indiana Poison Center
Methodist Hospital of Indiana
1701 North Senate Boulevard
Indianapolis, IN 46206
Emergency Numbers: (317)
929-2323; (800) 382-9097
(IN only); (TTY) (317) 929-
2336

Kentucky

Kentucky Regional Poison
Center of Kosair Children's
Hospital
P.O. Box 35070
Louisville, KY 40232-5070
Emergency Numbers: (502)
589-8222 (Metro Louisville
and southern Indiana only);
(800) 722-5725 (KY only)

Maryland

Maryland Poison Center
20 North Pine Street
Baltimore, MD 21201
Emergency Numbers: (301)
528-7701; (800) 492-2414
(MD only)

Massachusetts

Massachusetts Poison Control
System
300 Longwood Avenue
Boston, MA 02115
Emergency Numbers: (617)
232-2120; (800) 682-9211
(MA only)

Michigan

Blodgett Regional Poison Center
Blodgett Memorial Medical
Center
1840 Wealthy SE
Grand Rapids, MI 49506
Emergency Numbers: (800)
632-2727 (MI only);
(800) 356-3232; (TTY) (616)
774-7854

Poison Control Center, Children's Hospital
3901 Beaubien Boulevard
Detroit, MI 48201
Emergency Numbers: (313)
745-5711; (800) 462-6642
(MI only)

Minnesota

Hennepin Regional Poison
Center
Hennepin County Medical
Center 701 Park Avenue
Minneapolis, MN 55415
Emergency Numbers: (612)
347 3141; TTY (612) 337-
7474

Minnesota Regional Poison
Center
St. Paul-Ramsey Medical Center
640 Jackson Street
St. Paul, MN 55101
Emergency Numbers: (612)
221-2113; (800) 222-1222
(MN only)

Missouri

Cardinal Glennon Children's
Hospital Regional Poison
Center
1465 South Grand Blvd.
St. Louis, MO 63104
Emergency Numbers: (314)
772-5200; (800) 392-9111
(MO only); (800) 366-8888;
TTY (314) 577-5336

Montana

Rocky Mountain Poison and
Drug Center
645 Bannock Street
Denver, CO 80204-4507
Emergency Number: (800)
525-5042 (MT only)

Nebraska

The Poison Control Center
8301 Dodge Street
Omaha, NE 68114
Emergency Numbers: (402)
390-5555 (NE only); (800)
955-9119 (NE only)

New Jersey

New Jersey Poison Information
and Education System
Newark Beth Israel Medical
Center
201 Lyons Avenue
Newark, NJ 07112
Emergency Numbers: (201)
923-0764; (800) 962-1253
(NJ only); (TTY) (201) 926-
8008

New Mexico

New Mexico Poison and Drug
Information Center
University of New Mexico
Albuquerque, NM 87131
Emergency Numbers: (505)
848-2551; (800) 432-6868
(NM only)

New York

Long Island Regional Poison
Control Center
Nassau County Medical Center
2201 Hempstead Turnpike
East Meadow, NY 11554
Emergency Numbers: (516)
542-2323, -2324, -2325

New York City Poison Control
Center
455 First Avenue, Room 123
New York, NY 10016
Emergency Numbers: (212)
340-4494; (212) POISONS

North Carolina

Mercy Hospital Poison Control
Center
2001 Vail Avenue
Charlotte, NC 28207
Emergency Number: (704)
379-5827

Ohio

Central Ohio Poison Center
Children's Hospital
700 Children's Drive
Columbus, OH 43205
Emergency Numbers: (614)
228-1323; (800) 682-7625
(OH only); (TTY) (614)
228-2272

Regional Poison Control
  System
and Drug and Poison Information
231 Bethesda Avenue, M.L.
  #144
Cincinnati, OH 45267-01044
Emergency Numbers: (513)
  558-5111; (800) 872-5111

Oregon
Oregon Poison Center
Oregon Health Sciences Uni-
  versity
3181 SW Sam Jackson Park
  Road
Portland, OR 97201
Emergency Numbers: (503)
  279 8968 (local); (800) 452
  7165 (OR only)

Pennsylvania
Delaware Valley Regional
  Poison Control Center
One Children's Center
34th and Civic Center Blvd.
Philadelphia, PA 19104
Emergency Number: (215)
  386-2100

Pittsburgh Poison Center
Children's Hospital of Pittsburgh
1 Children's Plaza
3705 Fifth Avenue at DeSoto
  Street
Pittsburgh, PA 15213
Emergency Number: (412)
  681-6669

Rhode Island
Rhode Island Poison Center
Rhode Island Hospital
593 Eddy Street
Providence, RI 02903
Emergency Number: (401)
  277-5727

Texas
North Texas Poison Center
Parkland Hospital
5201 Harry Hints Boulevard
P.O. Box 35926
Dallas, TX 75235
Emergency Numbers: (214)
  590-5000; (800) 441-0040
  (TX only)

Texas State Poison Center
The University of Texas Medi-
  cal Branch
8th and Mechanic Streets
Galveston, TX 77550-2780
Emergency Numbers: (409)
  765-1420; (713) 654-1701
  (Houston); (512) 478-4490
  (Austin); (800) 392-8548
  (TX only, doctors and
  ambulance personnel only)

Utah
Intermountain Regional Poison
  Control Center
50 North Medical Drive:
  Building 528
Salt Lake City, UT 84132
Emergency Numbers: (801)
  581-2151; (800) 456-7707
  (UT only)

West Virginia

West Virginia Poison Center
West Virginia University
  Health Sciences Center
Charleston Division
3110 MacCorkle Avenue SE
Charleston, WV 25304
Emergency Numbers: (304)
  348-4211; (800) 642-3625
  (WV only)

Wyoming

Rocky Mountain Poison and
  Drug Center
645 Bannock Street
Denver, CO 80204-4507
Emergency Number: (800)
  442-2702 (WY only)

ENVIRONMENTAL PROTECTION AGENCIES REGIONAL OFFICES

WITH THE STATES EACH COVERS

EPA Region 1
JFK Federal Building
Boston, MA 02203
(617) 565-3424
Connecticut, Massachusetts,
    Maine, New Hampshire,
    Rhode Island, Vermont

EPA Region 2
26 Federal Plaza
New York, NY 10278
(212) 264-2515
New Jersey, New York, Puer-
    to Rico, Virgin Islands

EPA Region 3
841 Chestnut Street
Philadelphia, PA 19107
(215) 597-9370
Delaware, Maryland, Pennsyl-
    vania, Virginia, West Virgi-
    nia, District of Columbia

EPA Region 4
345 Courtland Street, NE
Atlanta, GA 30365
(404) 347-3004
Alabama, Florida, Georgia,
    Kentucky, Mississippi,
    North Carolina, South Caro-
    lina, Tennessee

EPA Region 5
230 South Dearborn Street
Chicago, IL 60604
(312) 353-2072
Illinois, Indiana, Michigan,
    Minnesota, Ohio, Wisconsin

EPA Region 6
1445 Ross Avenue
Dallas, TX 75202
(214) 655-2200
Arkansas, Louisiana, New
    Mexico, Oklahoma, Texas

EPA Region 7
726 Minnesota Avenue
Kansas City, KS 66101
(913) 236-2803
Iowa, Kansas, Missouri, Ne-
    braska

EPA Region 8
One Denver Place
999 18th Street, Suite 1300
Denver, CO 80202-2413
(303) 293-1692
Colorado, Montana, North
    Dakota, South Dakota,
    Utah, Wyoming

EPA Region 9
1235 Mission Street
San Francisco, CA 94103
(415) 744-1015
Arizona, California, Hawaii,
Nevada, American Samoa,
Guam, Trust Territories of
the Pacific

EPA Region 10
1200 Sixth Avenue
Seattle, WA 98101
(206) 442-1465
Alaska, Idaho, Oregon, Washington

BIBLIOGRAPHY

A Citizen's Guide to Radon: What It Is and What to Do About It. United States Environmental Protection Agency, U.S. Department of Health and Human Services, OPA-86-004, August 1986.

"Acute and Chronic Poisoning from Residential Exposures to Elemental Mercury—Michigan, 1989–1990." *Morbidity and Mortality Weekly Reports,* vol. 40, no. 23, U.S. Department of Health and Human Services/ Public Health Services, June 14, 1991.

Atwood, Charles, associate professor of chemistry, Mercer University. "How Much Radon Is Too Much?" Paper presented at the 201st national meeting of the American Chemical Society, Atlanta, Georgia, April 13, 1991.

Berthold-Bond, Annie. *Clean and Green, 495 Ways to Clean, Polish, Disinfect, Deodorize, Launder, Remove Stains—Even Wax Your Car— Without Harming Yourself or the Environment*. New York: Ceres Press, 1990.

Biological Pollutants in Your Home. U.S. Consumer Product Safety Commission and the American Lung Association, Washington, D.C., January 1, 1990.

Blakeslee, Sandra. "Research on Birth Defects Shifts to Flaws in Sperm." *New York Times,* p. 1, January 1, 1991.

Blumenthal, Dale. "Deciding About Dioxins." *FDA Consumer,* vol. 24, no. 1, pp. 11–13, Feb. 1990.

Bower, John. *The Healthy House: How to Buy One, How to Cure a "Sick" One and How to Build One*. New York: Lyle Stuart, 1989.

Budavari, Susan, ed. *The Merck Index*. 11th ed. Rahway, New Jersey: Merck & Co., Inc., 1989.

Carlton, William W., ed. *Fundamental and Applied Toxicology*. vol. 4, no. 3. San Diego: Academic Press, Inc., June 1984.

"Children's Exposure to Environmental Cigarette Smoke Before and After Birth." *Advance Data No. 202*. Vital and health statistics of the National Center for Health Statistics, June 18, 1991.

Citizen's Guide to Pesticides. United States Environmental Protection Agency, Office of Pesticide and Toxic Substances, OPA-88-108.

Cohen, Samuel, and Leon Ellwein. "Cell Proliferation in Carcinogenesis." *Science,* vol. 249, pp. 1007–1011, August 31, 1990.

Conolly, Rory B. "Biologically-Based Models for Toxic Effects: Tools for Hypothesis Testing and Improving Health Risk Assessments." Chemical Industry Institute of Toxicology, *CIIT Activities,* vol. 10, no. 5 (May 1990).

Current Federal Indoor Air Quality Activities. Prepared with the cooperation of the Interagency Committee on Indoor Air Quality (CIAQ), Washington, D.C., 1990.

"Elemental Mercury Vapor Poisoning—North Carolina, 1988." *Morbidity and Mortality Weekly Report,* vol. 38, no. 45, pp. 770–772. U.S. Department of Health and Human Services/Public Health Services, Nov. 17, 1989.

Ellenhorn, Matthew J., and Donald G. Barceloux. *Medical Toxicology: Diagnosis and Treatment of Human Poisoning.* New York: Elsevier Science Publishing Co., 1988.

Environmental Issues: Today's Challenge for the Future Proceedings. Fourth National Environmental Health Conference, U.S. Department of Health and Human Services, Public Health Service, Nov. 1990.

"Farming and Cancer." *Backgrounder,* National Cancer Institute, Sept. 4, 1986.

"Fiberglass—Another Asbestos?" Internal bulletin from HEIS, Berkeley, Calif., May 1990.

Fisher, Alexander A. *Contact Dermatitis.* 3rd ed. Philadelphia: Lea & Febiger, 1986.

Gates, Max. "Dad's Toxic Exposure Studied as Pregnancy Risk." *Star-Ledger,* May 25, 1990.

Goldsworthy, Thomas, Kevin Morgan, James Popp and Byron Butterworth. "Chemically-Induced Cell Proliferation." Chemical Industry Institute of Toxicology, *CIIT Activities,* vol. 10, no. 4 (April 1990).

Gosselin, Robert E., M.D. Ph.D., Roger P. Smith, Ph.D., and Harold C. Hodge, Ph.D., D.Sc., with Jeannette E. Braddock. *Clinical Toxicology of Commercial Products.* 5th ed. Baltimore: Williams & Wilkins, 1984.

Guide to Hazardous Products Around the Home: A Personal Action Manual for Protecting Your Health and Environment. Springfield, Missouri: Household Hazardous Waste Project, 1989.

Guide to Man-Made Fibers. New York: Man-Made Fiber Producers Association, Inc., April 1969.

HESIS Fact Sheet No. 2, "Fluorocarbons (Freons®)". Hazard Evaluation System and Information Service, Berkeley, Calif., January 1989.

HESIS Fact Sheet No. 4, "Lead." Hazard Evaluation System and Information Service, Berkeley, Calif., October 1989.

HESIS Fact Sheet No. 5, "Glutaraldehyde." Hazard Evaluation System and Information Service, Berkeley, Calif., May 1990.

HESIS Fact Sheet No. 6, "Formaldehyde." Hazard Evaluation System and Information Service, Berkeley, Calif., May 1990.

HESIS Fact Sheet No. 8, "Glycol Ethers." Hazard Evaluation System and Information Service, Berkeley, Calif., January 1989.

HESIS Fact Sheet No. 9, "Ethylene Oxide (ETO)." Hazard Evaluation System and Information Service, Berkeley, Calif., February 1989.

HESIS Fact Sheet No. 10, "Toluene." Hazard Evaluation System and Information Service, Berkeley, Calif., May 1989.

HESIS Fact Sheet No. 11, "Wood Preservatives Containing Arsenic and

Chromates." Hazard Evaluation System and Information Service, Berkeley, Calif., February 1990.

HESIS Fact Sheet No. 12, "Styrene." Hazard Evaluation System and Information Service, Berkeley, Calif., May 1990.

HESIS Fact Sheet No. 13, "Polychlorinated Biphenyls (PCBs)." Hazard Evaluation System and Information Service, Berkeley, Calif., February 1988.

HESIS Fact Sheet No. 14, "Isocyanates." Hazard Evaluation System and Information Service, Berkeley, Calif., October 1989.

HESIS Fact Sheet No. 15, "Methyl Bromide." Hazard Evaluation System and Information Service, Berkeley, Calif., May 1990.

HESIS Fact Sheet No. 16, "Mercury." Hazard Evaluation System and Information Service, Berkeley, Calif., October 1989.

HESIS Fact Sheet No. 17, "Perchloroethylene." Hazard Evaluation System and Information Service, Berkeley, Calif., March 1989.

HESIS Fact Sheet No. 18, "Epoxy Resin Systems." Hazard Evaluation System and Information Service, Berkeley, Calif., June 1989.

HESIS Hazard Alert No. 4, "Methylene Chloride." Hazard Evaluation System and Information Service, Berkeley, Calif., July 1985.

Human Ecology Action League. "Information Sheet: Consumer Tips." Atlanta, Georgia: Human Ecology Action League, 1990.

Indoor Air Facts No. 3, "Ventilation and Air Quality in Offices." United States Environmental Protection Agency, 20A-4002, July 1990.

Indoor Air Facts No. 4, "Sick Building Syndrome." United States Environmental Protection Agency, ANR-445-W, April 1991.

Indoor Air Facts No. 5, "Environmental Tobacco Smoke." United States Environmental Protection Agency, ANR-445, June 1989.

Indoor Air Facts No. 6, "Report to Congress on Indoor Air Quality." United States Environmental Protection Agency, RD-672, August 1989.

The Inside Story: A Guide to Indoor Air Quality. Washington, D.C.: Environmental Protection Agency and Consumer Product Safety Commission, 1988.

Kerosene Heaters. U.S. Consumer Product Safety Commission, August 1987.

Lioy, Paul, Ph.D., and Elaine Panitz, M.D. "Indoor Air Pollution." *New Jersey Medicine,* vol. 85, no. 11, pp. 921–926, Nov. 1988.

Man-Made Fiber Fact Book. New York: Man-Made Fiber Producers Association, Inc., Sept. 1969.

Marks, Thomas, senior scientist, the Upjohn Company. "Birth Defects, Cancer Chemicals and Public Hysteria: How We Got that Way and What We Can Do About It." Paper presented at the 201st national meeting of the American Chemical Society, Atlanta, Georgia, April 13, 1991.

McCann, Joyce. "In Vitro Testing for Cancer-Causing Chemicals." *Hospital Practice,* September 1983, pp. 73–85.

Medinsky, Michele, and Michael Gargas. "A Physiological Model for

Benzene Dosimetry." Chemical Industry Institute of Toxicology, *CIIT Activities*, vol. 10, no. 3 (March 1990).

National Research Council. *Toxicity Testing: Strategies to Determine Needs and Priorities*. Washington, D.C.: National Academy Press, 1984.

Nelson, Leonard, Medical College of Ohio. "Toxicants that Affect Sperm Cell Function May Have Fetal Consequences." Paper presented at the American Association for the Advancement of Science, annual meeting, Washington, D.C., Feb. 17, 1991.

"New Study Suggests Water Chlorination Linked to Bladder Cancer Risk." National Cancer Institute statement, Dec. 1987.

"Pesticides At Home: Uncertain Risks and Inadequate Regulations." California Senate Office of Research issue brief, April 1988.

Radon: The Health Threat With a Simple Solution. A Physician's Guide. Chicago: American Medical Association, AA15:90-594:400M, Sept. 1990.

Reproductive and Hematopoietic Toxicity of the Glycol Ethers: An Update with Emphasis on Derivative Compounds. Hazard Evaluation System and Information Service, Berkeley, Calif. March 1989.

"Research Contributions Made Possible by the NCI Cancer Atlases Published in the 1970s." *Backgrounder*, Office of Cancer Communication, National Cancer Institute, June 1987.

"Research News: Neurotoxicity Creates Regulatory Dilemma." *Science*, vol. 243, p. 29, Jan. 6, 1989.

Residential Air-Cleaning Devices: A Summary of Available Information. United States Environmental Protection Agency, Air and Radiation, EPA/400/1-90-002, February 1990.

Rosenberg, Jon, M.S. *HESIS Guide to Industrial Solvents*. California Department of Health Services and the Department of Industrial Relations, Calif., 1986.

Sax, Irving N., and Richard J. Lewis, Sr., eds. *Hawley's Condensed Chemical Dictionary*. 11th ed. New York: Van Nostrand Reinhold Co., 1987.

Sax, Irving, N., and Richard J. Lewis, Sr. *Rapid Guide to Hazardous Chemicals in the Workplace*. New York: Van Nostrand Reinhold Co., 1986.

Segal, Marian. "Determining Risk." *FDA Consumer*, vol. 24, no. 5, pp. 7–11, June 1990.

Seventh Annual Fiber Fabric and Fashion Guide. Compiled by Apparel Manufacturer and the Men's Fashion Association of America, January 1972.

Slavin, Raymond, and Dianna Ducomb. "Allergic Contact Dermatitis." *Hospital Practice*, pp. 39–52, April 30, 1989.

Understanding Toxic Substances: An Introduction to Chemical Hazards in the Workplace. Hazard Evaluation System and Information Service, California Occupational Health Program, Berkeley, Calif., 1986.

Walker, Cheryl, Ph.D. "Oncogenes and Tumor Suppressor Genes: Components in a Multistage Model of Carcinogenesis." Chemical Industry Institute of Toxicology, *CIIT Activities*, vol. 9, no. 11–12 (Nov.–Dec. 1989).

WaterTest^{sm}. "Volatile Solvents User's Manual." Manchester, NH.

Weekes, Donald, and Richard Gammage. *The Practitioner's Approach to Indoor Air Quality Investigations*. American Industrial Hygiene Association, 1990.

"What You Should Know About Lead-Based Paint in Your Home." *Consumer Product Safety Alert*. Washington, D.C.: U.S. Consumer Product Safety Commission, Sept. 1990.

Winberry, William, Jr., Linda Forehand, Norma Murphy, Angela Ceroli, Barbara Phinney, and Ann Evans. "Compendium of Methods for the Determination of Air Pollutants in Indoor Air." Project summary, United States Environmental Protection Agency, EPA/600/S4-90/010, May 1990.

Winter, Ruth. *A Consumer's Dictionary of Cosmetic Ingredients*. 3d rev. ed. New York: Crown Publishers Inc., 1989.

Winter, Ruth. *A Consumer's Dictionary of Food Additives*. 3d rev. ed. New York: Crown Publishers Inc., 1989.

Winter, Ruth, *Cancer Causing Agents: A Preventive Guide*. New York: Crown Publishers Inc., 1979.

Zamm, Alfred, M.D., with Robert Gannon. *Why Your House May Endanger Your Health*. New York: Simon and Schuster, 1980.

Zamula, Evelyn. "Contact Dermatitis: Solutions to Rash Mysteries." *FDA Consumer*, vol. 24, no. 4, pp. 28–31, May 1990.

Zeckhauser, Richard, and W. Kip Viscusi. "Risk Within Reason." *Science*, vol. 248, pp. 559–563, May 4, 1990.